Public Man,
Private Woman

Public Man, Private Woman

Women in Social and
Political Thought

Jean Bethke Elshtain

Princeton University Press
Princeton, New Jersey

Published by Princeton University Press, Princeton, New Jersey
In the United Kingdom: Princeton University Press,
Guildford, Surrey

Library of Congress Cataloging in Publication Data will be
found on the last printed page of this book

Clothbound editions of Princeton University Press books
are printed on acid-free paper, and binding materials are
chosen for strength and durability

Printed in the United States of America by
Princeton University Press,
Princeton, New Jersey

**For my parents
Paul G. Bethke and Helen Lind Bethke**

who taught me that life, often a laughing matter, is nonetheless deeply serious, to be treated neither carelessly nor with disrespect

**and for my children
Sheri, Heidi, Jenny, and Eric**

out of the mouths of babes comes noise—and sometimes wisdom—they gave me a generous share of both.

Posterity may know that we have not through silence permitted things to pass away as in a dream.
—*Richard Hooker*

Contents

Preface

On Thinking and Nastiness

A human being must be able to pull himself together to form a judgment, otherwise he turns into what we Viennese call a *guten Potschen* [doormat].—*Freud*

Ludwig Wittgenstein, in a letter to his friend and student, Norman Malcolm, made the following observations on the activity of philosophy and the vocation of the philosopher. "You see," Wittgenstein wrote, "I know that it's difficult to think *well* about 'certainty,' 'probability,' 'perception,' etc. But it is, if possible, still more difficult to think, or *try* to think, really honestly about your life and other people's lives. And the trouble is that thinking about these things is *not thrilling*, but often downright nasty. And when it's nasty then it's *most* important." [1] *Public Man, Private Woman* is a nasty book. It is intended to be. In the pages that follow I have attempted to think "really honestly" from the vantage point of a political theorist who has been influenced, for over fifteen years, by her involvement with the feminist movement. Wittgenstein was right: thinking "really honestly" has not been thrilling, if by that one means superficially titillating; rather it has been arduous, sobering, at times frustrating, and always difficult. I also share with Wittgenstein the conviction that real thinking is a form of "digestion," an almost literal incorporation of, and working through, the raw materials of reflection. Neither thought as digestion, nor as a journey to self-knowledge comes easily. But this process cannot be obviated. There are no shortcuts to conceptual clarity, and I have done my best not to take any in telling the story of the public and the private in political discourse.

If my path seems to the reader excessively circuitous, I urge patience. The trail of public and private is not like a modern

---

[1] Norman Malcolm, *Ludwig Wittgenstein, A Memoir*, p. 39.

superhighway, straight and smooth, providing few surprises. Instead there are twists and unexpected turns, retracings of earlier steps, wild, even dangerous bumps, dead ends, detours, and destinations uncertain. This must be so because when we talk about public and private, we tell a tale of how human beings have structured, guided, ordered, and imagined a life for themselves and others. The angle of vision from which I began my journey into public and private, past and present, owes much to Rousseau's insistence that the thinker who wishes to separate politics from morals will never understand either. By refusing to separate politics from morals I hope I have understood both. I see the task of the political imagination in our time as that of attesting as honestly as possible to the truth of the human condition, to its perils and its possibilities. Within the Christian tradition in which I was raised this process is called "bearing witness." One who bears witness voices the discontents of society's silenced, ignored, abused, or invisible members. The witness proffers reasons for that suffering in order that the silenced may find a voice, cry out for justice, demand to be seen. The witness is a disturber of the peace just as political discourse, if critique is its aim, must disturbingly shatter the artificial calm of official know-nothingness. The process of witness bearing is not a ruthless stripping bare of all social forms but a gentler, though no less determined, activity of unraveling knots, unpacking muddles, shedding the patina of mystification, and offering up moral and political judgments at each point along the way.

I started this book many times. I experimented with different ways to write it. I tried out alternative voices. Each rethinking and reworking gave me the courage to be more provocative and less abstracted from the wellsprings of my own thought and action as these revolve around the public and private theme. Without presuming to compare my efforts to those of our vexing forebear, Jean-Jacques Rousseau, I share Norman Jacobsen's views of Rousseau's linking of the personal and the political. He writes:

I mean . . . to suggest that the formal concerns of Rousseau's political theory are also intensely personal concerns. To miss this relationship is to miss a significant dimension present in all powerful political thinking. For the genius of all great political thinkers is to make public that which is of private concern, to translate into public language the more special, idiosyncratic vocabulary of the inner man in hopes of arriving at public solutions which might then be internalized by each of us. One sure test of the quality of a political theory is its universality, that is, the extent to which everyman responds to the statement of problems which originated, perhaps, as the vexations of a single soul. The great thinker, in other words, suffers the malaise common to an age and possesses the courage and the craft to translate that malaise into a public vocabulary, in the hope of discovering political remedies for what had previously been thought private ills.[2]

There will be readers who will be disturbed by my treatment of particular thinkers in the pantheon of the Western tradition. Some might also consider it unwise to analyze contemporary feminists with the same seriousness and detail as I do in my exploration of the "greats." There will be feminist readers, on the other hand, who will remain unconvinced that "patriarchal theorists" should be given sympathetic consideration at all. Should these two sorts of criticisms arise I would not be surprised: each of us prefers that someone other than ourselves, or those thinkers, or that tradition or movement to which we are committed, be the subject of critique.

A caveat: those readers whose primary concern is to use thought as a spur to immediate action, "what is to be done," will not find *Public Man, Private Woman* helpful as a goad to instant action. They are well advised to turn elsewhere. My discussion does serve as a touchstone for that reflective thought that, in time, becomes a constituent feature of political action guided by moral concerns and an insistence on limits. Indeed, self-revelation of the sort I intimate requires, as a moral imperative, action of particular kinds. But it is action devoid of the spirit of *ressentiment* that has so poisoned the politics of our century. Listen to the

---

[2] Norman Jacobsen, *Pride and Solace: The Functions and Limits of Political Theory,* pp. 100-101.

words of the pastor and theologian, Dietrich Bonhoeffer, writing from the prison where he would be martyred by the Gestapo: "Here and there people flee from public altercation into the sanctuary of private *virtuousness*. But anyone who does this must shut his mouth and his eyes to the injustice around him. Only at the cost of self-deception can he keep himself pure from the contamination arising from *responsible* action."[3]

The book uses two terms of ordinary discourse, public and private, as a conceptual prism through which to see the story of women and politics from Plato to the present. I did not uncover or discover an Ultimate Truth, or construct an Archimedean point to structure, guide, and settle all future questions. Instead I stalked the elusive trail of *meaning*. The meaning to which I refer is meaning *to* the subjects of their own actions and life-worlds as well as meaning *for* for the analyst or observer, from a necessarily different and removed vantage point, of those self-understandings, those meanings-to. Concepts like public and private constrain or enrich everday life and activity. We are, each of us, shaped to and for a way of life whose public and private forms, linked to or embodied within a grammar of basic notions and rules, either nourish or distort our capacities for purposive activity, either strengthen or rob us of the power (*potentia*) to love and to work. I begin, then, with the resources of ordinary language and move toward critique by unpacking latent meanings, nuances, and shades of interpretation others may have missed or ignored. In rethinking unreflectively held notions and concepts, our ability to sift out the more from the less important is enhanced. Slowly, as we begin to articulate more coherently an awareness of the connections between diverse activities, relations, reasons, and passions, our self-identities as active, meaning-bearing, and meaning-creating agents is enhanced. These considerations animate the "Introduction: Public and Private Imperatives."

In "Part I: Public and Private Images in Western Political Thought," I explore the images and themes clustered about the public and private distinction beginning with Plato and concluding with Marx. The problem for women is not simply their exclusion

---

[3] Dietrich Bonhoeffer, *Letters and Papers from Prison*, p. 27.

from political participation but the terms under which this exclusion has occurred. The reasons why women and men, public and private, personal and political, have been variously conceived are many: the presumption that some universally true, ubiquitous, and pervasive misogynistic urge explains everything is simplistic and wrong. My examination uncovers misogyny, to be sure, but I also discovered that among those who made it their task to conceive the political community and to structure a political order some were troubled, puzzled, even angered at received notions about men and women, public and private. I hope something of the feeling of their struggle comes through in my retelling of it.

The thinkers or schools of thought taken up in Chapters 1 through 4 are examined either because they are inescapable in any account of Western political thought, being so central to that enterprise that to omit them would be egregious, or because a thinker, though less than seminal, nevertheless exerted enormous influence within the framework of his own age. I have not ferreted out every incriminating reference to women in the texts I explored. Such an exercise would be tedious and depressing. Instead I examined major points of theoretical demarcation, those ideas without which the theorist's enterprise would be something other than what it is. I do not hold to the view that an entire logic of explanation can be discarded by a single, discrete piece of disconfirming or damning evidence. Besides, we now possess so many anthologies containing the collected sexist utterings of men through the ages that we have enough to keep us angry and miserable for years to come. Theorists must be understood and critiqued *as* theorists, first and foremost, for political theory is an activity of a particular kind to particular ends. To condemn or praise the thinker and ignore the thought is not the way the theoretical mind works. On the other hand, to ignore the thinker *in* the thought, as some advocate, is to perpetuate another sort of distortion, for one is unavoidably led to a picture of the man through the vehicle of his works. To judge the thought, therefore, is in some vital and deep way to judge the thinker. That is sufficient evidence for me to become perturbed and to judge harshly in a number of cases.

In "Part II: Contemporary Images of Public and Private: Toward a Critical Theory of Women and Politics," I bring the concerns of the theorist and of political thought to the task of critically evaluating competing feminist visions. One of my aims in Chapter 5, "Feminism's Search for Politics," is to draw out the inner connections between particular feminist logics of explanation and their implications for persons and politics. Feminists, too, are vexed with public-private dilemmas: indeed, that is the heart of the feminist enterprise. Because feminist thought, at least in America, rarely makes contact with Western political discourse, it has sometimes repeated old formulations. But at other times, imaginative and bold departures have been suggested. My final chapter has as its aim and justification making good on those promises the reader will find scattered throughout my critical appraisal of other thinkers, namely, that I would reconstruct in some fresh way the questions that stymied others. What I finally have to offer is an interconnected set of tentative formulations, a few as ragged around the edges as life itself, concerning our private and public travail, what we can do about it or what we should refrain from doing about it. I never lose sight of the fact that the questions I address and the formulations I pose might have effects on real people. Political theory is not about making the most efficient turbine engine, or constructing the sleekest giant skyscraper, or erecting the most monumental rocketship. It is about how people live their lives and create and recreate meaning anew with each waking day. Humility seems the best stance from which to approach questions whose answers may either enhance human meaning or further drain us of our capacity to seek meaning.

Acknowledgments

Friends, colleagues, and family members have offered their criticism, advice, and support for many years. I should like to acknowledge a few of these contributions.

George Armstrong Kelly, then Professor of Politics at Brandeis University, chaired what was at the time (1972-1973) a rather unorthodox project, my dissertation "Women and Politics: A Theoretical Analysis." That work served as the beginning of this one. Without his generosity with his time and with his luminous insights, it is unlikely that I would have had the opportunity to carry on. William E. Connolly, my friend and colleague at the University of Massachusetts, Amherst, read and commented at length on one of the first drafts of this text. His critical acuity and his impatience with muddled thinking helped me to sharpen my arguments. The late William E. Binstock, M.D., Cambridge, Massachusetts and the Boston Psychoanalytic Institute, read the entire manuscript in an earlier version and criticized it meticulously chapter by chapter. His intimate knowledge of psychoanalytic theory coupled with his desire to seek sophisticated and fruitful applications of that theory to political and social thought were a constant source of encouragement to me. Nannerl Keohane of Stanford read the manuscript and I have incorporated many of her criticisms and suggestions as well as those of Sanford Thatcher, my editor. Eli Sagan generously proffered insights and moral clarity. Robert Paul Wolff, Joan Landes, and Theodore M. Norton offered advice and encouragement.

My husband, Errol L. Elshtain, drew articles to my attention, undertook monumental Xeroxing assignments, picked books up and dropped them off, proofread, and suffered with me through my bouts of Angst. Vivian Goldman, who typed, was also involved in the manuscript as a vivacious voice and active friend. Dr. Paul R. Fleischman played a special role in helping me to think about silences as well as speech and to rediscover the ideas of what it means to have a vocation and what it means to be a witness.

With a group of similarly discontented women, all living in or near Boston, I shared for two years that exciting, troubling, sustaining process of discovery of self and Other which goes by the name of consciousness-raising. My debt to them is in the realm of the spirit and the trajectory of self-identity. I owe special thanks to Sue Miller and Esther Scott who, together with me, comprise a "postgraduate" remnant of that original consciousness-raising group. We pilgrims of mind and spirit convene in the flesh less often than we ought.

To Joanne, my best friend and the most blithe of spirits: still marvelous after all these years.

My colleague in the Economics Department at the University of Massachusetts, Jane Humphries, is the best pub partner one can imagine. Together we have muddled through a number of bad patches and emerged with our spirits intact.

Finally, although I have already acknowledged the noisy presences of my children in the dedication, I must add the following: I owe to Sheri, Heidi, Jenny, and Eric, precisely *because* they were never hustled out of sight, earshot, or mind as I struggled with this text (they wouldn't have stood for interdictions of silence anyway), whatever deep, enriching connection *Public Man, Private Woman* retains to what people call *real life* in all its untidy, concrete particularity. Special thanks to Jenny for her splendid help in checking references and quotations in the summer of 1980.

One note on style: because my bibliography is detailed and complete, I have shortened the references in the notes to include only the author, title, and page numbers. Place, publisher, and publication date can be found in the bibliography.

A book in the making for several years takes on the quality of a patchwork quilt. This makes errors, oversights, duplications, and what my elementary school teachers chidingly called "careless mistakes" unavoidable. I hope such lapses are few but should they occur I alone am responsible.

Public Man,
Private Woman

Introduction

Public and Private Imperatives

One is bound to employ the currency that prevails in
the country one is exploring . . .—*Freud*

Tolling for the tongues with no place to bring their thoughts
All down in taken-for-granted situations. . . .*—*Bob Dylan*

Several daunting tasks are part of telling the story of the public
and the private, evoking those images, those pictures of reality
(Wittgenstein might say) that have held us captive or merely
captivated us since they were first sketched by the august array
of fathers whose heritage, for better or worse, we know as Western
political thought. My way of giving a written account of what I
have seen requires a historical, interpretive, desimplifying method
that allows me to link the conceptual pillars, public and private,
to associated ideas and imperatives such as understandings of
human nature, theories of language and action, and the divergent
values and ends of familial and political life. The foundation of
this effort is an epistemology that places meaning and conceptual
analysis at the core of theoretical inquiry, debates on what it is
to be a human being at the forefront of moral vision, and the
claims of politics to primacy among human activities as the touchstone of political thinking.

Readers should not expect a neat, logical progression as I trace
the public and the private from past to present despite the (rough)
chronological ordering in Part I of the text. Instead, they will find
a tradition alive with competing alternatives and ways of seeing
clustered around the public and private as symbolic forms, what
John Gunnell calls guides to our orientation in the world.[1] Some

---

* © 1964 Warner Bros. Inc. All Rights Reserved. Used by Permission.

[1] John G. Gunnell, *Political Theory: Tradition and Interpretation.* See the
discussion in chapter 5, pp. 131-161.

of the thinkers I shall consider distinguished between public and private both as a way to describe social reality and as a theoretical, moral, and political exigency, a linchpin in their overall vision. The public and private recedes into the background of analysis for others, either because the existence of these spheres is simply assumed and therefore deemed not worth belaboring, or because their perspectives demanded the subordination or elimination of these particular basic notions in favor of alternative concepts and symbols. We shall also find as alternatives the insistence that the private world be integrated fully into an overarching public arena, that is, thoroughly politicized; an equally vehement demand for what might be called the "privatization" of the public realm with politics falling under its standards, ideals, and purposes; a rigid bifurcation between the two spheres with the private realm conceived instrumentally, treated as a necessary basis for public life but a less worthy form of human activity; finally, a call for retaining but recasting public and private boundaries as part of an effort to preserve each yet reach towards an ideal of social reconstruction.

I am aware of the fact that the terms public and private, as I have evoked them thus far, are evanescent notions that must be brought down to earth and anchored in the particularities of history and the specificities of theory. Let me begin to pin the concepts down further by issuing a caveat: to tell the full story of the public and the private would be the work of a lifetime. My aim is more modest. I shall tease out of the tapestry of past and present the meaning of that division as it appears in accounts of the relationship that pertains between that aspect of the public world deemed political and that contrasting dimension of social life called private, most often the household or the family. Images of public and private are necessarily, if implicitly, tied to views of moral agency; evaluations of human capacities and activities, virtues, and excellence; assessments of the purposes and aims of alternative modes of social organization. Readers will quickly discover that the way in which determinations about the public and the private and the role and worth of each is evaluated will gear a thinker's attitudes towards women. That is one way to put it. Another might be: a thinker's views on women serve as a foundation that helps to give rise to the subsequent determinations he makes of the public and the private and what he implicates and values in each. It is not easy to decide which way the vectors of personal and theoretical exigency move.

Although public and private are terms of ordinary discourse, one finds widespread disagreement over their respective meaning and range of application within and between societies. Brian Fay sees the public and the private as two of a cluster of "basic notions" that serve to structure and give coherence to all known ways of life and those individuals who inhabit them. The public and the private as twin force fields help to create a moral environment for individuals, singly and in groups; to dictate norms of appropriate or worthy action; to establish barriers to action, particularly in areas such as the taking of human life, regulation of sexual relations, promulgation of familial duties and obligations, and the arena of political responsibility. Public and private are imbedded within a dense web of associational meanings and intimations and linked to other basic notions: nature and culture, male and female, and each society's "understanding of the meaning and role of work; its views of nature; . . . its concepts of agency; its ideas about authority, the community, the family; its notion of sex; its beliefs about God and death and so on."[2] The content, meaning, and range of public and private vary with the exigencies of each society's existence and turn on whether the virtues of political life or the values of private life are rich and vital or have been drained, singly or together, of their normative significance.

No idea or concept is an island unto itself. Another scholar might explore the same issues—those having to do with women and politics—by tracing the meaning of nature and culture through the centuries. The point is that basic notions comprise a society's intersubjectively shared realm. Intersubjectivity is a rather elusive term referring to ideas, symbols, and concepts that are not only shared but whose sharing reverberates within and helps to constitute a way of life on both its manifest and latent levels. The particular meaning *to* each social participant of a concept inter-

[2] Brian Fay, *Social Theory and Political Practice*, p. 78.

subjectively shared may differ strikingly from its meaning to any other given individual, but a range of shared meaning must also be present. Wittgenstein claims that when we first "begin to believe anything, what we believe is not a single proposition, it is a whole system of propositions. (Light dawns gradually over the whole.)"[3] Similarly, when we learn to use a concept, particularly one of the bedrock notions integral to a way of life, we do not do so as a discrete piece of "linguistic behavior" but with reference to other concepts, contrasts, and terms of comparison.

Distinctions between public and private have been and remain fundamental, not incidental or tangential, ordering principles in all known societies save, perhaps, the most simple. (Though even in primitive societies exigencies based on the concepts of taboo and shame are found indicating an ordering of activities into those that can be seen by others and are sanctioned and those that are carried out under cover of darkness and considered impure.) To dissect and criticize conceptual categories central to a way of life within a particular linguistic community is inevitably, whether this is an explicit aim or not, to put pressure upon that society's web of intermeshed meanings. As soon as we lift one notion or another out of its mooring in a wider network so that we might take a closer look at it, we question established ways of seeing. The would-be conceptual rebel, whose explicit intent is to push the boundaries of a historically constituted language game towards alternatives she sees though others may not, may find herself in a position akin to that of Wittgenstein's hapless lion, who, if he "could talk, we could not understand him."[4] No one wishes to roar into a void. The best way to avoid that fate, I believe, is to approach the requirements of theory and the rigors of conceptual critique as the foundation on which to tell an interesting story.

[3] Ludwig Wittgenstein, *On Certainty*, ed. G.E.M. Anscombe and G. H. von Wright, p. 21e, par. 141.

[4] Ludwig Wittgenstein, *Philosophical Investigations*, trans. G.E.M. Anscombe, p. 223e. In Wittgenstein's view, one moves from the relative transparency of persons within one's own language game to the opacity of those outside it—people whom we either apprehend with difficulty or cannot understand at all. Wittgenstein's aim was a crystalline clarity which would lead to the dissolution of all philosophical problems. (*Philosophical Investigations*, p. 51e, par. 133). Such clarity, however, will always prove to be illusive.

Stories have a beginning, and I turn next to the speculative origins of the tale of the public and private.

PUBLIC AND PRIVATE SPECULATIONS

An amoeba has neither boundaries nor the capacity or need to define them. An amoeba cannot be said to inhabit distinct public and private spheres as it oozes along in its fluid world oblivious to questions of how and why. Those complex and marvelous social creatures, the giant cetaceans, roam the seas of the world, appear to delimit territory, and carry on a variety of activities which are essential to their survival and provide evidence of their sociality. Whales have social systems that include mating, nursing, nurturing, and protecting the young, and mutually guarding themselves against enemies. Whales communicate with one another, often across vast and awesome distances, through a meticulously structured series of clicks, whistles, and intricate sounds. They can send these messages to pinpoint food or their own locations, to warn of imminent danger, to announce a birth, to mourn, to indicate herd movement, and for all we land mammals know, simply to gossip. Given the nature of their fluid environment, the constraints and possibilities of their biology, and their marvelous but limited communicative abilities, it would be rather odd for us to insist that whales have public and private spheres within which discernible activities, those of a private sort and those of a public sort, occur. Whales are similar to us in many ways: they mate for life (*that* is getting less and less like us), they are loyal to their fellows, they have tightly knit family systems, and they have a need to communicate with their kind. But they can hardly be said to be, as we humans are, "twinned beings," creatures with clearly separated social loci for diverse activities within which we play a number of different roles.

Suppose we turn to our nearest evolutionary relatives, the higher primates. We would find, if we observed them outside the unnatural and often inhuman (or unprimate) confines of laboratory settings, that they have a complex, ongoing social order composed of a cluster of familial and kinship groupings which culminates in a dominant male; a rough division of labor based upon biological and survival exigencies; a tough-minded clarity about their territory; and an irrepressible need to explore their own habitats. Yet no chimpanzee social group has ever been observed holding a political caucus, taking a vote as to who should become the next dominant male, or whether an interloper should be accepted into the group, chased out, or assaulted.[5] Dominance is established in a manner that appears to have remained unchanged for centuries: a younger contender engages in aggressive behavior to taunt and arouse the group's dominant male who must meet the challenge through a ritualized struggle with clear-cut signals of victory and defeat. The chimpanzee mother-child relationship cannot be termed either a private or an intentional one although it is most certainly meaningful, if our understanding of meaning incorporates powerfully held and deeply felt ties of affection and devotion. Pregnancy itself is the result of an activity engendered by the involuntary production of hormones in a rigid cyclical pattern, the estrus cycle, and the bonding of mother and child emerges given certain endocrinological processes that serve as its motivational base. The female chimpanzee hasn't the reflexive powers of that enormously expanded forebrain which allows for a variety of alternative responses by human beings to neuroendocrinological pressure. Chimpanzees are tool-users but this is somewhat ad hoc and there is no technology for the transmission of increasingly sophisticated methodologies from generation to generation. Neither do we find law, religion, art, language—that layered and dense texture we usually call culture.

To begin to differentiate between public and private spheres requires, minimally, a shared language and tradition and human subjects sophisticated enough to orient themselves in the world through categories of thought which allow for comparisons, contrasts, and the establishment of relationships between one thing and another. That human beings appear to be the only beings that not only use but create and renew language; that create actively—

---

[5] If we saw politics, crudely, as coercion or force for the purpose of control of one group by another, something very like politics does go on, as Jane Goodall's remarkable book, *In the Shadow of Man*, points out. I reject this definition of politics, however.

will into being—political society; that pass on tradition in numerous formal and informal ways; and that mutually order their social lives as family members, kin, neighbors, colleagues, citizens, or foes—that is only the beginning of my tale. A prior consideration in the treatment of basic notions (and I would stress here the *basic* aspect) is that human beings are shameful as well as guilty. That is, certain activities or the thought of them induce emotions of a particular kind. Shame or its felt experience as it surrounds our body, its functions, passions, and desires requires appearances and symbolic forms, veils of civility that conceal some activities and aspects of ourselves even as we boldly or routinely display and reveal other sides of ourselves as we take part in public activities in the light of day for all to see.[6]

The august array of thinkers I shall take up as representative of the Western political tradition assumed and deployed *some* form of a distinction between the public and the private as conceptual categories and as private and public imperatives, to conceal as well as to reveal. As conceptual categories, public and private ordered and structured diverse activities, purposes, and dimensions of human social life and thinking about that life. As deeply felt imperatives, these resonant notions became the repository of people's most cherished dreams and wildest plans, their passions and prejudices, needs and interests, their fears and ambivalences, courage and values. The texts of great or representative thinkers are interesting both for what they find worthy or necessary or wise and for what they seek to push aside or out of sight. Although few of the thinkers I shall examine felt compelled to explain or to speculate as to why a public-private demarcation had emerged in the first place, each seems under an obligation to justify and to explain the particular division that exists in his own epoch and sustains ongoing social forms, whether to defend it or as a contrast model to his own alternatives.

The point for now is simply this: given human beings' capacity for social organization and innovation and their ability

[6] Freud's speculations on the emergence of shame are fascinating. I have borrowed from and expanded upon his discussion. See *Civilization and Its Discontents, Standard Edition*, vol. 21, pp. 99-100. Cf. Hannah Arendt's treatment of the "shameful" in *The Human Condition*.

to conceive and experience competing values and purposes, at one point in evolutionary history differentiations arose between activities which were public and those that involved a single person or a few persons that were not carried out in a public arena. Shared social existence predates by many centuries—indeed, we now know, by over three million years!—the creation of a stable language of politics in the fifth century B.C. Prepolitical social life was structured, ritualized, familial life. Our prehominid and hominid forebears were members of kin systems, hordes, clans, and tribes. They had social organization without having an activity called politics. Groups were held together by biological, sexual, and economic exigency and linked by shared memories passed on in an oral tradition. Family man and social man predates political man, Aristotle's *zoon politikon*, in both bioevolutionary and historic time. If no public life as a political life existed within rudimental social forms, what of a private sphere? Primitive methods of concealment do not in themselves comprise a private sphere but they can be construed as a private imperative, or, better yet, as a social imperative experienced as a private exigency. But no private sphere as a conceptually demarcated and socially determinant dimension within a wider social life can exist without some public world as a contrast. To see the lives of wandering hordes of bio-social, tool-using, hunting and gathering hominids through the prism of public and private would involve an anachronism distorting their world and obscuring our own.

My theoretical speculations locate the origins of our basic notions of public and private in a primitive, human social milieu. But these distinctions should not be seen as political ones in any simple sense, for politics required additional differentiations. As soon as man distinguished himself from other objects in the natural and physical world and began to see himself as the agent of his own destiny, a human imperative emerged to order social existence in more conceptual and intentional ways. Conceptual organization of social life always entails terms of comparison and contrast. Primitive comparative terms like big and little, dark and light, provided the linguistic basis for other, more abstract and complex, differentiations. This struggle for conceptual coherence begins anew with every human child who must, through his or her own thinking, make independent discovery of correct categories by means of observation.[7]

Human beings have and continue to divide their lives into one or more of a bewildering number of possible variants on the public and private. These divisions bear implications for women and politics. Some, in their desire to bring about changes for women, declare these divisions, since they have emerged historically, to be evidence of the imposition upon us of an arbitrary, culturally relative artifact that exists on the level of convention alone and which can be dispensed with if we are but rational and bold enough. Others, who may share similar ends, see the notions of public and private as complicatedly both natural and conventional, making contact on the deepest level with necessity. They argue that notions of the public and private are prerequisites for, and constitutive features of, social life itself. Whatever one's final determination on this vexing issue, public and private notions form one of the bases of explicit political theory in the Western tradition. I shall trace, briefly, the beginnings of those imperatives in Greek life and thought which arise on the basis of the public-private distinction.

THE GREEKS AND THE BIRTH OF POLITICS

A prephilosophical but increasingly sophisticated vocabulary emerged in the Homeric period, undergoing permutations in the pre-Hellenic and the Hellenic epochs in response to altered social realities and as a kind of anticipation of future exigencies. The distinction between nature (*physis*) and culture (*nomos*) became fixed, at least for the literate, privileged classes. With a division between the basic notions nature and culture secured, more sophisticated differentiations *within* culture became possible, desirable, or necessary.[8] Bear in mind that ideas about authority, sexuality, God, death, males and females were linked with one

---

[7] See Sigmund Freud, "On the Sexual Enlightenment of Children," *Standard Edition*, vol. 9, pp. 134-135. Freud explains what he sees as an epistemic drive in the human child.

[8] The most elegant treatment of these issues remains Sheldon Wolin's *Politics*

another to comprise, at one point, the intersubjective glue and texture of Greek life. The result of the Greek division and classification of cultural phenomena was the *polis*, the concept and reality of a structured body politic set off in contrast to the *oikos*, or private household.

Although I shall treat the Greek public-private imperative in detail in my discussion of Plato and Aristotle in Chapter 1, it is important to get our bearings now on several matters. First, the relations and activities occurring within and serving as the raison d'être of the *polis* were defined as existing outside the realms of nature and necessity.[9] Second, the free space of the *polis*, though apart from necessity, existed in a *necessary* relation to those activities lodged within the private realm, held by the Greeks to be the sphere of unfreedom. The sphere of the household was a sphere of production and reproduction alike. The public world of politics and free citizenry was conceptually and structurally parasitic upon the world of necessity, a realm downgraded and demeaned systematically by powerful public voices, including those of Plato and Aristotle.

The division of the social world into a public world of politics and a private world of familial and economic relations was made possible, in part, by the prior adoption of a vocabulary which allowed for terms of comparison and contrast, for demarcations into that which was open and revealed and that which was hidden and concealed, that which was free and that which was determined and unfree. The matters that were hidden and private in Greek society have remained surprisingly concealed in subsequent *treatments* of Greek society by political thinkers who have carried forward into later epochs not simply the categories public and private but much of the original content infused into those categories, thus enshrouding Greek misogyny, imperialism, and the exploitation of slaves behind the same ideological distortions deployed self-servingly by the Greeks.[10] This is the darker side of the Greek contribution to the story of the public and the private.

and Vision. Alasdair MacIntyre, in *A Short History of Ethics*, treats the emergence of a political vocabulary as part of his focus on terms of moral discourse.

[9] Interestingly, Aristotle was to blur this well-established distinction somewhat in his attempt to make of the *polis* an entity that was, in some sense, "natural."

[10] For example, one central feature of Greek, particularly Athenian, life, passed

A towering achievement, tied inescapably to the public-private division, is the notion of politics as a form of action, an activity carried out by individuals with agency within and upon the world, rather than creatures through or to whom things simply happened. Prehominid "natural man," who saw himself on a par with other objects, had no consciousness of himself as a being with causal efficacy within a world of objects. So long as the world was one in which no agentic imperative was thinkable, human beings resigned themselves to fatalism and saw the world through a prism of magical thinking in which capricious forces might, at best, be placated or tricked. The linguistic resources of rather noncomplex, largely oral rather than written languages frequently disallow certain distinctions, inferences, and the drawing of causal relations. There is a qualitative distinction to be made between language systems that provide for agentic imperatives and those that do not.

When the conviction emerged that men did have control over a portion of their lives, a revision of what it meant to be a member of the category human (or the male subtype of that category) followed or was coterminous with the conviction. It became necessary to characterize more accurately altered human realities and possibilities. Man's gain of partial autonomy, his emergence from the imbeddedness of "natural" determinism, meant that henceforth an individual could be seen as praiseworthy or could be blamed. Neither praise nor blame makes sense in a world in which man is no more responsible for his comings and goings than water surging over rocks is responsible for its tumbling and splashing. A subject as one who is praiseworthy or may be blamed contains within it the image of a being who, in acting in particular ways to given ends, necessarily thinks reflectively about himself, others,

---

over in silence by most later historians and political thinkers, is the nexus between Greek homosexuality and misogyny and their link-up with images of domination and subordination. The historian K. J. Dover has recently broken silence on this issue in *Greek Homosexuality*. He documents that the aversion to women and female sexuality was so pervasive in Greek life that the male who broke certain " 'rules' of legitimate eros detaches himself from the ranks of male citizenry and classifies himself with women and foreigners." The submissive male "by assimilating himself to a woman in the sexual act . . . rejects his role as a male citizen" (p. 103).

and his world. Mind's complexity was dramatically enhanced as more and more objects in the world became divisible along this criterion or that. But something curious happened along the way: not all that people thought could or (they decided) should be uttered as public speech. Speech and thought did not coincide. Just as various social and sexual human activities were carried on in secret, only a portion of what was thought actually got said.

PRIVATE SILENCES, PUBLIC VOICES

Man's public speech took place in that public realm par excellence, the *polis*. His private, albeit social, speech was carried on within the household, though that speech, tied to images of necessity, carried no public weight. (In addition, Plato provides for philosophic speech within the framework of a particular set of private male social relations, as treated in Chapter 1 below.) This led to—indeed it involved—levels of partially autonomous but interconnected spheres of human discourse. The question of what was appropriate to say, to utter, depending upon context— where one was and with whom and why—emerged not so much as a rule of etiquette (etiquette takes over when social forms begin to fray about the edges), but as a public-political, social, individual, even religious or mythopoeic imperative, broken only by gods, fools, madmen, the very bold or old or young.

Speech, too, had its public and private moments. Some categories of human subjects—in Greek society slaves and women were the most important—were confined to private realms of discourse. Truly public, political speech was the exclusive preserve of free, male citizens. Neither women nor slaves were public beings. Their tongues were silent on the public issues of the day. Their speech was severed from the name of action: it filled the air, echoed for a time, and faded from official memory with none to record it or to embody it in public forms.[11]

---

[11] I am not impressed with the claims made for powerful women who influenced public men through their private activities—in Athenian society this claim is frequently made for the *hetaira*, a courtesan or prostitute of high status. Although such private speech may, as taken over by the man and made public, have exerted

A question arises: were those denied a public role and voice properly human subjects at all? The answer to that question will turn on what one finds to be the foundation of our humanity and determines to be the forum which humanizes us. The answer will also depend on how one assays silences: whether one presumes the silent have had nothing to say because of their limited natures and roles, or whether one believes they may have had much to say about the meaning of human life but their thoughts and reflections were severed from public speech. Those silenced by power—whether overt or covert—are not people with nothing to say but are people without a public voice and space in which to say it.

Of course, years and years of imposed inaction and public silence strangle nascent thoughts and choke yet-to-be spoken words, turning the individuals thus constrained into reflections of the sorts of beings they were declared to be in the first place. But that is not the issue here. The question is one of silence and human subjects and the nature of public and private. A subtext running through these considerations is the nature of meaningful discourse itself. These questions are fundamental to what we understand when we speak of the individual or human dignity or moral purpose. How we discriminate between activities that are essential and necessary to our very humanness, those that are, however desirable, less essential, and those that are merely convenient, is at stake.

Because women have, throughout much of Western history, been a silenced population in the arena of public speech, their views on these matters, and their role in the process of humanization, have either been taken for granted or assigned a lesser order of significance and honor compared to the public, political activities of males. Women were silenced in part because that which defines them and to which they are inescapably linked—sexuality, natality, the human body (images of uncleanness and taboo, visions of dependency, helplessness, vulnerability)—was omitted from political speech. Why? Because politics is in part

an indirect public influence it remained private speech. Were such "women-behind-the-men" to have attempted to enter the public arena to speak with their own voices, they would have been roundly jeered, satirized, and condemned.

an elaborate defense against the tug of the private, against the lure of the familial, against evocations of female power.[12] The question to be put, then, is not just what politics is for but what politics has served to defend against. That question is best explored through the prism of the public and the private. Using public and private as my conceptual touchstones, I shall begin by tracing the powerful, public words of thinkers whose views helped to determine what was politics and, by implication, what was not politics and how we think and feel about each.

---

[12] A "defense," or "to defend against," must not be construed as meaning neurotic and therefore treated in reductionistic terms. Within psychoanalytic thought, there is continuing debate over the range, nature, and actual dynamics of defense mechanisms. As I use defense here it implies a set of ideas that must be fended off in order to deal with perceived threats and dangers. At which point such defense becomes a destructive falsification and distortion of reality rather than, importantly, a constructive way to deal with inner and outer realities will always be a matter for theoretical debate and moral judgment.

Part I

Public and Private Images in Western Political Thought

We know that the dead are mighty rulers . . .
—*Freud*

Chapter I

Politics Discovered and Celebrated: Plato and the Aristotelian Moment

. . . the argument is not about just any question, but about the way one should live.—*Plato*

A consideration of the prominent types of life shows that people of superior refinement and of active disposition identify happiness with honour; for this is, roughly speaking, the end of political life.—*Aristotle*

The introduction ended on a playful and provocative note with my suggestion that politics, including those normative ideals of collective life from Plato's time to our own, is never simply or exclusively *for* something but complicatedly a defense against something else. Should a reader cavil at this claim, or shudder in anticipation of an armchair psychoanalysis of Aristotle or Machiavelli, please rest assured. Although I shall not put any thinker on the couch I shall place each in turn on the table of critical dissection. Critique is the basis of an interpretive activity that allows one to put together, like the pieces of a puzzle, what it is a man celebrates and what he condemns, what he desires and what he fears, what he admires and what he abhors, what he looks towards and what he looks away from, which voices he listens to and which voices he silences. This process takes on greatest cogency at those points where a thinker seems to muddle or obfuscate his own position or engages in thin and inadequate arguments to defend it. That serves as a clue that he is fending off some idea, fear, or desire he finds incompatible either with his view of himself, his visions for society, or his understanding of the world.[1]

[1] See, for example, Eli Sagan's discussion of Thucydides in *The Lust to Annihilate: A Psychoanalytic Study of Violence in Ancient Greek Culture*, pp. 166-194.

DIVINE PLATO, DOWN TO EARTH

Because Plato's thought has been more thoroughly analyzed, interpreted, criticized, and celebrated than that of any other thinker in the Western political tradition, one wonders if there is anything new or interesting to report at this late date. Doubts are dispelled, however, as one enters Plato's world and finds him luminous, vexing, noble, and frightening by turns. Although I shall explore these issues at length in Chapter 5, there are among contemporary feminist thinkers some who would order all of human life under a single overarching rubric. These feminist authors do not cite Plato as inspiration for their reflections, yet his remains that body of thought which contains the most enduring and profound articulation of politics as a total aesthetic order. I shall unfold the nature of that order, as Plato pictures it, from the angle of vision afforded by the public-private prism. This allows certain dimensions of Plato's thought to stand out in bolder relief than they might under some alternative schema. One can ask: What urgent ends and aims, public or private, give vitality to his texts? Are the public and the private central to his concerns? What is the nature of public speech and private speech? Before tackling these and related questions head-on a précis of Plato's method is necessary, first, for those readers who may be unfamiliar with his categories of theoretical discourse, and second, because philosophic and political categories and imperatives are so thoroughly intertwined in Plato's work they cannot be examined apart from one another.

How and why did Plato carve up reality as he did? He urges in the *Statesman* that one "must only divide where there is real cleavage between specific forms" but insists that many divisions of the living world, seen and unseen, are sloppy and mistaken.[2] Plato claims that through his categories alone one may attain or grasp the highest reality, a world of invisible Forms, the *eidoi*, which lie outside history and time and of which only the wise can give an account. He observes: ". . . when a man tries by discussion—*by means of argument without the use of any of the*

[2] Plato, *Statesman*, ed. Martin Ostwald, trans. J. B. Skemp, p. 11.

senses [emphasis mine]—to attain to each thing itself that *is* and doesn't give up before he grasps by intellection itself that which is good itself, he comes to the very end of the intelligible realm just as that other man was then at the end of the visible."[3] Within Plato's system, the highest knowledge is a form of abstract philosophical knowledge unavailable in principle to the majority of humankind. He rejects other ways of knowing as foolish, inadequate, simplistic, even dangerous—a point I shall return to—particularly if these alternatives flow from emotion or passions rather than "intellection itself."[4]

For Plato the soul alone (*logistikon*), the locus (he believed) of the human capacity to speak, has a distinct identity. To reach the *eidoi*, those Forms of permanent, unchanging Truth, a particular kind of abstract dialectic was required. One begins in the realm of appearances with *doxa*, everyday unorganized knowledge; this sphere must be transcended and the novitiate moves into and then through *orthe-doxa*, concrete bodies of practical, organized knowledge, until at last, after much arduous mental and physical discipline, one reaches *episteme*, true knowledge of the Forms.[5] In the ideal state Plato creates "in speech," those who attain ultimate knowledge are given enormous power.[6]

The uninitiated in the Platonic world may wonder why Plato wished to transcend everyday reality and spend his time in a rarified sphere of extralinguistic Truth. We know that Plato despised the politics of his day and that he made several abortive

---

[3] Plato, *The Republic of Plato*, trans. Allan Bloom, Book 7, 530c-532d.

[4] Plato may have been one of those Freud had in mind when he observed that philosophy frequently "goes astray in its method by over-estimating the epistemological value of our logical operations." Sigmund Freud, *New Introductory Lectures on Psycho-Analysis, Standard Edition*, vol. 22, pp. 160-161. Cf. Mary Midgley, *Beast and Man: The Roots of Human Nature*, p. 44. She writes: "Fear of and contempt for feeling make up an irrational prejudice built into the structure of European rationalism."

[5] Cf. Bennett Simon, "Models of Mind and Mental Illness in Ancient Greece: I. The Platonic Model," *Journal of the History of the Behavioral Sciences*, pp. 398-404.

[6] James Glass notes that Plato "demystifies but in the course of his demystification he mystifies some of the impulses to power behind his philosophic arguments." (Personal communication with the author.)

attempts to create alternative political orders. We also know that Plato was coldly wrathful towards the political system that had put to death the man he revered above all others as the most just, most righteous: Socrates. (A democratic Athenian assembly sentenced Socrates to death.) Disheartened with the treatment accorded just men on this earth, Plato would create a world in which the just man is not only secure from the hounds baying at his heels but in which that man, and others of his kind, hold absolute power. Power conferred by knowledge of the Forms is its own

⟶ justification to set the terms of existence for others. Plato would preclude absolutely debate and controversy leading (inevitably, he believed) to social chaos and discord. He would do so with the certitude and finality afforded by ultimate Truth. It is only when Truth triumphs that the din created by the cacophony of disparate voices being heard in the land ceases.

I shall say more on Plato's means toward the end of order and justice below, but a prior question suggests itself. If Plato was spurred to construct his ideal city in part because the politics of his time was thoroughly debased, how was it possible for a righteous man who knows the Truth to come into existence at all within an unjust order? Plato anticipates the query by reminding us that his highest aim is not, first and foremost, the creation of a total system of justice but to save the souls of a few good men. If he achieves the latter goal his corollary aim will likely follow. Socrates says: ". . . the argument is not about just any question, but about the way one should live."[7]

Plato presumed that a good society provided the moral environment within which good men were nourished, although he allowed exceptions to this general rule. But what sort of society was good or might serve as the template of human virtue? In order to examine this question for Plato and, later, for Aristotle it is important to note that the *idion*, or the private, in contrast to that which was public or common, was accorded a much lower status in Greek life. The private person or *idiot* was a being of lower purpose, goodness, rationality, and worth than the *polites* or public citizen who belonged to and participated in the city. If his public

---

[7] *The Republic*, Book 1, 351a-352d.

world is in decay, the man who would be just cannot slip into a niche in a rightly ordered public world like a foot into an old slipper. Nor can the privacy of the household nourish a search for righteousness. Instead one would-be just man or several (such men will always be a minority for Plato) must begin a particular sort of private quest for wisdom as therapy for the individual soul. Later those few who have attained true knowledge serve as doctors, treating the public sickness of society. Despite it all, then, despite ignorance, confusion, the lure of selfish pursuits, the impulse of Eros, the just man may "live a private life, for that good life is . . . possible without the regime; it does not depend, as do the other ways of life, on ruling in the city. . . ."[8] The just man can exist without the just city but it does not hold in reverse: the just city cannot exist without at least a few just men.

By declaring that a nonpublic quest for justice, given a debased public world, may be the superior life, Plato appears to confound the Greek order of things. In his claim that under those conditions when a certain sort of private life is the preferred life, indeed the seedbed for ultimate public righteousness and justice, one might presume that women, private beings by definition, would enjoy an enhanced dignity and status in the overall scheme of things. Alas, this is not the conclusion that follows for Plato. What Plato requires for the creation and sustenance of the good man outside the good city is not the private world of the household or *oikos* within which women, children, slaves, and servants carry on that everyday production and reproduction which sustains life itself, but another sort of private space exemplified by the symposium, that all-male forum for philosophic discourse, pedagogy, and social intimacy that is the dramatic mise en scène for the Platonic dialogues. The dramatis personae of the symposia included older and wiser teachers—Socrates is the preeminent example—and a group of learners, frequently young males. These men engage in private (that is, not public in a political sense) philosophical speech

---

[8] See Allan Bloom's "Interpretive Essay" in his edition of *The Republic*, p. 415. Cf. Susan Moller Okin's treatment of Plato and Bloom's essay in *Women in Western Political Thought*. A provocative approach to Plato appears in Gunnell, *Political Theory: Tradition and Interpretation*.

which aims at the attainment of Truth and the achievement of a correctly ordered soul.

For Plato the private speech of households lacks either the form of prose or the form of poetry and is therefore without meaning—unformed, chaotic, evanescent, the speech of *doxa*. Household speech could be neither heroic ("at the beginning," Socrates reminds us, were "those who have left speeches")[9] nor partake in that quest for wisdom at which the private, philosophic male speech of the dialogues aims. The women of Plato's time were excluded from politics as a fact of social arrangements and historic tradition. But they were debarred as well from participating actively in the process of becoming a good person in the absence of a good society. Plato was after an alternative to the understanding of the true man (given a particular political order) as one "who has developed his male humanity and can participate in the highest functions of a man, politics and war."[10] To become good on Plato's terms a man must successfully fight and conquer Eros, the most dangerous desire, and sublimate through stern discipline his impulses into a pure and spiritual love of wisdom. One of the purposes of all those evenings spent by men of the symposium together was not just to absorb wisdom and be taught by the master, Socrates, but to discipline, as part of the route to wisdom, the homoerotic desires which would invariably be aroused by the presence of young among older men. Plato is unyielding on the issue of giving in to one's impulses. One must instead, through mastery of a situation fraught with temptation, rid oneself of "unnecessary" pleasures, for they are disruptive and undermine the quest for Truth. One must become the master of one's actions when awake and one's dream-thoughts when asleep in order to fend off those sordid desires ". . . that wake up in sleep when the rest of the soul—all that belongs to the calculating, tame, and ruling part of it—slumbers, while the beastly wild part, gorged with food or drink, is skittish, and pushing sleep away, seeks to go and satisfy its dispositions. You know that in such a state it dares to do everything as though it were released from, and rid

[9] *The Republic*, Book 2, 366a-367a.
[10] *The Republic*, Bloom ed., notes to Book 1, p. 441.

of, all shame and prudence. And it doesn't shrink from attempting intercourse . . . with a mother or with anyone else at all—human beings, gods, and beasts."[11]

The dreams of men did not surprise Plato for they provided additional evidence that human nature, on the whole, was rather weak, buffeted about by appetites and yearnings. One sort of man, democratic man, Plato found most offensive. In Plato's view, he was a creature at the whim of passions he had not learned, through discipline and education, to master. He would forsake civic responsibility at the surge of a hormone and corrupt the polity in selfish pursuits. If he were lucky, such passions might subside as he grew older. But in the meantime he will have made a mess of things and destroyed or weakened all that Plato held dear. The proud boast of democracies, freedom and free speech, is synonymous, Plato insists, with a "license in it to do whatever one wants."[12] Democratic man seduces the young into his false ways through "false and boasting speeches and opinions."[13]

Democracy contains no authentic or meaningful speech, only the silence of the privatized and the babble of the ignorant. Socrates: "And the ultimate in the freedom of the multitude, my friend . . . *occurs in such a city when the purchased slaves, male and female, are no less free than those who have bought them. And we almost forgot to mention the extent of the law of equality and of freedom in the relations of women with men and men with*

---

[11] *The Republic*, Book 9, 571a-571d. Shame is mentioned at several points in the dialogue of *The Republic* indicating that it was a concept with a widely shared meaning for the Greeks. For example: A decent man when "left alone" might "dare to utter many things of which he would be ashamed if someone were to hear . . ." (Book 10, 602d-604b). In a discussion of jokes, Plato notes that a person might be "ashamed" to make certain jokes himself but enjoy "very much sharing in comic imitation in private" (Book 10, 606b-608c). A difference cited by the Greeks as one bit of evidence for their superiority over the "barbarians" was their capacity to go about nude in appropriate settings, including athletic games and group exercises, without being "shameless" (Bloom's "Interpretive Essay," p. 458). It is interesting that Greek moves to defuse Eros required overcoming feelings of shame at one's nudity and that of others. Clearly, there would have been nothing to overcome had the emotion of shame, tied to tradition and social rules, not been internalized as a psycho-social imperative.

[12] *The Republic*, Book 8, 555d-557d.

[13] *The Republic*, Book 8, 559-561c.

women" (emphasis mine).[14] Clearly this overturning of social order and decency was so distasteful to Plato that it served as another mark against democracy. Unlike the Platonic good man, the democratic man minds not how thoroughly he wallows in lower pleasures. Proof of this lies in the fact that such men—something Socrates "won't allow those whom we claim we care for and who must themselves become good men"—go on "to imitate women," a degradation coupled with imitation of "slaves, women or men, who are doing the slavish things."[15]

Yet Plato refuses to grow faint-hearted for in any city exist "the more decent few" who can master desire. From this "smallest group" which comes to share in the only knowledge which "ought to be called wisdom,"[16] a city may arise even though "not one city today is in a condition worthy of the philosophic nature."[17] For now, "the good city exists only in speech"; it can be created in speech, and as we watch it come into being, "Would we also see its justice coming into being, and its injustice?" muses Socrates.[18] Plato's city with a foundation in speech ("I don't suppose it exists anywhere on earth") is available only to a few good men who alone can come to "see" in order to found a city *within* themselves on the basis of what they have seen.[19]

---

[14] *The Republic*, Book 8, 561c-563c.

[15] *The Republic*, Book 3, 395c-397c. Even Plato's feminist defenders, despite the famous arguments in Book 5 of *The Republic*, must see in this a tendency on Plato's part to equate the "imitation of woman" with debasement. The reader should note that "imitating a woman" in Plato's context did not mean performing a woman's household role or going about in female garb, but taking what was deemed the "womanly" submissive posture during homosexual intercourse.

[16] *The Republic*, Book 4, 428a-429d.

[17] *The Republic*, Book 6, 496a-498b.

[18] *The Republic*, Book 2, 367a-369b.

[19] *The Republic*, Book 9, 592a-592b. Plato adds: "It doesn't make any difference whether it is or will be somewhere." Or compare this exchange:

"Then, what about this? Weren't we, as we assert, also making a pattern in speech of a good city?"

"Certainly."

"Do you suppose that what we say is any less good on account of our not being able to prove that it is possible to found a city the same as the one in speech?"

"Surely not," he said. [Book 5, 371d-373d.]

The good man, the lover of wisdom, comes into being through a process of private speech from which women and lesser sorts of men are excluded. Private-philosophical speech, the prose form of the dialogues, aims at Truth, not meaning. The key to Plato's understanding of human speech is not so much that it is meaningful or has meaning, least of all to the majority of participants in a society, but that it can be deployed as a means to gain an ultimate Truth which has no voice in historic time. The exclusion of women from this lofty process could be laid, oversimply, on the doorstep of Athenian misogyny and the social structures and arrangements which sustained it. Yet we know, as I shall discuss below, that for the purpose of purely *abstract* argumentation Plato was capable of countering the prejudices of his time. His debarment of women from the search for wisdom can be explained both by the social milieu within which the search occurred, including its sanctioned homoerotic attachments between older and younger men, as well as the particular *nature* of the truth at which Plato aimed. That is, a particular homosexual ethos, framed within a society rife with fear of, and repugnance towards, women, especially Mother, fused with what we call the Platonic metaphysic.

Socrates always appears "in a strongly homosexual ambience; . . . Socrates' youthful friends are commonly—one might say, normally—in love with boys, and he fully accepts these relationships."[20] Socrates himself reports on the avid thumpings of his heart "at the sight of beautiful youths and boys";[21] however, for all the perfervid yearnings, ostentatious sighings, even flights, sulks, and tears evident in the dialogues, Socrates exemplifies Eros Denied as the route to Eros Bound.[22] One must, Socrates

---

[20] Dover, *Greek Homosexuality*, p. 154.   [21] *Ibid.*, p. 160.

[22] The reader is invited to turn to *The Symposium*, trans. Walter Hamilton, as one of several dialogues in which Plato's ideal of an immaterial Eros unfolds. Plato notes (pp. 46-47) that "the Heavenly Aphrodite to whom the other Love belongs for one thing *has no female strain in her*, but springs from the male, and for another is older and consequently free from wantonness. Hence those who are inspired by it are attracted towards the male sex, and value it as being naturally the stronger and more intelligent" (emphasis mine). The spiritual "children" of high love between men are declared to "surpass human children by being immortal as well as more beautiful. Everyone would prefer children such as these to children after the flesh" (p. 91). See also Philip E. Slater, *The Glory of Hera*, esp. pp. 4-14.

insists, exercise control by the rational principle over the demands of the body. The unseen wonders of Truth far excel the seen pleasures of earthly Eros; thus, all forms of copulation, particularly the heterosexual sort, deprive the soul of its capacity to pursue higher ends. The *erastes* or dominant senior partner in a homoerotic couple who forces himself on his *eromenos*, or junior and submissive partner, demonstrates in so doing his unsuitability for Eros as a sublimated quest of Truth. The hapless *eromenos*, on the other hand, is severely punished. Having broken the "rules of legitimate eros [he] . . . classifies himself with women and foreigners" and must forsake "his role as a male citizen."[23] That is, the junior partner who overeagerly permits or seeks penetration is shamed, "womanized," and must voluntarily relinquish or be deprived forcibly of his public existence as a citizen.

It is easy enough to see why women could not break through these highly charged layers of mystification, ritual, and ossified social practice which traversed pedagogy, philosophy, politics, and the temptations of pederasty in turn. What is more difficult to see, and more speculative to discuss, is Eros Bound, the outcome of a series of homoerotic temptations not yielded to, as the foundation of Platonic philosophy. It is clear that Plato downgraded heterosexual Eros and reduced human procreation to the level of an activity man shares with the beasts, with all "inferior," subrational existence.[24] No intimations of ultimate Truth lay within the heterosexual activities necessary to sustain life itself;

---

[23] Dover, *Greek Homosexuality*, p. 103. The following bit of dialogue is drawn from *The Republic*, Book 3, 403a-404d.

"Then, this pleasure mustn't approach love, and lover and boy who love and are loved in the right way mustn't be partner to it?"

"By Zeus, no, Socrates," he said, "this pleasure certainly mustn't approach love."

"So then, as it seems, you'll set down a law in the city that's being founded: that a lover may kiss, be with, and touch his boy as though he were a son, for fair purposes, if he persuades him; but, as for the rest, his intercourse with the one for whom he cares will be such that their relationship will never be reputed to go further than this. If not, he'll be subject to blame as unmusical and inexperienced in fair things."

"Just so," he said.

[24] Dover, *Greek Homosexuality*, p. 163.

however, these could and did emerge in a setting in which the beauty of younger males spurred the master, Socrates, to the highest realms of Eros-Bound thought. It seems not quite apt to term Socrates' male admirers and would-be lovers the handmaidens of Platonic wisdom but I can think of no masculine equivalent for this turn of phrase. Excluded from citizenship, relegated to the necessary but despised realm of necessity, defeated or undermined in the realm of Eros, Hellas' glories may not have been quite so obvious to Athenian women as they later were to Lord Byron from his distant shore.

But we cannot stop here, for the question will be put: did not Plato, despite all, dip into the font of wisdom and emerge at least partially redeemed (if not washed altogether of the misogynistic taint of his time) when he allowed a few good women to become Guardians in his ideal city? The conviction imbedded in the question is widely shared but it deserves serious qualification.[25] To explain my demurrer, it is necessary to reconstruct briefly and in broad strokes Plato's ideal state "in speech" asking, as I do, that the reader not forget that Plato's *Republic* is a form of discourse which emerged from a setting that not only *excluded* women but *included* relationships of dominance and submission among men. My point is not that we are thereby free to dismiss that discourse out of hand but that we remind ourselves that all human speech occurs in a particular time and place among specific groups of individuals, some of whom leave written accounts of themselves and others who are silent to us. Platonic speech cannot be exempted from considerations of historic specificity, nor from judgments based, in part, on such considerations. This means that one's final judgment of Plato's arguments must involve asking whether and in what important, not trivial, ways the *process* of reaching the *eidoi* infected the substantive conclusions that emerged. Did the symposia truly allow for uncoerced commu-

---

[25] See Bloom's "Interpretive Essay" in *The Republic*, p. 410. I am not unaware of the conviction expressed by Bloom, among others, that one must approach *The Republic* as a masterpiece of ironic discourse; however, one can appreciate Plato's irony without treating his conclusions ironically. I am proceeding on the assumption that *The Republic* should, indeed *must*, be taken seriously for the conflicts that spurred Plato to such drastic remedies are alive in our own troubled time.

nication and a dispassionate search for wisdom? Or were there covert constraints at work that had a silencing effect, preventing the raising of certain questions and distorting others? The reluctance with which we, from our safe and respectful distance, put such questions to Plato indicates that perhaps none of us wishes to bring divine Plato down to earth.

Of Plato's republic, "where public-spirited men rule for the common good," it can be said that its creation would require such drastic social surgery, all manner of disruptions, wrenchings, and griefs, that the vast majority of individuals, in his time or our own, would, if asked, prefer to remain in their unjust societies than to undergo Plato's cure.[26] Plato's new order is ruled by an elite whose knowledge gives them that right: they know all that must be known; they alone possess the political knowledge required to create and sustain the just city. The ruler's power and knowledge exempt him from certain of the moral injunctions which remain binding on other individuals, less powerful and knowledgeable than himself. Specifically, the ruler has the right to lie. "Then, it's appropriate for the rulers, if for anyone at all, to lie for the benefit of the city in cases involving enemies or citizens, while all the rest must not put their hands to anything of the sort . . . for a private man to lie to such rulers is a fault the same as, and even greater than, for a sick man or a man in training not to tell the truth about the affections of his body to the doctor or the trainer."[27] The rulers may lie in part because they are capable of distinguishing the "real lie" from those used in their public pronouncements as stratagems against enemies, or as preventive measures to stop some "madness or some folly." In order to dominate public speech effectively, to be the only public voices in the city, the rulers must censor or forbid speeches about the gods and expunge all tall tales of ancient heroes for ". . . the more poetic they are, the less should they be heard by boys and men."[28]

---

[26] Abigail Rosenthal, "Feminism Without Contradictions," *Monist*, p. 32. Cf. Midgley, *Beast and Man*, p. 76. Midgley finds that Plato's requirements for the ideal city involve "not just suppression, but an insolent and contemptuous *distortion* of a powerful emotional tendency."

[27] *The Republic*, Book 3, 389b-389e.

[28] *The Republic*, Book 2, 382a-382d; Book 3, 386c-387c.

The upshot is public silence from the vast majority, public duplicity when necessary from the rulers when they engage in political speech, and the silent perfection of the *eidoi* of whom no one speaks in historic time and space. The costs of Plato's just order seem rather high thus far. But there is more, including the chilling precondition that if the ideal city is to come into being, the rulers would take "the dispositions of human beings; as though they were a tablet . . . which, in the first place, they would wipe clean. And that's hardly easy."[29] Though Plato appears to want his reader to have empathy with the arduous task faced by his rulers, a more likely response is concern for who or what is to get "wiped clean." Another demand upon the elect: ". . . for a city that is going to be governed on a high level, *women must be in common*, children and their entire education must be in common, and similarly the practices in war and peace must be in common, and their kings must be those among them who have proved best in philosophy and with respect to war"[30] (emphasis mine). Here Plato is blunt and unembellished in addressing woman's lot as members of the elite in the ideal city. What is also clear is that socially and conceptually distinguishable public and private spheres must disappear for these distinctions exert a disunifying effect upon the social whole.

The achievement of the just state requires the creation of such a powerful, all-encompassing bond between individuals and the state that all social and political conflict disappears, discord melts away, and the state comes to resemble a "single person," a fused, organic entity. Clearly this vision can be attained only if private life, loyalty, and purpose are absorbed into the public domain. Away then with private marriage, family life, and child-rearing: this is the requirement for future Guardians designed to prepare each member of Plato's elite for the demand that his life in all its aspects be shaped in conformity to the ideal order. There is more to that ideal: a systematic meritocracy in which children are shunted about like raw material to be turned into instruments of social "good." For example: children from the lower orders (persons of iron and brass in the Allegory of the Metals) may per-

[29] *The Republic*, Book 6, 500c-501b.
[30] *The Republic*, Book 7, 543a.

chance, here and there, be gifted. As soon as the discernible sparks of future wisdom cross the tiny countenance, that child must be removed from his or her parents at once, "without the smallest pity," and moved upstairs with the persons of gold. Similarly, gold parents may give birth to a less than glittering offspring. This little infant is sent to the lower orders where he or she belongs. Children who are moved upward may one day become Auxiliaries or even Guardians.[31] Children sent below will do the things iron sorts do. There is a place for everyone and everyone must be in his or her place. "Surely," Socrates tells Glaucon, "we set down and often said, if you remember, that each one must practice one of the functions in the city, that one for which his nature made him naturally most fit."[32] Plato's explicit purpose with this social engineering is to prevent the emergence of hereditary oligarchies. But the drastic nature of his remedy seems out of proportion to the evil. One senses other impulses at work. I shall speculate a bit later as to what these may be, but first I shall turn to those women who are to be "held in common."

The female members of the Guardian class are corulers with the male brightest and best from whom their reproductive partners are selected. Plato's elaborate justification for incorporating women into the Guardian ranks, argued by Socrates in Book 5 of *The Republic*, is too well known to repeat in detail here. There are certain salient features of the argument which I shall probe. In the course of the debate, Socrates frequently makes his case against exclusionary, sex-linked practices that have no clear and necessary relation to the activities under consideration in terms that remain powerful.[33] The strength of Socrates' case on this level is not so much my concern here as the *costs* of female parity on the upper levels of the ideal state, for this parity with male rulers occurs under the terms of a thoroughgoing deprivatization. I shall explore briefly the arguments for sex parity and then turn to the terms under which Socrates insists it must be established.

Socrates counters Glaucon's and Admiemantus' objections to

[31] *The Republic*, Book 3, 414d-416e.

[32] *The Republic*, Book 4, 432c-433c. Cf. Rosenthal, "Feminism Without Contradictions," p. 36.

[33] See the argument in *The Republic*, Book 5 beginning 449c-491d.

his incorporation of women into the ranks of rulers by promulgating a notion of woman's nature which appears exemplary at first glance. Rather than consigning women to particular social outcomes based on biological categories, Plato insists that one may find within the category "woman" gifted individuals possessing all the qualities necessary to become a Guardian. Such unique women can undertake the same tasks and training as their male counterparts, for "If, then, we use the women for the same things as the men, they must also be taught the same things."[34] Plato does not envisage a social order in which individuals are evaluated and placed according to some a priori assessment of their higher or lower "natures" as members of a larger category. He insists that simply being born into a social class or biological sex does not in itself constitute prima facie evidence that any particular individual within a particular class or category has a higher or lower nature than any other. Plato's rationalist meritocracy requires that all considerations of sex, race, age, class, family ties, tradition, and history be stripped away in order to fit people into their appropriate social slots, performing functions to which they are suited. Should a male or female possess an aptitude for a particular occupation, for the female to enter that occupation along with a qualified male constitutes no violation of either wisdom or virtue.

Socrates concludes: ". . . we'll assert that it has not thereby yet been proved that a woman differs from a man with respect to what we're talking about; rather, we'll still suppose that our guardians and *their women* must practice the same things"[35] (emphasis mine). (Again the term "their women" is perhaps more suggestive than Plato appears to recognize.) The key phrase in the argument *for* parity is "with respect to what we're talking about." By that Plato means that possession of deft, skilled hands and fingers *would* constitute a relevant difference if the distinction in question were the occupation of a brain surgeon. But the possession of deft hands and fingers does not constitute a relevant difference for one who aspires to teach philosophy. In terms of

[34] *The Republic*, Book 5, 451d-452d.
[35] *The Republic*, Book 5, 453d-455c.

political rule, Plato declares: ". . . there is no practice of a city's governors which belongs to woman because she's woman, or to man because he's man; but the natures are scattered alike among both animals; and woman participates according to nature in all practices, and man in all, but in all of them woman is weaker than man."[36] It follows that one woman will be fit by nature to be a Guardian, another will not. But in each instance the "same natures," male and female, must be allowed identical pursuits.[37] For the purpose of running the commonwealth, a woman may have the same nature as a man.

Those who become part of the Platonic vanguard are disallowed private families and debarred from indiscriminate breeding. Instead a rigid sexual code is imposed which permits matings only when offspring are desired. A system of eugenics is devised to match up respective males and females with their most likely mates in order that vigorous, healthy offspring will result. Immediately after birth, the baby is removed from its biological mother and sent to a central nursery where it is entrusted to officers designated for child-rearing. Guardian women who have given birth do nurse when their breasts become engorged with milk, but are not allowed to nurse their own infants. Instead each mother nurses the "anonymous" baby presented to her when she enters the nursing home in the segregated children's quarter of the city.

Again, the nagging question: Why? What is this for? What is it a defense against? What has so roused Plato that the only solution he sees to individual malaise and social sickness is a thoroughgoing meritocracy, totally rationalized, in which individuals can be slotted into niches along purely functional criteria? Plato claims his moves are required to eradicate motives and occasions for discord and disunion. Private homes and sexual attachments, devotion to friends, dedication to individual aims and purposes notoriously militate against single-minded devotion to the ideal city or a quest for Truth. He cries: "Have we any greater evil for a city than what splits it and makes it many instead of one? Or a greater good than what binds it together and makes

---

[36] *The Republic*, Book 5, 455c-457a.
[37] Cf. Plato's *Meno*, trans. W.K.C. Guthrie, pp. 117-118.

it one?''[38] There are words scattered throughout *The Republic* that evoke a sense of chaos and disintegration: asunder . . . destroy . . . dissolves . . . overwhelms . . . splits . . . evil. And other terms are designated as potent enough to prevent anarchy: dominate . . . censor . . . expunge . . . conform . . . bind . . . make one. For Plato, every conflict is a potential cataclysm; every discussion in which differences are stated a threat portending disintegration; every sally an embryonic struggle unto death; every distinction a possible blemish on the canvas of harmonious and unsullied order, the purity of his aesthetically constructed ideal city. Plato offers not peace at any price but peace at a very high price. We should by now recognize that in most such bargains there is in fact no peace but individuals still pay the price, particularly, I shall argue, Plato's women.

Whatever nightmares rocked his sleep and terrors filled his days, Plato's solution is an overreaction in this sense: he created as his vision of the ideal city a kind of mirror image to the most thoroughly debased, incessantly chaotic, and haplessly disintegrated picture of social and political life one might imagine. If a thinker's contrast model to the creation of a new order is a scene of chaos and breakup and he truly believes that social orders that do not work smoothly under an overarching set of imperatives invariably tend to anarchy, his solution will have about it something of the final, total, ultimate. One wonders about Plato's Guardians and the task of being the wisest and best. Oh yes, they cultivate beautiful bodies with ascetic rigor, and do their mental gymnastics, but how joyless it must be, nearly as tedious as immortality. For Plato's Eros, the Bound Eros of the Guardians, is an Eros robbed of its heart, its potential for irrepressibility and innovation.

Plato continued to stress unity and organicity in his later work, *The Laws*, though there his solutions are less imposing, more workable. He repeats his litany on the evils of social disharmony, tying such evil once again to the peril presented by private women, homebound within the body politic. He conjures up the image of private wives, with their familial loyalties and values, undermin-

[38] *The Republic*, Book 5, 461e-462d.

contrast model —
question of how thinker
perceives change: in
extremes (black-and-white)
or more moderately

ing the common end and shared purposes of the city: again, there seems but one type of solution and that requires subjecting the private sphere to a thoroughgoing politicization and rationalization in order that it become a supportive buttress of the state. Plato accomplishes his purposes through enforcement of a complex set of regulations and controls of sexuality, marriage, pregnancy, childbirth and child-rearing, education, remarriage, and inheritance.[39] Plato's Athenian to Cleinias: "Take someone who proposes to promulgate laws to a state about the correct conduct of the public life of the community. What if he reckons that *in principle* one ought not to use compulsion—even in so far as one *can* use it in private affairs? Suppose he thinks that a man ought to be allowed to do what he likes with the day, instead of being regulated at every turn. Well, if he excludes private life from his legislations, and expects that the citizens will be prepared to be law-abiding in their public life as a community, he's making a big mistake."[40]

To fight the lure of disintegrative tendencies, Plato would educate women "in precisely the same way" as men for otherwise they will lack that common purpose without which the state is doomed to be but half a state. Plato's motive for equal education of the sexes was not primarily considerations of social justice, or equality, or individual rights (the notion as we understand it did not exist) but an instrumental drive, a means to his overriding end: social harmony and unity. He argues that because the woman's "*natural*" potential for virtue is inferior to a man's, she's a greater danger to social harmony than he. She "is inclined to be secretive and crafty" because of her "weakness."[41] She must not be left to her own devices or the state may lose control. Plato's insight here, later recast by Rousseau and contemporary feminists, is that a private realm in which women live lives of obscurity and retirement is not the best school for citizenship but a breeding ground of discontent. Why then do Plato's women,

---

[39] Plato, *The Laws*, trans. Trevor J. Saunders, *passim*.

[40] *The Laws*, pp. 261-262.

[41] *The Laws*, pp. 262-263. See also the discussion by Christine Garside Allen, "Plato on Women," *Feminist Studies*, pp. 131-138.

or many of them, protest the takeover and control of their domain from the outside if the result is to bring them closer to the public heart of things? Plato attributed this phenomenon to woman's "secretive . . . crafty" nature and to the fact that "a woman's natural potential for virtue is inferior to a man's." We know a bit more about human depth psychology than Plato did, and we could better explain the psychology at work.

There were, no doubt, many women of Plato's time who exhibited the characteristics he attributes to the private wives of *The Laws*. But the question is: Why? The key problem is not so much Plato's personal antipathy toward women but his conceptual adequacy to the task at hand. Here Plato's somewhat muddled treatment of the category "nature" becomes critical. As we have seen, he repudiated presumptions of human nature based solely on the notion that aggregate categories held sway for each particular individual within a category. He seems to perceive a thing's "nature" as the outcome of a developmental or maturing process, though there is some slippage on this point. But there is no doubt at all that Plato deemed it "better" (that is, more conducive to social harmony) for the majority of individuals to *believe* that natural or innate forces lay at the basis of a society's structure of rewards, statuses, privileges. To question this belief or to argue otherwise in political speech, whatever the truth might be, would promote skepticism and encourage disunifying tendencies.

I shall come full circle in this series of reflections on Plato by sketching what I see as the unacceptable price those women Plato admits to parity with male rulers must pay for the privilege. I begin with a claim: Plato's Guardians may have wisdom and power and rule in the ideal city but their human identity as males and females, but most especially females, is damaged in the process. (Remember that Plato's female Guardians go directly from a situation in which they are subordinate and have neither a public-political nor a philosophic voice to a world in which their voice is outside time. From the silence of subordination to the Silences of extralinguistic Truth!) First, the presumption that whether I am a woman or a man is an uninteresting, contingent statement about me rather than the essential and interesting bedrock of my identity is false.[42] Women suffer most heavily from Plato's denial of biological integrity as they can least escape biological imperatives. Now Plato may not wish to press the notion of "same nature" for the purposes of rule to the point where he means males and females have identical natures, though the depth connections in Plato's texts suggest very strongly that this is precisely what he intends. For Plato, in some profound sense, only the soul is real. His sexual asceticism reinforced the philosophic point that body and mind, desire and action, could be severed.[43] If my body is not the irreducible bedrock of whom I am—located as it is in time and space, having particular qualities, unique characteristics, and a developmental history—then the peculiar abstractedness and disconnectedness of the Guardian and his or her existence may well follow.

The terms under which Plato admits that elite group of women into parity with an equally elite group of men, for purposes he, not they, has chosen in a manner he, not they, has fixed, are

---

[42] Plato's arguments are based on the conviction that personal identity is not in some fundamental sense bodily identity. Peter Winch, however, observes that masculinity and femininity are not simply *components* of a life but its *mode*. "Now the concepts of masculinity and femininity obviously require one another. A man is a man in relation to women; and a woman is a woman in relation to men. Thus the form taken by man's relation to women is of quite fundamental importance for the significance he can attach to his own life. The vulgar identification of morality with sexual morality certainly *is* vulgar; but it is a vulgarization of an important truth." Peter Winch, "Understanding a Primitive Society," in *Rationality*, ed. Bryan Wilson, p. 110. See the following for further development of this complex theme: Sigmund Freud, *The Ego and the Id*, *Standard Edition*, vol. 19, pp. 3-66; Jean Bethke Elshtain, "Against Androgyny," *Telos*, pp. 5-21; Richard Wollheim, "Psychoanalysis and Women," *New Left Review*, pp. 61-70 in which Wollheim explicates the relationship between the body and ego development from a psychoanalytic perspective; Brian O'Shaugnessy, "The Id and the Thinking Process," in *Freud: A Collection of Critical Essays*, ed. Richard Wollheim, pp. 222-241. Bernard Williams' difficult essays on the subject are worth the reader's trouble, particularly "Bodily continuity and personal identity" and "Are persons bodies?" in his collection *Problems of the Self*, pp. 19-25 and pp. 64-81, respectively.

[43] See John L. Hodge, Donald K. Struckman and Lynn Dorland Trost, *Cultural Bases of Racism and Group Oppression* for a truculent but provocative discussion, beginning with Plato's "dualism," of those Western concepts, values, and institutional structures which support "racism, sexism, and elitism."

silencing terms. By definition and in advance, the woman gives up any hope of offering a coherent account of her social experience, the terms of her previous privatization, in a historically situated voice. For her the philosophic speech of the Guardian, Plato's ultimate reality, is surely an unreality, for it fails to touch the wellsprings of her bio-social, specific identity. In the realm of the ahistorical, eternal, and extralinguistic Forms there is no place for a finite, historical, language-using self. *The Republic* exemplifies a purely abstract vision of a future condition which bears no relation to humans-in-history, with no coherent connection to some recognizable past and the beings who lived in it.

Consider Plato's picture: women previously consigned to privatization and silence are suddenly thrust into a ruling elite (wives in common) presumably because they have survived a process leading to knowledge of the Forms and are not mired in *doxa* or even *orthe-doxa*. Surely, however, the woman who initially finds her voice following periods of socially decreed public silence will speak very much on the level of *doxa* as she pours out unsystematically what she has come to know and feel within her own world. Socrates makes a number of fine arguments to justify why women are suited for the task of rule in his city "in speech" but one senses that women, under the transformed silencing considerations as members of the elect, would know that they were there primarily because the Guardians needed to reproduce. Plato lets the cat out of the bag too often on this question. His ideal, perhaps, would have been a kind of parthenogenesis whereby male elites could give birth to themselves both metaphorically and actually. But that method, implied by the Platonic aesthetic, could neither yield biological offspring nor allow Plato to urge the transcendence of sexual identities in quite the same way. It is only at the cost of their sexual identity that the beings used routinely in the dialogues to evoke images of defilement, individuals having no public voice or role, are tapped in an abstract way for philosophic speech leading to political power. What woman would accept parity with an elite group of men on these terms—terms that dictate her homelessness and the stripping away of her psycho-sexual and social identity?

That Plato is sometimes seen as women's best friend among

political thinkers in the Western tradition before John Stuart Mill took pen in hand says rather more, I fear, about that tradition than it does about Plato, who appears to us, brought down to earth, with several warts—his intolerance of plurality, diversity, debate, or distinct human voices. Plato controls through superior wisdom but it is control all the same. To argue in behalf of woman that her nature is identical to man's for certain relevant purposes at hand is to offer, on one level, a convincing set of arguments imbedded, on another level, within a framework that promises only a pyrrhic victory in the service of ends women have had no hand in articulating. Plato's vision includes no dynamic and variable field of action. His aesthetic order is as unruffled as death if it is working perfectly.

In affirming the values of a static politics with order and harmony as its overriding raison d'être Plato must be given credit for refusing to shrink from the implications of his own thought. Lesser souls might consider some scheme logical, rational, even conducive to social order, yet reject what the cure requires. Plato, however, forges ahead with a vision of order in which the traditional web of social ties and relations has been cast aside in order to serve a larger purpose; in which human bodies are not fundamental to the identity of self; in which the relationship between child and parents is eroded to promote political ends; in which those embracing a different way of seeing are silenced or banished.[44] One senses that if Plato could have eliminated the beasts that bestir themselves in the night, he would. By demonstrating what a thoroughgoing rationalist, meritocratic order would require, namely, the application to, and assessment of, all human beings on a single set of formal and abstract criteria, Plato reminds us that the grounding of our lives can never be totally rationalized, *if* we consider our individual identities, our relations with others,

---

[44] Cf. Robert Paul Wolff, "There's Nobody Here But Us Persons," in *Women and Philosophy*, ed. Carol Gould and Marx Wartofsky, pp. 128-144. Wolff argues that a meritocracy within which only universalist criteria applied would transform all persons into "totally public persons," complete the destruction of traditional forms of social life, and serve as a monument to those "ideals and images of . . . classical liberalism" Plato strangely foreshadows. "It would also," Wolff insists, "be the ultimate denial of the humanity of man" (p. 141).

and our particular histories to be essential and important, not contingent and trivial, to us.

MAN'S POLITICS, WOMAN'S PRIVATIZATION: ARISTOTLE

Aristotle is something of a respite after Plato's great demands. He is not a thinker who would create a shining City on a Hill. Yet his reputation among contemporary feminist thinkers is lower than Plato's, based on widespread knowledge of Aristotle's unambiguous subjection of woman on the grounds that her nature required it. Aristotle absorbs woman completely within the *oikos* or household, denies woman any possibility of a public voice or role, and precludes the possibility for female self-transformation over time. Aristotle constructed this tidy arrangement under the terms of a set of teleological presumptions and an explanatory theory flowing from those presumptions which contain irresistible outcomes for women, men, and politics.[45] Those thinkers, including feminists, who would excise Aristotle from consideration given the unacceptable conclusions to which his method led him, may fail to make contact with other dimensions of his thought which continue to inspire those committed to creating and sustaining a participatory, normative ideal of political life. I shall turn to a condensed explication of Aristotle's method as a necessary first step in exploring his treatment of the public and the private.

It is Aristotle's view that the final cause of every thing can be determined by noting the actualization of those capacities inherent within it from the start. To the question: How does one know what capacities or potentialities inhere within a given entity, any single member of a category *x*, Aristotle points to an instance of the completion of that category as an empirically observable datum. In completion one reads potentiality. "What each thing is when its growth is completed," he writes, "we call the nature

[45] See Jean Bethke Elshtain, "Moral Woman/Immoral Man: The Public/Private Distinction and Its Political Ramifications," in *Politics and Society*, pp. 453-473. Although I draw upon this essay I arrive at somewhat more mixed conclusions on Aristotle than I did earlier.

of that thing, whether it be a man or a horse or a family.''[46] Aristotle's teleological determinism applied to natural and social objects and categories alike—both peafowl and *polises*. His empiricist approach led him to repudiate the existence of those immaterial entities Plato required in order to resolve his struggle with problems of the one and the many and to transcend his own age—in speech. Recognizing, however, that a crude empiricism was no alternative to Platonic metaphysics (one could not engage in conceptualization, if all that existed were congeries of disparate particulars),[47] Aristotle's solution was to formulate a method consisting of ''formal'' and ''material'' principles. The formal element is an ordering principle under which one grasps and makes sense of particulars. It has the force of a teleological imperative. Material principles, on the other hand, exist among qualities, relations, conditions—they cannot bring order to a whole.

For Aristotle each separate thing's end is predetermined: it is destined to fulfill its essence. It follows that to speak of the ''good'' of some x is always relative to its function and that function follows a fortiori from its inherent teleological principle. Aristotle assumes, with latter-day functionalists who have borrowed from his method, that one can determine what a thing (person, institution) is in terms of its function or ''end.'' To do so is to set up, simultaneously, standards of evaluation. That is, once we can state the function of any x we can say what a good x is, or we can say that x is good to the extent that it performs its function. Since the function of one x cannot by definition be taken over by another, Aristotle's system, for all its rigidity, does allow for some diversity within unity. He does not obliterate the many in the process of attaining one. He was appalled by Plato's blurring or obliteration of certain distinctions, including public and private, for this opened up all social spheres to reordering under a *single* rubric.[48] Aristotle's solution was to stay close to

---

[46] Aristotle, *The Politics*, ed. and trans. Ernest Barker, p. 5.

[47] Aristotle, *Metaphysics*, trans. Richard Hope, p. 51. Cf. pp. 19-20.

[48] *Metaphysics*, p. 44. In *Metaphysics* Aristotle comes down squarely in favor of a multiplicity of competing explanatory perspectives suited to many diverse sciences, including philosophy, ''the science of the end or good'' (p. 43). There are, he insists, ''many ways in which men may know the same thing. . . . Thus

what, for him, were the observable arrangements of various spheres and diverse activities within his and other societies and to recast or infuse at least some of these with a teleological insistency. As we shall see, teleology is indistinguishable from tautology at certain points in Aristotle's characterization of social life.

Although Aristotle believed in the gentlemanly Golden Mean and advised steering clear of extremes, the Greek society of his day was a civilization of extremes: founded on slavery, flourishing on imperialism of the most brutal sort, dedicated to misogyny in thought and practice, subject to conflict and crisis at each turn. Despite this, Aristotle's ordering of natural and social objects spun out a rationale for why things must be as they are. If they were not so civil and comfortable for the many, that was not his concern so long as certain equipoise held for the few, so long as things were functioning smoothly. What I am suggesting is that Aristotle's method has deep connections to an ideology that insulated him from the harsh realities of Greek life by providing simultaneously an explanation of, and justification for, those realities.

Several thinkers have commented on the class-bound nature of Aristotle's arguments. For example, Stuart Hampshire, discussing the *Ethics*, states: "Aristotelian theory entails that there is no very significant difference between manners and morals."[49] Or, Alasdair MacIntyre: "The list of virtues in the *Ethics* is not a list resting on Aristotle's own personal choices and evaluations. It reflects what Aristotle takes to be 'the code of the gentleman' in contemporary Greek society. Aristotle himself endorses this code. Just as in analyzing political constitutions he treats Greek life as normative."[50] If MacIntyre and Hampshire are correct, Aristotle was not only complacent with respect to the social arrangements

---

any one of these types of scientific explanations would seem to be a different type of knowledge and may yet give us wisdom" (p. 44). For a contemporary debate on the problems of epistemological monism and pluralism see the essays in *Criticism and the Growth of Knowledge*, ed. Imre Lakatos and Alan Musgrave.

[49] Stuart Hampshire, "Public and Private Morality," in Hampshire's book of the same title, p. 28.

[50] MacIntyre, *Short History of Ethics*, p. 67.

of his own society but also rationalized those arrangements. I shall examine this charge further by turning, first, to a somewhat schematic statement and critique of the central points of theoretical demarcation on public and private emerging from Aristotle's *Politics*, for his typologies have had an enormous influence on subsequent treatments of public and private. From this point of straightforward critique, I shall move to a more nuanced look at specific aspects of Aristotle's thought. Finally, I shall examine why among contemporary political thinkers there are those who find within Aristotle a concept of politics as a form of action, and citizenship as the touchstone of participatory public identity, that remains vibrant.

Given Aristotle's teleological method and functionalist framework, each separate thing's end is destined to fulfill functions it alone can fulfill. This is true of slaves by nature, women, even greater and lesser associations. Familiar with Plato's argument that woman's nature cannot be given *simpliciter* and stated categorically for individual cases, Aristotle remains unmoved. Although he is contrasted with Plato as a defender of diversity and a friend of pluralism, he is categorically inflexible on some issues. Woman's nature and her subsequent function is one of these. Aristotle cites the ''natural'' inferiority that, he avers, explains and justifies woman's lower social and political status by comparing so-called ''male'' and ''female'' elements to the formal and material elements of his epistemology. He writes in the *Metaphysics*: ''. . . for the female becomes pregnant from a single impregnation, whereas the male impregnates many females. So sex is an analogue of matter and form.''[51] The male, he continues, implants the human form during mating. He deposits within the female a tiny homunculus for which the female serves as a vessel until this creature matures. The female herself provides nothing essential or determinative. Aristotle buttresses his already strained teleology of female nature with a defective science of biological and reproductive processes.

Aristotle's prior teleological commitments suffuse his presumptions on public and private, women and politics. He begins

[51] *Metaphysics*, pp. 20-21.

with the claim that the good life is possible *only* in the "final and perfect association" and, for individuals, only through their participation in it.[52] Man (meaning the male) is by nature an animal intended to live in a *polis*.[53] All associations aim at some good, but it is only in the *polis* that the highest good is attained. It follows that only those free citizens, *polites*, who participate in this goodness themselves attain good.[54] Women, slaves, and children did not and could not partake in the full unfolding of goodness and reason which was the common heritage of coequal participants in the perfect association. There is an "essential difference" between greater (free, male) and lesser (unfree, female) persons although these two categories of persons are linked in relationships of necessary dominance and subordination. Aristotle justifies this relationship by finding a "community of interest" between "the naturally ruling element with the element which is naturally ruled" essential to the "preservation of both."[55]

Aristotle argued against the notion that power over others was *automatically* tied to goodness. He urged instead that "the superior in goodness ought to rule over . . . inferiors"; that power must be accompanied by goodness before it can become an element in a *legitimate* relationship between master and slave, or male and female; nevertheless, because the mere *fact* of such rule implied the existence of superior goodness in the dominant party, that is, a man could not become the slave of another were he not "capable" of becoming another's property and of "apprehending" the full reason and goodness in his master which he himself lacked,[56] power over another was (tautologically) accompanied by goodness in Aristotle's ideal state.

The household constituted a nonpublic sphere within which the female was subsumed and which therefore defined her. Because

[52] *Politics*, p. 4   [53] *Politics*, p. 5.
[54] Cf. MacIntyre, *Short History of Ethics*, p. 63. "The good of man is defined as the activity of the soul in accordance with virtue, or if there are a number of human excellences or virtues, in accordance with the best and most perfect of them."
[55] *Politics*, pp. 2-3.
[56] *Politics*, p. 15, including n. 1 and n. 3. Aristotle states that: "A man is thus by nature a slave if he is capable of becoming (and this is the reason why he also actually becomes) the property of another" p. 13.

the good at which the household aimed was a lesser good than that which was the end of the *polis*, the wife-mother achieved only the limited goodness of the "naturally ruled," a goodness different in kind from that of the naturally ruling.[57] Females possessed reason in a similarly incomplete, "inconclusive" form. Aristotle states:

The ruler, accordingly, must possess moral goodness in its full and perfect form [i.e., the form based on rational deliberation], because his function, regarded absolutely and in its full nature, demands a master-artificer, and reason is such a master-artificer; but all other persons need only possess moral goodness to the extent required of them [by their particular position].[58]

Those women, children, slaves, and "mechanics and labourers" Aristotle distinguishes from free, male citizens are the "necessary conditions" of the state. Although they do not share in public life per se, unlike the citizens who comprise the *polis'* "integral parts," they nevertheless provide the precondition upon which that public life rests.[59] Aristotle compares rulers and subjects to flute-players and flute-makers; one makes use of what the other makes.[60] Because the class or category "woman" is inferior to the class or category "man," women are debarred from citizenship and active participation in the *polis*. Men alone possess the necessary attributes for citizenship. A citizen is "best defined by one criterion, 'a man who shares in the administration of justice and in the holding of office.' "[61] The state "in its simplest terms, is a body of such persons adequate . . . for achieving a self-sufficient existence."[62]

Aristotle's commitment to the status quo is implicit in his argument for "natural" female inferiority and his conviction that the slave "by nature" was an article of property who "belongs

[57] *Politics*, p. 34.   [58] *Politics*, pp. 35-36.

[59] *Politics*, p. 108. Cf. Arendt's celebration of Aristotle's scheme of things in *The Human Condition*, esp. p. 29ff.

[60] *Politics*, p. 106.   [61] *Politics*, p. 93.

[62] *Politics*, p. 95.

entirely" to a master and "has no life or being other than that of so belonging."[63] Aristotle's women were *idiots* in the Greek sense of the word, persons who either could not or did not participate in the *polis* or the "good" of public life, individuals without a public voice, condemned to silence as their appointed sphere and condition.[64] A public voice was the right and privilege of those who were declared to possess reason and goodness to its fullest extent. The *imbecillitus sexus* of women fit them only for blank ruminations which put no strain on their limited faculties.

Politics, the sphere of action, the realm of the highest system of justice, was a space for that activity which served as the end of the *polis*. Public persons by definition were responsible, rational, and free. They shared fully in private life *and* the life of the *polis* as its integral parts. As such they participated in the ultimate moral good Athens had to offer given Aristotle's insistence that politics has a powerful claim to primacy among human activities. Ideally, the good man and the good citizen are coterminous, though there were, and could be, exceptions to the ideal. But Aristotle allowed no exceptions to the argument that the life of the whole was superior in nature, intent, and purpose to that of all "lesser" associations, including the family. Exclusively private persons, not fully rational, limited in goodness, women lived out their lives in the realm of necessity, a life deemed inferior in its essence, intent, and purpose to political life, but a functional prerequisite for the realm of freedom.

Aristotle's teleological principles coupled with his opacity as to social arrangements blinded him to certain phenomena another might have described under a competing point of view. Aristotle goes further than simply reporting what his epoch "looked like." In describing the woman, for example, as an inferior life form, a kind of misbegotten man (necessarily so given that her essence dictated her limitedness) Aristotle buttressed the prejudices of his age. His views held sway or proved persuasive long after the glory of Attica had been reduced to romantically mystified historic memory.

[63] *Politics*, p. 11. Cf. MacIntyre, *Short History of Ethics*, p. 60.
[64] *Politics*, p. 11ff.

Now I will move to another level by probing salient portions of the *Politics* and *Ethics*, treating the problems I find as the basis for an interpretive exercise. There are points, as one reads the *Politics* (less so the *Ethics*, though even there) when Aristotle's arguments sound particularly forced, even tendentious. At these points the fluid assurance of his prose falters. I suggest that these points, of which I shall take up a few, are areas of conflict for Aristotle—conflict he either refused to acknowledge, or recognized but chose to paper over. *The Politics*, Book 1, opens with the familiar discussion on the differences between a household and a *polis* I have just analyzed. But it should be noted that man is an animal meant by nature not only for the *polis* but for the family, a point stressed in the *Ethics*.[65] It seems not worth belaboring what cannot be finally settled, namely, whether man-as-male is more "naturally" a political or a familial animal for Aristotle; suffice it to say that he finds both "natural" in the sense that they meet human needs and fulfill certain human potentials, making a particular kind of life possible. But things begin to get curious when Aristotle contends (given that nature never makes anything in vain) that the reason man is meant for political association and the male alone is that he is "furnished with the faculty of language."[66] Through language, man declares what is advantageous and disadvantageous, and what is just and unjust. A capacity for language and the activity of its use essentially defines man—and, it must be observed, woman, for there is no evidence that women in Aristotle's time had been struck dumb.

[65] Aristotle, *The Student's Oxford Aristotle*, vol. 5: *Ethics* [*Ethica Nicomachea*], trans. W. D. Ross. See the discussion in Book 1. Aristotle is frequently less than clear on the precise relation of the *oikos* to the *polis*, despite the schematic ordering from Book 1 of *The Politics*. His position waffles somewhat. The household is declared part of a whole (the *polis*) which is necessarily prior to it. This is an abstraction that is of no help in characterizing the two realms and their respective activities, or in explaining anything. At one point Aristotle says the household is a "part of the polis" and women are "half the free population." The relationship of husband to wife is compared to that of a "statesman over fellow-citizens," according to Aristotle a relationship *lacking* clear-cut domination and subordination and a relationship devoid of a master/slave dynamic—more along the lines of *primus inter pares*. Yet that is *not* the overall thrust of his argument.

[66] *Politics*, pp. 5-6.

It might appear that if the human species, male and female, talks and that activity essentially defines the species, no a priori basis for segregating the sexes by activity and function is justified by "nature." What we learn from reading Aristotle, however, is that he never takes up that challenge, abruptly drops the focus on language, and slips soon thereafter into one of his "whole necessarily prior to the parts" refrains. The overall effect when Aristotle bogs down in his teleological discussion is to undermine the suggestive force of his undeveloped comments on language. Disquiet lingers: since woman is obviously a language-user and language is, in turn, evidence of man's reasoning capacity and a unique *human* quality, the means whereby humans can lodge the arguments and claims and embrace the values necessary to do politics, why are women methodologically and politically struck dumb by being shunted into a sphere Aristotle declares devoid of *significant* speech if not speech-less?

Matters get murkier when Aristotle, in Book 1, returns to man as the speaking animal and declares that the use of speech makes the "family and *polis*" alike possible. (Indeed, one could reasonably make the claim, which Aristotle does not given his commitment to the primacy of the public sphere, that it is the family, where children first use and respond to language, that essentially humanizes us, male and female alike.) At this juncture he declares that Nature, author of teleological imperatives, endowed man (meaning, it is clear from the context, only the male) with the power of *reasoned* speech for Nature had a purpose in mind—the making of the "political animal." The woman, also a speech-user, is not capable of reasoned speech: this makes her a household animal as her unreasoning speech along with her incomplete rational faculty, lesser goodness, and lack of authority fit her for the "lesser" sphere. The upshot is clear, however murky the path towards it—the political animal is a being who would be thought to be cowardly if his courage were only the same as that of a "*courageous woman*" (emphasis mine).[67] Women are missing something of courage as well.

The *zoon politikon*, blessed with a full complement of faculties,

----

[67] *Politics*, p. 105.

carries with him as a teleologic birthright of his class and sex the "goodness" of those who "naturally rule." The unearned "goodness" of the naturally ruling is used to provide one of Aristotle's less-than-compelling justifications for a Greek institution—slavery—when he insists that the superior in goodness, a goodness which has nothing whatever to do with what is usually understood by moral virtue, must preside over his inferiors in that quality. Aristotle's "goodness" (the term he uses is *kalokagathia*) is "the quality of one who is both handsome and good,"[68] and applied in his day to the character of the compleat gentleman. Such "goodness" commands sway over wives, inferiors, slaves. It seems rather a lot for Aristotle to peg on a trait or manner tied to class rather than to some substantive point of mind or spirit. In the *Ethics* Aristotle links all sorts of things to this "goodness," including happiness, felicity (the practice of which is excluded for women), and the excellence of the citizen. (There is also a general goodness, *arete*, construed as temperance, courage, and wisdom.) Women may be endowed with the power of speech but they are denied the capacity for rational deliberation, severed from what Aristotle considers the life of action, and precluded from the possession and practice of Aristotelian "goodness."

The most indelible impression left on the reader by Aristotle's belaboring of "natural rule" tied, in turn, to a thin notion of goodness is its inadequacy to the task at hand. He does struggle to develop an argument and justification for slavery. The position of women, however, never receives a full explication. Perhaps the lot of women was not a serious moral problem for the Greeks in the way slavery surely was, given Aristotle's more elaborate moves to justify and explain it. Whatever the truth of that speculation, Aristotle is a thinker comfortable with his lot and the "goodness that befits the gentleman," one free from the burdens of necessity. Although Aristotle's insistence on maintaining a plurality of social forms is admirable, the *particular* divisions he defends, and the justifications he proffers for their existence, appear from our vantage point as smoke screens to hide the abuse, exploitation, and infantilization of some persons so that others

[68] *Politics*, p. 34, see n. 2.

could participate in the "goodness" of those who rule "naturally."

As one thinks of who and what Aristotle excludes, expunges, holds at arm's length, or must subordinate, a cluster of class, sexual, and cultural prejudices come into focus. At least three imperatives are at work: (1) a commitment to a teleological schema which dictated certain outcomes; (2) involvement in a way of life that benefitted from extant social arrangements, if one were a participant in the realm of "freedom;" (3) a loathing of excess and strife. (The entrance into the public arena of any previously dispossessed group is likely to foment strife and, at least for a time, rather uncivil discourse.) In addition, one particular imperative operated as an aspect of Aristotle's political thinking which spurred a defensive posture. I refer to the widespread fear of the "private" power of women that permeated Athenian society, particularly fear of the mother. This fear compelled the man to leave home, not simply by removing himself physically but by fending off "home" emotionally, even politically. This fourth imperative finds textual support as one recalls the claims Aristotle makes for the "naturalness" of the *polis*—it exists to meet the precise measure of the needs of *particular* males, a point made again and again—together with the declared self-sufficiency of the *polis*. In other words, there is no need to go home to have one's needs met for there is nothing the household can provide that the self-sufficient *polis*, which can drain the household of what is necessary, cannot provide. It is as if the Athenian male were torn between two powerful fields of force: Mother and Market, household and *polis*, private and public, and chose to take his chances outside, to make his mark in public action, frequently warfare (fewer in the contemplative life), rather than to confront what John Knox would later term "the monstrous regiment of women."

If there were no more to Aristotle than a series of ideological justifications of a way of life, however, there would be little to commend him to contemporary political thought; however, Aristotle's smugness about Athenian social arrangements is only part of the story. There remains his image of the political realm as aiming at certain public, moral "goods" and citizenship as a form of action geared toward the good of the whole. He insisted that

"the end of the political community is . . . a greater thing to
attain and maintain, a thing more ultimate, than the end of the
individual,"[69] and that claim serves as the foundation for his
political thinking. One turns to Aristotle, then, not for his bad
teleology but for a vision of politics which remains alive. This
is where he might instruct feminism, which lacks a viable vision
of either politics or the political community and has thus far failed
to create an ideal of citizenship. (I take up these claims in Chapter
5.)

There is no small dose of irony in the fact that a thinker who
resolutely accepted and buttressed a politics of *exclusion* has become a symbol of a politics of participation. Brian Fay begins his
eager sketch of a normative ideal of politics by calling his efforts
part of "the Aristotelian conception of politics."

. . . according to this theory 'politics' refers to men's deliberate efforts to order, direct, and control their collective affairs and activities, to establish ends for their society, and to
implement and evaluate these ends. From this perspective,
what is fundamental about politics is the interaction and participation of men according to mutually defined and accepted
rules as they engage in this process of creating and adminis-
tering the laws of their community, which is to say that what
is most significant is the involvement of the citizens in the
process of determining their own collective identity.[70]

Fay concludes that "men can be free only when they participate
in determining the conditions of their lives":[71] all this and more
Fay calls "Aristotelian." Cornelius Castoriadis brings Aristotle
to the instruction of Marx, for the "question of Aristotle is the
political question, the foundation of the political community, of
society, as the creation of social individuals, as justice, as exchange—where *physis/nomos* meet."[72] Aristotle, not Marx, is the

---

[69] *Politics*, p. 355 (from Appendix 1, "Aristotle's Conception of Politics in *The
Ethics* and *The Rhetoric*").

[70] Fay, *Social Theory and Political Practice*, p. 54.

[71] *Ibid.*

[72] Cornelius Castoriadis, "From Marx to Aristotle, From Aristotle to Us,"
Social Research, p. 672.

key to politics insists Castoriadis, for politics is that activity central to a particular understanding of ourselves as free persons, citizens, and moral agents. Clearly Fay, Castoriadis, and others have implicitly if not explicitly settled for themselves the question whether Aristotle's logic of explanation is *necessarily* rather than historically linked to the exclusion of women, slaves, and unfree underclasses from political participation. In their view, Aristotle's participatory vision stands out as a towering contribution to our understanding of the continuing meaning, purpose, and nature of politics as a human activity.

That Aristotle himself excluded certain categories of persons from politics places no continuing claims on us if we determine that slave production and Aristotle's version of the production and reproduction of the *oikos* need not serve as structural supports for political activity. Of major contemporary thinkers only Arendt seems relatively unfazed by similar preconditions for citizenship.[73] Yet the manner in which explanatory theories in politics are assessed means that one can reject particular evaluations which flow from a general theory (Aristotle on slavery) without repudiating an entire logic of explanation (Aristotle on politics as a form of action). The key is to assay what one can drop without so eroding the overall structure of the theory that one's favored alternatives are dropped as particular dimensions of explanation are rejected.

This leaves the door open for feminist thinkers to turn Aristotle to their own purposes and to take up and insist upon a concept of citizenship as the touchstone of collective and individual public identities. Thus far such a vision is lacking in feminism, but it is embraced and echoed in other modes of contemporary thought, including one recent treatment of the human person as *actus humanus* whose potentiality (from *potentia*) can be actualized only through action "together with others."[74] This latter-day Aristotelianism, enriched with the complex edifice of another tradition of thought, recurs to Aristotle, as Karol Wojtyla (now Pope John Paul II) insists: ". . . participation as an essential of the person is a constitutive feature of any human community."[75] In a passage

---

[73] See Arendt, *Human Condition*.

[74] Karol Wojtyla (Pope John Paul II), *The Acting Person*, trans. Andrej Potocki, p. 275.

[75] *Ibid.*, p. 276.

replete with implications for feminist thinkers searching for alternatives to rigid functionalist definitions of the human being or equally rigid environmentalist determinism, Wojtyla writes: "Action gives us the best insight into the inherent essence of the person and allows us to understand the person most fully."[76] A wedge of social critique opens up, though it did not do so for Aristotle, if one follows through on a concept of action as revealing one individual to another and all to each other, for this possibility emerges only through participation. Thus barriers to participation, whether objective economic conditions; repressive social norms; or the noninvolvement of despair, bad faith, and cramped vision are opened up to debate and critique. Participation by the human person as *actus humanus* ideally gives individuals the possibility to discover their own potentialities combined with moral responsibility for a wider human network, a responsibility inseparable from the speech as discourse which aims at shared purposes. It is to the manner in which a tradition which has since its inception offered an alternative to the "Greek way," to Greek images of human beings, public and private, that I turn with a discussion of the Christian moral revolution and its political impact.

[76] *Ibid.*, p. 11.

Chapter 2

The Christian Challenge, Politics' Response: Early Christianity to Machiavelli

Happy the gentle; they shall have the earth for their heritage. . . . Happy the merciful: they shall have mercy shown them. . . . Happy the peacemakers: they shall be called sons of God.—*Matt. 5:5-9, Jerusalem Bible*

But when a prince is in the wrong, are his people bound to follow him too? I answer, No, it is no one's duty to do wrong; we ought to obey God who desires the right, rather than men.—*Luther*

Therefore it is necessary for a prince, who wishes to maintain himself, to learn how not to be good, and to use this knowledge and not use it, according to the necessity of the art.—*Machiavelli*

Feminists in our time have delved into the accumulated inheritance of two thousand years of Christianity and emerged with a list of horrors perpetrated by censorious prelates, zealous fanatics, repressive institutions, and the prejudiced faithful that would frighten any but the most stout-hearted. It is true, of course, that Christianity, like any powerful doctrine infused with a set of images, symbols, and ideas from which an awesome edifice of thought as well as diverse social practices and institutional forms have arisen contains its share of caprice, villainy, and dogmatism. There have indeed been those Luther condemned as "prurient and salacious" Churchmen whose denunciations afforded the secondary gain (not unknown to protectors of public morals in our own time) of requiring such men to spend their time reading and concentrating upon that which they condemned and forbade to others. It is true that Eve is tricked by the wily serpent and made responsible for introducing knowledge of good and evil into the world. (That never seemed to me as shameful as Cain's bringing murder into the world, however.) The entire edifice of church structure, particularly Catholicism, has been denounced from feminist pulpits as a haven of patriarchal privilege, though the existence of orders in which women rose to positions of great responsibility, power, and holiness is less often mentioned. The record is ambivalent. To quote Samuel Morse: "What hath God wrought?"

THE CHRISTIAN REVOLUTION: ARISTOTLE ON HIS HEAD

I shall begin with a salvo: Christianity ushered a moral revolution into the world which dramatically, and for the better, transformed the prevailing images of male and female, public and private. Because this moral revolution is rarely treated in depth in contemporary political theory, I shall articulate the most provocative reflections about the human condition along both spiritual and political vectors that emerge from early Christianity. Then I shall move to an exploration of Christian social thought in the works of St. Augustine, St. Thomas Aquinas, and the dramatic Martin Luther. A discussion of the Machiavellian counterrevolution against Christianity concludes this chapter.

My implicit and, at times, explicit contrast model to Christian social doctrine is the Greek world view taken at its apogee with Aristotle, not its retreat with the "unhappy consciousness" of the Stoics. My task is made more complicated by the fact that one important political theorist in our time who has discussed Christianity at length, Hannah Arendt, has denounced it as a destructive "life philosophy" (Marxism being another) which introduced into the world such politically pernicious notions as the sanctity of each human life and of everyday life. Arendt claims that Christianity cheapened politics by pronouncing the sacredness of all life and the dignity of human labor and work—all those persons and activities in the realm of necessity she, together with the apologists of Greek antiquity, disdains. Arendt laments: "The old contempt toward the slave, who had been despised because he served only life's necessities and submitted to the complusion of his master because he wanted to stay alive at all costs, could not possibly survive in the Christian era."[1] Arendt's heroes are Greek warriors who went off to battle, died young, and left beautiful memories. The slave who survived in a situation of utmost degradation receives, at Arendt's hands, a rather aristocratic contempt.

What, then, is this "life philosophy" Arendt quite perceptively sees as the antithesis of the Greek way? I have proclaimed a Christian revolution in thought. By that I mean that Christianity ushered in a dramatic transformation in our way of seeing the world, created a new vocabulary of basic notions with performative requirements, and posed answers to the question Socrates earlier asked: How might a human being live a just life? Previous notions of the public and private were wrenched from their Aristotelian straitjacket. Many other implications, some altogether worthy, others problematic, flow from the moral and conceptual transformation Christianity ushered into the West: Aristotle was indeed stood on his head.

First, the historic context must be secured. Christianity did not emerge nor did it flourish in a world overflowing with exemplary city-states, models of democratic probity with citizens searching for the common good—all killed off by the bacillus of Christian otherworldliness. Christ's mission began and ended in a dreary outpost of a corrupt, bloated, power-drunk empire already headed down a path from state worship to emperor deification and all the sordid evils of Caesarism. Simply because the "divine Augustus" occupied the imperial throne at the birth of Christ does nothing to efface the historic fact that the Roman Empire had, through guile, bloodthirstiness, and even genocide extended its sway over the then-known world. What "public life" was available to subjugated peoples? The only politics in the empire was the passivity of subjects quashed by fear and hopelessness or the power-machinations of the ambitious spurred by greed and ambition. Those few voices from the past who rose to condemn Caesarism and to lament the loss of the *res publica* passed or were forced from the

---

[1] Arendt, *Human Condition*, p. 316.

scene. (Yet it was precisely the charge that Rome's decline and fall was Christian handiwork that prompted St. Augustine's masterwork, *The City of God*, in the fourth century.)

Arendt hits the crux of what most disturbs her when she argues that Christianity accords each "individual life . . . [a position] once held by the 'life' of the body politic."[2] (A life held by some, including Aristotle, to be in some sense "natural.") One might recast Arendt's indictment thus: Christianity redeemed and sanctified both *each individual life* as well as *everyday life,* especially the lives of society's victims, and granted each a new-found dignity—a *dignitatis*—previously reserved only to the highborn, the rich, or the powerful. At the same time the private sphere, that "lesser" realm of necessity in Greek thought, was lifted from Greek contempt and elevated to an importance and honor once reserved exclusively for the sphere of "freedom," that public space within which male citizens debated important things and were heroes together. Making the last first in this case meant that the first became, if not exactly the last, then lower than the angels and no higher than the body of the faithful. Suddenly the public realm, politics, found itself (though not uniformly) condemned as the work of the devil (at worst) or an unfortunate, if not particularly ennobling, necessity (at best).

The heady drama of this moral revolution, with its politically jarring implications, is a part of the story of the public and the private that has lost none of its excitement. To effect a transvaluation so thorough that but a few centuries after Christ an emperor of Rome, under the moral suasion of a bishop of the Church, appeared in church to do an act of public penance for "crimes"

---

[2] *Ibid.*, p. 314. Marxism joins Christianity as a "life philosophy" which sounds the death knell to authentic politics in the Arendtian view. When human life is the ultimate point of reference, Arendt argues, politics is eroded. One hesitates to call Arendt's a "death philosophy" in contrast, although she is enraptured with heroes who died young. Arendt celebrates "aspiration toward worldly immortality" (p. 314) inseparable in Greek antiquity from what Eli Sagan, in his book of that title, has called the "lust to annihilate." Perhaps Arendt's views on this matter have escaped a full critique because of the reverence for ancient Greece which still pervades our thinking. Perhaps we, too, yearn to break free from the chains forged by Judeo-Christian ethics for what Arendt praises as "action for its own sake."

committed in the name of the state—what a spectacle! The public world now had to justify its power before another throne, had to face the wrath or censure of men of God and the threat of civil disobedience from the lowliest faithful.[3] Arendt is correct to see a decline here but it is not so much in politics, which had already declined even in her own vision of what it is to do politics, but in the *legitimacy* accorded the claims of politics. There is an imbedded premise in Arendt's argument that politics as a way of ordering life and political theory and symbols as the ultimate way to structure reality, have some automatic claim to primacy. Why is this so? The answer is that they have not—at least not without challenge. Politics, like every other human endeavor, must make its case. In our age, it must make its case before those Arendt, repeating Aristotle, calls *animal laborans* and relegates to private shadow boxes. Christianity challenged the primacy of politics. It did not relegate secular power to silence and shadows as secular power had formerly relegated the private, but the claims of the public-political world no longer went unchallenged. Caesar now had to confront the formidable figure of Christ. The match at the beginning appeared uneven yet it ended with an ecclesiastical monarchical church, the Church Triumphant (and Christ lost?), the bifurcation and decline of Roman order, and the stirrings of feudal forms and national pride throughout Europe. What became of the orientation of the public and the private?

[3] The last first and the first last invited Nietzsche's vitriol. He condemned Christianity as a "slave morality," its followers animated by *ressentiment*, an ugly spirit of revenge, which drained true grandeur and esprit from the world. Nietzsche is always provocative even when he is wrong, as I think he is here. Christianity's transvaluation is no *mere* reversal of the values of antiquity. The Christian moral revolution introduced *new* terms of moral evaluation rather than simply reversing the old. It ushered in a transformed synthesis with new and old interrelated or at tension in a number of complex ways. A simple reversal would represent no advance, simply a reaction-formation or a more sophisticated form of repression. Authentic moral change incorporates and transforms the old. It is also instructive that a morality that redeemed everyday life sanctioned "womanly" virtues at odds with visions of male heroism and bloodied glory. For Nietzsche's discussion of *ressentiment* see *The Birth of Tragedy* or *The Genealogy of Morals*, which appear in: Friedrich Nietzsche, *The Birth of Tragedy and the Case of Wagner*, trans. Walter Kaufman; and Friedrich Nietzsche, *On the Genealogy of Morals and Ecce Homo*, trans. Walter Kaufman.

The New Testament, especially the first four Gospels, that potpourri of incomplete doctrine, parable, beatitude, and homily, provides even today intimations of Christ's extraordinary appeal in a world in which power had utterly debased politics and there was simply no such thing as active participation, as a citizen, in public life. How could one possibly speak of a "common good" in a world composed of masters and slaves, victors and victims, imperialists and colonialists? Christianity advocated, as it always would, "rendering unto Caesar" that which was his, but it reconstrued what was his and it turned out to be minimal: obedience to laws aimed at public peace, payment of taxes, at first refusal to serve in armies, later a willingness to serve in a "just war." What was not Caesar's was control of life's ultimate purpose and meaning and the human being's vocation and calling on this earth. What was not under the purview of Caesar was how one chose to see oneself and the world and to live, breathe, and die within it. Christian doctrine drained the public state, the empire, of its claims to divinity and omnipotence and to being the only ordering principle in the world. Possessing free will, the bearers of responsible moral agency, Christians could do no less. But they could do more: they might be compelled to act against the state, to resist its claims and impositions upon individuals, their bodies, their minds. There was something new under the sun: the notion of principled resistance to secular power. Plato didn't allow for it; neither did Aristotle. Nor does such resistance begin, as common wisdom sometimes has it, with Socrates, for he accepted unquestioningly the right of an admittedly corrupt Athenian democracy to take his life and he reaffirmed, in his death, that the state was the author of his being. Christians might be martyred by secular power but they proclaimed in death that any power that arrogates unto itself the right to shed innocent blood is a blasphemy. Christians cannot, in clear conscience, join hands with those who set up the crosses of history. (It is, of course, true that official Christianity from Constantine on is frequently found with blood on its hands. But that, I am arguing, is at odds with original Christian doctrine which moved to revolutionize the moral climate of the Roman world.) The notion of moral revolt against public power opened up a range of options, duties, responsibilities, dilemmas, and reassessments not possible in pre-Christian epochs, implications—for women were citizens in the Christian community—for males and females alike.

Welcomed into that new community, the *res publica Christiana*, women shared in the norms, activities, and ideals that were its living tissue. She found (try to suspend time and place yourself as a woman of the first century after Christ in Judea hearing *this* message!) that qualities most often associated with her activities as mother—giving birth to and sustaining human life; an ethic of responsibility toward the helpless, the vulnerable, the weak; gentleness, mercy, and compassion—were celebrated. The realm of necessity generated its own sanctity. Women, like men, might be called upon to die for a cause, not as Homeric heroes wielding great swords, but as witnesses to the strength of their inner conviction and living sacrifices to the evil that absolute political power trails in its wake.

What of the charge that Christianity vitiated the Aristotelian vision of life as action and participation? That charge, too, is somewhat misplaced. First, no such Aristotelian ethos was available to participants in the early Christian era. Second, Christianity invited wider participation on the part of each individual male and female in its new community as following "the way" could best take place as a member of the body of the faithful. There were no more *polites* debating "whither Athens" but that, after all, was a distant, aristocratic, and exclusionary participatory vision. The Christian version of "withdrawal" from the world, as one option open to the faithful, was not a retreat into solipsism but a vocation that required contemplation and purification of the self, ideally in a life lived among others. Why this sort of withdrawal should be taken as a sign of civic contempt *simpliciter*, yet Aristotle's argument that a "life of action need not be, as is sometimes thought, a life which involves relations to others" should not, is problematic at best.[4] On Aristotle's scale of human virtues, the *vita contemplativa* was as admirable, in its own respects, as

---

[4] Aristotle, *The Politics*, p. 289. Also, "Actions cannot be good and outstanding unless the doer himself has a degree of pre-eminence over others as great as a husband has over his wife, or a parent over his children, or a master over his slaves" (p. 288).

the *vita activa*. Yet Aristotle's contemplative man had, according to Aristotle himself, nothing to contemplate. He engaged in "thoughts with no objects beyond themselves."[5] Solipsism is surely a more apt characterization of Aristotle's *vita contemplativa* than the Christian contemplation *of the world* through withdrawal from its temptations. It should also be noted that women were debarred from Aristotle's contemplative life and the pursuit of felicity given their defective rational principle, just as they were excluded from the *vita activa*. (In fact, Aristotle advocated mental inaction for the pregnant mother.) Christ himself never counseled a retreat into private virtuousness. The tree, he said, shall be known by its fruits, not the other way around. But he did bless acts of piety, carried out in private, with no aim at self-glorification and public honor.

Christianity's stance toward power in general affected profoundly its attitude on the questions of power in both its public and private aspects, Christianity at its inception, as I have indicated, challenged and questioned the power of force, command, and rule and demanded that such power justify its legitimacy. Ultimate power, *potestatis*, was reserved for God and that was a power none on earth could evoke save idolators. The singular voice of ultimate power was beyond the power of man to compel or to capture for himself. There was another sort of power— *potentia*—the latent power within each individual for action. That power was to be directed to God's glory and to the service of the faithful. Again, the reversal of the Aristotelian picture is startling. Recall for a moment Aristotle's teleological presumption that natural and social objects possessed an essence which categorically delimited ultimate possibility. This inner power was fully known when it culminated in empirical actualization: the proof was in the pudding. Because women's sphere was declared limited her nature a fortiori was limited. The free man, the citizen, possessed a greater (more complete, fuller) *potentia* and required a public environment within which his innate possibilities could be fully realized.

Christianity defied this rigid categorical separation of human

[5] *Ibid.*

beings by declaring that the *potentia* of every single human being was as great as any other and equal in God's eyes. Each individual was infused with the necessary power within him or her to do what he or she must: the most humble could challenge the mighty; the downtrodden achieve dignity. This *potentia* was unspecific as to environments most conducive to its realization, save that a body of the faithful, small or large, was the clearest route to the fulfillment of human power as possibility. Christopher Dawson argues that Christianity "made possible the ideal of a social order resting upon the free personality and a common effort towards moral ends."[6] The key words here—those that signify how dramatically things have moved from the *polis*—are "free personality," "common effort," "moral ends." All persons, by definition, are gifted with a "free personality." All could participate in a shared effort to common ends. But the ends had to be debated with reference to moral criteria; that is, the activity of participation *in itself*, though worthy, was not a complete *end in itself* but had an object in view and that object had to be evaluated along certain dimensions.

One reason the figure of Jesus remains important to political thought is his insistence that the realm of necessity, the nonpolitical or subpolitical realm, is not a despised forum for human endeavor, nor a vile and ugly beast to be tamed by the warriors of political order, but, simply and profoundly, that place where the vast majority of human beings find their homes and must be allowed to live with dignity and purpose in the conviction that they, too, have worth, uniqueness, immortal souls. The corridors of power found themselves reduced to a defensive posture: hereafter to maintain earthly order and to keep the civic peace could not, without a struggle, mean domination and coercion of that vast private world of individual conscience and everyday life. If the old politics of the *polis* was exclusionary and that of the Roman Empire a deadly imperialism, the new Christian community, though not political, was available to any who, like Socrates, had a hunger and thirst for righteousness. How different the

---

[6] Christopher Dawson, *A Monument to St. Augustine*, quoted in Frederick J. Copleston, S.J., *A History of Philosophy*, vol. 2: *Medieval Philosophy*, p. 105.

Christian band of men, women, children, the infirm, the "possessed," the crippled, even the criminal from the participants in Plato's symposium! One dimension was shared: the insistence that Eros Bound was necessary to attain righteousness, even as other scales of human virtue were turned around.[7]

That Christianity failed to live up to the promise of its early mission surprises no one in a skeptical and cynical time. We know the world is a most intractable place and human motivation a mixed blessing. But that Christianity secured a moral revolution and established a set of claims which must be faced and answered today, even if they are finally overridden, is a feature essential to any exploration of human identity, especially that of woman. There is more to the story of the Christian version of public and private, and I shall take it up with consideration of St. Augustine and his City of God.

St. Augustine: Citizen in a Heavenly City

Students of the great Wittgenstein, in their reminiscences of his life and work, tell us that St. Augustine's *City of God* was one of a very few books visible in Wittgenstein's sparsely decorated rooms at Cambridge and that he cited and referred to it often. This fact has always intrigued me. Either Wittgenstein, a philosophic skeptic and unbeliever, had a buried vein of mystery and piety running through his soul or, more likely, St. Augustine somehow nourished and sustained him as he struggled to develop a philosophy of language in which meaning, rather than truth according to certain narrow, logical criteria, was central. Wittgenstein looked at the play of words in everyday life and the way

---

[7] In his epistles to the Christian communities of Rome, Corinth, Galatia, Ephesus, and Philippi, St. Paul set forth a series of harsh strictures against sexuality. He regarded women as temptresses. Confronted with temptation, Paul adjures men to remain stalwart and single but (in 1 Cor. 7:9) he allows those who cannot "exercise self-control" to marry for "it is better to marry than to be aflame with passion." St. Paul's influence, which involved the infusion of the Greek philosophical tradition via Neoplatonism into Christianity, served to legitimate and to sustain within Christianity a current of suspicion of the human—particularly the female—body.

in which we, through words, create pictures of reality that orient
us in the world, structure, limit, or compel our thoughts and
actions alike. What did Wittgenstein see in Augustine's evocation
of the heavenly city? What Augustinian pictures captivated him?
I stated at the outset that the route of the public and private has
many detours. This is one, for if my hunch is correct and language
lies at the heart of this modest mystery, to probe Augustinian
views of the speaking human subject should lead us to Augustinian
solutions to publicity and privacy, freedom and necessity, politics
and the family.

It must be said, to avoid misapprehension, that St. Augustine
did not articulate a systematic, detailed political theory. He did
not do so for several good reasons, foremost among them the fact
that secular rule did not lie at the heart of his deepest passions
and concerns; moreover, as an African bishop, living on built-
over ruins of a once flourishing city-state utterly razed by Rome,
a witness to Roman perfidy and hollow pomp, he could well
remain unencumbered by a restless yearning for political life.
Some call him a pessimist and find his forays into secular theory
dour. Within the context of his age, I find him more realistic than
cynical, though one could certainly never view him as a celebrant
of the civic gods as the authors of our beings or the harbingers
of our salvation.

What was Augustine's earthly city, the city of man? First,
secular rule aimed at authentic goods, though its record of attempting to obtain them is a trail of tears. What had gone wrong?
Augustine locates the first and unerasable taint in the origin of
secular rule. Such governance would have been unnecessary, he
claims, had not sin entered the world with the Fall. (One could
reasonably view Augustine's account here, as many have done,
as a Christian version of state-of-nature theories.) Yet the city of
man must be granted great importance among human endeavors—
Augustine would not have Christians withdraw altogether from
the ''public thing''—for people yearn for earthly peace and security and earthly rule claims this as its end, though people's
hopes all too often are crushed as peace itself becomes a pretext
for war. True justice in its full completeness cannot be attained
on this earth—see the evils of slavery, not yet extirpated from

humanity—but one must nonetheless work for approximations to true justice. The Christian has a special duty to inform the actions of the powerful with moral restraint, to question the use of force, to resist empty pomp and demands for uncritical adulation of earthly authorities—all this is part of Christ's mission to Caesar. History itself can never be redeemed, however, for sin has entered the world. The human being *in* history can be and is redeemed, he argues, through Christ's humanity and the promise of a justice beyond that incomplete righteousness attainable in this world. The principle animating the earthly city all too often is *cupiditas*, a totally selfish impulse propelling the individual towards lust for dominion, economic gain, and hedonistic pleasure without regard for his fellows, God's commands, or the fate of his own soul. Augustine's contrast model for *cupiditas* is an opposing principle of conduct—both a standard and a substantive value—*caritas*, the unselfish love of one another, the glue that binds brother and sister in Christ's love, the love that reigns in the City of God when the just at last live in peace and righteousness. (It seems unlikely this is what inspired Wittgenstein. We must follow the trail a bit further.)

To make life on this earth less cruel and unjust some measure of civic order and secular justice, some regulation of human associations and affairs, is required. These social forms are not, crudely, what sin has brought into the world but what man, who is sinful, has created through the use of his God-given reason. What stands in the way of full use of human reason for good? St. Augustine provides a veritable hive abuzz with a swarm of explanations as to why earthly justice has never been attained and probably never will; however, I shall highlight the emphasis he places on language. In Book 19, Chapter 7 of the *City of God*, Augustine muses about the way in which all sentient creatures called human are divided by linguistic differences. These differences make it very hard for human beings to understand one another; to "get our feet" with each other is the way Wittgenstein would put it. States St. Augustine:

For if two men meet, and are forced by some compelling reason not to pass on but to stay in company, then if neither knows the other's language, it is easier for dumb animals, even of different kinds, to associate together than these men, although both are human beings. For when men cannot communicate their thoughts to each other, simply because of difference of language, all similarity of their common human nature is of no avail to unite them in fellowship. So true is this that a man would be more cheerful with his dog for company than with a foreigner. I shall be told that the Imperial City has been at pains to impose on conquered peoples not only her yoke but her language also, as a bond of peace and fellowship, so that there should be no lack of interpreters but even a profusion of them. True; but think of the cost of this achievement! Consider the scale of those wars, with all that slaughter of human beings, all the human blood that was shed![8]

How this passage must have saddened yet cheered Wittgenstein! But how do Augustine's comments on language bear importantly on the public and the private? Reread the sentence beginning "For when men cannot communicate their thoughts . . ." It is my claim that women historically have had no place to bring their thoughts, certainly no public arena to give them voice in the misogynist milieu of Greek antiquity. When they did speak, it was labeled so much reactive noise, devoid of meaning and significance. When we think of diverse languages we think of the kind of separation created by the linguistic differences between, say, Russian-speaking and English-speaking persons. But what of women and men in past epochs? They were separated by social arrangements and practices, ideologies, valuations, and the range and nature of spoken and written communication itself. The male literate class, a minority, was nonetheless the only literate class for all practical purposes. Cut off from philosophic speech of the symposia and the public speech of the *agora*, women's communications in classical antiquity would have taken on the very terms of their enforced isolation. The results of one sex almost exclusively inhabiting a public sphere and the other sex the private

[8] St. Augustine, *City of God*, ed. David Knowles, p. 861.

may help to explain why so many women and men literally could not (and cannot) ''speak'' to one another. George Steiner poses a possible explanation, one with which Augustine and Wittgenstein might concur, when he writes in *After Babel*:

> In most societies and throughout history, the status of women has been akin to that of children. Both groups are maintained in a condition of privileged inferiority. Both suffer obvious modes of exploitation—sexual, legal, economic—while benefiting from a mythology of special regard. Thus Victorian sentimentalization of the moral eminence of women and young children was concurrent with brutal forms of erotic and economic subjection. Under sociological and psychological pressure, both minorities have developed internal codes of communication and defence (women and children constitute a symbolic, self-defining minority even when, owing to war or special circumstance, they outnumber the adult males in the community). *There is a language-world of women as there is of children* (emphasis mine).[9]

St. Augustine is on to something vital when he discusses what happens when strangers meet. Surely there are also such ''strangers'' internal to any given society: witness the embarrassed encounter between a street-wise minority ''offender'' and a well-intentioned, neat, liberal, middle-class white. Someone usually gets taken for a verbal ride and it usually isn't the street-wise hipster. Language unites us, yes, but it also divides us. This is what links Wittgenstein with his forebear, St. Augustine, though Wittgenstein had greater hope that opacity could be overcome. The language of Christianity must have been so powerful and attractive to women emerging from the silence of the Classical era because the things Christ held dear and cherished were the terms of their own lives— forgiveness, succor, devotion. Christian terms of discourse and belief were simple and direct—told in the language of the people, cast in the forms of everyday speech, speech that communicated, speech with a liberatory moment.

[9] George Steiner, *After Babel*, p. 38.

Christ's was preeminently language that met the language needs and world of women of his time. He spoke their tongue, being the least "masculine" (if Roman centurians and Greek warriors are our standard) of men. He spoke the tongue of the dispossessed and used that language to call power to the test, shorn of the obfuscation in which it couched itself. Pontius Pilate found Christ unintelligible, a madman. There is more to be said on this topic, but I shall note for now (and develop in Chapter 6) that when feminist speech in our own time sounds wild and foreign it may be, in part, because it is as strange to our ears as an exotic tongue.

Having satisfied myself concerning the crux of Wittgenstein's devotion to Augustine, I shall take up the central features of Augustine's views on the public and private, stressing the links he finds between the family and political society. Augustine suffered not at all from Aristotle's need to categorize diverse types of human beings according to some teleological imperative. For St. Augustine, the entire sentient human race belonged within one category, the human, for God created us all, male and female, all diverse races, even bizarre creatures most of us would scarcely call human, though Augustine did. Celebrating God's diversity within the unity of creation, Augustine "even included the Sciopodes, who shelter themselves from the sun in the shade of one foot, and the Cynocephali, who had dogs' heads and barked. Whoever is rational and moral, regardless of color or shape or sound of voice, is certainly of the stock of Adam. None of the faithful (*nullus fidelium*) is to doubt that all the above originated from the first creation. God knew how to beautify the universe through the diversity of its parts."[10] God's natural law was written in the hearts of every human being. To celebrate unity within the diversity of sentient humanity was not only a joyous piety for St. Augustine, but an important feature of his recognition that all ways of life incorporated basic grammars of injunctions and prohibitions which regulated important things—the taking of human life, sexual relations, administration of justice—a kind of "nat-

[10] See Etienne Gilson's foreword to his abridged edition of St. Augustine's *City of God*, p. 25, n. 24. But note as well the excerpts from Augustine's "Of the Work of Monks" and "On the Holy Trinity" in *Not in God's Image*, ed. Julia O'Faolain and Lauro Martines, pp. 129-130 for expressions of ambivalence.

uralistic'' morality imbedded in the collective heart of humanity.[11] Rather than bifurcating the earthly sphere into rigidly demarcated public and private realms, Augustine finds in the household the "beginning or element of the city, and every beginning bears reference to some end of its own kind, and every element to the integrity of the whole of which it is an element, it follows plainly enough that *domestic peace has a relation to civic peace*—in other words, that the well-ordered concord of domestic obedience and domestic rule has a relation to the well-ordered concord of civic obedience and civic rule" (emphasis mine).[12] Every beginning carries within it a portion of the nature of the whole—in this instance civil society. (This can also be interpreted as Augustine's recognition that an inclusive and powerful whole will exert greater compulsion over those less powerful elements contained within it than the obverse. This makes the relation of *domus* [household] to *civitas* [civil society] necessarily asymmetric.) Most important: for Augustine, unlike Aristotle, the household and city, public and private, do not diverge as types or "in kind"; rather, aspects

[11] The dimensions of a "naturalistic" morality recognized by St. Augustine form the basis of much contemporary moral philosophy, e.g., Stuart Hampshire, *Morality and Pessimism*. Winch, in "Understanding a Primitive Society," comments on the centrality of birth, sexuality, and death to the rules and structures of human societies: "Their significance . . . is that they are inescapably involved in the life of all known human societies in a way which gives us a clue where to look, if we are puzzled about the point of an alien system of institutions" (p. 107). Birth, sexuality and death occupy this "central position" and "must be" constant factors, because these dimensions are the most powerful in human life. This leads Winch to conclude that the form such "limiting features" take "will necessarily be an important feature of any human society and that conceptions of good and evil in human life will necessarily be connected with such concepts" (pp. 110-111). The naturalistic dimension of Augustine's morality involves a strong presumption in favor of those acts which "seem" to us good and decent and against those that "seem" wrong or indecent. Augustine argues that all persons in every society, including those who commit it, feel and hence agree that murder is wrong; that, to him, constitutes prima facie evidence of God's universal law written in man's heart. Unfortunately, the introduction of sin into the world had done much to corrupt human desires and choices although it had not erased altogether God's law.

[12] St. Augustine, *The Political Writings of St. Augustine*, ed. Henry Paolucci, p. 151. See also John Neville Figgis, *The Political Aspects of St. Augustine's City of God*.

of the whole are borne into the parts, and the integrity and meaning of the part carries forward to become an *integral part* of the whole.

The duty Augustine assigns to the Christian father is to "frame his domestic rule" in accordance with the laws of the *civitas* in order that each might coexist in harmony with the other. (*Civitas*, within Augustinian discourse, is best understood as a generic term for human society, not as a reference to a particular form of secular government or unit of rule.) A father should injure none and do good to all. First and foremost among his duties is the care of those under him "for the law of nature and of society give him readier access to them and greater opportunity of serving them. And hence the apostle says, 'Now, if any provide not for his own, and specially for those of his own house, he hath denied the faith, and is worse than an infidel.' "[13] Augustine's admonitions to the Christian father are part of an ongoing effort to bind parents, mothers and fathers alike, together through those shared experiences which were given a transformed linguistic foundation and hence altered meaning as they were sanctioned by the Church.

The ground of relations of domestic peace is a well-ordered concord within the family. Both parents share responsibility for their children; women, however, should defer to their husbands, not because they are unequal to men in God's eyes or not fully rational beings, but because such deference is provided for in tradition and is necessary to promote the ends of domestic and civil harmony. Although he rejects a teleological argument on the inferiority of female nature to justify female segregation and subordination, Augustine does legitimate the rule of husbands over wives by granting considerable weight to tradition and the requirements for domestic concord. Augustine warns that the husband's rule over his wife and the parents over children must be neither absolute nor arbitrary for "even those who rule serve those whom they seem to command; for they rule not from a love of power, but from a sense of the duty they owe to others—not because they are proud of authority, but because they love mercy."[14] Augustine stresses the importance of households whose

---

[13] Augustine, *Political Writings*, p. 147.
[14] *Ibid.*, pp. 147-148.

foundations lie in compassion and justice tempered with mercy, as children first learn respect for law (and law must be respected only so long as it is just, for what is not just, Augustine insists, is not law) within the family.[15]

Why the concern with public and private order and concord? The *City of God* was occasioned by an event which shocked and benumbed the civilized world: the sack of Rome by Alaric and the Visigoths in 410. Christianity tapped the yearnings for community and citizenship in a fragmented world in at least three ways. First, it urged a righteous domestic order, under Christian terms of discourse, as a familiar *civitas* ruled by love, compassion, and authority in the person of Christian parents.[16] Second, it offered membership in the society of the faithful during their sojourn on this earth, a *societas Christianus*. Third, it promised a heavenly city when the faithful Christian citizen's earthly journey ended. That Augustine chose to deploy the concept "citizen" in his response to the travail of the breakup of imperial rule was wise, not simply as a strategy but in his profound recognition that old words had to become embodied in new social forms and levels of discourse if they were to survive the disintegration of the earthly city. Although some might find his use of the term "citizen" unacceptable—a jingle-jangle of disparate language games—it nevertheless makes sense, internal to Christian social thought, to find transformed meanings for those concepts that carried within them performative requisites (citizen being one) within a Christian context. The Christian was a citizen of the earthly city who must urge the applicability of moral law to reasons of state, and, as well, a cherished participant in the body faithful, the Christian republic, foreshadowing membership in the City of God, a citizenship whose full flowering awaited the transition from this world to the next. The concept "citizen" held forth the promise of meaningful involvement as an earthly symbol and as a sign of one's Christian vocation.

Augustine agreed with the main thrust of Aristotelian thought that the life of virtue must be a shared life. He located that sharing

---

[15] Augustine, *City of God*, (ed. Knowles) notes that it may even be the case that "safety is not to be found in the home . . . ," p. 859.

[16] *Ibid.*

in those ties that bind the faithful into a community on this earth and in the world to come: ". . . and how could that City have made its first start, how could it have advanced along its course, how could it attain its appointed goal, if the life of the saints were not social?"[17] He also recognized that human society is twisted by life within unjust and oppressive earthly dominions and the conceptions under which those dominions order their rule, conceptions that have a silencing effect on meaningful human speech. Thus, Augustine found Cicero's Aristotelian conceptions of a people offensive for their flat legalisms which he regarded as thinly disguised justifications of cupidity and narrow self-interest. Cicero defined a people as "the union of a number of men associated by bonds of common acknowledgment of right (justice) and the common pursuit of justice." Augustine argues that to be a genuine people those within a unit of rule must be seen, not as a collectivity of discrete particulars, but instead as beings who, united under one rule, share in "cherishing" the same things. He defines a people as "an assemblage of reasonable beings . . . bound together by common agreement as to the objects of love."[18]

Although Augustine doesn't focus on women as a separate consideration in his discussion of the earthly *civitas*, his enormously expanded definition of what it means to belong to the category "human," and his insistence on a basic grammar of morality internal to diverse ways of life, laws written on the human heart that iniquity could not altogether efface, touched women directly as these views altered the terms under which women were described, or could describe themselves, and were therefore evaluated. Augustine, taken all in all, is one of the great undoers of Greek misogyny which dictated a separate and inferior female nature and consigned women to a "lesser" realm of "necessity." More problematically, perhaps, he also undid Aristotle's vision of the polity as the home for man's highest aspirations and hopes on earth. St. Augustine's theory regarding the origin and nature of earthly rule and dominion precluded an all-consuming passion for politics. But his strictures on earthly rule

[17] *Ibid.*, p. 858.   [18] Augustine, *Political Writings*, p. 42.

and dominion did not, in fact, go on to become the prevailing view of Christian thinkers in the medieval period as the Church came to its accommodations with Caesar. It is to how the terms of that accommodation in the work of St. Thomas Aquinas—an accommodation which reintroduced in altered form certain Aristotelian distinctions—affected images of the public and the private that I now turn.

St. Thomas Aquinas: New Sanctity for the Secular

In the wake of that twelfth century Renaissance in the Christian West, which saw the infusion of Aristotle's works into medieval Europe via Arabic translators, Augustine's discursive approach to social thought receded into the background of philosophic and political discourse as did his deployment of ordinary language. The method of formal, abstract argumentation known as Scholasticism was perfected by St. Thomas Aquinas, its foremost exponent and the major figure in the rediscovery of Aristotle. I shall treat Aquinas' views on the public and the private beginning with that logic of explanation which formed the basis for his thought. How did a Christian thinker reconcile Aristotle's teleology (with its elitist outcomes) with his own views? Following an Aristotelian method, Aquinas' philosophy incorporated a concept of universals.[19] St. Thomas insisted that nothing existed in sensate reality outside the singular or particular, but that this did not mean the philosophic thinker was prevented from using abstract categories or posing conceptual universals. Although each particular thing

[19] Aquinas' method put him at odds with Ultra-Realists and Nominalists alike in the philosophic battles of the day. Ultra-Realists contended that logical and real orders were parallel. This meant, for example, that every particular woman in the world as a member of the logical category 'woman' was the same as every other woman. This conceptual muddle created hopeless problems for identity theory. Nominalists opposed to the Ultra-Realists sometimes careened so far to the opposite direction they emerged with the conclusion that general concepts made *no* reference to abstractions or universals. That is, every *general* category was a *particular* entity or individual. The radical Nominalist view, if applied consistently, boggles the mind and makes coherent thought an impossibility. See Copelston's fine discussion in his *History of Philosophy*, vol. 2, pp. 108-117.

did not exist in, or as, the abstract form of that thing, the mind could conceive of the universal categorical principle as an abstract form (like Aristotle's formal element) in a manner which made reference to, but could not be reduced to, particulars. The mind could make these particulars objects of knowledge *only* through the mediation of categories couched in an abstract, formal philosophical language.

Aquinas articulated a vision of the human being which, like Aristotle's, placed intelligence, the capacity for reason, at the apex of humanness. (Implicit within this view is a devaluation of the human being's emotional capacity as essentially defining the species.) Aquinas included women within "nature's intention" as part of the category human. The image of God "in its *principal signification*, namely the intellectual nature, is found both in man and in woman" (emphasis mine). Aquinas doesn't stop here but goes on to add that "in a secondary sense, the image of God is found in man, and not in woman: for man is the beginning and end of woman." Aquinas here relies on Aristotle's flawed biology which tied male and female to formal and material principles with the formal-male element implanting a fully formed *homunculus* into the female-material who gave it a place to grow until it emerged *through* but not *of* her body. Aquinas buttresses his own teleological argument for female insufficiency by indicating that he regards each woman, in her biological nature, as "defective and misbegotten" for "the production of woman comes from a defect in the active force or from some material indisposition."[20]

Although women are burdened with secondary disabilities that help to explain their less active, complete, and fully realized natures, they do belong within the category human nature as coequals with men in the chief sense in which Aquinas defines human beings: the possession of a rational faculty. Reasoning human beings must live together and assist one another in the attainment of knowledge, for such a pursuit requires "different discoveries—one, for example, in medicine, one in this and an-

[20] Aquinas' *Summa Theologica*, quoted in *Not in God's Image*, ed. O'Faolain and Martines, pp. 131-132. Cf. Aristotle, *Metaphysics*, pp. 20-21. Bentham was later to take note of the secondary characteristics of the female sex.

other in that.''[21] Yet women, by definition, cut off from pursuits that involve arriving at knowledge through individual reason, are precluded by Aquinas from that essential human endeavor: their ''disabilities'' keep them in that place which has long been their traditional province.

Although Aquinas does not make this point explicitly, it is clear from the texts that ''the use of speech'' which he deems ''a prerogative proper to man'' is also a realm in which women are found wanting. Why? Aquinas' theory of language is important here for it is dramatically at odds with Augustine's. Where Augustine emphasizes the difficulties in the way of full transparency of human beings to one another as individuals are separated by linguistic differences, Aquinas stresses language as the ''means'' whereby ''one man is able *fully* to express his conceptions to another.''[22] Woman's social situation has always been one infused with what Rosenthal calls ''silencing considerations,''[23] a silence induced by the existence of ''power-over'' them that may not be acknowledged fully by social participants. Women will always fall short as language-users, *if* the test is the *full* expression of conceptions to one another. Deprived of a vocabulary to convey her historically situated social experience, including her feelings at the ambivalence with which Western culture viewed her, the speech available to Aquinas' women would lack the crystalline clarity he sees as the nature of speech itself. Clearly, Aquinas' reintroduction of features of the Aristotelian teleological approach to female nature represents a retrogressive dimension of the West's ''return to Aristotle.''

Insisting on the dignity of politics, Aquinas recasts Aristotle's dictum that man is a political animal, or one destined to live in a *polis*, by demanding a further ''socializing'' of that formulation: Man is a *political* and a *social* being. Aquinas writes: ''Yet it is natural for man, more than for any other animal, to live in a group. . . . This is clearly a necessity of man's nature. . . . It is therefore necessary for man to live in a multitude so that each

[21] St. Thomas Aquinas, *The Political Ideas of St. Thomas Aquinas*, ed. Dino Bigongiari, p. 176.
[22] *Ibid.*
[23] Rosenthal, ''Feminism Without Contradictions,'' *passim.*

one may assist his fellows.''[24] *De Regimine Principum*, Aquinas' single, albeit incomplete, political text, offered Western Christendom a new sanctity for the secular order. He revivified the concept "citizen," long eclipsed in the Christian West, as a substantive ideal, by the image of the dutiful "subject." (Although medieval Christian thought did accord this "subject" a right to revolt against tyrants.) Aquinas defines politics as an activity that requires a body politic having as a public, moral end the achievement of justice through obedience to moral law.

Against St. Augustine, Aquinas argues that the state's origins did not lie in original sin and were not primarily maintained by a "lust for dominion." With Aristotle, he declares the state "natural"—an outgrowth of, and necessary to, man's nature. (It should be noted that a theorist may accept a social theory of human nature, as did St. Augustine, and yet disagree that secular rule is some "natural" outgrowth of that sociality. Instead, he may posit a "golden age" when man's social nature alone pro-

[24] Aquinas, *Political Ideas*, pp. 175-176. Arendt, who indicts St. Thomas as one of those culprits responsible for undoing the glory that was Greek thought, notes Thomas' "unconscious substitution of the social for the political," which "betrays the extent to which the original Greek understanding of politics had been lost." See *Human Condition*, p. 23. Arendt is mistaken on several counts. First, Aquinas did not substitute the "social" for the "political"; rather, he incorporated aspects of human social existence, of lives shared with others, into his political vision. Second, Aquinas and Arendt do not share the same understanding of "social." For Arendt the "social realm" is the sphere of unfreedom; the home of *homo faber* who does not have and can never attain a genuine life, that of the *vita activa*. Arendt defines "social" as a world without "sufficient dignity to constitute . . . an autonomous and authentically human way of life" (*Human Condition*, p. 13). Aquinas incorporates the sentient human race—including *homo faber*—into his "human way of life" and "social" category. Aquinas' inclusion of the concept "social" in his gloss on Aristotle was his way of stressing a theory of the natural sociability of human beings. This social nature meant that humans had needs that were social, including work, love, worship, and play with others. Thus the restructured, virtuous Christian *civitas* would be bound together, not so much through the reflected glory of heroic warriors, but by those social ideals Aquinas considered worthy but Arendt did not—indeed she scorns them throughout her work. Cf. Dante, *Monarchy and Three Political Letters*, p. 25: ". . . mankind is at its best in a state of concord; for as man is at his best in body and soul when he is in a state of concord, the same is true of a house, a city and a kingdom, and of mankind as a whole."

vided the basis for order, before the fall from grace that introduced, simultaneously, sin and a need for secular governance into the world. The belief that human nature, male and female, is social need not go hand in glove with a high regard for secular politics, nor optimism concerning it.) By reaffirming a foundation in Christian doctrine for the exercise of secular authority away from sin and towards shared human ends, both social and political, Aquinas recasts Aristotle's claims for secular rule in Christian form.

Because all persons—male and female—share in human sociality and rationality all (presumably) could become citizens within a reconstructed Christian polity. Aquinas neither affirms nor denies this hope; indeed, the references to how he would go about structuring and governing the polity are scattered and incomplete. Several public-private themes emerge clearly, however. First, Aquinas ties the good of the private sphere, the family, to the good of the civic order, the public realm. He shared Augustine's conviction that the household should exist in harmony with the larger order—as an ideal—yet remain, in some meaningful sense, distinct from it. Within the household the wife belongs to her husband yet retains her own personality. She is an individual separate from her husband more than a slave is from his master or a son from his father, for "she is received into a kind of social life, that of matrimony." Husband and wife "have an immediate relation to the community of the household . . . between them there is *domestic justice* rather than *civic*."[25] Aquinas was correct that husband and wife have immediate ties within the private sphere. But there is a difference: traditionally only a single status is open to the wife. The husband shares in both the family as a participant in domestic peace and, as well, participates as a public citizen. It is in his *public* capacity, as a citizen, that he enjoys civic justice and shares in its "universal" dimensions.

Aquinas refines Aristotle's theory of the public-private split with important provisos on the enhanced dignity of the woman.

[25] Aquinas, *Political Ideas*, p. 103. Cf. Dante, *Monarchy*, p. 10. Dante writes: "If we consider a home, the purpose of which is to train its members to live well, we see that there has to be one member who directs and rules, either the 'pater familias' or the person occupying his position, for, as the Philosopher says, 'every home is ruled by the eldest.' "

The family as a little Christian commonwealth cannot crudely be a realm of forced coercion and constraint. Aquinas, unlike Aristotle, must grant activities *within* the private sphere a sanctity as well, not simply because they carry over into the public realm but because they express certain Christian virtues and values. Christian morality has a profound effect on the nature and dignity of the public sphere as well. Human activities and forms of behavior considered sinful take on an additional import as they are seen as a threat to the virtue of the Christian commonwealth in its public aspect. In deciding what activities should be proscribed as being *sinful* and *socially destructive*, activities, therefore, in which the public has a legitimate interest and voice, Aquinas repairs to that natural reason and morality he sees written on all human hearts.

The practices he deems most destructive are those viewed as contrary to, or as a threat to, human sociality and community ties. If not checked, regulated, or prohibited, they weaken the ties that bind social-political communities, large and small. Aquinas singles out usury, drunkenness, gluttony, suicide, murder, breaking of promises, adultery, and homosexuality as antisocial acts. The prohibition against adultery holds for both sexes. (This is not to say that adultery did not remain, in practice, a more serious offense for the woman than the man.) Breaking promises, murder, and usury are clearly antisocial practices. But what of those activities or "vices" considered private within liberal society—drunkenness, gluttony, suicide, homosexuality? Is the later view of liberal tolerance and civility correct that such activities are private and of no concern to anyone else? Aquinas would respond to this suggestion by arguing that these activities are both the individual's private affair—a matter of the immortal soul—as well as a public affair, for within the framework of a community that takes as its foundation a concept of civic virtue (whether this community is Christian, democratic, or socialist), activities ordinarily viewed as private within liberal conceptions of persons and politics take on a highly charged public and political dimension. To sin within medieval Christianity, whether one was male or female, was never a totally private concern as it involved one's place in the moral community. Luther was to sever a tight connection between prohibited individual acts and the political community and later liberal theorists bifurcated a whole range of human activities from the sphere of public concern, regulation, and interest—developments with ambiguous implications for women and politics. Aquinas' insistence on a legitimate public interest in activities which may be seen as antisocial or as eroding the moral fabric of community remains an ongoing challenge to the political imagination and moral conscience.

LUTHER: PRIVATE PIETY, POWER POLITICS

Although Luther's chief passions did not lie in the realm of the political, the impact of his work on Western political thought is critical. He is a key figure in the emergence of a new concept of the human subject, hence the evolution of terms of public and private reality. Luther's work breaks with Catholic Christianity's focus upon externals—public acts of penance, pilgrimage, prayer. Luther's pietistic soul is "justified and saved by faith alone." His "free Christian" can be saved by faith even as the traditional moorings of community and social life give way before the forces of nationalism, early capitalist accumulation, and the disintegrating *res publica Christiana*.

The insistent focus in Catholic social philosophy that the Christian life should, ordinarily, be a shared life involving external evidence of inner conviction, faded from Luther's vision. He seems untouched by Aquinas' sanction of earthly rule and the dignity and purposes accorded secular rule by St. Thomas. (Aquinas was too much the Aristotelian for Luther who, an avid student of the classics, read Aristotle and detested him. He considered Aristotle's *Ethics* the worst book ever written.) Luther's "free Christian" had no need of institutions and offices, canonical laws and rituals, Popes and priests. Learning, too, could be a trap set by the devil (this from one of the sixteenth century's most learned men); the learned may speak with a silken voice but lie within his soul. No one can compel another in matters of faith. Each person has, or should have, access to the Word of God. Reduce the Christian life to its irreducible dimensions, he cries, and keep one's distance from all institutional forms of rule. All God's faithful servant needs is faith and the Word. ". . . it is clear," he writes in his essay on "The Freedom of a Christian," "that the inner man cannot be justified, freed, or saved by any outer work or action at all, and that these works, whatever their character, have nothing to do with this inner man."[26] The pious man or woman wears no external insignia proclaiming, "I am one of those saved by faith." He simply hears the Word preached, falls on his knees before the awesome God Almighty in private, and tends to his soul.

Responding to the social dislocation around him, a chaos refracted in the interstices of his soul, Luther responded by constructing a tiny, redeemed point of order amidst the turbulence and change. He would not build an external community. He would refuse to create yet another swollen structural edifice, a monument, he believed, not to man's piety but to his pomposity. He lived in the midst of a political jigsaw puzzle with grasping princes and last-gasp emperors trying to keep the pieces together or redraw them. There was no "Germany" save in the hearts and minds of some Germans and in a powerful language he would do more than any other individual to refine, solidify, and proliferate. In the meantime, Luther's point of order shrunk to the thinnest thread, a tensile strand he hoped would hold tight in the shipwrecked social world of his age. Clinging to the anchor of the Self, the Christian subject, male or female, dramatically turned inward, for there, Luther said, the Kingdom of God was truly to be found. No matter what winds blew about in the storm, the free Christian could live in the midst of saints or satyrs, criminals or citizens, decay or delight for his "true transformation . . . is entirely internal."[27]

For Luther to claim, as he does, that an individual's works—his deeds—have, or may have, "nothing to do with this inner man," is an unsettling claim. If one took Luther at his word, the person who, say, tortures his pets tells us nothing about himself in so doing: neither does the woman who spends a lifetime min-

[26] John Dillenberger, ed., *Martin Luther: Selections from His Writings*, p. 56.
[27] MacIntyre, *Short History of Ethics*, p. 122.

istering to the untouchables and dying. Surely Luther cannot have meant this, yet it remains a linchpin in Lutheran theology. This despite the fact that Luther exhorted the faithful, in terms almost jolly, to engage "in activity, in deeds, in works and exercises. God does not want hearers and repeaters of words, . . . but followers and doers, and this occurs in faith through love."[28] Or: "Faith is directed toward God, love toward man and one's neighbour, and consists in such love and service for him, as we have received from God without our work and merit."[29] Luther's argument would follow a line of reasoning thus: I have patiently explained that the righteous are saved by faith alone. I meant it. Though external signs cannot be presumed to tell us anything about the inward man, the just, one saved by faith, will be compelled to do good works, to live his faith; however, some who do good works are not saved as they have no faith.

Whatever one finally determines as to the relationship between faith and good works in Lutheran doctrine, it is clear that there is in Luther's thought a retreat from public life with social forms and institutions as their moorings even as the sinew of established networks unravelled and gave way. If one cannot turn to the Pope, nor the emperor, nor the king, nor the priest, nor a settled community, to whom then can one turn? The answer is either to oneself or to a shrunken "we" in the form of a Christian family. (It is the case that Lutherans built communities of the faithful. My point is that these are not as *central* to Luther's vision as such communities are within Catholic social doctrine.)

I argued in my Introduction that the fortunes, relative strengths, and spheres of operation of public and private ebb and flow depending upon their respective fates in changing historic contexts and their diverging relationship to one another. The era of the Reformation represents an ebb tide in the normative import of public institutions and the social locus they provided. As the legitimacy of these traditional institutions was shaken, it occurred in a world in which new forms had not yet solidified to orient men and women. Because Luther did not live in a society with

[28] "Extracts from the Wittenberg Sermons, 1522," in *Martin Luther*, ed. E. G. Rupp and Benjamin Drewery, p. 100.
[29] *Ibid.*, p. 101.

a well-governed and clearly justified public-political world, it is more difficult to determine how and in what ways the private sphere served to oppose, complement, or support the public. There were feudal princes ruling under feudal law over large areas of German soil. All men were either subjects of a prince or the Holy Roman Emperor or both. Final determinations as to spheres of influence depended largely on force. It is not surprising, then, that for Luther the political sphere was little more than a realm of coercion and unfreedom. Princes can either destroy you or protect you, no more, no less. But this world of externals is inessential to the faith of the Christian. The true epicenter of his existence is a pietistic, ever-scrutinized *vie intérieur*.

Because the Lutheran was in the world, not out of it, he had to take some stands towards secular rule. That stance was simple: unless an attempt was made to compel one in a matter of faith, one obeyed, for order was a great good and anarchy a hideous evil. Obedience in externals compromised one's freedom not at all, for freedom belonged to the inner man. The outer or public man was subject to the powers that be. "A Christian," Luther writes, "is a perfectly free lord of all, subject to none. A Christian is a perfectly dutiful servant of all, subject to all."[30] Luther pronounced no male-female distinctions in his free Christian's bondage and bound Christian's freedom. Both were subject to secular authority. Both enjoyed inner Christian freedom and spiritual equality no matter what their earthly external status. Each believer was equal to all others; indeed, the most powerful, public person may be less worthy than the most humble, private person: with regard to inner worthiness the lowly person may even be superior.[31]

One could no longer evaluate a person by his or her social role, status, or function. Luther's "priesthood of all believers" drained the aura which previously surrounded various statuses. The lowliest man in Christendom might get to heaven before the Pope in all his majesty and splendor.

As heady and subversive of hierarchy as this seems to be, Luther simultaneously gave up on whatever direct moral suasion

---

[30] Dillenberger, ed., *Martin Luther*, p. 53.   [31] *Ibid.*, p. 65.

Christ, via the spiritual sword, could bring to Caesar, for that suasion required a powerful social institution. Such institutions, for Luther, could not authentically do God's work. The Christian could only pray that individual rulers would be pious or cautious as they went about their dirty work, a vocation Luther called that of "God's hangman." God needed such hangmen, according to Luther, because human beings were frequently seditious, rebellious, and given to irrational transports and raging disorders. This tumult is destructive: it kills the innocent along with the guilty, cheapens social life, throws fear into the hearts of the innocent and the faithful, and makes a mockery of that dutiful obedience in all external things which is the mark of a good citizen. In Luther's writings on secular power we get the first glimmerings of Hobbes' irresistible secular God, his awesome Leviathan. The hangman is a terrifying and bleak enough vision of what a public world is all about. For Luther, the public world could never serve as the locus of human identity and a place within which human beings could act communally towards worthy shared ends. Luther's public Self lost the name of action. Like Augustine before the awesome downfall of Rome, he retreated unto himself and contemplated the City of God. Unlike Augustine, Luther's city lay primarily within his own being.

Did Luther enrich or reconstruct the private realm when he gave politics (for the most part) over to the Devil? The answer is yes, although the matter is not entirely clear-cut. At various points, Luther assigns a variety of purposes to the Christian family which can only be held in tension with one another.[32] Luther calls

---

[32] John Calvin, who is not discussed in the text because his views are not as innovative or seminal as Luther's, nevertheless shared Luther's view that Christian marriage was a blessed institution which ordered lives of mutual virtue for pious men and women. His discussions of domestic piety take a more stern and legalistic turn than Luther's, however; they are more straightforwardly patriarchal. Calvin's image of the Christian father is less the ambivalent and sometimes tortured creature portrayed by Luther, a man bound by affection to love his children and by responsibility to instill in them a sense of authority, than a paterfamilias with no doubts as to where his duty or authority lie. Calvin's father has a fearful majesty. Man himself, for Calvin, is a less responsible and complex creature than he is for Luther. Calvin's version of the equality of Christians, unlike Luther's that presumed a universal human capacity for spiritual understanding and right conduct,

the family the heart of human existence and his views on women are robust and remarkably enlightened for his time. Within the private arena, human discourse and speech—speech within an intimate, social setting cemented by strong bonds of affection, responsibility and promise-keeping—could be turned to what Luther called "the natural desire of sex" as one of the fundaments of Christian marriage, together with mutual respect and the rearing of Christian offspring. A Christian marriage would never come to fruition, Luther argues, were males and females not propelled towards union by their sexual appetites and desires, needs Luther accepted as God-given and natural. There is, in Luther, little pious sighing for a totally otherworldly divine love as a substitute for a worldly, human love. Luther declared that human love had about it something of the divine.

In the matter of speaking one's desires, Luther emerges as a liberator of human speech: frank, openly vulgar, honest enough to admit he had human appetites, tweaking the public pomposity of the mighty with irreverent earthiness, Luther ripped the veils of pious denial off subjects previously tabooed or whispered about in prurient secrecy. For example, outraged at the royal pomp and ritual surrounding the papacy, Luther spoke of the Pope sitting quietly "like a gracious lord when the sacrament was passed to him on a golden rod by a bowing cardinal on bended knee." Yet all other members of the Christian faithful must kneel before the holy sacraments. Luther thunders: "As though the holy sacrament were not worthy that a pope, a poor stinking sinner, should rise

stresses an equal depravity of all in the eyes of God. Thus the parent-child relationship focuses almost exclusively on instilling obedience and the fear of both God's and the father's wrath. The family is the child's first "subjection to earthly rule" and such subjection alone helps unruly human children learn to submit to authority. The lordly power of the father is collapsed into the fatherly power of the Lord. Calvin's Christian citizen is the obedient subject whose liberty consists in submission to a natural righteous order, whether family or state, public or private. His political ideal was a hierarchy in which state and church, like paternal and secular authority, were fused into an ordered unity. Calvin's denial of a social theory of human nature or an equality other than a shared depravity, and his insistence on the "law of the fathers" tied the nature and purpose of politics to "the due maintenance of religion" within a tradition in which only men ruled. See John Calvin, *On God and Political Duty*, pp. 46-47 and *passim*.

to show God honor, when all other Christians, who are much more holy than the most Holy Father, the pope, receive it with all reverence!''[33] In this same letter, within a three-page span, the Pope is condemned by Luther for his devilish pride, his pretension to lordliness, his servicing by obsequious courtiers, his shamelessness, his improprieties, his wicked doings "devised by the devil" and his "ridiculous and childish . . . perverted and deluded reasoning."[34]

How the initially shocked faithful must have loved such blunt talk from one of their own, not silenced by his awe of powerful spiritual and temporal authorities, nor silent on simple human appetites. Luther transformed the possibilities of meaningful public and private discourse by demonstrating that serious attention should be paid to important and vital questions through the vehicle of the vernacular, the down-to-earth language of the ordinary person. This was a bedevilment of power in the bargain. Earthy public and private talk: What if a woman attempted it? The question, once stated, jars, for one cannot attribute the absence of such "female talk," whether public or private, to female illiteracy and the widespread absence of education. The language of the vernacular was women's language. Instead one must look to the double standard taking shape, gearing expectations for, and guiding normative judgments of male and female speech along public and private vectors alike.

A Martin Luther might boast that he could "cut wind" in Germany and Rome would "smell" it. No woman, particularly no Christian woman and member of the faithful, could address either worldly secular power or the husband, to whom Luther believed she must defer (though to whom she was not subjugated), with such boldness. One person's truculent, irrepressible speech (the brave man) is another's brazen, irrational, immoral speech (the uncontrollable or slatternly woman). Because speech is the central way we come to know ourselves, to reveal ourselves to others and to express our own identities, for the more powerful to repress the speech of the vernacular simply because propriety or tradition dictates it, or for individuals to repress such speech in themselves because, alas, they "never think such things"

[33] Martin Luther, *Three Treatises*, p. 58.   [34] *Ibid.*, pp. 53-54.

(shorthand for repress or deny them) is to impoverish possibilities
for transformative human discourse that gives expression to human
discontents. Luther's ambiguous heritage, despite his personal
defiance, does not challenge political power and distinguishes
private voices depending on whether the speaker is male or female.
The Christian wife must speak in the voice of piety and house-
wifery, though Luther did allow her, within the privacy of spiritual
counsel, to voice the language of frustrated desire.

Luther's refusal to repudiate and revile the human body, particularly the *female* body which had been the particular target of
prurient and salacious Churchmen, led him to attack those
"schoolmen, the monks, and such other" who "never felt any
spiritual temptations, and therefore . . . fought only for the re-
pressing and overcoming of fleshly lust and lechery, and being
proud of that victory which they never yet obtained, they thought
themselves far better and more holy than married men. . . . Under
this holy pretence they nourished and maintained all kinds of
horrible sins, as dissension, pride, hatred, disdain, and despising
of their neighbors, trust in their own righteousness, presumption,
contempt of godliness and of the Word of God, infidelity, blasphemy, and such-like."[35] Luther's defense of the naturalness of
sexual desire prompted him to save some of his choicest vitriol
for those Schoolmen who declared the female body repugnant.

> Crotus . . . wrote blasphemously about the marriage of
> priests, declaring that the most holy bishop of Mainz was ir-
> ritated by no annoyance more than by the stinking, putrid,
> private parts of women. That godless knave, forgetful of his
> mother and sister, dares to blaspheme God's creature through
> whom he was himself born. It would be tolerable if he were
> to find fault with the behavior of women, but to defile their
> creation and nature is most godless. As if I were to ridicule
> man's face on account of his nose! For the nose is the latrine
> of man's head and stands above his mouth.[36]

---

[35] Dillenberger, ed., *Luther*, p. 147.

[36] Quoted in *Not in God's Image*, ed. O'Faolain and Martines, p. 197. Sadly,
many contemporary radical feminists are guilty of repudiating female biology as
well. See Chapter 6 for a full discussion.

Luther's response to the sexual and moral problem of a young wife may serve as an example of his enlightened attitude on sexuality in general and female sexuality in particular. Luther was troubled over the torment of a young woman who discovered she was married to an impotent man. He, not surprisingly, had no wish to beget a child although his wife yearned for one. What should she do? If a woman finds herself in such a situation and is "unable to remain continent," Luther advises "her to seek a divorce in order to marry another, as she was content, in her conscience to do so, and after ample experience on the part of herself that he was impotent." Should her husband (whom Luther considers a husband "in name only" at this point, merely "a man who lives in the same house") refuse her right to divorce, Luther suggests that she have coition "with another man, say her husband's brother, but keep this 'marriage' secret . . . ascribing the children to the putative father, as they call such a one."

Luther goes on to say that a woman who follows such a course of action need have no fear for her immortal soul. She is in a state of salvation for it is the man's condition and stubbornness which first created the impasse and prevented the marriage to work properly. Ideally, the husband "ought to coincide" with her right to have intercourse with another and to bear a child as she has become his wife in the legal sense only. Should all else fail, the wife, long since "free" in the genuine sense, may, without obtaining a divorce, marry another and flee to a foreign country. "What other counsel can be given to one constantly struggling with the dangers of her natural emotions?" To the faithful who would be astounded at what they might perceive to be immoral encouragement of adultery on Luther's part, Luther replies that such persons never seem to consider the husband's deceit of the wife, for it was he who defrauded her "totally in body and life" and that is a "greater sin" than her alienation of his estate.[37] Luther, in this instance, comes down squarely in favor of natural sexual desires, simple human values, and the freedom of a Christian should these values clash with property values and the formal laws of the state.

[37] Dillenberger, ed., *Luther*, pp. 337-338.

As I noted above, for Luther the Christian family was the epicenter of human social existence. The family was an arena of compassion, concern, kindness, and emotion but Luther also located learning obedience to authority within the family. The Bible commands children to honor and to obey their fathers and their mothers. Luther not only finds the source of parental authority in that commandment, he goes further: "For all authority has its root and source in parental authority. For where a father is unable to bring up his child alone, he takes a teacher to teach him; if he is too weak, he takes his friend or neighbour to help him; when he departs this life, he gives authority to others who are chosen for the purpose. So he must also have servants, men and maids, under him for the household, so that all who are called master stand in the place of parents, and must obtain from them authority and power to command. Wherefore in the Bible they are all called fathers.'' Luther went so far as to prophesy ''the end of the whole world'' should the ''rule of the parents'' be lost.[38]

If the child does not learn obedience in the home the temporal order is threatened as that child will be a willful and rebellious subject. Like the political liberal Alexis de Tocqueville some three centuries later, Luther tied the *nature*, *structure*, and *purpose* of secular order to that of the family. Unlike de Tocqueville, Luther saw the family not simply as an analogue or microcosm of the state; he found the origin of all authority in the scriptural injunction to parents. Luther's views resemble political theories of patriarchy but there are important differences. Luther refused to mesh paternal and temporal authority as did later theorists of patriarchy, and he did not find a grant of unlimited absolute dominion to fathers in scripture. Instead he adopts a perspective which seeks the origin and prototype of secular rule in the rule of fathers, declares that an important relation between the two exists, but insists that political rule is not, like that of parents, natural. The rule of parents in practice must be ameliorated in its harshness, threaded through and through with bonds of love and compassion for that power is both ''natural and voluntary . . . . But the rule

---

[38] *The Large Catechism*, quoted in Herbert Marcuse's *Studies in Critical Philosophy*, p. 75.

of government is forced, an artificial rule.''[39] Within the family as a natural and voluntary society, conjugal equality reigned. Juliet Mitchell has observed that once ''formal conjugal equality (monogamy) is established, sexual freedom as such—which under polygamous conditions was usually a form of exploitation—becomes, conversely, a possible force for liberation.''[40] Luther's sanction of human sexual desire as both natural and good reinforced this development.

I would prefer to conclude my reflections on Luther with that note, but I must return to and take up that dynamic within Luther's vision of the private home, namely, the rearing of a dearly beloved yet sternly disciplined child to be, above all, one who obeys. To be sure, obedience is ''external'' in Luther's view of mind and emotion and the child cannot be compelled in matters of faith. So why this unyielding, obsessive stress on obedience? This takes me to the defensive dimension of Luther's politics, or, in this case, his apolitical stance which is nonetheless infused with political resonance.

Luther's own rebellion was a rebellion against Church and state, sacred and secular authority, and he took it to the top. He would answer to no one save God and Holy Scripture. His rebellion over, his revolution secured, Luther denounced repeatedly the evils of sedition, rebellion, disobedience to authority—all the activities in which he did engage or was said to have engaged. The man who threw Western Christendom into tumult hated social dissension and saw it as the work of the Devil; thus, he teaches his children to obey their elders. He insists repeatedly that earthly secular rulers can command, and expect to receive, obedience in things external. During the Peasant Uprising of 1525, which was inspired in part by his own teachings, Luther, rather than giving the peasants support or even sympathy (or, perhaps, silence) instructed the secular arm to put the rebels down without quarter. The peasants—a ''faithless, perjured, lying, disobedient'' lot of ''knaves and scoundrels''—should be smitten. They ''deserved death in body and soul''; indeed, everyone who can is ordered,

[39] *Luther als Pädogog*, quoted in Marcuse, *Studies in Critical Philosophy*, p. 77.

[40] Juliet Mitchell, *Woman's Estate*, p. 113.

with justice, to "smite, slay and stab, secretly or openly, remembering that nothing can be more poisonous, hurtful or devilish than a rebel. It is just as when one must kill a mad dog; if you do not strike him, he will strike you, and a whole land with you."[41] If these troubling outbursts were mere exemplars of Luther's individual distress, we could note them and go on. But his intemperance embodies larger public and private issues, so I shall spend another moment on explication.

When politics is given over to the Devil, as Luther gave it, one ought not be surprised that the Devil takes over politics. Without assemblies to curb, citizens to debate, a dense thicket of laws, precedents, and tradition to chasten, instruct, and defuse power, it may be unleashed on the very person or persons who themselves have a history of ambivalence toward it. Luther defied earthly and spiritual authority from his father Hans, to the Holy Roman Emperor, to the Pope himself and emerged triumphant. Rather than becoming, unambiguously, one of humankind's liberators he took on, as one aspect of his complicated and turbulent nature, the vocation of jailer. He would tolerate no public rebellion, this former rebel. Luther's is an instance of a *politics of displacement*, that dynamic that comes into play, connecting and interweaving public and private imperatives when, in this instance, a series of public events arouse a deeply felt, perhaps unconscious, private conviction. Such a politics is volatile and dangerous. It is more likely to occur when certain conditions prevail: (1) established public and private, secular and religious, institutions and rules are in flux and people have a sense that the center will not hold; (2) there are no clearly established public insitutions to focus dissent and concern in an ordered way; (3) private values, exigencies, and identities come to take complete precedence over public involvement in the secular realm as a citizen. If these characteristics remind the reader of our epoch, the resemblance is quite intentional. Luther is a prototypical modern in many recognizable ways, though that ambiguous accolade usually goes to his Italian contemporary, Machiavelli, whose thought aims to administer the coup de grâce to the power of the spiritual sword (*sacerdotium*)

---

[41] "Against the Robbing and Murdering Hordes of Peasants, May 1525," quoted in *Martin Luther*, ed. Rupp and Drewery, p. 122.

in matters of the secular sword (*regnum*). Luther, with reluctance, saw the necessity for God's hangman. Machiavelli's counter-revolution, on the other hand, seeks to "corner Christianity," to reduce it to harmlessness at the hearth with Christ becoming simply one of the penates.

MACHIAVELLI MAKES HIS MOVE

Early modern political theorists, responding to disintegration of the *res publica Christiana* and growth in the power of states freed increasingly from intervention in their affairs by the Church, were inspired to elaborate justifications of political sovereignty and *raison d'état* which became constitutive of the very practices they either described or intimated. It is Machiavelli, however, who articulated a theory of political action which continues to resonate—I shall argue with dire consequences—for public and private reality alike. As with most of the texts we have considered, Machiavelli's were *livres de circonstance*, reactions to a turbulent and unstable political situation within sixteenth-century Italy, an Italy torn apart by fratricidal wars between and within its various duchies and city-states. This internal bloodletting made Italy peculiarly vulnerable, in turn, to attacks from the outside by Spanish, French, or imperial armies. Machiavelli's response to disorder, as every student of political thought knows, was to shift the ground of the political enterprise away from medieval Christian concerns with legitimacy and the righteous exercise of kingly authority to the problem of political *power* itself: how to get it and how to keep it.

MacIntyre notes: "For Machiavelli the ends of social and political life are given. They are the attainment and holding down of power, the maintenance of political order and general prosperity, and these latter, in part at least, because unless you maintain them, you will not continue to hold power. Moral rules are technical rules about the means to these ends. Moreover, they are to be used on the assumption that all men are somewhat corrupt,"[42] and, it must be added, so are all women. Human nature, for

---

[42] MacIntyre, *Short History of Ethics*, p. 127.

Machiavelli, is a constant—unchanging from one historic period to the next—and it presents a bleak and dangerous image. ''For it may be said of men in general,'' he writes, ''that they are ungrateful, voluble, dissemblers, anxious to avoid danger, and covetous of gain; as long as you benefit them, they are entirely yours; they offer you their blood, their goods, their life, and their children, as I have before said, when the necessity is remote; but when it approaches, they revolt.''[43] These untrustworthy persons are subject to laws of history. Much of their behavior is governed and determined although they remain largely ignorant or unaware of this fact.

Machiavelli's theory of human nature, together with his belief that *virtù*, a particular form of civic virtue, was necessary to a brave and united people, spurred him to articulate a theory of political action which could be justified, not within Christian morality, but from the vantage point of a divergent ethic. The perspective which prevailed in Christian social thought had not involved bifurcation of politics from the pursuit of justice and righteousness: Machiavelli, however, placed force rather than legitimate authority at the heart of his political vision. Force permeated all political levels up to the pinnacle of an armed state of militant, mobilized citizens, geared towards defense or the extension of its sway. That Machiavelli's personal preference was a republican state, long since dead and silent to his time, is a consideration which must not ''be allowed to confuse the issue'' in an evaluation of his theory of politics;[44] moreover, the view of the citizen in his idealized prior epoch was that of an *armed* citizen-soldier. Machiavelli reaffirmed on alternative grounds Aristotelian distinctions between public and private spheres and rigidified divergent terms of evaluation for public and private activities. Thus, within Machiavelli's world, a man could be a good ruler but a wicked person if private morality were set up as the criterion by which to judge his public actions, an alternative Machiavelli rejects as suicidal to political survival.[45] Rules of

---

[43] Niccolò Machiavelli, *The Prince and The Discourses*, p. 61.

[44] MacIntyre, *Short History of Ethics*, p. 127.

[45] Machiavelli, *Prince and Discourses, passim.* See also an article celebrating Machiavelli's ''public morality'' by Isaiah Berlin, ''The Question of Machiavelli,'' *New York Review of Books*, pp. 20-32.

conduct appropriate to the sphere of "private morality" were declared inappropriate to the new morality of a politics which turned on holding and exercising power. "Good" and "bad" as these terms of evaluation had previously moved within public and private discourse were denuded of much of their previous meaning and force.

In the midst of this transformation, women were confined to a private world where softness could be practiced and the voice of womanly piety be heard without doing irreparable harm to a public domain where martial vigor must reign supreme. Machiavelli did politicize the private sphere to the extent that he saw it, too, as a battleground for a kind of war, the war between the sexes, which involved its own power plays, stratagems, advances, retreats, and a language game of coquetry and deception for male and female participants.

What emerges from Machiavelli is a series of partial or whole, public and private, mirror images which depend on one another within the framework of a conflicting interplay of forces. A "bad" man can be a "good" politician but he can also be a "good" man in private. What is moral in the public realm cannot be judged by the standards of private moral conduct; therefore, public persons are judged one way in their capacity as public persons and another way in their existence as private persons. Politics is the realm of public power, the sphere of justice and systems of law. The state is a body of citizens, instilled with civic virtue and subject to laws. Political leaders are also subject to laws but not bound by them in the exercise of power. Women are not of politics per se, but provide, in their capacities in the private sphere, a refuge from public life for men when they share in the private sphere. A "good" woman makes a "bad" citizen by definition. The woman who is a "good" citizen cannot, in the private sphere, be a "good" woman. She is judged in each instance by standards of so-called private morality, Christian morality without teeth. She is not to share in public (im)morality. Women are morally superior *because* they are publically inferior. The private realm of feeling and sentiment is not subject to laws and not judged by public standards. If there is power in this sphere, it is power as covert manipulation, deceit, and cunning. This realm is not properly part of the public sphere but provides a base for it. Women are nonpolitical and so are men in their private capacities.

The nature of social structures and arrangements of Machiavelli's time was such that the private sphere became a perfect defensive foil for his purposes. Machiavelli's politics can be seen in large measure as a defense against the softer, "womanly" Christian virtues. Machiavelli assigns to the private sphere an already socially decreed function, but he deprives that function of any vector *moving outward*. Christian social thought, though Luther is a partial exception, required that the Christian, taught piety within the home and among a public body of the faithful, take the measure of the public world, condemn its excesses, and temper the harshness of its justice with mercy. Christ, in this view, might challenge Caesar, reject *raison d'état* and the blandishments and threats of power. This potentially critical and seditious wedge of Christian doctrine, already blunted, was shorn by Machiavelli of any powerful, public weapons by which privacy could measure publicity. Machiavelli's bow in the direction of private virtue is not a gesture of respect but a signification of the ineffectuality of such virtue in the public arena. Not only were women left out of the councils of government, their duty frequently lay in ministering to the victims of public policy and acquiesing in a public language, through their silence, whose key words were fear, duplicity, necessity, power, will, *Realpolitik*, and *raison d'état*.

In order to inject vigor into a decaying and shattered political order, Machiavelli advocated a politics which required that the actions of men be judged, not by their intentions, motives, or purposes, but by their consequences. He writes in *The Prince*: "Therefore it is necessary for a prince, who wishes to maintain himself, to learn how not to be good, and to use this knowledge and not use it, according to the necessity of the case."[46] Or, ". . . it will be found that some things which seem virtues would, if followed, lead to one's ruin, and some others which appear vices result in one's greater security and wellbeing."[47] The prince does what is required. He takes the necessary steps in the assurance

---

[46] Machiavelli, *Prince and Discourses*, p. 56.   [47] *Ibid.*, p. 57.

that all other considerations are overridden by the imperatives of *raison d'état*.

Sheldon Wolin, with restraint, characterizes Machiavelli's political thought as an "economy of violence," rather than, as some have seen it, the advocacy of unrestrained evil and duplicity.[48] Yet that "economy" is a strategic, not a *moral* setting of limits, and can readily be foresworn for reasons of state. What is central to my purposes as the cutting edge between images of public and private is first, Machiavelli's bleak denial of a social view of human nature and second, his defense of a powerful and amoral concept of political action grounded in an armed state and citizenry. Machiavelli's armed virtue not only excluded women from politics, it deemphasized women's traditional private sphere. The home, with its softer virtues, came in for the scorn of the powerful rather than the blessings of the pious. The ideal of the citizen with which Machiavelli finally emerged "implied a totally different conceptualization of the modes of political knowledge and action from that implicit in the scholastic-customary framework."[49] The political community for Machiavelli, as for Aristotle, involved a life of action. The authentic, uncorrupted *res publica* was that structure which grounded men's lives on this earth. Machiavelli insisted that the rules for the polity be judged by a non-Christian vision of morality.[50] The citizen who participates in the revitalized polity shares in its universality, for the polity is the most inclusive association in a world of like associations: this, at any rate, is Machiavelli's Aristotelian ideal as outlined in *The Discourses*.

But Machiavelli faced a dilemma: how could one create or infuse civic virtue (*virtù*) within a republic which was demoralized, corrupt, and disunified, in which such *virtù* was absent? If the political times are decadent and corrupt, what can serve as

---

[48] Wolin, *Politics and Vision*, "Machiavelli: Politics and the Economy of Violence," pp. 195-238; and his essay, "Political Theory as a Vocation," in *Machiavelli and the Nature of Political Thought*, ed. Martin Fleischer, pp. 23-75.

[49] J.G.A. Pocock, *The Machiavellian Moment*, p. 49.

[50] *Ibid.*, p. 73. Pocock notes: "Virtuous republics were at war with one another. For this reason the Christian virtues and the civic could never coincide; humility and the forgiveness of injuries could have no place in the relations between republics, where a prime imperative was to defend one's city and beat down her enemies," pp. 213-214. Cf. Berlin, "The Question of Machiavelli," *passim*.

the basis or wellspring of the *virtù* necessary to a noncorrupt politics? Machiavelli solves this problem by interjecting the concept of the *will*. Popular participation, he decides, is lodged, not so much in the political knowledge, acumen, and dedication to shared purposes of its citizens, but to the state of will of each and all.[51] For Aristotle's male citizens, governed by public rules and reason, Machiavelli substitutes the armed popular state whose principles he believed he had uncovered in the history of the Roman republic. He observes:

Although I have elsewhere maintained that the foundation of states is a good military organization, yet it seems to me not superfluous to repeat here that, without such a military organization, there can neither be good laws nor anything else good. The necessity of this appears on every page of Roman history. We also see that troops cannot be good unless they are well disciplined and trained, and this cannot be done with any troops other than natives of the country; for a state is not and cannot be always engaged in war, therefore troops must be trained and disciplined in time of peace.[52]

J.G.A. Pocock concludes that Machiavelli's "militarization of citizenship makes the *Discorsi* in an important sense more morally subversive than *Il Principe*."[53] Throughout the *Discourses* Machiavelli celebrates the classical vision of *virtù* but he justifies and implements a life of armed preparedness and vigilance, the artifact of human will.

The occasional references to women within *The Discourses* and *The Prince* are of little major theoretical consequence although they reaffirm Machiavelli's ability to combine a fatalistic pessimism with a voluntarist will to power. He mentions *Fortuna*, an archetypal female principle, the bitch goddess of Caprice, several times. She is said to govern about one-half of all human affairs leaving the remainder to human artifice. (But not quite, as human behavior is ruled by determinative laws of history as well.)

---

[51] Pocock, *The Machiavellian Moment*, p. 212.
[52] Machiavelli, *Prince and Discourses*, p. 503.
[53] Pocock, *The Machiavellian Moment*, p. 213.

Machiavelli compares *Fortuna* to an impetuous river or a fickle woman who must be mastered and conquered by force.[54] Machiavelli also credits women with having served as the precipitating cause for disastrous wars in much of past history; indeed, he devotes a chapter in *The Discourses* to an account of "How States are Ruined on Account of Women." He recounts, from classical sources, the methods by which women have achieved the distinction of bringing about the downfall and ruin of their states. But these anecdotal references are relatively unimportant. What is central is the manner in which Machiavelli's language structures a vision of politics which places a dissembling, untrustworthy human subject, governed by laws or a fate he cannot control, yet capable of making a voluntarist effort to achieve *virtù* by will, at its heart. Politics revolves around the terms power, force, and violence.

Machiavelli's politics eliminates women by definition from the most important field of citizen involvement, military exploits. Juliet Mitchell observes that ". . . historically it has been women's lesser capacity for violence as well as for work that has determined her subordination. In most societies woman has not only been less able than man to perform arduous kinds of work, she has also been less able to fight. Man not only has the strength to assert himself against nature, but also against his fellows."[55] I am not

[54] Machiavelli, *Prince and Discourses*, pp. 91, 94. There is no extended discussion of the relation of family to polity in Machiavelli but he does devote a chapter in *The Discourses* to "How States are Ruined on Account of Women." He recounts a tale from Roman history in which a "rich heiress" becomes the focal point of a dispute which leads to war. Men must struggle in behalf of their ravaged and ill-treated wives and daughters. In this manner "women have been the cause of . . . great damage to those who govern them." Another illustration drawn from Roman history details how the "outrage committed upon Lucretia deprived the Tarquins of their throne," and so forth. Machiavelli also counsels "absolute princes and rulers of republics" to tend to this subject and to "well reflect upon the disorders that may arise from such causes, and . . . see that proper remedies be applied in time, ere they involve their state or republic in loss and shame" (p. 489). Machiavelli provides no guidelines for this vigilance. The passages noted above are unimportant theoretically but instructive insofar as they hold victims responsible for the damage done when men must seek revenge of their honor.

[55] Mitchell, *Woman's Estate*, p. 103.

lamenting Machiavelli's failure to incorporate women within his vision of the armed state nor questioning whether or not women are capable of full armed combat. These considerations are not the most important in a moral and political assessment of his politics, a politics which requires attaching value to consequences or states of affairs.

All social ties and relations suffer as the split between public and private widens into a gap and then a chasm. Within the domain of *Realpolitik* intractable terms like "power, force, coercion, violence" structure political action and consciousness. On the other side of the chasm, softness, compassion, forgiveness, and emotionality are allowable insofar as they do not intervene with the public imperative. The private world is called upon to "make up" for the cold (but necessary) inhumanity of the public. Yet it, too, suffers from the politics of amoral consequentionalism, [56] for the private sphere exists within a "space" permeated by that politics and within a political consciousness that—to the extent that it accepts the theory that all men are wicked, that politics is power and the promotion of self-interest, and that this is the "way things are"—will systematically vitiate transformative possibilities as these will be neither seen nor understood within its tough, hard world.

[56] Machiavelli's consequentialisms cut the heart out of theories of individual moral agency.

Chapter 3

Politics Sanctified and Subdued: Patriarchalism and the Liberal Tradition

The lordship which Adam by creation had over the whole world, and by right descending from him the Patriarchs did enjoy, was as large and ample as the absolutest dominion of any monarch which hath been since the creation.—*Sir Robert Filmer*

The end of obedience is protection.—*Thomas Hobbes*

If therefore these words give any power to Adam, it can be only a Conjugal Power, not Political. . . . —*John Locke*

The family, justly constituted, would be the real school of the virtues of freedom.—*J. S. Mill*

method

summary

Aristotle

Plato

I indicated in the previous chapters that where a theorist draws lines and makes divisions, how he categorizes the structure of reality, which notions he finds basic and which less essential, are critical to an examination of his ideas on the public and private and their implications for women and politics. Aristotle articulated a rigid public-private split along teleological lines. The family or household comprised an unfree realm, a necessary condition for the *polis*, but not one of its integral parts. Public life for Aristotle was that arena within which free, coequal males performed the responsibilities and garnered the privileges and glories of citizenship. Earlier Plato, having recognized the importance of the private world to the public, had resolved potential tension between them by eradicating or controlling the private familial sphere totally. As a corrupted imperial politics gave way to religion as the center of human life and purpose, the position of women within

Christianized homes grew in dignity and honor, even as images of women remained fraught with ambivalence. At the same time, Christian men and women were enjoined to be obedient and dutiful subjects of God the Father and of the emperor or, later, the king, so long as the ruler's authority was legitimate. As subjects, neither men nor women possessed genuine public duties and responsibilities; thus the question of active participation in political decisions and affairs of state was submerged.

Christianity

With the twelfth century revival of the works of Aristotle in the West and the rise of civic humanism, a concept of the public-spirited citizen who embodied, in Machiavelli's phrase, civic *virtù*, was revived. But the resurgence of a notion of political action merged with the notion of an armed citizen within Machiavelli's thought. Women again were excluded from the public stage and citizenship for men was militarized. The private world remained; indeed, its importance was enhanced by the exhortation and example of such Protestant reformers as Martin Luther. The gentler virtues of family life, however, were no match for the bold and forbidding doctrine of *raison d'état*, which became the paradigmatic political notion of early modern Europe. I take up the public-private thread with a discussion of patriarchalism in political thought.[1]

12th c.

---

[1] Although my discussion on patriarchalism shall center on Sir Robert Filmer's *Patriarcha*, there are other important thinkers associated with this tradition. One of these is Jean Bodin who, in the context of sixteenth-century France, articulated a theory of political sovereignty which took the nation-state ruled by a kingly patriarch for granted. Bodin is identified with the concept of sovereignty (*puissance soveraine*) in its full-blown modern panoply, defined as the unlimited authority to make and to enforce law within a given unit of rule. For Bodin, law was the command of the sovereign king and lord that subjects were required to obey. In *Six Books of the Commonwealth*, Bodin linked public and private through that authority exercised by patriarchal fathers within the family and a patriarchal king within the state. Both the lordly father and the fatherly lord had a divine right to demand unquestioning obedience from their respective subjects. Like Aristotle, Bodin distinguishes the state from all other forms of association and considers its end ("justice") different in kind from that of lesser associations such as the family. The family necessarily lacks the *telos* of the state; therefore, the ruler of the family does not and cannot possess the perpetual and absolute sovereignty which belongs to the king alone. The family is a kind of image of the state, "the model of right order in the commonwealth." To the father should be restored the power of the

FILMER AND THE PATRIARCHAL TRADITION

"And God said . . ."—for Robert Filmer, no more need be said. In his *Patriarcha*, the most uncompromising, complete, and bold statement of political patriarchalism, all individuals, male and female, are privatized and silenced save the king, the Supreme Father, whose words are cast by and for him in the mold of the Father of All.[2] "The Prince," he writes, "whom you may justly call the Father of the country, ought to be to every man dearer and more reverend than any Father, as one ordained and sent unto us by God."[3] For Filmer, the earthly authority of all fathers and of the king is identical in kind, not simply analogous. It should be noted that a family analogy need not lead to patriarchalism of Filmer's sort. An analogy does not presume an identity. What type of patriarchalism emerges from family-polity, public-private analogues and metaphors will depend upon how the family itself is conceived. A thinker might go on to drop the familial analogy as controlling for politics, preserving patriarchy in the private sphere even as he excises it from the public sphere.[4] One of the

---

Roman *paterfamilias*, of life or death over the members of his household. Bodin accepts Aristotle's teleological explanation for, and justification of, woman's separate and unequal nature. For Bodin women are useful for reproduction but little else. The power, authority, and command a husband exercises over his wife is "allowed by both divine and positive law to be honourable and right" for only he has a "natural right to command." The father is the image of God, Father of all things. This state of affairs within families and states exists, not through human design nor invention, but by nature. (Jean Bodin, *Six Books of the Commonwealth*, trans. M. A. Tooley, pp. 6-7, 10-12.) Bodin's theory is one variant on the theme of patriarchalism. It does not constitute the strongest and most uncompromising version of patriarchal explanation, however, for Bodin drew back from categorizing the family *in its essence* as a *political* as well as a *natural* unit. He refused to equate the patriarchalism of the sovereign father-king with the "natural" patriarchalism of the private lordly father.

[2] Sir Robert Filmer, *Patriarcha and Other Political Works*, ed. Peter Laslett, p. 241.

[3] *Ibid.*, p. 325.

[4] See R.W.K. Hinton, "Husbands, Fathers and Conquerors: I," *Political Studies* (pp. 291-300), for further exploration of dilemmas within the logic and tradition of patriarchalism. Hinton also notes another possibility which might emerge from a familial analogy when he observes that it is a "great mistake . . . to assume that the analogy of the family necessarily led to patriarchalism,"

great political and theoretical dilemmas of sixteenth- and seventeenth-century political thought was the attempt to reconcile voluntarism in politics with "naturalism" (the family as a natural-patriarchal institution) in the private, social, but prepolitical sphere. In this context, Filmer exemplifies patriarchal thought at its apogee which is also, historically, the beginning of its decline.[5]

Filmer's key conceptual touchstones, terms of a public language that was privatized, are *natural authority*, *absolute power*, *will*, *subjection*, and *obedience*. In Filmer's world there is no split between, or even a drawing of public-private lines; indeed, there is no private sphere—in the sense of a realm demarcated from politics—nor political sphere—in the sense of a realm diverging from the private—at all. Filmer so thoroughly politicizes the family and familializes the commonwealth that there is no room for individuals, whether male or female, to conceive of themselves as having a number of diverse roles to play.

Using God's grant of dominion to Adam in Genesis 1:28 for scriptural and divine sanction, Filmer locates absolute power and authority at the beginning of time. He finds this power "natural" and patriarchal. Men did not come together voluntarily to create politics, he argues, whether motivated by fear or inconvenience or some urge to attain a chosen good. All power, all authority, and with them unquestioning obedience, are imbedded in the original grant of dominion at the Creation. The commonwealth has its origins in the Garden of Eden. Within Filmer's patriar-

---

and cites as evidence the work of one Sir Thomas Smith entitled *De Republica Anglorum*. Smith "describes marriage . . . charmingly: it is a partnership." Using the family as a metaphor to stress "two elements of consent and co-operation," a very different set of implications emerges for politics than in political theories based on a hard patriarchalist view of the family (pp. 292-293). Cf. Mary Lyndon Shanley, "Marriage Contract and Social Contract in Seventeenth Century English Political Thought," *Western Political Quarterly*, pp. 79-91.

[5] I am not treating explicitly the question of patriarchal theory as an ideology emerging from a specific historic reality, a defense mounted by an old agrarianism with its landed aristocracy and concept of justice as entitlement based on rules of primogeniture and entail, against the rising forces of commercialism and capitalism. For a brief discussion of seventeenth-century England as a patriarchal society see Laslett's introduction to Filmer's *Patriarcha* (pp. 1-43). Laslett's discussion is also helpful in classifying various understandings of patriarchalism within anthropology.

chalism there are only subjects, never citizens. Each father in his little domain "lords" it over wives, children, and servants. But the individual father, in turn, is subjected to the lordly king. Filmer's world is one long chain, from its apex to its lowliest part, within which an endless cycle of command and obedience is repeated timelessly yet through and in time.

One can reasonably see in Filmer's treatment of the family a thoroughgoing politicization, though it seems to me there is no genuine politics at all in Filmer's universe. But I shall stay with the claim for a moment in order to make an important point that looks forward to my discussion of variants on contemporary feminist theory in Chapter 5. If a thinker incorporates the private realm of the family into a total politicized structure of explanation, and flattens out all distinctions between what is public and what is private, the following dilemma necessarily emerges: if all relationships and activities, including our most intimate ones, are political in their essence, if politics is everything and everywhere, then no genuine political action and purpose is possible, as we can never distinguish the political from anything else. This imperative is at work in the writings of feminist analysts who urge that "the personal is political" totally and *simpliciter*. It is interesting to note, looking ahead, that there are similarities between Filmer's arguments and those of certain radical feminists to whom his views would be anathema. Each finds a free flow between public and private, politics and family. All spheres and activities are characterized in a *single, "privatized" public language*. Although radical feminists, writing four centuries after Filmer, draw different implications from their own collapse of public and private, they nonetheless preserve, with the dictum that the personal is political and the political personal, one of the basic notions of patriarchal theory.

Within Filmer's patriarchal world, to borrow from Peter Laslett's statement of Filmer's conclusions: there is no Form of Government, but Monarchy only; there is no Monarchy, but Paternal; there is no Paternal Monarchy, but Absolute, or Arbitrary;[6] nobody ever "leaves home." Royal government by divine monarchs

---

[6] Laslett's introduction to Filmer's *Patriarcha*, p. 20.

was intensely personal. The kingdom was also the king's private domain; his body and the body politic were separate, yet fused into the concept of an overarching, single will. "I am the husband, and all the whole island is my lawful wife," says King James.[7] As Michael Walzer points out, the king was the "only public person."[8] All history became a kind of domestic history, an unbroken chain of patriarchal-personalized rule. This domestication of politics under patriarchal principles operated in Filmer's *Patriarcha* and other defenses of royalism and divine right, not as a series of analogies or metaphors but as an overarching *Weltanschauung* which linked public-private, nature-convention, family-politics in a total system.

The patriarch within Filmer's vision was not a kind and forgiving father who provided succor for his "children" and might even allow them to "speak." The prevailing image of the Divine Father and Christian king in medieval Christendom had been considerably softened in belief and practice, in part through devotion to the Holy Mother. The Church itself was conceived as a "feminine" institution (Holy Mother Church) despite the fact that Church governance, though not all religious orders, consisted of male hierarchies. Christianity is also a religion in which the Son of God, though sacrificed, is ultimately triumphant and who himself embodies such "feminine" qualities as mercy, forgiveness, and compassion.

With the breakup of the medieval synthesis and the demise of the power of the spiritual "sword" over the secular, lines of division hardened within Christian Europe along vectors of nationalism sanctioned, in some instances, by a state church governed by a lordly father. A more stern and forbidding image of the patriarchal God emerged. Filmer's God is fiercely Old Testament in his wrath, his capacity for vengeance, and his demand for absolute obedience. The softening influences of the New Testament fade into the background. Filmer defends against any feminine influence as well as any possibility of questioning authority—for this leads inevitably, he fears, to anarchy and rebellion.

---

[7] Quoted in Michael Walzer, *Regicide and Revolution: Speeches at the Trial of Louis XVI*, p. 22.

[8] *Ibid.*, p. 23.

He creates, from this defensive posture, a tight organic theory of society regressive in its implications for persons and politics. There is one voice in the land which thunders and demands as others, quivering and silent, obey.

To counter Filmer's patriarchalism most effectively it would have been necessary to make the case that the family Filmer finds natural, political, and patriarchal *in its essence* is a more complex and various institution which cannot be subsumed within a set of terms that tap only command, obedience, power and authority—all the hard coinage of the absolutist realm. That which Filmer sees as given and unchanging, particularly the family which exists in every known society and has throughout history, has in fact taken a variety of forms and has served changing, although not totally changing, purposes.

Unfortunately, the contractarian, constitutional, and voluntarist theories of politics that superceded Filmer's patriarchalism, including the Hobbesian solution which fused absolutism with consent, failed to treat the family in a full and coherent manner. As these thinkers recast distinctions between public and private in order to take the family out of the politics and politics out of the family, they found that the remnants of patriarchalism were not so easily expunged. The image of the human being which emerged triumphant in postpatriarchal political thought was in tension with, yet parasitic upon, the person as family man or woman. Hobbes' *Leviathan*, for example, features an uneasy coalescence of contractualism and obedience to absolute authority. He returns the family to prepolitics but argues that absolute obedience pertains both in this privately contracted sphere as well as in the public world. Locke's *Two Treaties* locate the family in the state of nature, but in this, his rejoinder to Filmer, Locke fails to engage Filmer's arguments at their conceptual root—in the problem of what weight one ought, or must, give to tradition and to what is deemed natural. By failing to come up with a vocabulary rich enough to account for the centrality of the social relationships of the family, even as they "depoliticized" these relationships, thinkers within the liberal tradition adopted a set of assumptions which required the "systematic setting to one side of the fundamental facts of birth, childhood, parenthood, old age, and death."[9]

Despite its relentless power-riddenness and celebration of subjection which disallowed any individual, male or female, to "grow up," there were some strengths in Filmer's account. The most important of these was his insistence that human beings are defined by relationships and traditions that are neither reducible to prudential calculation nor to human artifice. Filmer had some sense, however distorted, of the power of familial images, and of history as a force which militates against sudden and wholesale changes in the way a society structures its human relationships. For example, he counters Hobbes' claim that all obligations, including familial, emerge through contract: "I cannot understand how this right of nature can be conceived without imagining a company of men at the very first to have been all created together without any dependency one of another, or as mushrooms (*fungorum more*) they all on a sudden were sprung out of the earth without any obligation one to another, as Mr. Hobbes's words are in his book *De Cive*, Chapter 8, section 3."[10]

As for the suggestion that children consent to the exercise of paternal dominion, Filmer evinces incredulity: "How a child can express consent," he writes, "or by other sufficient arguments declare it before it comes to the age of discretion I understand not."[11] Filmer never forgot that all human beings begin life in a state of helplessness and unchosen dependency. Unfortunately, this led him to conclude that people were not "born free" and, as well, that they could never outgrow the tutelage of a powerful "parent." The lordly father in his own domain lived in a state of simultaneous subjection and arbitrary control over others. Given Filmer's declaration that all power on earth "is either derived or usurped from the fatherly power,"[12] it was impossible for him to see any alternative. Gordon Schochet is correct to insist that beliefs such as these "had to be overcome before constitu-

[9] Wolff, "There's Nobody Here But Us Persons," p. 133.
[10] Filmer, *Patriarcha*, p. 241.
[11] *Ibid.*, p. 245.   [12] *Ibid.*, p. 233.

tional liberalism could become a dominant ideology,"[13] but it is also true that such beliefs were never overcome altogether. As liberalism emerged as the dominant mode of Western political thinking, less consideration was given to whether Filmer had been answered convincingly, or simply successfully, by liberal theorists.[14]

HOBBES, LOCKE, AND THE LIBERAL TRADITION

The discussion which follows interweaves several themes. First, I take up Hobbes' and Locke's alternatives to patriarchal political thought. I explore the manner in which Hobbes recasts patriarchal argument and creates a public and private language devoid of moral terms. Locke, in turn, renders his liberalism parasitic upon surviving patriarchal forms in a sphere he saw as private and prepolitical. After a discussion of the survival of patriarchal political language, I pick up the thread of liberal argumentation with those nineteenth-century heirs to Locke, Jeremy Bentham and John Stuart Mill.

Thomas Hobbes' importance for political thought goes much beyond his areas of agreement with and divergence from Robert Filmer. His structure of explanation represents a dramatic and bold break with the Platonic and Aristotelian traditions which had permeated Western thought. Hobbes' radical nominalism, an approach Steven Lukes calls "methodological individualism," requires that every complex whole be broken down into its simplest components. The whole is declared to be no more than the aggregate of isolated particulars, its parts. Lukes writes: "Methodological individualism is a doctrine about explanation which asserts that all attempts to explain social (or individual) phenomena are to be rejected (or, according to a current, more sophis-

---

[13] Gordon Schochet, *Patriarchalism and Political Thought*, p. 121.

[14] Prior to the publication of Laslett's edition of Locke's treatises it was generally believed that Locke was answering Hobbes' *Leviathan*, because Filmer's *Patriarcha* wasn't considered worthy or important enough for a full-blown set of counterarguments. See "Introduction," John Locke, *Two Treatises of Government*, ed. Peter Laslett, pp. 15-135 inclusive.

ticated version, rejected as 'rock-bottom' explanations) unless they are couched wholly in terms of facts about individuals.''[15] Statements about human nature are reducible in principle to statements about molecules in motion.

In Hobbes' view only particulars exist and are real. Knowledge of such entities emerges, not as a result of a systematic, categorical exploration on several levels, nor even via empirical observation, but from the acquisition by men of the right definition of names. Truth is nothing but "the right ordering of names." Human reason is reduced by Hobbes to "nothing but *reckoning*."[16] True knowledge is correct definitions. False and senseless tenets are synonymous with wrong definitions. If Hobbes' epistemology is methodological individualism, his ontology is abstract individualism. Hobbes' method, his theory of human nature, and his creation of a polity in which each consents to be ruled absolutely, entail and reinforce one another. For Hobbes, a life suitable to human needs is possible "only in the context of the state, and that the state can exist only where there is sovereign authority of a sort which is as absolute as it is possible to conceive."[17] Hobbes rejects a social view of human nature and denies that relations between persons are in any way essential and intrinsic rather than contractual and artificial.[18] With others conceived as potential obstacles or instruments which impede or abet one's own way, the relations of Hobbesian beings to one another are guided by an instrumentalism shorn of sentiment.

Hobbes' central concern was order. The manner in which he conceived alternatives—either anarchy or absolutism—precluded

---

[15] Steven Lukes, *Individualism*, p. 110. Hobbes' mechanistic cosmology—matter in motion—reduced mind to matter.

[16] Thomas Hobbes, *Leviathan*, ed. Michael Oakeshott, pp. 36-41.

[17] Peter Winch, "Man and Society in Hobbes and Rousseau," in *Hobbes and Rousseau*, ed. Maurice Cranston and Richard S. Peters, p. 233. In Hobbes' commonwealth the supreme civil power is also the supreme pastor and "author" of all other pastors. As head of the church, he not only appoints judges and has absolute power over church law (as well as civil law) he is the final arbiter of scriptural interpretation.

[18] Wolff, "Nobody Here But Us Persons," p. 131. Wolff writes: "In the liberal tradition, the relationships between persons are characteristically represented as extrinsic rather than intrinsic, accidental rather than essential."

any consideration of other possible "goods" that might be the ends of diverse human activities. For Hobbes, the end of political life—order—is pregiven and all else melts away before this overarching imperative. His key concern in exploring public and private spheres is to figure out how every arena of life can be brought under the purview of the all-powerful sovereign. "Hobbes could not possibly hope to succeed," writes Norman Jacobsen, "by imposing his solution upon the public sphere alone."[19] Why? The answer lies in Hobbes' theory of human nature and his understanding of man's prepolitical state. He writes: "For I ground the civil right of sovereigns, and both the duty and liberty of subjects, upon the known natural inclinations of mankind, and upon the articles of the law of nature; of which no man, that pretends but reason enough to govern his private family, ought to be ignorant."[20] Human beings, for Hobbes, are anxious, fearful, threatening to themselves and others, full of inherent destructive passions. Hobbes views life before the creation of commonwealths as a terrifying and conflict-ridden state of nature despite the fact that he locates families in this prepolitical state.

The existence of families does not succeed in taming the savage heart of Hobbesian man, in part because with the birth of each child the state of nature, a seething within, is reproduced.[21] The "dominion" of the father within the family is not some smooth order passed on from generation to generation; instead, each father must make his children submit to him, through a struggle, by use of 'natural force." He can destroy them should they refuse to obey. The threat of destruction is the basis of the Hobbesian solution to the problem of order on all levels and in each arena of human intercourse. Sovereign power is acquired by force or forced consent, not simply derived from paternal authority—here we find Hobbes' intermingling of absolutism and consent—beginning with children, who, within the private realm, consent to be ruled absolutely.

The child in the family, like the subject of the Hobbesian com-

[19] Jacobsen, *Pride and Solace*, p. 56.
[20] Hobbes, *Leviathan*, p. 509.
[21] This discussion owes much to Jacobsen's wonderfully evocative characterization of Hobbesian man and the Hobbesian Leviathan.

monwealth, agrees to his or her subjection, motivated by fear and the threat of death. The child's consent is forced and is based on the power parents, particularly the father, hold over life and death. The family's relationship to later political society is as a kind of microcosm of the system of order, subjection, and obedience; it must induce its members to become subject to the command of the sovereign within the commonwealth. (I shall take up the way in which Hobbes' theory of political education deprives the child of a moral education and the mother of any central role in that education below.) The family, itself, "is not properly a commonwealth."[22]

In order to prepare the child for his role as the dutiful subject of an awesome, all-powerful earthly lord, one parent must rule in the family. Hobbes states that the "one" can be either man or wife.

The right of dominion by generation, is that, which the parent hath over his children; and is called PATERNAL. And is not so derived from the generation, as if therefore the parent had dominion over his child because he begat him; but from the child's consent, either express, or by other sufficient arguments declared. For as to the generation, God hath ordained to man a helper; and there be always two that are equally parents: the dominion therefore over the child, should belong equally to both; and he be equally subject to both, which is impossible; for no man can obey two masters. And whereas some have attributed the dominion to the man only, as being of the more excellent sex; they misreckon in it. For there is not always that difference of strength, or prudence between man and the woman, as that the right can be determined without war. In commonwealths, this controversy is decided by the civil law; and for the most part, but not always, the sentence is in favour of the father; because for the most part commonwealths have been erected by the fathers, not by the mothers of families.[23]

---

[22] Hobbes, *Leviathan*, p. 155.
[23] *Ibid.*, p. 152.

Hobbes' apparent willingness to accept the "equality" of the mother to command within the family is little more than a formal imperative, however, as Hobbes goes on to observe, that the force of tradition and greater male strength will suffice, in most instances, to make that "one" the male.

A contractual agreement allocates power between husband and wife and over children. Hobbes presumes that before the age of maturity the child has given his tacit consent to being governed absolutely; in effect, the child consents to acquiesce to a power that might destroy him for the sake of escaping from a condition that would certainly destroy him. Thus in the state of nature, paternal power is "naturally" absolute; in civil society it is contractually absolute. It is for this reason that R.W.K. Hinton argues that Hobbes has not moved very far from his contemporary Filmer with his welding together of voluntarism and absolutism; Hobbes' theory, Hinton states, involved "taking patriarchalism for granted and inserting the act of consent."[24]

If there were no more to Hobbes than an uneasy coalescence of contractual obedience and absolute dominion permeating through the interstices of all spheres of society, he would seem, like Filmer, an artifact of a past time. But Hobbes remains gripping in part because there are, in our own day, those who would seek Hobbesian solutions to public and private questions by depriving us of a grammar of moral discourse and forcing all of life under a set of terms denuded of any critical edge.[25] In so doing, they would deprive the human subject of the capacity to think, to judge, to question, and to act, for all these activities are constituted by

[24] R.W.K. Hinton, "Husbands, Fathers and Conquerors: II," *Political Studies*, p. 56. Cf. the alternative view suggested by Richard Chapman who sees the chief virtue of Hobbes on the family in the "premise that the family can be viewed in political terms." This, of course, is no unalloyed blessing. Chapman, however, labels the politicization, unambiguously, an advance because once having politicized the family one can criticize it "according to political values"—surely an empty imperative unless one articulates the political values under which this critique takes place. To see the family "in political terms" has both regressive and progressive dimensions which Chapman appears not to recognize. See Richard Allen Chapman, "Leviathan Writ Small: Thomas Hobbes on the Family," *The American Political Science Review*, passim.

[25] See Winch, "Man and Society in Hobbes and Rousseau."

an ordinary language infused with moral terms. Because one of my concerns in unraveling concepts of the public and private is to assess who has a public voice and what sort of voice that is, Hobbes' moves to strip us of our linguistic capacities, and the social relations and ways of life they presuppose, take on great urgency. If no one has a public voice, if only one voice, that of the secular god, is heard in the land, the public-private distinction hardly matters, as no one can debate the competing worth, purpose, and value of each. The price of civic and domestic peace is to give up the power of individual speech, judgment, and understanding.

I shall backtrack for a moment in order to explain the Hobbesian basis for the Great Silence, his solution to our public and private travail. All individuals are cursed with "a perpetual and restless desire of power after power, that ceaseth only in death."[26] Though God is the first author of speech, man cannot rely on his own words to bring order: "the bonds of words are too weak to bridle men's ambition, avarice, anger, and other passions, without the fear of some coercive power."[27] Words are not only "too weak," but also a positive inducement to private avarice and public sedition. Human speech is riddled with absurdity and senselessness, a "sort of madness" when words lose precise signification, when names are full of sound and fury but signify nothing.[28] This accursed abuse of words has no meaning and bears no truth: it is, for Hobbes, babbling and "wandering amongst innumerable absurdities" of metaphor and ambiguity. Now speech, of course, is what uniquely defines us as a species and it is within the family setting that our potential for speech is first, quite literally, heard and realized. To silence seditious speech, public and private language must be controlled. All human beings must be subjects and subjected, must quell the inner voices of passion and thus disarticulate the connection between thought/speech/action. To defuse the power within, Hobbes would impose upon us a new vocabulary: one dispassionate, neutral, "scientific."[29]

cf Althusser

---

[26] Hobbes, *Leviathan*, p. 80.   [27] *Ibid.*, p. 108.

[28] *Ibid.*, pp. 34-37.

[29] Jacobsen, *Pride and Solace*, p. 57. Cf. the discussion in Albert O. Hirschmann, *The Passions and the Interests*, pp. 31-32.

Hobbes' search for "truth" along radical nominalist criteria erodes the meaning to human subjects of their own lives, which can no longer be couched in the rich terms of everyday language but must, like everything else that "can intelligibly be said . . . be reducible to a statement about the motion of a material substance."[30] All children and all citizens must be taught this scientific language, all must be indoctrinated in "the right ordering of names."[31] Human discourse begins and ends, for Hobbes, not with a restless search for meaning but with correct definitions of words shorn of meaning. The notion that the Hobbesian vocabulary, given its reductive, mechanistic quality, is somehow "neutral" is a dangerous view that implicitly (for Hobbes, explicitly) sanctions the silencing of human speech by the all-powerful— those with the power to "name names." To that single will and voice, the mortal god, Hobbes' subjects must surrender their plurality of wills and voices. The "poison" of seditious doctrines is eradicated. The "absurdity" of private babbling ceases. What has been lost along public and private dimensions in the Hobbesian deal?

The human subject is deprived of the power of individual speech: a *potentia* destroyed by the external imposition of an absolute power, *potestatis*. Although that is a loss too great to be borne by any, those most particularly deprived would be groups previously silenced, at least in public language, by their absorption within private reality. Having begun to enter the public world in large numbers the debate, for women, is: under what terms does this public activity occur? Can the traditional concerns of women in the private realm "speak" to the public world? Should they? How? These possibilities are eradicated by the great Hobbesian silence as women are deprived (together with everyone else) not only of a public-political voice but of their traditional role in moral education through the activity of mothering. Hobbes' scientific vocabulary is one drained of terms of *public* moral evaluation— duty, justice, right, equality, liberty, legitimacy, resistance—and deprived of terms of *private* moral sentiment and emotion—affection, responsibility, love, mercy, compassion, decency, kind-

---

[30] Winch, "Man and Society in Hobbes and Rousseau," p. 234.
[31] Hobbes, *Leviathan*, p. 36.

ness. Good and evil, central to an evaluative moral grammar, are defanged and reduced to names that signify no more than human "appetites and aversion." Under the terms of the Hobbesian deal, it is possible that women would enjoy the terrible equality of the silenced and subjected, and that no individual man in concrete social reality would enjoy a social, economic, or political advantage over her. But no moral agent would accept those terms in order to transform public and private reality.

The insidious seduction of putative neutrality—the search for a neutral "scientific" vocabulary—goes on, inside and outside political thought. Perhaps one example, this drawn from the realm of Skinnerian behaviorist psychology, a psychology built upon notions of language not unlike Hobbes', will suffice to terrify us into *not* accepting Hobbes' solution to our public and private riddles. The passage is drawn from Peter Singer's *Animal Liberation*. Singer quotes an article by Alice Heim:

The work on "animal behavior" is always expressed in a scientific, hygienic sounding terminology, which enables the indoctrination of a normal, non-sadistic young psychology student to proceed without his anxiety being aroused. Thus techniques of "extinction" are used for what is in fact torturing by thirst or near-starvation or electric shocking; "partial reinforcement" is the term for frustrating an animal by only occasionally fulfilling the expectations which the experimenter has aroused in the animal by previous training; "negative stimulus" is the term used for subjecting an animal to a stimulus which he avoids, if possible. The term "avoidance" is O.K. because it is an observable activity. The terms "painful" or "frightening" stimulus are less O.K. because they are anthropomorphic, they imply that the animal has feelings—and that these may be similar to human feelings. This is not allowable because it is nonbehavioristic and unscientific (and also because this might deter the younger and less hard-boiled researcher from pursuing certain ingenious experiments. He might allow a little play to his imagination).[32]

---

[32] Alice Heim, *Intelligence and Personality*, quoted in Peter Singer, *Animal Liberation*, pp. 45-46. Cf. Midgley, *Beast and Man*, pp. xv-xvi.

Enter Silence. John Locke broke with Hobbes' uncompromising and thoroughly reductive method. His own logic of explanation turned on an empiricist theory of knowledge and meaning which formed the basis for the classical liberal version of the abstract individual. Liberalism historically has opposed "an ideal and abstract humanity . . . to a real and concrete one."[33] I shall examine first aspects of Lockean epistemology that lead to a kind of free-floating vision of the self.

After unfolding Locke's views of the individual, of particular importance to his version of the relationship between public and private (indeed, neither is separable from the other in Locke's thought), I shall take up Locke's discussion of paternal, or parental, and political power and conjugal and political life, drawing primarily upon his *Two Treatises of Government*. Finally, I shall turn to the problem of the public language of classical liberalism.

Locke's empiricist epistemology can acknowledge the existence of other minds only as alien objects: we are not intrinsically connected to others. Our thought processes—the way we acquire knowledge and speak to, and of, what we have come to know—occur as a kind of solipsistic activity. Language, for Locke, is a system of external signs and symbols rather than a complex social activity that links inner and outer, helping to constitute both our internal and external realities.[34] The activity of the mind occurs abstractedly. The logical separation of mind and body, reason and passion, leads to an image of an individual as unsituated in time and space, as not located in a body which matures, grows old, and dies. Mind and body enjoy a contingent rather than a necessary relationship to one another.[35] Reduced by Hobbes to "matter in motion," the human subject as a reflective, purposive being is not resurrected by Locke. Instead we get the image of a passive observer whose social obligations are derived from a series of

[33] Roberto Mangabeira Unger, *Knowledge and Politics*, p. 58. Although I had completed the first draft of my discussion of liberalism before reading Unger's volume, I found his arguments in places paralleled my own and in revision I have drawn upon him to buttress my own case.
[34] Norman Malcolm, *Problems of Mind, passim.*
[35] Cf. René Descartes, *Meditation on First Philosophy, passim.*

rationally conceived—on Locke's view of the "rational"—obligations.[36] The excesses of Filmer's unreflective naturalism are replaced with an excessive rationalism. Fully human beings are lost in either case: reduced to a living prototype of encrusted tradition in the one instance, and to fragmented beings whose reason, sundered from passion, implicates the reasoner in a process of reckoning consequences and behaving prudentially, at least in the realm of "understanding," in the other.[37]

The split in Lockean epistemology between reason as formal rationality and passion as scarcely contained desire, and the notions of human personality erected upon it, *require* a public-private split of a particular kind, one that allows human beings to exist in two divergent spheres. These spheres, in theory, have only tenuous connections to one another but they are, in fact, internally related, thoroughly dependent upon one another in a deeper sense. A dialectical relationship between public and private is denied, yet the terms of that denial bespeak the parasitic nature of the ties between them. This is an important but difficult claim.

Locke's epistemological split between reason and passion is reflected in, and refracted through, his version of a public-private

[36] See the discussion in Unger, *Knowledge and Politics*, of the unreflective view of mind and personality liberal theory "vindicates and refines" (p. 30). According to Unger, liberal theory is based on: the separation of understanding and desire; the views that desires are arbitrary; the notion that knowledge is acquired by a combination of elementary sensations and ideas that, in the acquisition of knowledge, the whole is simply the sum of parts. Cf. John Dunn, *Western Political Theory in the Face of the Future*, p. 41, and the very brief treatment of Locke by Okin, *Women in Western Political Thought*, in which epistemological issues do not figure centrally.

[37] ". . . the psychological principles of liberalism make it impossible to formulate an adequate conception of personality" (Unger, *Knowledge and Politics*, p. 55). But see Dunn who argues that Locke's "[r]eductive egoistic liberalism . . . turns out to be predicated on an explicitly transcendental and extra-human order of value." Dunn also finds Locke, in fleeting moments, dropping "the language of stolid bourgeois utility" for a "flashier and more aesthetic language of existential self creation." (*Western Political Theory in the Face of the Future*, p. 40.) It should be noted that Locke's attempts to soften the hard staccato of his rationalism with references to "sentiment" may indicate his recognition of the inadequacies of that rationalism to define the self fully but do not lead to an epistemological recognition of an alternative way of seeing tied to a way of being in the world completely, not as an amputated self.

split. Locke celebrates the rationalization of human life in the transition from status to contract. The liberal version of the public-private split is a fundamental distinction in this process. Locke's human beings—I shall examine male-female distinctions in a moment—exist in separate spheres whose connections to one another his presumptions about the human personality disallow him to explore or even to acknowledge fully. The implications of this stance are profound and occur on several levels. One might characterize Lockean epistemology as the division of human beings along one boundary or marker into "public minds" and "private desires." Within the public arena, the sphere in which individuals, free and equal in the formal legalistic sense, go about protecting certain rights and serving certain interests, making contracts and reaching agreements of mutual benefit, Locke presumes that *the same knowledge is shared by all* and that the public sphere is the *only* sphere in which this holds. In Roberto Unger's characterization: "Men differ by what they desire, but they are capable of knowing the world *in the same way*. Particular desires felt by the individual are arbitrary from the standpoint of the understanding."[38] (The "world" in which men are held to have that capacity is, of course, the public realm only.) Another way to express the point might be this: the epistemological developments of the seventeenth and eighteenth centuries carried the implication that all minds, for the purposes of nonprivate activity and understanding (reason), are in the same epistemological position. This view served as an underpinning for the claims of a particular class and grew, in part, out of the interest of that class in establishing a sphere in which all individuals could be said, in some formal sense, to be equal.

The presumption that human beings are rational, metaphysically free, prudential calculators of marginal utility—and all think alike in this regard in the public sphere of politics and understanding—is used as a contrast model for the qualities and activities in a private world from which the public sphere is bifurcated theoretically. The public realm and "public mind" exist as defenses against the private sphere in which desire, conceived as uncon-

[38] Unger, *Knowledge and Politics*, p. 50.

trolled and arbitrary, is held to rank supreme. Again, Unger: "In our public mode of being we speak the common language of reason, and live under laws of the state, the constraints of the market, and the customs of the different social bodies to which we belong. In our private incarnation, however, we are at the mercy of our own sense impressions and desires."[39] The fact that women were denied a public voice within seventeenth- and eighteenth-century liberalism meant that the "voice" of woman was necessarily that of privatized, irrational desire.

There is, surely, another defensive element within Lockean liberalism, one necessary to effect a certain kind of break from the past and from the enforced filiopiety of patriarchalism. It is that the only way to "kill the father" was to argue that the most powerful God the Father had given men minds which, if used in the mode of reason rather than desire and private obedience, could attain a passionless, deprivatized sameness of true understanding. This uniform understanding had the benefit of effecting a break from the authority of the past, sundering man's eternal subjection to the twin rules of the father (traditional authority) and desire (privatized reign of the passions in a sphere populated by women).[40]

The effect of these splits was to further privatize the private world and to reduce the language of women to that of cloying sentiment as the private world was cut off even further from public discourse. No legitimacy was granted to the possibility that the way the human mind works and human lives are lived serves powerfully to undercut, even to falsify, Locke's arguments. One could certainly make the opposite case from classical liberalism's, namely, that it is *only* in a private sphere of highly charged intimate relationships persisting over time that the possibilities for understanding are the greatest and the greatest understanding is possible. The abstract relations of the market and liberal citizenship do not and cannot allow for the possibilities of mutual recognition and intersubjective understanding characteristic of long-term intimate human ties in the private sphere. One could also quite plausibly

[39] *Ibid.*, p. 59.
[40] See Norman O. Brown's provocative treatment of this theme in *Love's Body*, pp. 4-7.

argue that human beings differ from one another less by what they desire and need—as we all desire and need (unless we have been terribly damaged in our early years) love, recognition, intimacy, sexual satisfaction or some resonant sublimated equivalent, mutual sharing based on moral "instincts," avenues for self-creativity and outlets for curiosity, and other *outgrowths* of the desiring part of the human personality—than by what they "understand" in an abstract and formal sense, but may neither need nor desire. Human desire is far less arbitrary than what we come to "know," which diverges dramatically depending upon our particular social situations (rich or poor, male or female, black or white, industrial or underdeveloped, educated or illiterate, and so on). Yet all human beings everywhere, on the level of desire and passion, share a great deal. This view, of course, is incompatible with liberal epistemology and the politics which flows from it: it is not even recognized as an alternative which should be argued. One additional strength of my contrasting perspective is its ability to see the public world, particularly in its market and political aspects, as preeminently a realm of passions of the most divisive and crude sort. In cautioning against this possibility, liberalism, paradoxically, winds up sanctioning much of the horror of public passion by simply denying it and sweeping passion into a bin called "private." In Jacobsen's words: "Locke smooths some of the rough edges and induces us to forget the mounds of bodies upon which the modern state rests."[41]

I shall now turn to Locke's discussion of the nature of political society and conjugal society, respectively, folding in along the way his images of male and female subjects. Men, for Locke, are "free by nature," that is, they do not require political society in order to be free. In the state of nature they were free but, guided by calculation and a desire for security, they were "willing to quit a Condition, which however free, is full of fears and continual dangers." They united for "mutual *Preservation* of their Lives, Liberties and Estates, which I call by the general Name, *Property*."[42] These "free" men, who were not members of an ordered

---

[41] Jacobsen, *Pride and Solace*, p. 70.
[42] Locke, *Two Treatises of Government*, p. 395.

society prior to the social contract, sign an original compact creating political society which requires that they give up that "natural political right" which was theirs in the state of nature.[43] Consenting to the bonds of civil society, they are obligated to submit to the rule of the majority, to give up all absolute power (for Locke, a form of tyranny) and to join in a mutually beneficial contract which ushers in the rule of law and of reason. Political power is based on consent; it is not "natural." Locke dismisses the patriarchalist insistence that men are born into a subjection that is both "natural" and political with the following words: "Tis plain Mankind never owned nor considered any such *subjection*."[44] Instead men consent freely to create political society, thereby establishing public means to private ends by providing for the sanctity of contract and the maintenance of civic order. In an interesting partial reversal of Aristotle, the state can now be seen both as the sphere of freedom and as a necessary condition for certain private, publicly sanctioned ends.

Locke is silent on the question of women's participation in that mutual act of consent which brought political society into being— this despite the fact that women are granted the possibility of formal property rights in the public sphere. Melissa Butler accounts for Locke's silence by attributing it to Locke's fear of "alienating" his audience given his self-identity as a "good enough propagandist."[45] Yet if women had the same natural freedom and equality as men—which Butler also argues—given that they could earn, make contracts, and own property, it seems clear

---

[43] *Ibid.*, p. 380. Cf. Carol Pateman, "Sublimation and Reification: Locke, Wolin, and the Liberal Democratic Conception of the Political," *Politics and Society*, p. 455.

[44] Locke, *Two Treatises of Government*, p. 389.

[45] Melissa A. Butler, "Early Liberal Roots of Feminism: John Locke and the Attack on Patriarchy," *American Political Science Review*, pp. 146-147. Butler finds Locke much more the feminist than I, in part because I disagree that Locke's introduction of "rationalist arguments" represents an unambiguous advance, given the *form* of rationalism inherent within his position, which had a corrosive effect on the development of a compelling account of the human personality. That Locke would educate boys and girls alike in the "use of reason" must be evaluated with reference to the fact that all human beings, for Locke, begin as blank slates to be written upon.

there is something more going on than a strategic consideration on Locke's part. Public grants of parity to women have gone hand in glove within liberalism from Locke's time to our own, with extraordinary disparity in the distribution of goods and services and in the concrete allocation of economic and social power. Locke's abstract grant of property rights is in some important ways tendentious in a social situation in which the female portion of the population is propertyless. If past history is patriarchal—in this Locke agrees—and the chief motive for the formation of civil society is the preservation of property (understood as a variety of "goods," not simply economic), it is difficult to see how women can emerge, simply by a grant of formal rights, from a condition of propertylessness and subjection to one of public parity. Of course, they cannot, and this is the crux of one of Marx's critiques of liberalism.[46]

Where does the family belong in a liberal contractual society? Do human beings enter the world as unfree subjects within the family? Or do they come into life with a contract in one hand and a pen in the other, stipulating carefully their own and their parents' reciprocal contractual duties, rights, and responsibilities? That, presumably, would be the ideal: "free" consent from birth. But Locke recognizes its impossibility and, in some ways, its undesirability. He declares the father's paternal power and authority to be natural—exercised over children only through their minority.[47] "Every Man's Children being by Nature as *free* as himself, or any of his *Ancestors* ever were, may, whilst they are in

---

[46] What of those born into society following the signing of the original compact? Are those who never had a choice, who never actually consented, bound by its rules and regulations? Locke says "yes," for by remaining in the society each individual gives his tacit consent to the contract: the commonwealth—love it or leave it. MacIntyre comments on tacit consent: "Locke's doctrine is important because it is the doctrine of every modern state which claims to be democratic, but which like every state wishes to coerce its citizens. Even if the citizens are not consulted and have no means of expressing their views on a given topic, they are held to have tacitly consented to the actions of governments" (*Short History of Ethics*, p. 159). The concept "consent" is eviscerated of its full meaning in Locke's system of thought. Consent within ordinary language implies an active process.

[47] Locke, *Two Treatises*, p. 354.

that Freedom, choose what Society they will join themselves to, what Common-wealth they will put themselves under."[48]

The core of Locke's arguments on families and politics appears in Chapter 6 of the *Second Treatise*. He begins by giving both parents "parental power" over their children. Parents have a responsibility to care for their children but neither mother nor father has absolute dominion over them. There is no absolute paterfamilias in Locke's vision. Parental power, which Locke shortly reverts to calling "paternal," is temporary.[49] As parents are obligated to raise their children, children are obligated to honor their parents. Although conjugal society is a freely contracted one, voluntary and shared, it does not serve as the model for a freely contracted political state. Locke calls political and paternal power "perfectly distinct and separate . . . built upon so different Foundations, and given to so different Ends."[50] Although governments may have originated historically from the authority of fathers within families, even then absolutism did not prevail as sons gave their (tacit) consent to be governed. The power of the father-husband is no model for sovereign power in political society for sovereign power, Locke notes, includes the power of life and death which fathers do not possess. The power a father has to "order the things of private Concernment in his Family" is a "Conjugal Power, not Political,"[51] but it does allow him to pass on his estate. There are only superficial similarities between a family and a commonwealth. In political society the supreme power has the right to make laws with penalty of death, to regulate

[48] *Ibid.*, p. 358. Locke in this passage again exhibits his view of an abstracted universal human nature. He would have us believe that switching societies is a genuine possibility for all free citizens—as if making the choice of becoming Chinese, Russian, British, or American were not unlike picking out a suitable garment or a favorite ice cream flavor. He seems incognizant of the manner in which our languages and cultures emerge from and help to structure not only our social arrangements but our *selves*.

[49] Wolff, "Nobody Here But Us Persons," p. 132. Wolff writes: "Despite all the treatises on education in the liberal tradition, there is little recognition that childhood is an essential stage in the life of each person, and not merely an irritating infirmity, symmetrical with the infirmities of old age, save that childhood, unlike old age, is to be got over as quickly as possible."

[50] Locke, *Two Treatises*, p. 357.   [51] *Ibid.*, p. 210.

and preserve property, and to defend the commonwealth ''and all this only for the Publick Good.''[52]

As a party to the patriarchalist debate, Locke believed he was countering ''the strongest patriarchalism because it was based on consent.'' Thus Locke easily wrote off Filmer's derivation of a grant of dominion from Genesis by insisting that no ''natural law'' ever existed to subject a woman to her husband, if her circumstances or a contract exempt her from it. Locke denies women's subjection to an authoritarian patriarchal father as something natural and inevitable, and the fountainhead of political government. But, curiously, he then suggests that there is a foundation in nature for the woman to be subordinate to the male for the man is the ''abler and the stronger.''[53] His long passage on this is worth citing in full:

. . . but a Punishment laid upon *Eve*: and if we will take them as they were directed in particular to her, as their representative to all other Women, they will at most concern the Female Sex only, and import no more but that Subjection they should ordinarily be in to their Husbands: But there is here no more Law to oblige a Woman to such a Subjection, if the Circumstances either of her Condition or Contract with her Husband should exempt her from it, then there is, that she should bring forth her Children in Sorrow and Pain, if there could be found a Remedy for it . . . for the whole Verse runs thus, *Unto the Woman he said, I will greatly multiply thy sorrow and thy conception; In sorrow thou shalt bring forth Children, and thy desire shall be to thy Husband, and he shall rule over thee.* 'Twould, I think, have been a hard matter for any Body, but our A. to have found a Grant of *Monarchical Government to Adam* in these Words . . . God, in this Text, gives not, that I see, any Authority to *Adam* over *Eve*, or to Men over their Wives, but only foretels what should be the Woman's Lot, how by this Providence he would order it so, that she should be subject to her husband, as we see that generally the Laws of Mankind and

[52] *Ibid.*, p. 308.　　　　　[53] *Ibid.*, p. 364.

customs of Nations have ordered it so; and there is, I grant, a Foundation in Nature for it.[54]

Although a grant of dominion to the partiarch is denied as having any basis in nature, woman's subordination to man is explained as a result of the curse laid upon Eve, the laws and traditions of mankind, and the foundation of nature. Locke in this instance is trying to have his cake and eat it. He ridicules naturalistic arguments for political society which ground patriarchalism in history, scripture, and tradition, and slips in via the Garden of Eden the notion that women's subordination within the conjugal, not political, society of marriage may be understood and defended on the basis of nature.

It is true, nonetheless, that the analogy of the family is shoved into the background of political debate with Locke. Hinton goes so far as to argue that this "line of reasoning ceased to play an important part in political reasoning."[55] Schochet contends that it "was precisely Locke's polemical purpose to show how irrelevant the Filmerian analysis of politics was!" and that Locke's attack on the political relevance of the family was the most interesting "and important aspect of the anti-patriarchal doctrine."[56] Both Hinton and Schochet overshoot the mark in writing finis to patriarchalism. If Hinton, for example, means that patriarchalism ceased to play a central role in the self-conscious articulation of systematic theories of politics, he—and Schochet—are largely correct. But if one looks instead at actual social relations and at metaphors, analogies, symbols, and themes as a line of reasoning within ordinary language and history, patriarchalism remained imbedded in human life and thought.

Patriarchalism lost its credibility as a full-blown justification for, and theory of, politics. But because language, meaning, and knowledge are social activities which alter slowly over time, patriarchalist terms continued to resonate through both public and private vocabularies. The reason that patriarchalist notions did not

[54] *Ibid.*, pp. 209-210.
[55] Hinton, "Husbands, Fathers and Conquerors: II," p. 67.
[56] Schochet, *Patriarchalism*, pp. 267, 271.

disappear when they "rationally" should have is quite simple but extraordinarily complex: self-conscious political theory is an activity that is, at one and the same time, part of, yet aloof from everyday life. Changes in theory seep slowly into the political consciousness and vocabulary of an age and when they do they do not transplant totally what is there; instead new concepts, terms, and the meanings they convey enter the dense and diverse stream of human language, shaped and molded by history, tradition, and homely truths. It should come as no surprise that patriarchal terms gave way slowly for they are tied to our earliest memories as dependent and helpless children in families—this fact of life did not change although classical liberal theorists may have forgotten it or denied its significance.

The public language of liberalism, based on Locke's rejection that "in the beginning God said" (although God had endowed man with the powers of reason which allowed him to speak in the voice of sweet public understanding), remained dependent upon a private world "silenced" to the public.[57] That is an argument I have already made. But there is another problem with the public language of liberalism, namely, that the incursion of a language of marginal utility and "reckoning consequences" into the private sphere upon which that public world is erected, may erode and coarsen private social relationships, recasting them along crude contractual lines. To infuse the public language of liberalism into the private world is to replace older patriarchal perspectives, of which Filmer's is the paradigmatic case, with another distortion, one that decrees that *all* social obligations are derived from the rationally conceived obligations of individuals whose motivations are seen as narrowly egoistic.[58] Even if private social relationships could not be coherently characterized by the language of contract and exchange, even if women held the line against allowing market language to dominate private meaning, a process of erosion began that seems to be culminating in our own time.

Within the family, Locke's deployment of the language of parental or paternal authority, his statement of women's participation

[57] Locke, *Two Treatises*, pp. 243ff.
[58] Dunn, *Western Political Theory*, p. 37.

in the conjugal society, together with his grant of formal rights to her in the public sphere, offered no immediate wedge women could drive into public power. Women later were to use the language of rights to press claims. Their arguments had to be compressed within the linguistic forms of the liberal tradition. This meant that woman's "reason" as a public presence couldn't give voice to the private, social bases of female identity, couldn't allow woman's experience to "speak to" the public realm. Thus woman's experience of herself was distorted. She had no vocabulary, in public speech, to describe the nuances and textures of her actual social relations and social location. She lacked terms that might have afforded her a heightened, reflective understanding of herself and her world. The options left open to women were to speak the public language of liberalism and to conceive of their entry into politics on those terms; to speak, in private, the language of sentiment, a language increasingly cloying as it lost part of the force of the Christian ethic of caring and responsibility and was shorn of its power to beard power; or, alternatively, to seek remedies to social ills and to define their entrance into the public world along the lines of a frequently censorious moralism. The effects of the particular public-private split inherited from the liberal tradition will be treated fully in Chapter 5 below.

The Fate of Patriarchal Language: Private Survivals, Public Reverberations

In the discussion of Filmer, Hobbes, and Locke I argued that although the image of an absolute patriarch who demanded and received unquestioning obedience from passive subjects retreated before liberal contractarianism, images and themes of patriarchalism retained a resonance and vibrancy which continued to play a role in political metaphors, symbols, and terms of discourse. There are no absolute monarchs left who claim to rule by divine right. Yet our long historic experiences in families dominated by men (if not patriarchs in the strict sense) continue to structure our response to politics and political relationships.

A political language can never be the sole and original creation of a few philosophers. The defeat in England of the concept of monarchical absolutism meant that one powerful ideological anchor of patriarchalism, the absolute dominion by the kingly father, was removed. But thinking about politics familially and families politically was not. The traditional family (much as we know it today in terms of size and composition—father, mother, and children) flourished and life went on. This leads to a consideration of the politics of language and the language of politics—indeed, the two are inseparable. If one agrees that language is imbedded within and helps to order social reality and, further, that a powerful feature of our social reality is the dynamic relationship between father, mother, and children, it follows that language appropriate to the family sphere may migrate to other areas, including the political, just as the family's shared reality becomes impregnated with those concepts and values which derive from thought and action on the public level.[59]

Any society beyond the most primitive contains an array of associations, institutions, structures, and relationships organized to various purposes and ends. Those purposes are described and understood in certain ways; thus political activities, their meaning and explanation, "must be thought of as existing in many contexts and on many levels simultaneously."[60] It should not be surprising—indeed it would be surprising were this not true—that our political vocabulary resonates with terms whose meanings are drawn from our earliest social relationships within families. Nor should the fact that terms appropriate to altered social and political conditions which first emerge within the public sphere filter eventually, if less thoroughly and powerfully, into family life surprise us.

The victory of liberalism and the rejection of all modes of "naturalism" was carried out systematically on the level of abstract theory and constitution-making, but was only a partial success if one looks to the resistance of the family to the rationali-

---

→ [59] J.G.A. Pocock develops this theme in his essay "Languages and Their Implications: The Transformation of the Study of Political Thought," in *Politics, Language and Time*, ed. Melvin Richter, pp. 3-41.

[60] *Ibid.*, p. 18.

zations of its inner life and relationships. Within seventeenth- and eighteenth-century families, for example, the godly father continued to discipline his rebellious young. Work by Michael Walzer and others on family history stresses the frequent emphasis on duty and the demand that children obey their "political fathers" who were God's magistrates performing a sacred duty by instructing their children in "the first principles and grounds of government and subjection."[61]

The newer political fathers of nineteenth century America reflected the breakdown of older theories and practices of patriarchalism. They were fathers in a somewhat different mode: stern but forgiving, strong but open. They listened to their children and even humored them. They educated as well as demanded obedience. Like the new democratic father, the American political father or leader didn't lord it over his people. Subjects, transformed into citizens, were not required to bend the knee or stand in awe. (It took many years to learn the lesson, if indeed we have learned it.) The leader was owed respect and, if he urged a course of action upon his fellow citizens following proper consultation and consideration, they had a patriotic duty to follow.

Alexis de Tocqueville's discerning eye perceived the changing relationships between public and private in mid-nineteenth century America. He observed that great care was taken "to trace two clearly distinct lines of action for the two sexes" in American life.[62] Within the family, father was the "natural head." Americans believed that although men and women had the duty and skills to perform different tasks, an "equal regard" for both must be shown: "they consider both of them as beings of equal value."[63] Unfortunately, such equal regard did not lead to social and political equality—a fact Tocqueville glossed over or lost in the midst of his praise for America's success in raising the moral and intellectual level of women. Although America's women were

---

[61] Michael Walzer, *The Revolution of the Saints*, p. 191. The Mother was viewed as a sentimentalizing force whose influence could not be allowed to dominate lest children "go soft." See also John Demos, *A Little Commonwealth: Family Life in Plymouth Colony.*

[62] Alexis de Tocqueville, *Democracy in America*, ed. Phillips Bradley, 2:223.

[63] *Ibid.*, p. 225.

confined within a "quiet circle of domestic employments," they nowhere, Tocqueville insisted, occupied a loftier position. Americans, unlike his European counterparts who sought to level all sex distinctions, knew enough to seek sex equality through diversity.[64]

Tocqueville's most interesting contribution to an understanding of the public and private resides not so much in his gloss on the virtues of American womanhood, but in his insight that domestic institutions, in some way, mesh with or reflect the higher political order. Tocqueville ties up the internal governance of the family, which molds adult behavior and character through childhood development patterns and practices, with aristocratic and democratic systems respectively. In patriarchal authoritarian societies no authority but the father's is recognized within the family, just as the larger society is governed by an authoritarian "father" whose power is unquestioned.[65] Within the patriarchal authoritarian family system, the "parent not only has a *natural* right but acquires a *political* right to command them (i.e., children); he is the author and the support of his family, but he is also its constituted ruler" (emphasis mine).[66] In a democratic society, on the other hand, the father's authority is never presumed to be absolute and his authority is considerably softened in its exercise. The mother plays an important role as the inculcator of democratic values in her young—values they will need in a system characterized by a wide measure of flexibility, participation, freedom, and the absence of absolute rule. Thus aristocratic and democratic systems are mutually reinforcing on all levels.

The formulation is a bit neat and pat as it stands: Is the family more determined by the overall order, or determining of that order? Tocqueville sees most of the influence flowing from the

---

[64] *Ibid.*, p. 223.

[65] Can a people, once it becomes cognizant, destroy powerful political myths and symbols which have come to be seen as oppressive? Michael Walzer justifies the beheading of King Louis XVI because public regicide was the only decisive way of destroying the myth of the inviolability of the royal patriarch and the patriarchal ancien régime. See Walzer, *Regicide and Revolution*.

[66] Tocqueville, *Democracy in America*, 2:203-204.

public world into the private. Families, he argues, labor under a strong compulsion to pattern themselves on the structure of the public power. But Tocqueville never explores the dynamics of this process. He simply insists that women, in their separate but equal private worlds, are important to the workings of democracy. He writes: "No free communities ever existed without morals, and as I observed, . . . morals are the work of woman. Consequently, whatever affects the condition of women, their habits and their opinions, has great political importance in my eyes."[67] Families then and now serve as the locus of our most intense, highly charged, and important human relationships. Indeed, many have argued that as the alienation and impersonality of the modern public world, including the pressures of market society, have increased, the family's function as a haven and a reminder that human beings can transcend cash exchange relationships has been enhanced. The family today is both a resilient and a vulnerable institution.

Do we continue to deploy patriarchal symbols and themes? Yes, in a somewhat attenuated form. We portray the leader as a kind of father—or he thinks of himself as one. Former President Nixon referred to Americans as being like "children in the family" who needed to be told what to do. We invoke the "family of man" and speak, more recently, of "the brotherhood and sisterhood of Americans." Many of our loaded and contested terms of discourse, public and private, derive from our experience in families: trust, obedience, authority, punishment, betrayal, cooperation, jealousy, grief, remorse, anger. Our concepts of fairness and sharing are bound up with learning the "rules of the game" and experiences with "cheating," "not being fair," "winning," and "quitting" as children. All of these terms are translated into adult discourse and used politically. That political leaders understand this (on some level) and use it or abuse it (on some level) is also no doubt true.

It is to the attempt of two key spokesmen of nineteenth-century liberalism to treat these and other public and private issues that I shall now turn.

[67] *Ibid.*, p. 209.

NINETEENTH CENTURY LIBERAL SONS:
JEREMY BENTHAM AND JOHN STUART MILL

Neither Bentham nor Mill transformed in major ways the empiricist theory of knowledge and meaning which underlay Locke's
thought; indeed, Bentham carries the imperative of instrumentalist
rationality to its extreme within a utilitarianism which portrays
human beings exclusively as prudential, efficient calculators dominated by a simple, single calculus to maximize pleasure and to
avoid pain.[68] Bentham's theory of mind features hapless individuals, prey to the twin forces of pleasure and pain, conceived
as free floating abstractions that make no necessary reference to
social and historical reality. What matters is that the individual's
quantity or yield of aggregate pleasure should be greater than the
yield of pain. An external calculus is applied to all of human
life and thought. The utilitarian "attaches value ultimately to
states of affairs."[69] In Bentham's famous salvo, push-pin is *au
fond* as good as poetry—prejudice apart.[70]

In *The Principles of Morals and Legislation*, Bentham gives
some consideration to the public and the private in his discussion
of the relationship of women and married couples to the law. He
finds sex a "secondary circumstance" influencing human sensibility.[71] He offers a few of the traditional encomiums to womankind: the female is more sensitive, delicate, moral, religious,
and sympathetic than the male. Her coarser counterpart, however,
is stronger, hardier, superior intellectually, and firmer in mind.
Bentham discerns other differences which are ultimately significant to his utilitarian calculus. A woman's affection, he declares,
does not embrace the welfare of her own country, much less all
humankind, but is limited either to her own children or to young
children generally. It follows that a woman's biases conform less
to Bentham's principle of utility than those of man, owing to

---

[68] J.J.C. Smart and Bernard Williams, *Utilitarianism For and Against*, p. 95.

[69] Sensibility for Bentham is the disposition an individual has to feel a quanity
of pleasure or pain upon the application of a cause or given force; it can be
measured in quantums or degree.

[70] Cited in Dunn, *Western Political Theory*, p. 41.

[71] Jeremy Bentham, *The Principles of Morals and Legislation*, pp. 58-59.

"some deficiency in point of knowledge, discernment, and comprehension."[72]

Why is this "lesser" capacity of women on the utilitarian scale significant? It becomes important in case of marital conflict—particularly should such conflict fall under the province of law. Bentham pleads for a "common sense" approach to marital strife. How, he queries, should competition between man and wife be decided? Sadly, there are no guidelines save physical force. The facts are simple: power must be lodged in one or the other of the parties in cases of irreconcilable conflict. An example of such conflict, which tells us rather more than we might wish to know about Bentham's utilitarianism, is the following: "The man would have the meat roasted, the woman boiled: shall they both fast till the judge comes in to dress it for them?" That would be silly, so the legislator must determine who has power to settle the dispute. If the legislator follows utilitarian logic, he begins by ruminating on the fact that (1) men and women were living together long before there were legislators; (2) the male is almost everywhere the stronger of the two, and therefore possesses already, by purely physical means, "that power which he is thinking of bestowing on one of them by means of law"; (3) ergo, he may as well acquiesce in the status quo and place legal power in the hands of the more powerful.[73] It makes the legislator's task much easier, for were he to vest legal power in the physically weaker (even if she were clearly "in the right"), the stronger would be in a state of perpetual transgression of the law. No question of justice or reason ever enters in.

Bentham closes with the faint piety that the legal vestment of such power in the hands of the physically stronger will result in "the producing of a benefit to somebody."[74] He expresses the

[72] *Ibid.*, p. 59.

[73] *Ibid.*, p. 259, n. 1. Cf. Herbert Leonidas Hart, *Women's Suffrage and National Danger: A Plea for the Ascendancy of Man.* Hart says that in the case of "every permanent relation between two or more human beings . . . the right to command . . . is necessarily possessed by one or some number less than all"; moreover, "anarchy and Lawlessness" are as reprehensible in the family as they are in the state and the "supreme power" to prevent this unhappy condition is required in both societies (pp. 121-123).

[74] Bentham, *Principles*, p. 260. Note that Bentham does not posit a complete

hope that in cases of marital contention the interests of both parties will be consulted. But there is nothing to preclude legal rationalization of brute force in his conceptual schema. As Bernard Williams points out, utilitarianism can't make "any sense of integrity and has trouble with justice."[75] Bentham's approach disallows conceptual clarity on the relation between public and private worlds. He does not, for example, note a discrepancy between his justification of domestic one-man rule and his arguments against the legal wardship of women; nor does he consider the possibility that justifications of the power of the stronger in our intimate adult relations might serve as a foundation for the use of force in our public relations. For Bentham the family is sealed off from the public world and relations between the sexes are explored as if they were unrelated to public problems.

Bernard Williams has termed utilitarianism in its paradigmatic form a great simple-mindedness with "too few thoughts and feelings to match the world as it really is."[76] The self is reduced to a kind of mirror of societal instrumentalism. Williams also taxes utilitarians for their boundless but impersonal benevolence, their expressed desire to change the world in accordance with the presuppositions of utilitarian doctrine, and their willingness to be, in some diffuse way, responsible for everything which, in practice, means that they have "no genuine moral responsibility for anything."[77] Utilitarianism denies that substantive reason that must be an integral dimension within a theory of individual moral agency. For a utilitarian, acts are good or bad based on external criteria and can be judged without reference to individual reason. Bentham is guilty of these serious flaws. John Stuart Mill's case is a more ambiguous one.

Mill is a complex thinker whose acceptance of the principle of utility, together with his rather abstract view of persons, impov-

---

harmony of interests between husband and wife. He does at least recognize the possibility of strife. But his solution is a domestic *Faustrecht* [club-law]. The appearance, if not the fact, of domestic harmony must be preserved.

[75] Smart and Williams, *Utilitarianism*, p. 80.

[76] *Ibid.*, p. 149. It is not important for the purposes of this inquiry to explicate the differences between "rule" and "act" utilitarianism.

[77] *Ibid.*, p. 110.

erished his understanding of the full power and texture of intimate human social relationships and of the nature of political life as the arena of power and passion. All of these limitations weaken his analyses of the public and the private, including his feminist tract, *On the Subjection of Women*, which nonetheless remains one of the clearest and most intelligent statements of liberal feminism. Mill's rational empiricism led to a thin explanation for the traditional subjection of women and an inadequate means to end that subjection and to alter the terms of public and private. I shall explore Mill's perspective, beginning with a brief consideration of the underlying presumptions he brings to inquiry.

Mill's empiricist utilitarianism is built upon that split between reason (or understanding) and desire (or passion) I have already treated in the discussion of Locke. That which is not Reason is Instinct, Mill writes, and "the worse rather than the better parts of human nature."[78] Mill assumes a sharing or unity of moral and political beliefs among those individuals who are dominated by reason. His goal is to couch the principles of moral and political "science" in the form of natural science, a kind of streamlined language of rationalism. For ultimately, according to Mill, "reason speaks in one voice." In practice this meant that the ignorant or the irrational would have to defer to those who had attained enlightenment and spoke in the voice of reason.[79] Given his bifurcated understanding of mind which dictated that one must attain an "apotheosis of Reason" and reject utterly the "idolatry" of Instinct, an idolatry "infinitely more degrading than any other, and the most pernicious of the false worships of the present day," Mill was muddled about what human beings finally are, have been, or can become.[80]

This confusion is apparent in Mill's account in his *Autobiography* of the "Crisis in My Mental History." Mill describes how he learned that happiness comes only to those who have their "minds fixed on some object" other than personal happiness.

---

[78] John Stuart Mill, *On the Subjection of Women*, p. 18.

[79] Graeme Duncan, *Marx and Mill: Two Views of Social Conflict and Social Harmony*, p. 262.

[80] Mill, *Subjection of Women*, p. 18. Cf. Dunn, *Western Political Theory*, p. 52. Mill, Dunn argues, had "no coherent conception of human personality at all."

"The only chance is to treat, not happiness, but some end external to it, as the purpose of life."[81] One must, along the lines of a nonreflexive empiricist view of mind, avoid scrutinizing one's feelings and purposes. Self-consciousness must be thoroughly externalized. The "anti-self-consciousness theory" of Carlyle, Mill continues, which demands that the individual eschew reflections on his own happiness by "forestalling it in imagination, or putting it to flight by fatal questioning" became "the basis of my philosophy of life."[82] Mill's is the philosophy of the external man. Not only does this help to explain some of the flatness of his style and thinness of his analysis—of which more below—but it also leads directly to the role model theory of social explanation in contemporary social science, a type of explanatory framework which simply cannot account for how inner images, ideas, and fantasies become our "very nature." I shall explore this problem at greater length in my discussion of liberal feminism in Chapter 5. At this point I shall turn to the vexing question of human motivation as it emerges in Mill's discussion of woman's subjection.

Mill, the liberal optimist, holds to an extraordinarily bleak view of human motivation—or male motivation—which is frequently unacknowledged, yet necessary to his entire perspective. He speaks of an original "law of force" and "law of superior strength" as the basis of human society and the relations between the sexes.[83] This law of strength was the rule of life in unenlightened epochs. Mill finds only an "odious source" for traditional relations between men and women. He refuses to countenance the worth of *any* appeal to history or tradition. His repudiation of the human past is so total that he never sees tradition as a presumption in favor of any human relation or institution but always as a powerful argument *against* such relations or institutions. He sees the past as time when status and force, not contract and free choice, formed the bases of social life. Mill does not consider whether women's motivations may have been involved in helping to create familial life, nor does he take up in detail in his major texts whether the family may be a prerequisite if any form of

[81] John Stuart Mill, *Autobiography*, p. 92.   [82] *Ibid.*
[83] Mill, *Subjection of Women*, p. 22.

social life is to exist at all, given the extraordinarily long dependence of human infants upon the adult care of specific others. He speaks of a pride in the possession of power which is "common to the whole male sex,"[84] and that this "desire of power is the strongest" over "those who are nearest to him."[85] Why?

Mill's explanation of what motivates man to dominate woman in the first place is the sheer desire of males for power over females—a monocausal theory of human thought and action. He also speaks of a "value attached to her by men" but he explains this no further, begging the question.[86] Inequality between the sexes persists, Mill argues, because it does not proclaim its "own origin" in force and because discussion "has not brought out its true character"; therefore, women's subjection "is not felt to jar with modern civilisation."[87] In other words: there is an original law of the jungle, a law which persists because it remains unacknowledged by social participants, male and female. Why should the female have a stake in the continuance of a set of social relations of which she is, in Mill's view, *simply* a victim? Again, Mill has no coherent explanation. His way out of this state of affairs is a rational leap to a relationship of "perfect equality" between the sexes. If such a relation were given a "trial" on a rationalistic basis, people would choose to accept it.[88] The result of deliberation, then, is pregiven by Mill and it would end in the foreclosure of the old way and the triumph of the rational and new. Mill predicts that once a superior way of life is established,

---

[84] *Ibid.*, p. 25.

[85] *Ibid.*, p. 26. Mill's bleakness extends to his notions of why the more powerful first began to acknowledge "any right in inferiors," namely, "when he had been ordered, *for convenience*, to make some promise to them" (p. 22; emphasis mine). Mill fails to specify who did this ordering. The important point is his presumption that convenience, or some aspect of utility, was the motive that spurred moral advance.

[86] *Ibid.*, p. 19.

[87] *Ibid.*, p. 21. Cf. "Society, from its highest place to its lowest, is one long chain, or rather ladder, where every individual is either above or below his nearest neighbor, and wherever he does not command he must obey. Existing moralities, accordingly, are mainly fitted to a relation of command and obedience" (Mill, *Subjection of Women*, p. 62).

[88] *Ibid.*, pp. 19-21.

when true equality between the sexes is instituted, privileged males will give up their old ways, as they will see that sex equality is conducive to happiness.

Mill fails to convince us because we cannot understand from his account why human beings, male and female, act as they do. Or, if we accept his pure power analysis of male behavior we are left in the dark as to female motivation—unless we make recourse to a rather unflattering view of female masochism through the ages. Women go from being male victims to being the beneficiaries of male beneficence but we cannot appreciate, from Mill, why women would suddenly desire this change or why men would undertake it. Let me explain a bit further. In a discussion of the way in which the confinement of women to a private world of domesticity becomes a hindrance to public morals as ''an active and energetic mind, if denied liberty, will seek for power,'' Mill writes:

> Where liberty cannot be hoped for, and power can, power becomes the grand object of human desire; those to whom others will not leave the undisturbed management of their own affairs, will compensate themselves, if they can, by meddling for their own purposes with the affairs of others. . . . The love of power and the love of liberty are in eternal antagonism. Where there is least liberty, the passion for power is the most ardent and unscrupulous.[89]

As one unravels the presumptions imbedded in Mill's claim, something like the following emerges: (1) if liberty is denied, power is pursued; (2) where there is least liberty the urge for power is most forceful and least controllable; (3) women, confined to domesticity, turn the domestic arena into a field of force in which they play the unscrupulous game of private power over others; (4) if women received public *liberty* (not power!), their quest for private power would cease, having lost its raison d'être. Does this make sense? In addition to the contestable presumptions concerning the relationship of power to liberty, there are hidden

[89] *Ibid.*, pp. 123-124.

premises in Mill's argument that he could not bring out or his claims would have been undercut. These covert views have to do with male motivation. Mill is inconsistent. He has already claimed that those individuals who have long held *public liberty*—males— continue to be driven by the desire for *private power*. Yet, on his own view concerning females and the vectors of power-liberty, the female drive for private power should cease once the arena of public liberty is achieved. Are we then stuck, however implicitly, with a set of notions that male and female motivations differ, that their natures are, in some sense, disparate? Clearly so, though Mill doesn't say so. But this, despite his environmentalist arguments I shall consider in a moment, is the only possible way his claims concerning males and females, power and liberty, cohere.

Mill insists, under the terms of liberal externality, that the environment makes us what we are. He therefore claims that an examination of the particular *forms* of male-female relationships historically, including an exploration of those qualities women have exhibited through the ages, would tell us *nothing* about female nature because males have, in a sense, rigged the experiment.[90] The past tells us only about male nature: that this nature is driven by an unexplained (by Mill) "value" attached to women and a need (also unexplained by Mill) to dominate women. But the past tells us *nothing* of women's nature, a nature Mill insists is at present "an eminently artificial thing."[91] The only way to

[90] Cf. the discussion in Rosenthal, "Feminism Without Contradictions," pp. 34-35. See also John Stuart Mill's discussion of the "despotism of custom" in *On Liberty*.

[91] Rosenthal, "Feminism Without Contradictions," p. 38. Benedict de Spinoza, towards the conclusion of his *Political Treatise*, devotes himself briefly to a consideration of women's subordination to men. If that authority of men existed simply by "mere institution," Spinoza would find no compelling reason to exclude women from government. But he consults experience, history, and tradition and the evidence seems to him so overwhelming that he goes along. He presumes that some natural basis underlies the empirical tradition. I shall cite the passage in full:

But, perhaps, someone will ask, whether women are under men's authority by nature or institution? If it has been by mere institution, then we had no reason compelling us to exclude women from government. But if we consult *experience* itself, we shall find that the origin of it is in their

set things right, to evaluate what woman's nature might be, is to alter the environment, particularly that most "universal and pervading" of all relationships, the one between male and female, and to guide that relationship henceforth under terms of "justice instead of injustice."[92] So convinced was Mill on this score that he attributed the source of all "the selfish propensities, the self-worship, the unjust self-preference, which exist among mankind" to the "present constitution of the relation between men and women."[93]

If one accepts Mill's conclusion as to the source of the difficulty (which I do not, certainly not under the terms Mill describes it), the next step is determining an effective way to get at the problem. At this juncture Mill falls into an environmentalist naiveté. The

---

weakness. For there has never been a case of men and women reigning together, but wherever on the earth men are found, there we see that men rule, and women are ruled, and that on this plan, both sexes live, in harmony. But on the other hand, the Amazons, who are reported to have held rule of old, did not suffer men to stop in their country, but reared only their female children, by killing males to whom they gave birth. But if by nature women were equal to men, and were equally distinguished by force of character and ability, in which human power and therefore human right chiefly consist; surely among nations so many and different some would be found, where both sexes rule alike, and others, where men are ruled by women, and so brought up, that they can make less use of their abilities. And since this is nowhere the case, one may assert with perfect propriety, that women have not by nature equal right with men; but that they necessarily give way to men, and that thus it cannot happen, that both sexes should rule alike, much less that men should be ruled by women. But if we further reflect upon human passions, how men, in fact, generally love women merely from the passion of lust, and esteem their cleverness and wisdom in proportion to the excellence of their beauty, and also how very ill-disposed men are to suffer the women they love to show any sort of favor to others, and other facts of this kind, we shall easily see that men and women cannot rule alike without great hurt to peace. But of this enough.

Benedict de Spinoza, *A Theologico-Political Treatise and Political Treatise*, trans. R. H. Melwes, pp. 386-387.

[92] Mill, *Subjection of Women*, p. 103. Cf. John Stuart Mill, *Auguste Comte and Positivism*, pp. 91-92.

[93] Mill, *Subjection of Women*, pp. 103-104. In *Auguste Comte and Positivism* Mill writes: "All experience testifies that regularity in domestic relations is almost in direct proportion to industrial civilization" p. 93.

relations between men and women, he argues, will transform in the *private sphere* once the *public grant* of equal rights is afforded women. This solution is curiously out of step with the articulation of the problem: these include, remember, "desire of power," "law of force," and "law of superior strength." The gap between problem, on the level of private sexual relations (riddled with power in Mill's own estimation) and Mill's public solution strikes our less innocent age as excessively simple. I shall consider problems of his public vision, tied to a quest for formal-legalistic equality, but first it is important to note that Mill's vision of male and female relationships, as he posits his future of "perfect justice," is strangely devoid of power and lacks a recognition of the deep human emotions at work in our most intimate relations.[94] Mill writes as flatly about male-female relationships as he does about Saint-Simon's philosophy or proposals for parliamentary reform. He can do no other given his commitment to a split between reason and desire. Once human relationships are uplifted to the sphere of understanding they are, as they must be, drained of passion.

Another turn of this issue: Mill knows that teleological arguments of the Aristotelian sort gerrymander analysis and wind up justifying as "natural" modes of domination of one group, sex, or class by those who benefit from such domination. He also understands, at least in part, that women occupy a position different from that of all other subject classes, as he rather daintily notes that men want women's "sentiments" as well as their

[94] Ernst L. Freud, ed., *The Letters of Sigmund Freud*, pp. 75-76. Freud, who had translated Mill's *On the Subjection of Women* into German when he was still a student, commented on Mill's style in a letter to his fiancé, Martha Bernays, dated November 15, 1883:

. . . I found fault with his lifeless style and the fact that in his work one could never find a sentence or a phrase that would remain in one's memory. But later on I read a philosophical work of his which was witty, epigrammatically apt, and lively. Very possibly he was the man of the century most capable of freeing himself from the domination of the usual prejudices. As a result—and this often goes hand-in-hand—he lacked the sense of the absurd. . . . His autobiography is so prudish or so unearthy that one would never learn from it that humanity is divided between men and women, and that this difference is the most important one.

"obedience."[95] Mill, however, goes astray in his account—and this is why Rousseau's story of male and female relations is richer, as I will argue in Chapter 4—because he fails to accord women *any* active role in helping to create and to constitute social relations through the ages. In Mill's world, women have just fallen into line. Mill also fails to understand another extraordinarily complex dynamic which psychoanalytic theory has helped us to describe and to explain.

What women have had to contend with all these years is not simply or only the fact that men have been in a position of greater power over women, or that women have lacked appropriate role models to help them aspire to something other than what they are, but that women, as do all human beings, quite literally incorporate or "take in" and make part of their inner world aspects of external reality. This external reality is not only what is crudely "out there" but also a dimension of perceived reality that may have begun as an inner image, fantasy, fear, or desire that is projected outward, then taken in as if it were, simply, external reality.[96] What women and men must attempt to understand is man's inability to tolerate the feminine side of his nature—an intolerance projected into, and helping to constitute, external social forms.[97] (This is a central male motivation that Mill, given his thin psychology, misses.) The problem, then, isn't simply *between* the sexes but internal to the minds of both sexes, particularly that of the male.

I suggest, knowing it is controversial, that the dynamic I refer to works along the following lines: Men fear the sexual and reproductive power of women. This is reflected in the lengths to which they have gone to protect themselves by projecting that fear outward into social forms, by imbedding the need to defend themselves against women in institutions and activities, including those called "political," historically inseparable from war-mak-

[95] Mill, *Subjection of Women*, p. 30.

[96] See the discussions of projection in Sigmund Freud, *The Psychopathology of Everyday Life*, *Standard Edition*, vol. 6, pp. 1-279; Sigmund Freud, "The Unconscious," *Standard Edition*, vol. 14, pp. 166-204; and Sigmund Freud, *New Introductory Lectures*.

[97] See the provocative discussion on which I have built my own argument in Richard Wollheim, "Psychoanalysis and Women," esp. pp. 68-69.

ing. (To argue this is *not* to state that politics is only a reaction formation or serves only defensive purposes.) In this complex inner-outer dialectic, rejected or hostile feelings are expelled. Their embodiment in an external form is one way the male mind works unconsciously to denude images of women of much of their force—especially the image of Mother. On the other hand, operating on a level both conscious and unconscious, is the conviction that women are weak and soft. Men define themselves by that which is "not-woman," therefore not vulnerable. To fend off both the unconsciously imbedded image of female power and the recognition of the "weakness of woman" as that which one cannot accept in oneself, men have, over the years, created hard, external institutions of enormous power both as a match for the vision of the powerful Mother within and as a protection, a hedge against their own "weak, female" self. (My argument assumes with Freud that all human beings are psychically bisexual.)[98] This perspective affords the political imagination the advantage of being able to link inner and outer realities in a complex overall perspective not available to Mill, given his epistemological limitations.

The inadequacies of Mill's analysis extend to his prescriptions on the public level for attaining equality between the sexes. But several important aspects of Mill's liberal solution to public-private ills must be noted. Mill is committed to the liberal theory of progress within which each age is seen as more enlightened than the preceding one. The move to grant full equality of formal rights to women is not only put forth as the solution to women's subjection on all levels, public and private, but is also regarded by Mill as part of the spreading rationalization of human society, a rationalization that requires setting aside the force of various distinctions based on considerations of sex, among others. For Mill human society is the sum total of individual interests, wants, and choices made with reference to certain external goals. Equality for women is part of a desirable state of affairs to which Mill

[98] Important references to Freud's theory of psychic bisexuality may be found in Sigmund Freud, "A Child is Being Beaten," *Standard Edition*, vol. 17, pp. 179-204; Sigmund Freud, *Three Essays on the Theory of Sexuality*, *Standard Edition*, vol. 7, pp. 130-243.

cheerily looks forward, indeed to which Mill can look forward by blanking out various weaknesses or inadequacies in his own approach.[99]

Mill both wants to have his cake and eat it. Even as he embraces full equality of rights and citizenship for women in the public sphere, seeing this as the wedge whereby patriarchal domination of women by men in marriage will also disappear, his analysis runs ashoal on the rock of the traditionally structured family. Mill seeks equality *within* the family yet wishes to retain much of the traditional ambience of family life tied to women's domestication and men's assumption of public responsibilities. He would expel from the family that inequality which made it a "school of despotism" in order to transform the family into "the real school of the virtues of freedom."[100] This new family, in order to serve as a "school of sympathy in equality," features parents "living together in love, without power on one side or obedience on the other."[101] Although for children the family must always be, in part, a school of obedience and command, Mill continues, children must be taught the sentiments of freedom. This can best be done within a transformed domestic life.

Where Mill becomes unconvincing is in the means by which he would attain his ends. He fails to see, or at least he does not give full credence to, those sources of male power over women that lie outside legal forms or may ever operate behind or underneath the cover of legality. I refer, for example, to man's economic power. Here Mill retreats to a defensive and transparently inadequate argument given his recognition of power disparities. He grants women full *liberty* in the political realm, thereby freeing them from ignoble private power quests. But he embraces a traditional division of labor *within* the family based on males being actively employed *outside* the home. Women remain private albeit "free" beings and continue to exert their traditional softening effect upon men whereby "the desire of young men to recommend themselves to young women" remains an important agency of character development, responsible for "some of the chief steps

---

[99] Robert Paul Wolff, *The Poverty of Liberalism*, p. 184.
[100] Mill, *Subjection of Women*, p. 63.   [101] *Ibid.*

in the progress of civilization."[102] Mill did not find women's employment a desirable state of affairs. He writes:

The great occupation of woman should be to *beautify* life: to cultivate, for her own sake and of those who surround her, all her faculties of mind, soul, and body; all her powers of enjoyment, and powers of giving enjoyment; and to diffuse beauty, elegance, and grace, everywhere. If in addition to this the activity of her nature demands more energetic and definite employment, there is never any lack of it in the world: If she loves, her natural impulse will be to associate her existence with him she loves, and to share *his* occupations; in which, if he loves her (with that affection of *equality* which alone deserves to be called love) she will naturally take as strong an interest, and be as thoroughly conversant, as the most perfect confidence on his side can make her.[103]

Clearly, Mill was ambivalent about thoroughgoing alterations in private social arrangements between the sexes. His way out was a grant of equality of citizenship and civil liberty, together with a formal grant of the *right* to public power to women, knowing full well that the structure of social arrangements forbade the implementation of these rights. Surely in Mill's work there is a recognition, on some deep and tacit level, that the public world of bourgeois liberalism was dependent upon a particular vision of the private world in which women played the role of softeners and civilizers, and the family was the haven in a heartless world. To make of the family a little civil society was, for Mill, even with his sanguine view of that society, clearly intolerable. So he accords women a grant-to-power in a public world most women were not in a position to enter, hoping that such a grant in itself would serve to expel from familial life those aspects of domination incompatible with conjugal equality and, for Mill, true love.

[102] *Ibid.*, p. 108.
[103] John Stuart Mill, "On Marriage and Divorce," quoted by Richard W. Krouse, "Patriarchal Liberalism and Beyond: From John Stuart Mill to Harriet Taylor," in *The Family in Political Thought*, ed. Jean Bethke Elshtain.

I am not suggesting that there is an easy way out of Mill's dilemma; rather, I am arguing that the thinness of Mill's approach precludes either a way out of the binds in which he finds himself (and women) or, alternatively, a more complete statement of the problem. In the next chapter I shall take up three of the most bold writers in the history of political thinking and ask if they did any better with the daunting questions that confounded Mill.

Chapter 4

Politics and Social Transformation: Rousseau, Hegel, and Marx on the Public and the Private

There can be no patriotism without liberty, no liberty without virtue, no virtue without citizens; create citizens and you have everything you need; without them, you will have nothing but debased slaves, from the rulers of the state downwards.—*Rousseau*

The state is the actuality of the ethical idea.—*Hegel*

The state is based on the contradiction between *public* and *private life*, between *general interest* and *private interest*.—*Marx*

The no-nonsense self-assurance of latter-day liberals and the dolorous solemnity of the patriarchalists I examined in the preceding chapter comprise a rather neat contrasting set of arguments: the former bristling with promises of progress and a future of unending human improvement and rationality; the latter heavy with notions threaded back through a tradition of centuries lived among lordly fathers and fatherly lords under the omniscient eye of God the Father. Having traced the vagaries of the theme of public and private in both schools of thought, liberal and patriarchal, I shall now move to a consideration of three theorists whose works provide alternatives to each. I shall explore the chief points of theoretical demarcation in the writings of Rousseau, Hegel, and Marx insofar as they touch in interesting or important ways on my central theme.

The tradition of political discourse to which Rousseau, Hegel, and Marx responded and to which they made major contributions was, as I have shown, a complex and by no means consensual one. Politics was viewed as the fulfillment of man's nature and the apogee of moral life or as an unfortunate necessity brought into being by, and serving to curb, man's cupidity and capacity for rapacious mischief. Citizenship in the polity was deemed the highest calling and chief good to which man could aspire, or a poor thing compared with citizenship in the City of God. The private realm of intense personal relationships was seen as a potential risk to political harmony, and thus a dimension of human life to be checked or even eliminated if political concord was one's overriding aim, or the central good of life on earth. Human nature was viewed as intrinsically social or as atomistic and asocial. Human aims and purposes were seen as virtuous insofar as they partook of a general good or depicted, even celebrated, as narrow self-interest. Rousseau, Hegel, and Marx alike share the common denominator of standing within the broad stream of Western political discourse even as each adopted certain views in opposition to that tradition. I begin with the provocative figure of Jean-Jacques Rousseau.

JEAN-JACQUES ROUSSEAU:
VIRTUOUS FAMILIES AND JUST POLITIES

To the political thinker with feminist sensibilities, Rousseau is an inexhaustibly rich, if vexing thinker.[1] The first and most indelible impression Rousseau leaves on the femininst thinker is the manner in which he insistently, even obsessively, concentrates on dilemmas identical to, or closely linked with, those that lie at the heart of her own enterprise.[2] To be sure, Rousseau's answers

[1] There are feminists who see Rousseau as an example of the Western patriarchal tradition at its misogynistic worst and who read his works, unambiguously, as chauvinist tracts. A case in point is Eva Figes' assault on Rousseau in her book, *Patriarchal Attitudes*. In a chapter on "Rousseau, Revolution, Romanticism and Retreat," Figes treats Rousseau as beneath contempt, a figure of derision and scorn whose *Social Contract* is so "illogical" she is puzzled as to how it could have had such "enormous influence." An interesting alternative may be found in Elizabeth Rapaport, "On the Future of Love: Rousseau and the Radical Feminists," in *Women and Philosophy: Toward a Theory of Liberation*, ed. Carol Gould and Marx Wartofsky, pp. 128-144.

[2] Rousseau is not all alone, among classical political theorists, in having treated

to many of the dilemmas posed by the relationship between the sexes, and the public and private spheres, are frequently less than satisfactory to the contemporary feminist.

What are the dilemmas, puzzlements, and tangles shared by Rousseau and contemporary feminist thinkers? They include exploring human nature, male and female, and establishing the grounds on which this human nature can be debated; dissecting the resonant terms and affective symbols that structure intimate relationships between the sexes with particular emphasis on the nexus between sexuality and power; tracing the lines of reciprocal mediation and influence between the public and private spheres; questioning whether, and how, one can raise and educate children to become good persons, good citizens, or both, and whether the one necessarily entails the other; drawing distinctions, or defending analogies, between familial and political authority; and establishing the bases, if any, for social transformation with special emphasis on female discontents within civilization.

In pursuing these and other resonant matters Rousseau recognized that in order to exemplify the varied and lively diversity of human existence a supple and evocative vocabulary was required. The characterization by Freud of his own work might have been uttered by Rousseau: ''. . . it has been my chief aim to make no sacrifice to an appearance of being simple, complete, or rounded off, not to disguise problems and not to deny the existence of gaps and uncertainties.''[3] A thinker who neither disguises problems nor makes sacrifices to an appearance of being simple, complete, or rounded off, is frequently a thinker whose conceptual touchstones and moral sensibilities demand that he or she be one of that small number who make it their task to confront and articulate dilemmas, paradoxes, and human absurdities. The core of ''dilemma discourse'' involves a number of fundamental questions. How, for example, does one go about setting the terms under which social arrangements, relations, or institutions may be assessed in order to determine whether they express forms

sexual and developmental questions, but he is unique in that those questions are central to his discourse.

[3] Freud, *New Introductory Lectures*, p. 6. See also Jacobsen's treatment of Rousseau in *Pride and Solace*.

specific to a particular social system, and therefore are subject to change, or whether one is confronted instead with a cluster of ineluctable givens, imperatives that have always pertained and shall as long as a recognizably human existence is to survive? Faced with an intricate mosaic within which relatively immutable givens are so thoroughly fused with social forms that are, in principle, transformable, the theorist must attempt to tease apart the interstices of these "givens" within their institutional loci, explore the tissue of social relationships, and reflect on the fabric of personal identity. The dilemmas which serve as the focus for this book present complexities of the sort sketched above. I shall turn first to Rousseau's use of certain key concepts in order to develop his account of women, nature, and public-private dilemmas.

Rousseau deploys the terms "nature" and "natural" to a number of diverse ends and purposes within his key political texts.[4] "Nature" is used, in what I shall call the first sense, to present a picture of reality, a vision of the natural state of human beings. This beginning carries implications for Rousseau's views of men and women in history and civil society, but unlike the social contract theorists he criticizes, Rousseau does not deploy the notion of a "state of nature" as an abstract or logically necessary postulate. Rather, he urges that his condition of "nature" represents a plausible reconstruction of an actual epoch, a period of time in which not yet fully human hominids were solitary wanderers on the face of the earth. Rousseau presumes a "truly natural," prepolitical, presocial existence, an "original historical condition from which the human species evolved."[5] Rousseau's wandering forest child is prompted to form bonds with other solitary hominids given the promptings of basic natural desires.

[4] Jean-Jacques Rousseau titles and editions consulted for this discussion include the following: Jean-Jacques Rousseau, *Emile*, trans. B. Boxley; Jean-Jacques Rousseau, *The First and Second Discourses*, ed. Roger D. Masters; Jean-Jacques Rousseau and Johann Gottfried Herder, *On the Origin of Language*, trans. J. Moran and A. Gode; Jean-Jacques Rousseau, *Politics and the Arts: Letter to M. D'Alembert On the Theatre*, trans. Allan Bloom; Jean-Jacques Rousseau, *On the Social Contract*, with *Geneva Manuscript and Political Economy*, ed. Roger D. Masters; Jean-Jacques Rousseau, *The Confessions*, trans. J. N. Cohen.

[5] Roger D. Masters, *The Political Philosophy of Rousseau*, p. 198.

The role Rousseau assigns to the passions in the evolution from man-in-nature to a culture in which human nature has become, in part, social, cannot be underplayed. His insistence on the centrality of passion places him at odds with the abstract rationalist models of man that played a key role in liberal contractarian and utilitarian theories. Rousseau is closer to Freud than to Locke and the utilitarians with his claim that one "does not begin by reasoning, but by feeling."[6] The passions serve as the catalyst for culture as they prompt the first attempts at human speech. In Rousseau's words, "the passions stimulated the first words," and the words appropriate to these passions are "love, hatred, pity, anger."[7] Rousseau disagrees with celebrants of self-interest as the chief motivating force of human existence. The need for human communication, he argues, cannot be explained solely with reference to self-interest or self-preservation. We can slake our hunger and thirst on our own, he insists; "One stalks in silence the prey on which one would feast."[8] Indeed, competition over prey and scattered vegetation tends to separate, not unite, natural beings. It is love, hate, pity—powerful feelings—that serve as the impetus to create ties that bind. By tying the emergence of human social existence to "affairs of the heart" and the tongue rather than to prudential calculations of marginal utility, Rousseau drives a wedge between himself, the liberal contractarians, and the radical nominalist, Hobbes.[9]

Rousseau's second image of the "natural" man, woman, or way of life is deployed in order that Rousseau may characterize those traits which have emerged in evolutionary history and become, as it were, humankind's "second nature." "Natural," in this second sense, is also used to convey desired outcomes or

[6] Rousseau, *On the Origin of Language*, p. 11.

[7] *Ibid.*, pp. 11-12.

[8] *Ibid.*, p. 12.

[9] The most powerful elaboration of Rousseau's tentative arguments and insights was to come many years later, not from the pen of a political theorist but from the work of a thinker as familiar as any with the wondrous and terrible workings of the human heart. Freud, in *Civilization and Its Discontents*, supports Rousseau's stress on powerful and ambivalent feelings and passions in the self-creation of human beings. See also Robert Wokler, "Perfectible Apes in Decadent Cultures: Rousseau's Anthropology Revisited," *Daedalus*, pp. 107-134.

preferred relations, social forms, and ways of life. It enables Rousseau, as I shall explain below, to indicate notions of what is appropriate and proper for human beings once social forms are created and human nature becomes, in some sense, social even as it remains, in some sense, natural.

Within Rousseau's original natural state, the isolated monads who populate it, male and female, come together for brief couplings only to break apart and continue on their respective ways. In this presocial natural condition, there is no marriage, no family life, no long-term love nor friendship, no property. One of the most compelling grounds for Rousseau's critique of the social contract theories of Locke and Hobbes is his insistence that the contractarians were guilty of presuming that patriarchal families, not unlike the families which pertained within their own historic epoch, existed in the state of nature. They had, Rousseau argues, simply read back into a state of nature a social form that emerged within history.

Much turns on this debate, for what theorists locate in a state of nature, or presume to exist a priori, and what they see as creations in history through human activity will help to determine their stance towards social change. It is, of course, the case that traditions which emerged at one point in history begin to take on the appearance of having always existed ''by nature'' and individuals may come to believe things have ''always been this way.'' The humanly constituted origin of the practice, rule, belief, or tradition lies shrouded behind a veil of historic myth and the accretion of time. Rousseau knew this and recognized it as one of the most tormenting of dilemmas: How is one to tell what really existed by nature and what emerged historically? Furthermore, what difference does the locating of an institution, practice, or tradition in time make?

A matter of immediate concern to the feminist thinker is whether a theorist presumes that a particular male-dominated family form is given, pertaining in and by nature and therefore not subject to revision through conscious human intention and action, or whether the theorist denies the patriarchal familial form such a status, thus leaving open the question as to whether the family can be transformed. By repudiating the vision of the social contractarians,

Rousseau aimed to distinguish carefully what is "established by nature" from what is merely "advantageous." His original natural state featured a rough-and-ready parity between the sexes, in which women reared the offspring resulting from casual couplings in the absence of a settled family life. The bonds of reciprocal affection and mutual involvement in reproduction are missing and the woman feels no passion of love for the man after her child is conceived.[10] Rousseau's hominids live at peace with nature and as friends of their fellow creatures in their prepolitical, presocially organized world.[11] These beings can be said to be social in the sense that they are driven to express powerfully felt passions for one another. In the earliest glimmerings of moral "feelings" in the human heart, Rousseau locates the basis for a naturalistic morality.

In his *Second Discourse*, Rousseau provides his most detailed tracing of man's natural-social, social-natural evolution from an original state of nature through successive stages or epochs in that state of nature, stages in a bio-historical process, which led to organized civil and political society. Rousseau situates these stages or epochs in the realm of convention and, in increasingly mediated and less transparent ways, in natural dispositions and sentiments. For Rousseau to insist, as he does, that the family serves vital biological and cultural functions as human beings make themselves in history does not logically commit him to any *particular* evaluation of woman's nature as distinct from man's. That the pure state of nature is altered with the establishment of fixed abodes and stable families, a condition Rousseau terms "savage society," represents a momentous transformation from the presocial hominid state. Tools, speech, and clusters of residences are created and human beings, speaking and laboring, grow more truly human and social even as they retain their ties to the original "natural" condition.

Savage society, the second stage in man's evolution from the original state of nature, is Rousseau's own preferred stage because it is a social organization which retains its ties to the natural

---

[10] Rousseau, *The First and Second Discourses*, p. 216.
[11] *Ibid.*, p. 130.

wellsprings of human life and action as human sociality becomes "second nature."[12] A question occurs: Why should the isolated beings of Rousseau's first image assent to evolution from a solitary, family-less existence to one in which the family predominates and fixed abodes become the social rule? First, it is clear that Rousseau's natural being is not governed by "rational choice" along prudential lines; moreover, there were no organized social or political avenues through which the matter could have been debated. So the question is moot: an anachronistic concern. More to the point are the reasons Rousseau himself gives for this momentous change in the overall process of civilization. He links the shift to revolutionary "developments of the heart" which helped human beings to become more truly human by giving rise to the "sweetest sentiments known to men: conjugal love and paternal love. Each family became a little society all the better united because reciprocal affection and freedom were its only bonds." At this point and not before, "the first difference was established in the way of life of the two sexes, which until this time had had but one. Women became more sedentary and grew accustomed to tend the hut and children, while the man went to seek their common subsistence. The two sexes also began, by their slightly softer life, to lose something of their ferocity and vigor."[13]

In the second stage of the state of nature there is no systematic

[12] All subsequent stages in man's natural-social and historic evolution represent an advance on the previous stage. Gradually arts, education, laws, religion, civil society, and political government emerge. But a degeneration sets in as jealousy, cruelty, vengeance, the shift from innocent *amour-soi* to vain *amour-propre* rises and all the evil effects of property-holding emerge. Discrepancies of wealth and privilege, the gradual corruption of government institutions and a degeneration made inevitable by extreme inegalitarianism follow—it all adds up to a pretty bleak view of human "progress." This is set in vivid contrast to Rousseau's preferred epoch of savage society in which family units and organized social existence prevail but human beings are still bound by simple ties of pity and compassion. Man is not yet at odds with himself and his inner nature, and his extant social forms are simple and uncomplicated avenues of human expression. See Roger D. Masters, "Jean-Jacques is Alive and Well: Rousseau and Contemporary Sociobiology," *Daedalus*, pp. 93-106.

[13] Rousseau, *First and Second Discourses*, p. 147. Cf. Masters, *Political Philosophy of Rousseau*, p. 170.

inequality lodged in social structures, no political domination nor unjust privilege. Although women and children are dependent in part on men for provisions, they, too, perform necessary and equal household and agricultural work. Rousseau demonstrates that a division of labor *simpliciter* does not suffice as a system of domination. There are other reasons for the shift to a settled way of life. Rousseau finds these reasons in the increased complexity of human needs and the rise of more differentiated social forms. Human beings could no longer be solitary wanderers. Rousseau, citing Locke's *On Civil Government*, disagrees with Locke's characterization of the state of nature, his insistence that the woman's biological constitution means she is "commonly with child again and brings forth, too, a new birth, long before the former is out of a dependency for support on his parent's help, and able to shift for himself; whereby the father, who is bound to take care for those he hath begot, and to undertake that care for a long time, is under an obligation to continue in conjugal society with the same woman by whom he has had them, and to remain in that society much longer than other creatures."[14] Instead Rousseau sees this imperative as operative when humans have evolved to a more complex stage.

Savage society, the second stage in evolutionary history, is one stage in a number of subsequent transformations of the original natural state. Those who claim that Rousseau's use of "natural" man or woman within the second stage of evolutionary history either constitutes carelessness on his part, or is logically indefensible given his first usage of "natural," seem to presume that Rousseau is constructing an abstract formal model. Instead, he is attempting to create what Wittgenstein would call a "picture of reality," in this case an image of the past of the human species. It is clear from the texts that Rousseau strove to maintain a dynamic interplay between biological and social, natural and historical, internally and externally determined human beings. This being the case, there comes a point on the evolutionary trail when it is impossible to tease out with precision the person-as-such from the person-as-socially-constituted. This subtle point is a critical

[14] Rousseau, *First and Second Discourses*, p. 215.

one for feminist thinkers who are searching for a vocabulary and mode of theoretical reflection which allows them to open up the nature-culture, biological-social debate in a manner that is fruitful and illuminating rather than dead-end.

If Rousseau's version of the state of nature puts pressure on the more ahistorical constructs of Locke and Hobbes, his arguments concerning the nature, purpose, and relation between paternal authority and political authority distance him from Locke's protagonist, Robert Filmer. Filmer saw political power as the absolute and unquestioned authority of the ruler, a direct outgrowth of God's grant of dominion to Adam which was passed on to all subsequent fatherly lords and lordly fathers. Patriarchal authority, for Filmer, is thoroughly political and political authority is thoroughly patriarchal on all levels. Rousseau will have none of this and he knocks at least some of the conceptual props out from under patriarchal political theory.

In contrast to Filmer, Rousseau argues that paternal authority acquires its principal force *from* civil society; that political authority is neither deducible from, nor an outgrowth nor mirror reflection of, paternal authority. Although Rousseau claims in *The Social Contract* that the family is the "most ancient of all societies, and the only natural one,"[15] this passage should not be seen as a rapprochement with a hard-line patriarchalist position. It should not be interpreted in this manner because Rousseau is quite careful to posit an analogy, not an identity, between familial and political societies. The ruler, he argues, corresponds "in some sense" to a father and citizens to children. But an identity between each analogue is inappropriate and ultimately destructive, for, in Rousseau's words, "in the family the father's love for his children rewards him for the care he provides; whereas in the State, the pleasure of commanding substitutes for this love, which the leader does not have for his people."[16] In the state, love gives way to pleasure in domination.

For Rousseau, the authority of the body politic is grounded in a social compact which brings it into being and grants it power over its members through the vehicle of the general will. Legit-

---

[15] Rousseau, *Social Contract*, p. 47. [16] *Ibid.*

imate power alone is sovereign and right and only this sort of power—legal, publicly vested power—is properly political. The illegitimate use of force is mere physical power without moral effect. "Yielding to force," Rousseau observes, "is an act of necessity, not of will. . . . In what sense would it be a duty?"[17] No man has *natural political* authority over his fellows (as in patriarchal theory). As might does not and cannot make right, "there remain only conventions as the basis of all legitimate authority among men."[18] Politics is an activity brought about and constituted in history which has as its raison d'être the attainment of certain purposes and ends common to all.

But the basis of familial government is not legalistic, contractual, or sovereign. Within the family love and duty, not domination, is the glue which binds it together. The basis of family government or authority lies, in large measure, in the superior strength of the father who deploys it to protect his children and to command their obedience. This paternal authority "is correctly thought to be established by nature." No legislature has, can, or should decree it. No law proclaims it. It predates the creation of civil society, going back to an earlier stage in human evolutionary history, one in which there was a closer identification of social man with natural man. The father's duties are dictated to him by no external authority but are prompted "by natural feelings, and in such a way that he can rarely disobey."[19] "Natural" is deployed here as roughly synonymous with an imperative anchored in the biological and social evolutionary history of the species; it has a basis in biology but serves a desirable and necessary end in human social existence. The father, "in very nature," ought to command.

Is there any hypocrisy on Rousseau's part in granting no moral imperative or legitimacy to force within political society, yet lodging the right of the father "in very nature" to command in familial society in part because of his admitted physical advantages? If Rousseau's intent were a straightforwardly misogynist one, he wouldn't have tied himself in so many knots in his exploration of these matters. He could, for example, have quite easily postulated a state of nature in which male domination exists by def-

[17] *Ibid.*, p. 48.   [18] *Ibid.*, p. 49.   [19] *Ibid.*, p. 169.

inition and allowed this patriarchal dominion to go unchanged and unchallenged in civil society. By insisting upon a reexploration of male-female relationships and positing an ambivalent relationship between the family and the polity, Rousseau opens up a range of questions others failed to ask.[20]

Yet Rousseau emerges with a surprisingly tedious conclusion: the man is physically superior; the man should have the final say. Actually, his position is not quite that simple, for the father's right "from the nature of things" to command is further justified on the grounds that parental authority "should not be equal."[21] Rousseau feared and despised parental divisiveness—families in which there was endless recrimination, dissension, and discord. He would put a finger in the dike of familial disruption by retreating behind a notion of the indivisibility of familial authority. In this respect Rousseau is at least consistent in tracing lines of influence from state to family and in demanding unity from them both.

One final justification for the domination of the father within organized family life is proffered by Rousseau:

. . . however slight the incapacitations peculiar to the wife are thought to be, since they are always an inactive period for her, this is sufficient reason to exclude her from primacy, because when the balance is perfectly equal, the smallest thing is enough to tip it. Furthermore, the husband should oversee his wife's conduct, because it is important to him that the children he is forced to recognize do not belong to anyone other than himself.[22]

Rousseau has not helped his cause in the eyes of feminist critics by layering onto a serious bio-social set of considerations a mor-

---

[20] See also John Charvet, "Individual Identity and Social Consciousness in Rousseau's Philosophy," in *Hobbes and Rousseau*, ed. Maurice Cranston and Richard S. Peters, pp. 462-483; Ernst Cassirer, *The Question of Jean-Jacques Rousseau*; Ronald Grimsley, *Jean-Jacques Rousseau*; and Masters' *Political Philosophy of Rousseau*, for alternative articulations and development of these questions in Rousseau's thought.

[21] Rousseau, *Social Contract*, p. 170.   [22] *Ibid.*

alistic injunction. I can only suggest the following, not to justify Rousseau's position but to attempt to penetrate the nature and motivation behind his fear of familial discord and cuckoldry. Recall, if you will, Rousseau's expressed opposition to forces that might disrupt or divide political authority, dilute sovereign power, and erode the general will. It is important to situate Rousseau's concerns with familial authority and discord within the wider ambience of his thought as a whole. He had been convinced for some time, before he penned this defense of paternal authority, that social life, in its public and private forms and modes of expression, was running aground on the shoals of envy, petty jealousy, and corruption. He would stave off these dangers as long as possible by preserving some appearance of stability and virtue in the private world.

Two fears seem to be at work in the passages just explored: a fear that the more "civilized" humans became the less human they might one day be, for their ties to their early bio-social, natural past would grow thinner, more impoverished, and less resonant with each succeeding epoch. Rousseau's pessimism as to public possibilities, the preservation of space for authentic civic virtue, is the perennial pessimism experienced by one who would transform a corrupt order but, given its corruption, can't determine the base from which to launch his struggle. The second fear expressed in Rousseau's grant of familial authority to the father is a fear of the sexual and psychological resources of women, their reproductive capacities, their seductiveness, their vulnerability, and their openness to human intimacy. Rousseau believed that women already possessed power on so many levels vis-à-vis men and children, simply by virtue of their being what they were, that they neither "needed" nor could be trusted with power of a public, political sort. Women were volatile and must be reined in, forced to be content to wield their power "privately." That a man of Rousseau's sensitivity could fail to experience empathic identification when women were denied the dignity that is attendant upon public participation and speech; that he could place women in circumstances in which they had no rights but only revocable privileges; that he could force them into patterns of repetitious emptiness, indicates both the limits of his capacities to transcend his own age and his deep and abiding fear of women.[23] Nevertheless, any serious contemporary feminist thinker must take up the challenge Rousseau has laid down to explore, in terms adequate to the complexities involved, the inner relationship between familial and political authority.

Rousseau's chief hope for attaining a balance of private and public virtue lay in education. He devised a very different course of study for his Emile and his Sophie respectively. Indeed, Rousseau's account of male and female development and educational processes and requisites highlights the tension in his thought as well as his concessions to an environmentalist posture. There seems little doubt that Rousseau would have preferred, had he been able to justify, a tighter connection between biological givens and social outcomes. If the education of the sexes simply followed predetermined biological patterns, the different educative fates that awaited male and female infants would not need to have been pursued with such rigor, nor would the process have been so fraught with pitfalls. But Rousseau refuses himself this consolation as he sets about devising an educational method for boys, who are in training for citizenship, and girls, who are preparing for their roles as virtuous and noble wives.

Although mind and body, male and female, do not follow biological dictates in an unmediated manner, the biological substratum for sex differences in behavior cannot be ignored. The educations of Emile and Sophie are designed to equip them for the diverse stations, purposes, and obligations in life which their biology does not dictate but to which it contributes.[24] When Rousseau calls the dynamics and purposes of his educational program "natural," he means there is a basis in biology for the activities that take place pedagogically. It is Rousseau's view that divergencies in the roles and responsibilities of males and females had

---

[23] The key texts are *Politics and the Arts*; *Emile*; and, of course, *The Confessions*, although this theme emerges as a kind of subtext in all of Rousseau's work.

[24] For discussions which differ somewhat from my own see Nannerl O. Keohane, "The Masterpeice of Polity in Our Century: Rousseau on the Morality of the Enlightenment," *Political Theory*, pp. 421-456; Allan Bloom, "The Education of Democratic Man: Emile," *Daedalus*, pp. 135-154; and William Kessen, "Rousseau's Children," *Daedalus*, pp. 155-166.

a basis in the human bio-social constitution and evolution. In an interesting reversal of the way in which he construed the relationship between family and civil society (civil authority does not derive from familial authority, but instead the authority of the familial head takes its principal force from the institutions of civil society), Rousseau argues that sex distinctions arise and occur in nature prior to the pressures of civilization. Within the epoch of savage society, men and women established a division of labor that made biological sense given their respective reproductive roles. It was actual sex distinctions, then, occurring in nature, that set the basis for later socially constituted and buttressed distinctions. Distinctions between the sexes, both social and natural, are not for Rousseau "the result of mere prejudice, but of reason."[25] Emile's and Sophie's education is, then, "natural": it builds on a biological base; it is anchored in centuries of historic tradition; and it is morally preferable as the best means to preserve the public and private spheres alike. This is Rousseau's view of the matter.

Rousseau is afraid that women will demand to become educated like men. The more frequently this occurs, he notes ominously, the more women will indeed become like men and the less influence they will have over them. At that perilous juncture, "men will be masters indeed,"[26] rigid and immovable, untouched by the more compassionate sex. To forestall this eventuality, little girls must be disciplined; they must "early be accustomed to restraint. . . . All their life long, they will have to submit to the strictest and most enduring restraints, those of propriety."[27] Rousseau's emphasis on the nurturance of children places him squarely in yet another dilemma: women are a softening influence; they purvey moral values and sentiments to the young; they are the civilizers of children and, sometimes, of men. It follows, according to Rousseau's logic, that when women are unchaste, unfaithful, unseemly, vain, or frivolous, their ostensibly private

---

[25] *Emile*, p. 324, Book 5 is the major source of Rousseau's reflections on this matter. The superior Bloom edition of *Emile* became available only after this section was written. See Jean-Jacques Rousseau, *Emile or On Education*, ed. and trans. Allan Bloom.

[26] *Ibid.*, p. 327. [27] *Ibid.*, p. 332.

behavior is suffused with public implications. Why? Because the basis of male public citizenship would disintegrate if his private world collapsed, as the citizen is also, necessarily, a husband-father, the head of a household.

The flip side of a coin that features the public-spirited visage of the male citizen and dutiful father is the profile of the loving, virtuous, chaste, selfless wife, "enduring restraints," particularly "those of propriety." Yet, paradoxically, Rousseau believed that this image was already fading when he penned his most idealistic portrait of it—his paean to a public and private world that perhaps never existed, nor could be brought into existence if for no other reason (and this alone would suffice) than the fact that women, placed as Rousseau places them, within an intolerable hothouse of propriety, piety, and chastity, will inevitably constitute an unhappy, repressed, and hence subversive population. Women, yearning for something more, perhaps they know not what, will be miserable and the temptation to act out in selfish or irresponsible ways in the private world, their only forum for action, will be too great. Rousseau surely knew all of this.[28] In *La Nouvelle Héloïse*, for example, the harder Rousseau strives for a happy resolution the more threatening things become. Tony Tanner concludes that the *Héloïse*, is ". . . a book that not only bespeaks some kind of imminent crisis in the particular family structure on which society is based, but carries with it a sense of doom concerning the very emotions and institutions that book strives to celebrate."[29]

Rousseau observed the power of women and that power, at base, was sexual. "Do you want to know men? Study women. . . . Chasteness is nothing. It is only an invention of the social laws to protect the rights of fathers and husbands and to preserve order in families."[30] Rousseau admits that the sexual needs and desires of women are as powerful and basic as those of men. Yet

---

[28] The anxiety that runs through his discussions of these matters—in *Emile*, *Politics and the Arts*, *The Confessions*—provides abundant textual evidence of Rousseau's awareness of the problematic situation into which women were placed.

[29] Tony Tanner, "Julie and 'La Maison Paternelle'; Another Look at Rousseau's *La Nouvelle Héloïse*," *Daedalus*, p. 23. Cf. the account of Rousseau's heroines in Okin, *Women in Western Political Thought*.

[30] Rousseau, *Politics and the Arts*, pp. 82-83.

he continues to demand a double standard, for the consequences of unfaithfulness are not the same on both sides. Besides, Rousseau continues (the argument here wears a bit thin), ". . . even if it could be denied that a special sentiment of chasteness was natural to women"—just a few pages earlier Rousseau denies precisely this—"it would not be any less true that in a society their lot *ought* to be domestic and retired life" (emphasis mine).[31] When a woman deviated from her appointed station, Rousseau was quite capable of lashing out and sketching that woman as simultaneously passive and feeble, domineering and manipulative. As Judith Shklar points out, Rousseau blamed corrupt women, especially the women of Paris, for much of the moral corruption and decadence in his society, a decadence that threw him into despair.[32] Women spoiled civilization.

Despite the fact that Rousseau repudiates the empiricist epistemology of Locke and later liberal thinkers by tying together reason and passion, he nonetheless sees their separation as an unfortunate but ineluctable product of civilization. The first languages were languages of passion and simplicity. But, as civilization develops languages grow less passionate. They no longer speak to the heart but become "duller and colder." This is a process Rousseau declares "entirely natural,"[33] yet it results finally in the abstract language of civilized and educated men, a language which is "the parent of deceit."[34] The public language of the virtuous citizen must nonetheless be a language which reflects the change in man's nature which he has undergone once he takes on his social identity as a citizen.[35] Somehow transfor-

[31] *Ibid.*, p. 87.

[32] Judith N. Shklar, *Men and Citizens*, pp. 144-145. For a dire view of these matters see William H. Blanchard, *Rousseau and the Spirit of Revolt.*

[33] Rousseau, *Origin of Language*, p. 16.

[34] Jacobsen, *Pride and Solace*, p. 107.

[35] Cf. *ibid.*, p. 121. Also see Jean-Jacques Rousseau, *Government of Poland*, trans. Willmoore Kendall, where Rousseau lauds the ancients' methods of binding citizens to the fatherland, "that fatherland in whose behalf they were kept constantly busy" (p. 8). These methods, including the horror of various "public spectacles" Rousseau celebrates, are surely at odds with other qualities Rousseau praises in his characterization, in other texts, of the bourgeois household and the "natural" man.

mation from instinct to justice in man's nature, a transformation detailed in Rousseau's *Social Contract, First Discourse,* and *Discourse on Political Economy,* allows man-as-citizen to remain closely in touch with his original true nature (before civilization spoiled it) in order that he may speak in the voice of simple sense and civic virtue. It might seem as if women, cut off from that language of abstract ideas Rousseau finds the "parent of deceit" by their social situations and the segregated education of the sexes Rousseau demands, would be more in tune with "true nature" and less likely to speak with a dissembling tongue. Rousseau disallows the possibility of virtuous *public speech* to women, however, offering women three main possibilities for public and private discourse: Rousseau's dominant female images are the slatterns and high society decadents of Paris, the "good girls" who give in to temptation and pay a terrible price, or the noble, selfless mothers in bourgeois households. If, for Rousseau, humans are the speaking animals, his women also speak but in the voice of romantic excess—all tears, swoons, and wastings away— or domesticity. Rousseau's romantic men sound just as exaggerated to our less romantic age, but they are allowed a greater range of diverse possibilities in terms of the voices with which they may speak to, and of, that which they have come to know, believe, or desire. The depth of Rousseau's mistrust of women is apparent in the fact that those closer to original nature, by his own logic, are not allowed to speak in the always-to-be trusted voice of that nature.

The question we must put to Rousseau, having placed him in a tradition whose task it is to face and articulate paradoxes and dilemmas, is whether or not the binds his women experience in the public and private spheres are attributable primarily to extant social institutions and forms which are, in some ways, unjust (women, therefore, being victims of injustice), or primarily to an inescapable human dilemma, the burdens of which women have, disproportionately, had to bear. I refer here to the tensions, conflicts, and frequently irreconcilable demands of family love and full-time citizenship, of expressive sexuality and monogamous intimacy versus public duty and devotion, of the not fully harmonious demands of being a good person and a good citizen at the same time.

One dilemma presented immediately lies in determining whether the price paid for Rousseau's vision of the just polity *necessarily* turns on the privatization and exclusion of women from citizenship, or whether this is a peripheral issue, expressive of Rousseau's own sexual prejudices but not tied, in deep ways, to the inner structure of his theory. The latter possibility would be a tidy way out but it would also be too facile a solution. Rousseau requires that a resonant, vibrant, constant private world be sustained as one of the *necessary* social preconditions of his ideal polity. If women participated in Rousseau's public sphere on a par with men, the complexly interrelated structure of public and private alike would erode: without someone to tend the hearth, the legislative hallways would grow silent and empty, or become noisily corrupt. This is Rousseau's conclusion.

It is quite possible, even feasible, to incorporate women into citizenship along the lines of a formal-legalistic, social contract model: a thin concept of citizenship demands little save looking out for one's self-interest and occasionally tending to public matters. Rousseau's citizen rejects prudential rationality as an unworthy touchstone of public thought and action, for social purposes cannot be reduced to a mere aggregation of private purposes.[36] Rousseau's public world takes up a great deal of space. But it leaves room for, indeed it is in a fundamental way dependent upon, a virtuous private sphere that serves as the training ground of future citizens and protectors of private values alike.

Without women to guard, nurture, and renew the private sphere, Rousseau's public world cannot exist. I am not suggesting that it is impossible to posit an arrangement which allows men and women to be coequals within interrelated and valued public and private spheres for which they both bear burdens and undertake responsibilities. I am claiming that within the concepts and demands of the public and private world as set forth by Rousseau, such an arrangement is impossible and doomed to failure. Yet it may be the case that by articulating clearly the public and private restrictions confronted by women, and by locating some of his

---

[36] See, in addition to Rousseau's full discussion in *The Social Contract*: Keohane, "The Masterpiece of Polity in our Century"; Kessen, "Rousseau's Children"; and the discussion of Rousseau's contributions to a radical notion of moral autonomy in Charles Taylor's *Hegel*.

female heroines within impossible situations, Rousseau helped to coalesce and to focus the very discontents whose unpromising results and portents he feared, discontents we may see as no less complicated than he, though perhaps we find them less frightening.

This leads me to reflections on one of Rousseau's knottier knots. The ethical polity, in its public and private aspects, can be sustained only by persons who are committed to the twin values and worth of each. But what happens (and this is by no means merely a hypothetical problem—it is our contemporary dilemma) to these public and private commitments in the absence of a polity which can serve as the moral touchstone and vibrant focus of the allegiance of its citizens? Rousseau states the problem in *The Social Contract* thus: "In order for an emerging people to appreciate the healthy maxims of politics, and follow the fundamental rules of statecraft, the effect would have to become the cause; the social spirit, which should be the result of the institution, would have to preside over the founding of the institution itself; and men would have to be prior to laws what they ought to become by means of laws."[37] If we determine that our social order is corrupt and corrupting, what shall serve as the basis for moral action? Where does one discover principles to live and act by? How does one nurture the ideal of the "citizen" which lies, as yet, beyond one's reach? Can a wellspring for change be sustained within private spheres existing as enclaves of respect for persons, autonomy, decency, diversity, and caring despite their being surrounded by an impoverished world?

The best way to approach Rousseau's classic dilemma is by asking what Rousseau requires if a people is to cherish the principles ("effects") of life in polity. They must adopt those principles as *reasons* that serve as *causes* for action, giving rise to the very ends from which they "ought" to have derived. Rousseau's meaning, while not concise, is clear: those individuals outside the bounds of the ethical polity may yet adopt as reasons the principles which would animate life in such a polity. These reasons can then serve as the animating principles for present action. How is this possible?

[37] Rousseau, *Social Contract*, p. 69.

Rousseau believed that the ends for moral action did not inhere in the extant social institutions of his time, nor were these ends implicit in contemporary forms of social life as lived. Here he overstates his case, for one cannot (as MacIntyre points out) answer the question, "What ought I to do?" until one has answered the question, "Who am I?" One's answer to the latter question will involve specifying or locating oneself "in a nexus of social relationships, and it is within these and the possibilities which they make available that ends in the light of which actions may be criticized are discovered."[38] In our own time the nexus of social relationships which retain the possibility for affection, tenderness, responsibility, moral duty, obligation, and caring are, for the most part, those we call or know as "private," relationships under sustained pressure to succumb to the contentious and instrumentalist presumptions of our civil society. But the possibility remains, and the importance of that possibility cannot be overstressed. Without a set of early experiences which allow for multiple, enriching human identifications, individuals will have only thin, contingent connections to others and will be more likely to capitulate to the temptation or demand for destructiveness, pity, and contempt. I agree fully with those, including Rousseau and, later, Freud, who stress the power and importance of human emotions and those psychic identifications which link us in a kind of sisterhood and brotherhood and who go on to claim that this dimension of reality is essential for a just society. The private sphere can serve as a kind of template upon which our most powerful political sentiments are patterned.[39]

For sound principles to be cherished as reasons which might, in turn, animate the moral fiber and social life of persons, must the home become a kind of just polity, a little commonwealth? Can political ideals—public law, freedom, justice, equality—prevail in a private arena? What then of nurturance, mercy, forgiveness, succor? Rousseau has not solved the problem, for he has

[38] MacIntyre, *Short History of Ethics*, p. 187.

[39] Stephen Salkever quotes Rousseau as insisting that even if the life of civic virtue is "not a likely possibility" given the present order of things, "a happy social life is still possible today in the setting of an ordinary household," for the family is one source of virtue and happiness. Stephen G. Salkever, "Rousseau and the Concept of Happiness," *Polity*, pp. 42-43.

expunged, in his effort to achieve some sort of answer, certain dimensions of the question. Constitutional principles for an ethical polity are not implementable within the private sphere. Were the attempt to be made it would be disastrous for both spheres alike. Children can be schooled in certain images of civic virtue, not in any strict sense, but in the sense of keeping alive those qualities of mind and spirit that would help to give birth to a polity within which civic ideals could be realized, should the time ever be ripe.

Given the corrupt social order, Rousseau observes that: "I shall have to discover the ends for moral action . . . in a form of social existence which does not yet exist." This strikes me as an avowal of the possibility that the ends for action must sometimes be sought in the activities of one's imagination, as a kind of play, or drama, or dress rehearsal, an envisaging that requires the qualities of mind and spirit I have evoked above. I shall remind myself, before others do, that public speech and action require more than one person; that moral reason-giving must be done to and with others in a social situation. If one reposes the ends for moral action in imagined social situations, doesn't one open up the possibility of turning individuals into pawns of the political fantasist or social engineer run amok? If so, that would make things little different than they have ever been, for we have all too often become the playthings of men of action animated by regressive fantasies of rage. The pitfall is present. Let me grant the danger and move on to resituate an alternative view of fantasy as a form of creative, moral political thought in which the person who would become a participant in the ethical polity may hold on to certain "ends for moral action."

First: when Rousseau seeks to ground principles in a yet-to-exist way of life he isn't starting from scratch. He's building from the ground up but he is standing on a particular foundation. The political imagination, like that of the artist, draws upon a repertoire which "consists in knowledge of or beliefs about what or whom I imagine." Neither I, nor Rousseau, nor the reader of this book is "quite untrammelled in my imaginings. . . . I am constrained by *whom* it is whom I imagine, and I am constrained by *what* it is that I imagine their doing."[40] The vision of a better life draws

---

[40] Richard Wollheim, "Identification and the Imagination," in *Freud: A Col-*

upon an extant way of life. A vision or fantasy of a better world, an ethical polity, need not involve the utter destruction of the old, nor become stuck in unchecked interiority; rather, what starts out as a kind of inner dialogue may become transformed through contemplation and action, as reasons become causes, into public speech and principles. This is part of what Rousseau was about in *The Social Contract*. Our mistake is to think of locating or finding ends only in precise plans of action or thoroughly worked out constitutions. We may think of the work of the political imagination as a species of fantasy of a particular sort, tapping moral and aesthetic impulses and public and private identities: a dynamic concatenation of individual psychic states, wishes, fears, desirings, and reasonings which, transformed first to envisaging, may finally manifest themselves in and through action on the public level. Once this complex process has been worked through, states of mind have ceased to be merely or simply individual and have become something more.

Each of us has the responsibility of making judgments between competing visions of the political imagination, rejecting those which tap primitive rage. Only in this way can fantasies of hope, civil and virtuous, be kept alive, fantasies which the more clamorous images of the rageful would expunge from our world. It is possible that our language of philosophical and political inquiry is not yet adequate to the task of uniting the sensual and the spiritual, of achieving a dialectics of choice, variability, and possibility which disallows absolute certitude and the destruction it brings in its wake. This task of the political imagination is possible only if civility is not utterly destroyed, only if a private sphere which allows for playful experimentation from deep seriousness of purpose exists free from totalistic intrusion and control. For even when justice is not realized and public ethics are an unattained ideal, freedom preserves the human communication necessary to attain and to realize both.

I shall argue in my concluding chapter that it is possible to appropriate aspects of Rousseau's concept of the citizen as an active moral agent, one who has rejected prudential rationality

---

lection of Critical Essays, ed. Richard Wollheim, pp. 182-183. Cf. Benjamin R. Barber, "Rousseau and the Paradoxes of Imagination," *Daedalus*, pp. 79-95.

and calculating self-interest as unworthy bases for human thought and action, without accepting Rousseau's argument that the achievement of such citizenship requires the exclusion of women from the public realm. But the thorny questions suggested by Rousseau's work remain: Is it possible for men and women to be coequals within interrelated public and private spheres for which they share burdens and responsibilities? Feminism's response to this question is taken up in Chapter 5, but now I shall turn to the imposing figure of Hegel.

G.W.F. HEGEL: SELF-CONSCIOUS SUBJECTS AND PUBLIC AND PRIVATE IDENTITIES

In order to understand Hegel's views on the public and the private, it is necessary to delineate the Hegelian mode of inquiry. Hegel's epistemological imperatives, like Rousseau's, serve as the basis for a critique of those modes of political explanation which presume an abstract individual related to his society in ways that are external and instrumentalist. By "external" I mean that being a part of society is not seen to alter persons in any fundamental or meaningful way. By "instrumental" I mean that social institutions are seen to exist in order to preserve, protect, and defend the self-interests of individuals.

Hegel's conclusions on human nature and politics flow directly from his conceptual categories and his method: a logic of explanation which presumes that human beings come to know that which they call reality through the dynamic interplay of contrasts and negations.[41] In Hegel's view, the human subject moves via concepts from the relative abstractedness of sense-certainty and particularity to the relative concreteness provided by those categories within which sense perceptions and particulars are incorporated and transformed. In other words, the immediate particular available to human senses is rendered more, not less, concrete and thus available in a meaningful way to the cognizing human subject through the concept within which it is absorbed.

---

[41] Taylor, *Hegel*, see chap. 9, "A Dialectic of Categories."

At the heart of Hegel's account of history and political society lies the complex depiction of the human subject's capacity for consciousness and self-consciousness. Hegel, to put it oversimply, holds that human self-consciousness is possible because the human mind works actively upon material given to it through the senses. Human beings can experience reality from a reflective perspective. Insofar as he or she is self-aware, the human subject comes to recognize that the stock of inherited notions available (e.g., the classical liberal tradition) comprises a perspective which "both illuminates and misrepresents; so the conceptual schemes of individualist society are genuinely illuminating in that they bring out authentic features of that society and of its characteristic modes of theorizing, but misrepresent in that they conceal the limitations of individualism, partly by representing as universal and necessary features of moral life what are only features of individualism."[42] It is in the very nature of human consciousness as potential self-consciousness not to remain passive and fixed, but to discover the possibilities immanent within a given historic situation. Reason, for Hegel, is "purposive activity."[43] Hegel's account of reason and the mind constitutes a powerful and compelling alternative to those passive accounts embraced by liberal empiricists. Hegel connects human consciousness to the subject's historic situation. At the same time, however, he leaves room for critical reflection *on* that situation; indeed, it is in the fissure between social being and social consciousness that critical self-awareness may emerge.[44]

[42] MacIntyre, *Short History of Ethics*, pp. 206-207.

[43] G.W.F. Hegel, *The Phenomenology of Mind*, trans. J. B. Baille, p. 83. Hegel notes in another context:
Consciousness knows and comprehends nothing but what falls within its experience; for what is found in experience is merely spiritual substance, and, moreover, object of its self. Mind, however, becomes object, for it consists in the process of becoming an other to itself, i.e. an object for its own self, and in transcending this otherness. And experience is called this very process by which the element that is immediate, unexperienced, i.e. abstract—whether it be in the form of sense or of a bare thought—externalizes itself, and then comes back to itself from this state of estrangement, and by so doing is at length set forth in its concrete nature and real truth, and becomes too a possession of consciousness [p. 96].

[44] *Ibid.*, p. 805. The distance between social being and social consciousness is healed when absolute knowledge—"Spirit knowing itself as Spirit"—is at-

Like human consciousness, human freedom, if it is to have any authentic meaning at all, must be grounded historically. In some of his most devastating and heavily ironic passages, Hegel criticizes the "unhappy consciousness" of the ancient Stoics who held that there could be "free consciousness" in a world of slaves and fetters. Hegel observes that the Stoics' "freedom" is the *idea* of freedom couched abstractly rather than its substance embodied concretely.[45] Freedom, like subjectivity, is "necessarily situated in life, in nature, and in a setting of social practices and institutions."[46] Thus a motive for self-consciousness is imbedded within Hegel's theory of human nature and politics; the Hegelian subject is a purposive being capable of taking the world and himself as the object of reflective thought. He can tend to his own thoughts and actions—a process which is both liberating and painful[47]—

tained. Hegel reintroduces, via Kant, an antimony between reason and desire, nature and spirit, but he attempts to resolve this antimony as he rejects Kant's formalism. Hegel develops overlapping spheres of identity in which, as one moves to the higher levels, reason-spirit come to dominate. (See Taylor, *Hegel*, p. 369.)

[45] The free-floating abstractions celebrating freedom and consciousness which Hegel criticized are reminiscent of the doggerel printed on greeting cards. Coy phrases mandate devotion, affection, appreciation, and eternal love. Greeting cards offer a currency of emotion; they *represent* the feeling, but they do not *embody* it and may, in fact, exist at odds with authentic emotion. Cf. William Gass, *On Being Blue: A Phenomenological Inquiry*; and D. H. Lawrence, *Stories, Essays and Poems*, ed. Desmond Hawkins, pp. 377-378. Criticizing a poem, Lawrence complained that it "is the currency of poetry, not poetry itself."

[46] Taylor, *Hegel*, p. 567. A question often put to the analyst who would incorporate Hegelian insights or deploy the Hegelian method is whether it is defensible to pick and choose from Hegel what one finds most important and helpful to one's own ends and purposes, thereby evading Hegel's ontology and his teleology of history. Taylor raises this issue in his study. He indicates that he feels compelled to treat the question because no one in the contemporary world "actually believes his [Hegel's] central ontological thesis, that the universe is posited by a Spirit whose essence is rational necessity." If a rejection of Hegel's ontology required dropping his theory of self-consciousness or repudiating his dialectical method, Hegel would remain unavailable to many (like myself) who turn to his works to sharpen and to enrich their understanding of the human subject as a reflective, historical agent. I believe that one can extricate the dynamics of self-consciousness from Spirit unfolding in history, if one offers an alternative account of the impulse or motive for that self-consciousness. I develop such an account in my concluding chapters.

[47] Jean Bethke Elshtain, "The Social Relations of the Classroom," *Telos*, pp. 91-110.

and the self-knowledge which results must always be cast in historical form.[48] I shall return to Hegel's view of the human subject and link it to consideration of public and private identities and language following an examination of Hegel's account of the relationship between public and private social arrangements and relations, and of male and female "natures."

Hegel's views on the public and the private—the relationship among those spheres he terms the family, civil society, and the state—are indebted to Aristotle's conceptual bifurcation of the household from the *polis*. Hegel, too, would separate the realm of "necessity" from that of "freedom." *Where* Hegel locates women in his scheme of things is prior to *why* he places them there. (Within Hegel's thought the *why* is related internally to *where*.) In the case of women, Hegel's *where* is the sphere he calls a "*natural* Ethical community,"[49] namely, the family. In a passage whose meaning will be clarified as the discussion proceeds, Hegel contends that the family

. . . as the inner indwelling principle of sociality operating in an unconscious way, stands opposed to its own actuality when explicitly conscious; as the basis of the actuality of a nation, it stands in contrast to the nation itself; as the *immediate* ethical existence, it stands over against the ethical order which shapes and preserves itself by work for universal ends; the Penates of the family stand in contrast to the universal spirit.[50]

For Hegel, the natural ethical element serves as "the medium in which . . . Spirit finds . . . its realization or its objective existence."[51]

[48] Rosenthal, "Feminism Without Contradictions," p. 42. Cf. R. C. Solomon, "Hegel's Concept of Geist," in *Hegel: A Collection of Critical Essays*, ed. Alasdair MacIntyre. Solomon contends that Hegel is none too clear on the status of his human subject, his "I." Descartes' "*cogito*" is a thinking mind, neither person nor body. Kant's "I" is a formal transcendental principle. Solomon demonstrates convincingly that Hegel concurred with Kant's position on the "nonsubstantiality" of the "I think" although both recognized "the importance of the differences between a transcendental 'I think' and an empirical self or person" (p. 143).

[49] Hegel, *Phenomenology*, p. 468.   [50] *Ibid.*   [51] *Ibid.*, p. 473.

What does Hegel mean by this passage? He begins his account of the family as a natural ethical community by insisting that the ethics of the family do not lie in any "sentiment or the relationship of love" which pertains between and among family members.[52] Instead, the family's ethical importance derives from the relationship of the family to that universality embodied within the state. Yet Hegel also states that the "Penates of the family stand in contrast to the universal spirit." How can the family take its ethical importance from "universal ends" even as it "stands over against" those ends? Hegel's answer takes shape as one considers his differentiation of family members on the basis of their relationship to the familial and universal spheres: the nearer to the universal order, the more significant the family member becomes. In Hegel, as in Aristotle, the public world predominates and gives meaning to the private. The public life of a society is the locus of human action in the world.

Not all may aspire to ethical universality and significance, however. Like the inhabitants of Orwell's *Animal Farm* who learn that all animals are created equal but some are more equal than others, the inhabitants of Hegel's conceptual universe are ethically significant but some are more significant than others. Hegel, like Aristotle, excludes women from involvement in the "good" of the public realm. Instead, women are defined by the family: the family is a woman's beginning and her end. For the man, the family is that ethical relationship which serves as the basis of all others, including citizenship. The male alone can become a "real and substantial" citizen. Should he abrogate citizenship, should he sink back into the family, he becomes "merely unreal insubstantial shadow,"[53] a companion to those incomplete shadowy female forms who call the family "home."

In order to do justice to Hegel's rich account, I shall pick up his strand of argument and follow it through his logic of explanation. Hegel regards the relationship of husband to wife as "the primary and immediate form in which one consciousness, recognizes itself in another . . ."; a recognition he calls "natural self-knowledge."[54] This self-knowledge *is* available to women

[52] *Ibid.*, p. 468.   [53] *Ibid.*, p. 470.   [54] *Ibid.*, p. 474.

but it falls short of genuine self-consciousness. The male begins with the same natural self-knowledge, but for him this immediate consciousness serves as a template upon which full self-consciousness develops. The woman is stuck with the immediacy of natural self-knowledge—a feature of her necessary and unalterable absorption within the particularity of the family. Hegel's account of brothers and sisters reaffirms this position.

Although both brothers and sisters are individuals, the sister bears or embodies a "feminine element" or form. She cannot, by definition, actualize a full ethical life; "the law of the family is her inherent *implicit inward nature*, which does not lie open to the daylight of consciousness but remains inner feeling. . . . The feminine life is attached to these household divinities (Penates), and sees in them both her universal substance and her particular individuality" (emphasis mine).[55] Thus in the passage above, the woman, in her devotion to the penates of the family, is positioned "in contrast to the universal spirit." In paragraph 166 of the *Philosophy of Right*, Hegel recasts Aristotle's distinction in the *Metaphysics* between these male and female elements he depicts as the analogue of form and matter whereby the male provides the human form during mating and the female serves as a vessel within which the male-created *homunculus* incubates. Hegel likens the differences between men and women to that between "animals and plants. Men correspond to animals, while women correspond to plants because their development is more placid and the principle that underlies it is the rather vague unity of feeling."[56]

---

[55] *Ibid.*, p. 476. Cf. par. 166 of Hegel's *Philosophy of Right*, trans. T. M. Knox, pp. 114-115. "Women," Hegel insists, "are not made for activities which demand a universal faculty such as the more advanced sciences, philosophy, and certain forms of artistic production. Women may have happy ideas, taste, and elegance, but they cannot attain to the ideal." Hegel goes on to compare men to animals and women to plants.

[56] Hegel, *Philosophy of Right*, p. 263. Hegel goes on to warn of the jeopardy in which states would be placed should women be allowed to take over government. A woman's regulations of her actions, not having been incorporated within the imperatives of universality, are bound to be particular, arbitrary, capricious. I would not wish to dismiss Hegel's observations as *simple* misogyny—there are

The sister, limited by her inward nature, goes on to realize her ethical significance in her role as wife and mother, but not, Hegel insists, in her *particular* relationship to her *own* husband and children ("this particular husband, this particular child"). Instead, she must be tied to what Hegel terms a husband and "children *in general*,—not to feeling, but to the universal."[57] For Hegel, the relations of a woman to her own husband and children have no deep ethical importance *in themselves*. Only as these particular relationships are assimilated to, or within, the abstraction of husbands-in-general and children-in-general does the real relationship achieve importance. The man has no problem. He bears the *form* of universality and "possesses, as a citizen, the self-conscious power belonging to the universal life, the life of the social whole."[58]

In the male child alone the family has a member "in whom its spirit becomes individualized, and enabled thereby to turn towards another sphere, towards what is other than and external to itself, and pass over into consciousness of universality."[59] The male is "sent forth by the spirit of the family into the life of the community, and finds there his self-conscious reality."[60] The family discovers "in the community its universal substance and subsistence" and the community, in turn, "finds in the family the formal element of its own realization."[61] Hegel's complex, reciprocal public-private dialectic is a dynamic but "stable equilibrium of all parts."[62] Although there is no public-private split in Hegel's account in the sense of a radical separation of one sphere from the other, the public and the private *are* differentiated and ordered as higher and lower, with the lower spheres of first the family and second civil society (as we learn below) serving as necessary foundations of the state. The reciprocal, if asymmetrical, relationship between spheres requires connecting links or mediations. These are provided by males in their roles as brothers, husbands, fathers, and property-owners.

---

serious problems when any previously excluded group enters the public's sphere because the terms of that entry will reflect their prior privatization.

[57] Hegel, *Phenomenology*, p. 476. [58] *Ibid.*, p. 472.
[59] *Ibid.* [60] *Ibid.*, p. 478.
[61] *Ibid.* [62] *Ibid.*, p. 480.

What is one to make of Hegel's arguments thus far? First, it should be noted that the presumptions Hegel brings to inquiry, including a teleological view of male and female natures, serve as the foundation for his political perspective. Unlike Rousseau, Hegel is not tormented by the indeterminancy of the relationship between nature and nurture in the development of human (both male and female) nature. Hegel has already settled this question before he articulates his views on the family, civil society, and the state. Second, it should be noted that within the constraints of his presumptions on male and female natures, Hegel positions women as near to the universal as his perspective allows. In this effort, Hegel is forced by the logic of his argument to deny that any intrinsic worth and significance inheres in the lives of women as wives and mothers, even as he celebrates the worth and significance of the everyday lives of men as citizens.[63] A woman's worth reposes in her tenuous connection to the universal via the male; without this nexus the family, and thereby the woman, lack ethical significance by definition.

Suppose a woman were to internalize Hegel's perspective on women, their familial relationships, and their importance. She would be required to abstract from her intense, ongoing relationships with those particular, real human beings who are *her* children and *her* husband in order that she might instead realize ethical significance through a relationship to those abstract universals, husbands-in-general, children-in-general: transcendental forms of Children and Husband. As one couches the argument in this manner, it seems strained. No human being, as Hegel knew, can have a relationship with an abstract category; moreover, the rules which govern our moral life quite properly attach greatest importance to those obligations we have to the persons with whom we share a social existence.

Hegel's public world is composed of the differentiated, yet linked, realms he terms "civil society" and the "state." I shall examine the purposes Hegel assigns to the state by exploring the second foundation upon which his state builds (the family being the first), a realm of anarchic economic competition Hegel calls

---

[63] Wolff, "There's Nobody Here But Us Persons."

"civil society." Civil society, like the family, is a particularistic sphere. The raison d'être of civil society is private property and self-interestedness. Although the state is erected on the basis of the family and civil society, it is reducible to neither of them; indeed, the more comprehensive category, the state, gives to civil society as it does to the family its genuine meaning and worth. The family's tie to civil society lies in private property. Property gives the family its *external* existence which, as it "takes the form of capital . . . becomes the embodiment of the substantial personality of the family."[64]

To put it another way: private property and the "universal principle of freedom," tied to the protection of private property, act as powerful lures to draw the male individual "from his family ties" in order that he might realize his role as *homo economicus* within the individualistic realm of civil society. The apparent destruction or dissolution of family ties serves a necessary end: it prepares the male—for he alone is individuated from the family—for his subsequent involvement as a citizen in "the actuality of the ethical Idea," the life of the state. The state, in transcending the conflicts of civil society, embodies a concrete and authentic, rather than illusory and abstract, freedom. In the state alone, as in Aristotle's *polis*, man attains his highest individual and collective good and his most noble ends. "Everything that man is he owes to the state; only in it can he find his essence. All value that a man has, all spiritual reality, he has only through the state."[65] Once again: the public and the private coexist in a complex dialectic. The private, or nonpublic, realms acquire their meaning and worth via their links to the public sphere of the state. Outside the ordering context provided by the state, the family shrinks to a shadowy insubstantiality. Although the family and civil society comprise the necessary foundations for the state, they do not define the state in any important way. Quite the opposite: the state, in order to be a state, can be defined by nothing save itself. It is, to recall Aristotle's characterization of the *polis*, the "final and perfect association."

[64] Hegel, *Philosophy of Right*, p. 116.
[65] Cited in Taylor, *Hegel*, p. 379.

Yet Hegel ultimately fails to provide a believable account of how the ethical state is to come into being and, having come into being, maintain itself. The most serious flaw in Hegel's account of the public and the private does not lie in his failure to incorporate women within his universal category (this is a particular evaluation which may be rejected without abandoning Hegel's logic of explanation altogether), but precisely where Marx locates it: in Hegel's insouciance regarding the realities of economic power and the manner in which a predatory civil society vitiates the possibilities for a just public order. Although Hegel is haunted by the unity-destroying potentialities of private loyalties and purposes, he allows such a wide berth to the individualism of *homo economicus* that his political vision is imperilled.

There are other problems. A brief example will serve to illustrate one limitation of Hegel's political perspective. Hegel warns that "insular families" may impede a young man's transition to citizenship, and thus to universal consciousness, by goading the youth into a premature, exaggerated, tough individualism within civil society.[66] Hegel laments any "spirit of individualism" severed from "the universal purpose." He proposes to combat this individualism, not through a form of persuasion that calls the youth's capacity for reflexive self-consciousness into play and allows him to choose the more worthy alternative instead, through coercion. Deploying the state as the sole repository of the legitimate means of violence, Hegel would pack the individualistic young man and others like him off to war. In war, he observes, self-interestedness is banished and the collective predominates.[67]

[66] Hegel, *Phenomenology*, p. 497. Hegel observes that the community "gets itself subsistence only by breaking in upon family happiness" and "dissolving" it into the universal. In so doing, however, "it creates its enemy for itself within its own gates, creates it in what it suppresses, and what is at the same time essential to it—womankind in general. Womankind—the everlasting irony in the life of the community—changes by intrigue the universal purpose of government into a private end, transforms its universal activity into a work of this or that specific individual, and perverts the universal property of the state into a possession and ornament for the family."

[67] Hegel's discussion is chilling in part because his abstract proposal has been put into practice so often by governments who cynically conspire to achieve internal cohesion and national unity by going to war. This was standard practice

At this juncture the image of the citizen governed by public rules and reason fades to make way for an image of armed virtue and a public unity created, not through mutually shared social purposes, but through mutually shared external enemies.

I shall now come full circle by returning to the Hegelian subject, the terms of public and private identity, and the role of language in constituting and expressing each. For Hegel, man is the public being and woman the private being. But matters are more complex than that if we take Hegel's account of identity seriously. Just as the public world predominates and gives meaning to the private, for Hegel public identity is central because the public realm is preeminently the realm that fully defines and humanizes man. In serving the state, the man "is not serving an end separate from him, rather he is serving a larger goal which is the ground of his identity, for he only is the individual he is in this larger life."[68] Yet it is not only males whose identities are necessarily tied to the public world given Hegel's insistence that language is essential to a shared way of life and to linking public and private experiences, both of which are in some sense linguistically structured. Although man is the public being par excellence, woman experiences the public world through the mind-constituting medium of language as well. For if language gives form to our experiences of ourselves in culture and if public experiences and private experiences penetrate one another, then women, as language-using beings, will be linked directly (if passively, being denied an active role in the public realm) to the wider culture through their participation in a linguistic universe. All of us are tied in powerful, frequently unconscious but deeply felt ways, through wishes, desires, and dreams to a whole people. These intrapsychic links, which need not lead to action although they are a necessary feature of action, implicate both women and men.

Hegel doesn't allow for such a connection explicitly though it is a logical outgrowth of his method and his views on language. All participants in a linguistic community share a common tongue

---

of the Romanov tsars for centuries. Hegel blames willful and selfish mothers for rearing sons ill fit for their public destinies, thereby confirming his view that women are implacably resistant to universalism.

[68] Cited in Taylor, *Hegel*, p. 380.

and thus necessarily share in public meanings even if some are deprived of the possibility for public action.[69] (I am not implying that meanings are shared perfectly—only that they are shared importantly.) Man becomes alienated, Hegel continues, if his public experiences are drained of meaning. Such alienation must be woman's lot as well, at least in part, because even if women cannot act within the public world, they can still act, or believe they are acting, *for, or in the interests of* that world—sending off sons to die in war is one grim example. But if Hegel is correct, men, as the essentially defined public beings, should suffer a greater alienation and more serious loss of identity if public experiences fail to engage their highest meanings and define their highest aspirations. One might, at that point, see women as a kind of "saving remnant" who, given public decay, uphold the values and importance of the private sphere. But Hegel does not allow for this Rousseauian possibility: the private sphere is so thoroughly defined by the public that it, too, is denuded of its raison d'être with the breakdown of public meaning.

What happens when the public sphere as a unifying force and moral paradigm collapses? Hegel sees individualism as the result. Persons come to see themselves qua individuals, not as beings defined essentially by their membership in a political community. Paradoxically this development, which Hegel deplores, may arguably be the *only* means available to the woman to attain an identity other than a thoroughly privatized one. Unfortunately, the public identity of individualism is so readily absorbed into that predatory variant that predominates in bourgeois civil society, it may become a stopping point rather than a trajectory into a higher sense of self as a participant in the political community. That is, the terms under which identity as an individual is attained may vitiate the possibility for achieving a shared, social, political identity. This is a problem not yet confronted within contemporary feminist theory, and I shall turn to it in Chapter 5 below.

The political imagination informed by feminism is placed in an extraordinarily difficult position as one follows through on the implications of Hegel's position. The alternatives seem to come

[69] Cf. *ibid.*, p. 381.

down to this: (1) women may reject the individualism of contemporary society—the terms of predatory individualism including the "How to Get Yours" versions of feminism—but for what? (2) A possible alternative *in thought* would be the articulation of what a public identity for individuals would involve or require, including a revitalized concept of citizenship that could tap higher human motivations and serve as the locus of a political community. In the absence of such a political identity, women are left with: (3) interest group liberalism, a politics which draws out and requires self-interestedness as the supreme motivating force, or (4) a retreat into the private sphere (for feminists this must be viewed as at least in part a retreat given their concepts of the family), into a nonpublic existence as the central locus for the creation of self-identity.

Although these seem to be the alternatives Hegelian analysis allows, there are other possibilities. There is the religious identity which Hegel believed had been transcended historically, namely, membership in the city of God which ties individuals on this earth to a larger community of the faithful. This provides a public identity, not simply or merely a private one, but it is inadequate under the terms of Hegel's robust celebration of the state. Life as an aesthetic pursuit, a life of art, is yet another alternative. Hegel recognized art as a form of thought but argued that art could not attain the highest level of spirit and the clarity of philosophy.[70] Yet one finds intimations of art as a way of life in Hegel's work given the crucial role he assigns to it, and the fact that aesthetic experiences and consciousness are necessary steps in the struggle to attain full self-consciousness. In the absence of a vibrant public sphere, the life of art may be a worthy alternative. A third option is the vocation of the political theorist. To be sure, such an identity loses the name of action as "the theorist often plays out a kind of private politics."[71] For Hegel none of these possibilities is a fully worthy alternative to a public identity, as a citizen, in an ethical state. But for us to accept Hegel's judgment we must also agree to his conviction that the public sphere is altogether more

[70] My arguments here are based on my understanding of Hegel's aesthetic theory. See G.W.F. Hegel, *Aesthetics: lectures on fine art*, trans., T. M. Knox.
[71] Gunnell, *Political Theory*, p. 142.

noble and of greater purpose than the private. We must also agree that a political identity alone embodies and embraces the sphere of freedom and reason—this despite the fact that states have more often engaged in wars as a shared public purpose than in any other kind of public activity. We must also agree (for this is the only way to move from privatization to a public identity, even if we have given up on the attainment of Universal Spirit) that there is still room in our public sphere for World Historic figures, for heroes and founders, guardians and legislators. Yet John Gunnell suggests that a theory which requires such heroic figures may not be compatible with an open society, a society comprised of individuals with diverse, potentially conflicting public and private purposes.

I shall conclude my reflections on Hegel by returning to language and speech. Hegel's ideal is the full transparency of thought and of human speech. Abigail Rosenthal states: "It is the method of Hegel to show that breakdowns in speech . . . are needless."[72] Few of us would be willing to accept the possibility of full transparency as the chief criterion and end point of rational speech. If, however, one keeps the notion of clarity of discourse before the mind's eye as an ideal, even if unattainable in practice, it helps one to listen for *silences*, for breakdowns in human discourse, and to go on to ask *why* these silences occur. In this sense, Hegel remains vital in any move towards social transformation that pivots on the morally autonomous, speaking human subject.

KARL MARX: SPECIES-BEING AND AN END TO POLITICS

Marx's most forceful observations on the public and the private emerge within his condemnation of bourgeois society.[73] In Marx's view, the liberal state celebrated by Hegel as an ethical community is instead an illusion which fails to transcend the conflicts of civil society. Indeed, the state exists to serve the wealthy and the powerful. But its role in this process is masked by an ideology

---

[72] Rosenthal, "Feminism Without Contradictions," p. 38.

[73] Frederick Engels' *The Origin of the Family, Private Property and the State*, the key Marxist text on public and private, is examined in chapter 5 below.

which presumes a rigid split between the "private world" of business and commerce, as well as the private sphere of the family, and the "public world." According to liberal ideology, all distinctions of wealth, education, occupation, religion, race, class, and sex are left behind when bourgeois man enters the public realm in which all are formally equal to one another: one citizen, one vote. In fact, Marx declares, the distinctions the citizen supposedly leaves behind, all those matters which are social or private and hence not political, are the grounding of his objective reality: they are his real social relationships. Spheres of economic domination and subordination, exploitation and competition, are left untouched or are buttressed by the notion of a separate political realm in which such distinctions do not figure.

Liberal ideology presumes an abstract human being stripped of the attributes of his social existence; man is viewed as privatized and self-seeking, "withdrawn into himself, into the confines of his private interests and private caprice, and separated from the community."[74] Yet, combined with other similarly abstracted beings, he is said to be part of a political community. The "sophistry" which celebrates the bourgeois state as a genuine community helps to bring into being an individual who "not only in thought, in consciousness, but in *reality, in life*—leads a twofold life, a heavenly and an earthly life: life in the *political community,* in which he considers himself a *communal being,* and life in *civil society,* in which he acts as a *private individual,* regards other men as a means, degrades himself into a means, and becomes the plaything of alien powers."[75] Marx rejects the demarcation of public from private spheres as they are understood in bourgeois society and liberal ideology. Having "unmasked" the bourgeois state and shown that powerful interests are served by the bifurcation of the public sphere of politics from the private spheres of economics and the family, what alternative does Marx offer? Does he transform the relationship between the public and private as conceptual categories and social realities? Marx is not easy to pin

[74] Karl Marx and Frederick Engels, *Collected Works,* 3:154. The ups and downs of Marx's position on nearly everything are explored brilliantly in Jerrold Seigel's *Marx's Fate: The Shape of a Life.*

[75] Marx and Engels, *Collected Works,* 3:154.

down on these issues. I shall begin by considering his rejection of the public sphere and go on to explore his treatment of the family.

There is a clear shift between Marx's early and later views on the state. In an 1842 article for the *Rheinische Zeitung*, Marx writes with deep emotion of those powerful bonds which link the citizen to the state.

> Is not the state linked with each of its citizens by a thou-
> sand vital nerves, and has it the right to sever all these
> nerves because this citizen has himself arbitrarily severed *one*
> of them? Therefore the state will regard even an infringer of
> forest regulations as a human being, a living member of the
> state, one in whom its heart's blood flows, a soldier who has
> to defend his Fatherland, a witness whose voice must be
> heard by the court, a member of the community with public
> duties to perform, the father of a family, whose existence is
> sacred, and, above all, a citizen of the state.[76]

Marx later heaps scorn upon superstitious reverence for the state and declares that at such time as a generation has been reared in "free" social conditions it will be possible to have done with the state entirely—to throw it on the "scrap heap." He insists that the "existence of the state and the existence of slavery are in-separable."[77] One of Marx's goals was the abolition of politics and its replacement by administration.

Despite his apparently unequivocal condemnations of the state as an inherently evil and coercive organization erected as an in-strument of class domination, Marx leaves the door open for the creation of a real, not illusory, community. Unfortunately, Marx provides no compelling description of such a viable political com-munity. We know what it would not be: it would not be the state as arbiter between vying interest groups, nor the state as the means whereby a hegemonic class justifies and maintains its dominance.

The logic of Marx's analysis requires that the bourgeois private

[76] Marx and Engels, *Collected Works*, 1:236.
[77] Marx and Engels, *Collected Works*, 3:198.

sphere disappear with the downfall of the bourgeois state, for they turn on and require one another. Marx writes (in "Critical Marginal Notes on the Article by a Prussian") that if "the modern state wanted to abolish the *impotence* of its administration, it would have to abolish the *private life* of today. But if it wanted to abolish private life, it would have to abolish itself, for it exists *only* in a contradiction to private life."[78] By "private life of today" Marx refers not simply, or only, to the family, but to that entire economic sphere which, according to bourgeois thought, was located in an apolitical sphere as well. My concern for the purpose of this inquiry is with the private life of the family—that realm which chiefly implicates women. If one seeks a fully realized critique of the bourgeois family in Marx, one shall seek in vain. He does not take up the question explicitly. His views on the family must be teased out of his work.

Marx's most complete position on the family appears under his byline in an early article in the *Rheinische Zeitung*. In a discussion of a proposed Divorce Bill, Marx comes down squarely and unhesitatingly *for* the inviolability of the family *against* the individualists who, he claims, think only of rights, not of duties, and thus favor relaxing laws on divorce.[79] Marx embraces the Hegelian view that marriage is an ethical relationship which cannot be reduced to the terms of the legal contract with which it begins. Proponents of easier divorce laws forget, Marx continues, that they are dealing, not with *individuals*, but with *families*. Those who enter into marriage (here Marx reminds his opponents, somewhat disingenuously, that "no one is forced" to marry) are "compelled to obey the laws of marriage" which "cannot be subordinated to . . . arbitrary wishes; on the contrary . . . arbitrary wishes must be subordinated to marriage."[80]

Marx's repudiation of his early effusiveness on the mystical bonds which enmesh the citizen with the state is relatively clearcut; however, no similar rejection of his early position on the family exists. Marx's strictures against the bourgeois family are not a repudiation of the family per se. Those who wish, for their

[78] *Ibid.*

[79] Marx and Engels, *Collected Works*, 1:308.

[80] *Ibid.*

own purposes, to find a wholesale rejection of the family in Marx often cite the *Communist Manifesto* as proof that Marx believed that the family had already been eliminated among the proletariat and that the bourgeois family's days were numbered. Marx's depiction of the downfall of the family is regarded as an expression of his own antifamily views. This literal and credulous approach to a document like the *Manifesto* would no doubt amuse Marx. The *Manifesto* thunders with rhetorical flourishes and bristles with biting irony. Marx and Engels pile one purposeful distortion upon another. The *Manifesto* is intended to arouse the exploited and to infuriate their exploiters. A series of masterfully couched exaggerations proceeds in an unabated staccato throughout the text. For example, Marx claims that the bourgeoisie has reduced the family to money relations; that the bourgeois exploits his wife as "a mere instrument of production"; that "bourgeois claptrap about the family and education, about the hallowed co-relation of parent and child" is especially "disgusting" given the fact that modern industry has torn asunder "all family ties among the proletarians"; and that the children of the working class have been "transformed into simple articles of commerce and instruments of labor."[81] Each of these claims takes a portion of the truth and in the best tradition of political rhetoric makes it the whole.

It is clear from what Marx is raging against—turning children and women into instruments, ripping apart family ties among the proletariat, degrading social relationships into exchange relations—that he remains devoted to some ideal of a family life, untainted by the corrosive effects of exploitation. Indeed, his excoriation of the damage done to families under capitalism is inexplicable in the absence of such a commitment. Marx's criticisms make sense if one presupposes that in unmasking the bourgeois ideology of the family, which covers up both the reality of the self-interestedness of bourgeois private relationships and the destruction by the bourgeoisie of proletarian family ties, Marx appeals implicitly to an alternative state of affairs.

Further evidence for the view that Marx aimed at the transfor-

[81] Lewis S. Feuer, *Marx and Engels: Basic Writings on Politics and Philosophy*, p. 25.

mation or restoration of family life, not its eradication, may be found in *Capital*, Volume One. Marx observes that the English Parliament's moves towards legislation designed to assuage the worst abuses of child labor by proclaiming "the rights of children" is made necessary by the fact that "modern industry, in overturning the economic foundation on which was based the traditional family . . . had also unloosened all traditional family ties."[82] Misuse of parental authority and subsequent abuse of children did not create capitalist exploitation, including child labor; "on the contrary, it was the capitalistic mode of exploitation which, by sweeping away the economic basis of parental authority, made its exercise degenerate into a mischievous misuse of power."[83] Although this process is both "terrible and disgusting," Marx does not regret it entirely. He believes that the absorption of women "outside the domestic sphere," and of young persons of both sexes into the process of production will help to create "a new economic foundation for a *higher form of the family* and of relations between the sexes" (emphasis mine).[84] Marx fails to pursue this suggestion. He nowhere proffers a coherent vision of the structure and shape of relations between men and women, parents and children, within that "higher form of the family" he hopes industrialization will bring into being.

Finally, there is the passage from Marx's essay on "Private Property and Communism," one cited frequently by Marxist feminists. Marx argues that the nature of a society's relationships between males and females demonstrates the "extent to which the human essence has become nature to man, or to which nature to him has become the human essence of man. From this relationship one can therefore judge man's whole level of development."[85] The meaning of Marx's claims that there is some "human essence" that is, or ought to be, natural, and a nature that is, or ought to be, "human essence" is unintelligible without an explicit review of Marx's theory of human nature. I turn, therefore, to the question: What, in Marx's view, is human nature? Is that nature shared by men and women alike?

[82] Karl Marx, *Capital*, ed. Frederick Engels, 1:489.
[83] *Ibid.*   [84] *Ibid.*, 1:490.
[85] Marx and Engels, *Collected Works*, 3:296.

Marx, like Rousseau and Hegel, espouses a social theory of human nature. I have already contrasted a social theory of human nature with the abstract individualism of classical liberal contract theories. That Rousseau, Hegel, and Marx embrace an alternative to abstract individualism does not mean that their respective views on human nature are shared; indeed, each differs from the other in his account of the characteristics of human social nature and the relationship which pertains between and among social beings and their personal and political worlds. Following Rousseau, Marx observes that man as a member of civil society often appears as "natural man" when he is, in fact, man as constituted within history. Man does have a "natural essence" according to Marx. This essence is termed "human" even as man's humanity is characterized as "natural."[86] Marx writes of a "*human* essence of nature or the *natural* essence of man."[87] He begins with man in the generic sense—he does not pose divergent and separate natures for men and women—as a natural being, "a real, corporeal man,"[88] a repository for "certain powers" made known to him through felt "needs" which force their way to the attention of his consciousness.

Marx presumes that an individual will feel a need for whatever is necessary in order for him to realize his powers,[89] but he fails to provide evidence for this claim—he simply endows man with a need to realize his powers. Nature and its objects become the medium through which man's needs are met and his true essence is realized. Marx's human nature emerges finally as a composite: a quasi-Aristotelian teleology of givens ("needs" and "powers" and the "need" to realize "powers"), together with the shaping of man's nature in history and the presumption that man's nature is Protean, a reservoir of varied and nearly limitless potentialities which will be fully realized only when man's individual life and his species life "are not different," when the individual's "consciousness of species man confirms his real social life,"[90] a process that presumably implicates both male and female. When individ-

---

[86] *Ibid.*   [87] *Ibid.*, 3:303.   [88] *Ibid.*, 3:336.

[89] *Ibid.*, 3:303. For a full discussion see John McMurty, *The Structure of Marx's World-View.*

[90] *Ibid.*, 3:299.

ual life and species life have become an identity, man will be returned to himself: all splits will be healed. Communism (the only "fully developed humanism" which "equals naturalism") will come into being, for communism is "the *genuine* resolution of the conflict between man and nature and between man and man—the true resolution of the strife between existence and essence, between objectification and self-confirmation, between freedom and necessity, between the individual and the species."[91] Man as species-being is also a being for himself.[92]

Marx's perspective on human nature entails the claim that the authentic realization of that nature within history requires the elimination of *all* distinctions between the general and the particular, the universal and the individual, public and private, nature and culture, man and citizen, freedom and necessity, species-life and particular existence. Boundaries, divisions, tensions, conflicts, and limiting conditions melt away as Marx evokes a utopian vision of the restoration of man to "himself." He writes:

> Only when the real, individual man re-absorbs in himself the abstract citizen, and as an individual human being has become a *species-being* in his everyday life, in his particular work, and in his particular situation, only when man has recognized and organized his *"forces propres"* as *social* forces, and consequently no longer separates social power from himself in the shape of *political* power, only then will human emancipation have been accomplished.[93]

Marx's argument presumes that the "real, individual man" will somehow "re-absorb" into himself the "abstract citizen." How is this to come about? What personal or political imperatives will bring about such reabsorption? Is social life on any order of complexity possible without somewhat abstract ties between persons in their various social roles and capacities within diverse institutions? The painful conflicts Rousseau confronts are assumed away by Marx. We must ask, therefore, whether Marx's vision is coherent as it stands. He presumes and requires a thoroughgoing

[91] *Ibid.*, 3:296.　　[92] *Ibid.*　　[93] *Ibid.*, 3:168.

and total socialization of the individual (man's *forces propres* must be organized as social forces) within an emancipated human community. This community will require no structures of governance, no laws, no rules to adjudicate and adjust humanity's mutual relations, for Marx is assuming that all distinctions, boundaries, tensions will have melted away. Total harmony prevails. His community requires neither the vocabulary of traditional political discourse, nor the political activities concepts such as rights, order, and law helped to constitute.[94]

I shall pose one argument against Marx's account. If one adopts a view of the individual as complex, self-conscious, and potentially self-reflective, a being engaged in relationships with other beings within the framework of a particular historical, linguistic community, one has already undermined Marx's presumptions. One has set the stage for conflict as common meanings are never shared fully. If the human mind is active, not passive, one can never erect a political vision on the presumption that a uniformly shared, fully transparent, and uncritically created social consensus can be achieved on any important public or private issue.

Marx contrasts his version of species-life with the Hegelian perspective he found unacceptable insofar as it rested on those distinctions he would eliminate. Within the Hegelian framework, species-being is an abstract category which allows Hegel to move from individual particulars to this universal category. As deployed by Hegel, species-life is the combined totality of the activities of human beings within society. Because of the level at which the concept operates, Hegel does not presume that species-being requires concrete embodiment in each and every particular individual. If his vantage point shifts down to individuals, categories appropriate to that level of explanation are deployed. None of this is as obscure as it may seem. The following example should illustrate my point. In his twelfth-century tract, *De Monarchia*, Dante urged the notion of a *humana civilitas*, a concept he used to encompass Western Christendom. All persons in the Christian West were members of the *humana civilitas*, a totality greater than the sum of its parts. Yet no individual nor group of individuals

[94] See Duncan, *Marx and Mill*, p. 139.

could be singled out as embodying *humana civilitas* any more than an individual or group could embody species-life within Hegel's explanatory framework.[95]

In turning Hegel's concept of species-being on its head, Marx winds up in a muddle. Marx treats an abstract Hegelian category as one that can be located on the particularistic level; thus Marx requires the attainment of species-being, a universal category, *by* and *in* each and every *particular* individual if human emancipation is to be achieved. The effect of Marx's requirement that individual man and generic man must be identical if human emancipation is to be achieved has several important implications for theories of community and politics. Marx solves the problem of the public and the private Rousseau struggled with by eliminating the distinctions. With his eradication of the state, Marx drops politics and individuals as conscious political actors from his vision of the future; thus Marx avoids paying serious attention to the problem of political power and the need for safeguards against that power.[96] Marx rejects any effort to articulate a vision of politics as an arena within which individuals, in their roles as citizens, strive to achieve some common good. Just as he sweeps away the concept of the individual as a bearer of rights or a being of unique dignity and worth when he repudiates or undermines the philosophical and moral systems which served as the seedbed of such concepts, he denies politics, and with it the citizen, any role in his future society. There will, he insists, be no need for such activities and relations in communist society for politics exists only as a form of estrangement of man from himself in class society; politics is incompatible with human emancipation; politics serves only to protect privilege; politics, it follows, can never be transformed into a worthy human endeavor. This means that women who aspire to a public, political role are simply enacting a charade of false-

[95] Klaus Hartmann, "Hegel: A Non-Metaphysical View," in *Hegel*, ed. Alasdair MacIntyre, p. 110. For Dante's discussion of *humuna civilitas*, see *De Monarchia*, in *Monarchy and Three Political Letters*.

[96] Duncan, in *Marx and Mill*, says of Marx that he "contemptuously dismissed political safeguards against power and the powerful in such terms as 'the hackneyed forms of routine parliamentary democracy' " (p. 205). For Duncan, Marx is the most antipolitical of social theorists.

consciousness in Marx's view. The result is a thin notion of the human community and loss of the individual within an all-encompassing "social" category. Marx's incomplete accounts of his future community fail to make contact with concrete observations of various divisions of human powers and public and private activities in historic experience. Instead, one is left with the rhetorical claim that human beings may constitute and reconstitute themselves and their societies from a stance of naiveté, a kind of innocent eye blind to the force of social tradition and political passion.[97]

With the eradication of a world of necessity, all barriers to the full exercise of human powers would be removed. Man would be free insofar as his essence is freedom. But where does Marx locate this freedom? What is its substantive content? Marx urges that freedom is realizable in a community of persons who have been restored to themselves as "social" beings. "It is the positive transcendence of *all* estrangement" (emphasis mine).[98] Marx's myth of *Aufhebung* poses the dream of a return to some mythopoeic fusion of man and nature. Bertell Ollman admits that there are "few developments in communism which are as difficult to grasp or as far reaching in their implications as the substitution in people's minds of man the species for the separate and independent individuals each of us takes himself to be."[99] Ollman

[97] Stuart Hampshire, *Thought and Action*, p. 232.

[98] Bertell Ollman, *Alienation: Marx's Conception of Man in Capitalist Society*, p. 135.

[99] *Ibid.*, p. 110. Ollman goes on to speak of the individual's "integration" into the group and of the absorption of the particular within the general as the realization of human "freedom." He believes that exertions of the creative will in the future society will be "joyful, satisfying and fulfilling . . . rather than unpleasant and draining of the individual and of his capacities" (p. 119). It is difficult to see why this should be true unless one presumes that effortless achievement will be one byproduct of the attainment of communist society. Ollman also defends Marx's theory of community by insisting that the communist community will involve the realization of a "sincere and multifaceted relationship binding each individual to everyone else in his society. Such a bond can only come into existence after all artificial barriers to the mutual involvement of people have been torn down" (p. 118). The problem here is the lack of specificity as to what constitutes an *artificial* barrier and the concomitant lack of recognition of *real* constraints, including those of time, space, and the limitations of the body.

here reformulates Marx's claim rather than specifying it critically. How does one substitute "man the species" for the particularities of individuals? Do we simply "take" ourselves to be separate individuals, or are we not, finally, individuated entities who exist in particular bodies in time and space? Even if one finally resolves these issues a more serious problem looms. The processes of ego development require that a child, in order to learn a language and thereby become a social being, must learn to separate, individuate, classify, and identify particular objects of reference. Should a child fail in this task, his world would remain an inchoate stew, a blur of whirring images. Language use involves, by definition, a mode of classification and differentiation, and among those entities classified and differentiated we number, most importantly, human beings.

The absence of any account of human beings as creatures who give a spoken account of themselves is a serious blow to Marxism's claims to be a comprehensive social theory, for any such theory must provide for this "centrally human capability."[100] It is easy enough to see why language had to be expunged from Marx's discussion of the future emancipation of the human species. He ties language, including the terms of public and private discourse, too closely to the particular relations of class society. That is, language for Marx serves largely if not exclusively to cover up the harsh realities of capitalist exploitation. The Hegelian dialectic of self-conscious awareness is dropped as a linguistically grounded activity and with it the speaking subject disappears from view. The result, for women, is that their public silence is no more serious a question for Marx than the distorted public speech of men is. If the only voice in which man can speak is the voice of rationalization or false-consciousness, for women to be silenced does not assume the importance it must for the theorist committed to explaining public and private orderings of the world given in language, through a language which does not mystify those relations.

Taylor offers the following critique of Marx:

[100] Dunn, *Western Political Theory*, p. 106.

. . . Marx himself, early and late, held to a terribly unreal notion of freedom in which the opacity, division, indirectness and cross-purposes of social life were quite overcome. It is this picture of situationless freedom which underlies the unviable synthesis of expressivism and scientism, and which allows Bolshevik voluntarism to masquerade as the realization of freedom. . . . Now this freedom without situation is what Hegel called 'absolute freedom.' . . . This situationless notion of freedom has been very destructive. . . . Marx's variant of 'absolute freedom' is at the base of Bolshevik voluntarism which, strong with the final justification of history, has crushed all obstacles in its path with extraordinary ruthlessness. . . . [the notion that] our only situation will be that of generic man, harmoniously united . . . is not only unbelievable, but arguably unliveable. It would be an utterly empty freedom.[101]

When the individual, male or female, has no value outside the social whole, when no part of the human being is declared unavailable to social forces, "there is no theoretical barrier against social surgery of all kinds."[102] Like Plato, Marx eliminates the distinction between the public and the private but the cost is too high. He loses along the way the reflective subject central to any theory of politics which would serve both as a concrete historical analysis and as a force for nonrepressive social change.

Rousseau, Hegel, and Marx illustrate the complex and diverse possibilities which inhere within the Western tradition on the public and the private. Each, in his own way, is committed to social transformation and to some ideal of social life. Each recognizes the necessity of ordering or reordering public and private social relations and arrangements to attain his transformative or reconstructive goal. Each does it differently. Rousseau posits a number of ideal ways of life—virtuous citizenry, bourgeois households, natural unspoiled man and woman—but each requires, in

---

[101] Taylor, *Hegel*, pp. 557-558.
[102] Hampshire, *Morality and Pessimism*, p. 31.

a central way, the subordination of women to men. Rousseau's strength lies in his recognition that not all of social life can be brought under one overarching imperative and that there are diverse goods which can only be attained through alternative modes of public and private activity. He recognizes, however inchoately at times, that the qualities required for the patriotic citizen diverge from those qualities of forebearance and compassion which should animate the family. Rousseau's alternative to the empiricist way of seeing imbedded within liberal contractarianism enriches our understanding of the reasoning and passional human subject.

Hegel would solve Rousseau's dilemmas by ordering and giving meaning to all "lesser" institutions through their mediated connections to the state as an ethical community and the embodiment of reason and spirit. Like Rousseau, he privatizes and subordinates women. Unlike Rousseau, Hegel refuses to consider the ways in which foreclosing a public identity to half the population in his ideal state bodes ill for public ethics and private virtue alike. Hegel's commitment to an ideal of the state forces the attention of contemporary theorists, particularly those concerned with public and private issues, to the possibilities and pitfalls of a "political solution" to our contemporary malaise. The strength of Hegel's account lies in his rich articulation of the processes of human self-knowledge and consciousness tied to and constituted by language. Although Hegel himself doesn't allow women to attain full self-awareness, feminist thinkers in our time can appropriate his concept of the knowledgeable human subject in their articulation of a motive for, and legitimation of, modes of feminist inquiry and protest.

Finally, Marx deals with the problem of public and private by eliminating the distinctions altogether, or seeing the distinctions as dispensable. He contrasts an altogether unjust and exploitative present with a totally harmonious and free future but provides no coherent way for human subjects, male or female, to get from their current malaise to their future utopia. The weakness in Marx's account is his lack of attention to the language-using human subject and to the complexities of human self-consciousness; moreover, by repudiating political terms of discourse, Marx does not allow for *political* struggles, over time, to sustain as well as to achieve just societies. A strength of Marx's account is his recognition that the bourgeois private sphere, including the structure of work life and a society's economic relations, does not exist in some hallowed repose apart from and untouched by the public. By exposing the hypocrisy of the celebration of the family under capitalism even as family ties are weakened and eroded and family members exploited, Marx not only performed a vital theoretical and political service, he helped to lay the basis for considerations of questions of oppression, exploitation, and class that cut through the public and private conceived as bifurcated realms.

My examination of the public and the private in Western political thought has arrived at neither definitive answers nor conclusive definitions; instead, I have nurtured a complexity which is possible only as one gets inside alternative images of reality. I shall use that complexity as the touchstone of my critique and interpretation of contemporary perspectives on the public and the private which comprise Part II of this inquiry.

Part II

Contemporary Images of Public and Private: Toward a Critical Theory of Women and Politics

Reformers, martyrs, revolutionists, are never fighting against evil only; they are also placing themselves in opposition to a good—to a valid principle which cannot be infringed upon without harm. . . . Wherever the strength of man's intellect, or moral sense, or affection, brings him into opposition with the rules which society has sanctioned, *there* is renewed conflict between Antigone and Creon: such a man must not only dare to be right, he must also dare to be wrong—to shake faith, to wound friendship, perhaps to him in his own powers.—*George Eliot*

Chapter 5

Feminism's Search for Politics

The structure of the mind is being battered from the
inside. Some terrible new thing is happening. Maybe it'll
be marvelous. Who knows? Today it's hard to distinguish between the marvelous and the terrible.
—*Doris Lessing*

There are no neatly defined limits on the boundaries of politics.
Boundary shifts in our understanding of "the political" and hence
of what is public and what is private have taken place throughout
the history of Western life and thought. Minimally, a *political*
perspective requires that some activity called "politics" be differentiated from other activities, relationships, and patterns of
action. If all conceptual boundaries are blurred and all distinctions
between public and private are eliminated, no politics can exist
by definition. The relatively open-textured quality of politics
means that innovative and revolutionary thinkers are those who
declare politics to exist where politics was not thought to exist
before. Should their reclassifications stick over time the meaning
of politics—indeed of human life itself—may be transformed.
Altered social conditions may also provoke a reassessment of old,
and a recognition of new, "political" realities. Sheldon Wolin
observes: "The concepts and categories of a political philosophy
may be likened to a net that is cast out to capture political phenomena, which are then drawn in and sorted in a way that seems
meaningful and relevant to the particular thinker."[1] The thinker
who casts such a net must be prepared to set forth and to defend
the criteria she deploys when she sets about capturing political
phenomena. Under what rules does she sort the catch and to what
ends and purposes?

[1] Wolin, *Politics and Vision*, p. 21.

Feminist analysts—radical, liberal, Marxist, and psychoanalytic—share at least one overriding imperative: they would redefine the boundaries of the public and the private, the personal and the political, in a manner that opens up certain questions for inquiry. They would "break the silence" of traditional political thought on questions of the historic oppression of women and the absence of women from the realm of public speech. This silence-breaking takes a variety of forms depending upon the presumptions any particular feminist thinker brings to inquiry and the purposes she has in mind—issues which touch upon a number of vital debates. It should be noted at the outset that the leading articulators of feminist perspectives in our time have *not* seen as one of their major tasks making contact with what Wolin terms that "ancient and continuous discourse that began in the fifth century B.C. with the public life of the Athenian *polis* and the political discourse which centered around it and often against it."[2] This has been both a strength and a weakness: a strength because feminist thinkers have not felt constrained by the heavy legacy of "the fathers" and thus have moved in more innovative directions than they might have otherwise; a weakness because many of the vital concerns of political theory, of *any* political theory, including notions of citizenship and the basis of order in the political community have either been ignored or slighted.

In my treatment of thinkers and schools of thought in the Western tradition I brought to bear questions of one attuned to feminist issues. In this chapter I intend to bring the concerns of the political theorist to bear on feminism. This means, first of all, that I shall spell out the implications for politics of feminist accounts, implications which may remain unexplored by the analyst herself. It also means that the nature and meaning of feminist discourse becomes a subject for critical inquiry. What sort of language, public and private, do feminists propose women begin to speak? What public and private identities do feminists embrace as alternatives to previous social and personal definitions of women? How do feminists propose to redescribe social reality and expe-

---

[2] Sheldon Wolin, "The Rise of Private Man," *New York Review of Books*, pp. 25-26. Wolin argues that notions of the "public" are tied to other concepts, including citizenship, authority, the state, freedom, law, and civic virtue.

rience in order to reflect on what makes this reality and experience what it currently is, whether what is must be, or whether dramatic alterations are either possible or desirable? Another way to put this final question might be: how do feminists sort out which public and private experiences are ineradicably involved in what it means to be a human being within a world of others, and which alternatives can and should be transformed in order to reconstruct human identity, social experience, and reality itself?[3]

I sketched a number of alternatives for ordering the basic notions, public and private, in my Introduction. These included the subordination or elimination of public and private in favor of alternative concepts and symbols; the demand that the private world be integrated fully within, or subsumed by, an overarching public arena; the insistence that the public realm be "privatized" with politics controlled by the standards, ideals, and purposes emerging from a particular vision of the private sphere; or, finally, a continued differentiation or bifurcation between the two spheres treated either symmetrically or asymmetrically. It is important to keep in mind that notions of public and private have served to reveal as well as to conceal a multiplicity of human desires, purposes, fantasies, and activities. Just as politics is, in important ways, a defense against the pull of the private, it follows that the private, or better, understandings of "privatization" as they have emerged historically, serve to defend against the public. Feminist thinkers who propose to reorient themselves and others to and within the social world deal, whether implicitly or explicitly, with public and private imperatives which cut a number of ways—for and against traditional understandings of men, women, and their shared, yet separate, universes.

The chapter which follows is divided into four sections in which I take up, in turn, radical, liberal, Marxist, and psychoanalytic feminist perspectives in order to explore what happens within each to public and private speech, identity, and action. In my concluding chapter I develop the basis for an alternative to each of the perspectives I explore, drawing from each as I do. It is im-

---

[3] This question is suggested by a reading of Fay, *Social Theory and Political Practice*.

portant to note that the division between competing feminist approaches is not a precise one, having emerged over the past fifteen years in feminist thought and practice. There is some overlap between and among positions, but there are also important, not trivial, differences between each—differences that do not allow for easy resolution or some happy synthesis into one grand overarching feminist theory. A second observation is necessary: because feminist thought rarely takes the form of explicit political thought, by which I mean thought that takes as its object of inquiry and concern some entity called "the political community," it may seem, to some readers, unfair or strained for me to draw out of each feminist perspective such a political stance. For example: the radical feminist writer whose chief concern is to evoke passionate images of "woman" as the human embodiment of Nature, and to do so in the form of a poem, a metaphysical treatise, or a utopian vision, may claim that she is exempt from the sorts of questions and criticisms traditionally aimed at political theorists. She is creating a new universe; she has quit the old. But surely this will not do, for every feminist writer I shall examine is making the case for a reordering and restructuring of individual and social life. Anyone engaged in that activity touches politics and thus opens herself up to political critique. I begin with the radical feminist perspective.

RADICAL FEMINISM: "THE PERSONAL IS POLITICAL"

The radical feminist perspective emerges in a variety of forms or modes of discourse. It will be my task to state or to tease out the political implications imbedded in radical feminism whatever the form in which the perspective is presented. A simple way to clarify my interpretive and critical task is to state, and then go on to argue, that good poetry sometimes makes very bad politics; that evocative metaphors may bear within them disturbing implications for public and private identities even as they startle and illumine the individual in certain ways; that a stance of rage, incorporated within a utopian political urge, may bode ill for that

*ontological arguments =
typological thinking?
essentialism?*

civility necessary to a democratic politics.[4] I shall explore these and other questions by examining radical feminist views on male and female natures and their account of the history of human social relations, these two touchstones being inseparable and necessary to one another. As I move through the landscape of these complex issues I shall tie in questions of public and private identity and language in radical feminist thought. More disturbingly, I shall explore the key terms or categories of radical feminist discourse insofar as these usher in a debasement of the present and a call for a future utopia which shares certain roots with what might be called the antidemocratic impulse in politics.[5]

The radical feminist portrait of man represents, in some ways, an inversion of misogynist views of women. Even as woman has been portrayed historically as an evil temptress or a fount of idealized goodness rather than as a complex flesh-and-blood creature who is both noble and ignoble, radical feminists sketch a vision of the male that is unrelenting and unforgiving in its harshness. The view of male and female natures, respectively, forms the core of radical feminist thought. It is important to note that the radical feminist position on male and female natures is frequently couched on the level of ontology, that is, male and female being (or Be-ing, as some prefer to put it) is given a priori. Men and women, for some leading radical feminists, are born ''that way.'' The problem historically has been that the male, an aggressive and evil being, has dominated, oppressed, exploited, and victimized the female, a being of a very different sort.

By returning to ontological arguments, radical feminists turn back the philosophic clock. In effect, they repudiate what is called ''the epistemological turn'' in philosophy ushered in with the

---

[4] It should be noted that what might be called the ''facts'' of women's oppression—for example, the relative annual salary discrepancies between full-time male and female employees across all levels of employment—may be assimilated within a number of competing explanatory frameworks. The meaning adduced from such facts will differ depending upon the logic of explanation within which the facts are lodged. Facts are given meaning through their absorption into a conceptual framework.

[5] One work which treats the problem of social movements and fascistic imperatives is James Gregor, *The Fascist Persuasion in Radical Politics.*

breakdown of religious and theological domination of philosophical discourse.[6] In ontic discourse, being is prior to knowledge; therefore it has a status which renders it unamenable to questions of the human being as a being who comes to know concretely, in history and through time. The "epistemological turn" made possible the creation of a view of human beings as self-conscious subjects whose identity is not given but emerges as a result of each individual's attainment of subjective consciousness. The shift from ontology to epistemology opened the way for consideration of forms of mind, theories of the constitutive role of the subject in the construction of objects of knowledge, and, eventually, consideration of the social origin of different beliefs. This development was essential in the evolution of the modern subject. By repudiating the philosophic tradition that historically provided the basis for women to break free from the constraints of ontological definition, radical feminists play a very dangerous game. One dimension of this game is the implicit, at times explicit, contention that human beings are to be judged not by what they do or say but by what they *are*. In the case of men, what they are is corrupt to the core. No man can escape the taint of this original sin.

An early statement of radical feminist politics, that of Ti-Grace Atkinson, begins by declaring that all men qua men are ontologically "insecure and frustrated," beings who *must* (they have no choice about it) alleviate their frustration *through the oppression of others*.[7] Atkinson calls the process whereby men devour and dominate women "metaphysical cannibalism." She posits a nightmarish scenario in which men invade and take over women, creating a "sex-class" system. Atkinson then explains all of human history, including every society in the present, with reference to the features of the two sex-classes, male and female. (I shall

---

[6] This epistemological turn is associated with Descartes, Leibniz, Berkeley, Hume, Kant—all of whom turned the previous relation between ontology and epistemology upside down by deriving ontology, or being, from knowledge, with knowledge given primacy. I owe this insight to Robert Paul Wolff, though what I have made of it for the purpose of this discussion is my own responsibility.

[7] Ti-Grace Atkinson, "Theories of Radical Feminism," in *Notes from the Second Year: Women's Liberation*, ed. Shulamith Firestone, *passim*.

discuss below how Atkinson proposes to get out of this ontological iron cage.) All known societies, past and present, were or are nothing but the "ultimate outgrowth" of the nature of the male sex-class. Society "conforms" to male nature.[8]

In a second early discussion of male and female natures, men were called an

. . . obsolete life form. He is an anachronism in this technological context. His muscles are no longer needed. The built-in obsolescence of his physical and emotional nature is now apparent. The aggressive, destructive drives of man lack proper reasonable outlets. He is being phased out by technology. Sperm banks and test-tube babies can take over his last function, his only function that has positive effects for the human race.[9]

Men, the author continues, sustain their lives "at the expense of other better life forms. Until he gives up his existence, either voluntarily or by force, there will be no relief from suffering nor any moral progress on this planet."[10]

Susan Brownmiller's men (in *Against Our Will*) come into the world tainted from the start with an inherent lust for power. But women, in their inner core, remain unsullied.[11] Brownmiller de-

[8] *Ibid.* One ethological account with potentially reactionary implications is Lionel Tiger and Robin Fox's *The Imperial Animal*. Edward O. Wilson's *Sociobiology: The New Synthesis* is the key text in the "new" argument from biology. For a sympathetic but critical philosophic discussion of ethology and sociobiology see Midgley, *Beast and Man*.

[9] Betsy Warrior, "Man as an Obsolete Life Form," *No More Fun and Games: A Journal of Female Liberation*, p. 77. Three anthologies published around the same time give a sense of the thinking on women's liberation a decade ago. See Joanne Cooke, Charlotte Bunch-Weeks, and Robin Morgan, eds., *The New Woman*; Betty Roszak and Theodore Roszak, eds., *Masculine/Feminine*; and, the best of the the three, Vivian Gornick and Barbara K. Moran, eds., *Woman in Sexist Society: Studies in Power and Powerlessness*.

[10] Warrior, "Man as an Obsolete Life Form," p. 78. It is possible that Warrior is being ironic along the lines of Swift's famous proposal for ending the Irish famine. The problem, however, is that her essay hasn't the form of ironic discourse which involves at least two implied audiences.

[11] Susan Brownmiller, *Against Our Will: Men, Women and Rape*, p. 131. See

fends her move to ontic thinking by arguing that the use of the categories "all women" and "all men" as concepts given *in nature* with ineluctable social outcomes leads to a "higher political understanding" that she does not go on to specify. There is a problem with the abstracted nature of the categories—"all women," "all men"—that Brownmiller and other radical feminists give a universal, pan-cultural status. But for the moment I shall focus on her presumptions concerning human nature. What follows from man's lust for power, coupled with his "biological capacity to rape," is, according to Brownmiller, a set of factors "*sufficient* to have *caused* the creation of a male ideology of rape" (emphasis mine). This male rape ideology, she continues, is a "conscious process of intimidation by which *all* men keep *all* women in a state of fear."[12] To answer the question why a man is motivated to rape, Brownmiller simply repeats the claim which prompts the question in the first place: men rape because they can and because they are incorrigible by nature. The man who repudiates rape and does not engage in the activity nevertheless *covertly* approves of and benefits from the practice. His condemnation is skin-deep; his corruption goes to the depth of his being.

As I indicated, women are untouched by this male lust for power. But if, as Brownmiller insists, the male lust for power is a biological given, if it is coded into the genes, women must share in it too as they receive a full complement of genes from one power-mad creature, their biological fathers. Brownmiller never confronts this problem. We are left with the vision of a remorseless male with "just one thing on his mind." As a corollary, the image of women that emerges is that of an asexual innocent, a vision not unlike the nineteenth-century Victorian ideology of "good women." Brownmiller shares the tendency within radical feminism to portray women as Universal Victims. I discuss below the language of victimization and the implications for women themselves should they accept a description of social experience and history grounded in an unrelenting portrait of women as exploited

my critical review, Jean Bethke Elshtain, "Review of *Against Our Will*," *Telos*, pp. 327-342.

[12] Brownmiller, *Against Our Will*, pp. 14-15.

and demeaned, contributing nothing to culture, stuck in nature, forced to do "shitwork."

In Mary Daly's radical feminist theology we enter a dark, pre-rational nether world in which males are not so much power-mad avengers as ghastly, ghostly vampires. Daly's "demons" are pro-pelled by a need to suck the lifeblood of women. Men, she pro-claims, feed "on the bodies and minds of women . . . like Dracula, the he-male has lived on women blood."[13] In her latest text, *Gyn/Ecology*, an exercise in "metaethics," Daly further develops her demonology. Women, to become Hags, Spinsters, and Crones, to create a "Hag-ocracy," must "exorcise" those "demons who attempt to block the gateways to the deep spaces of this realm," demons who "often take ghostly/ghastly forms, comparable to noxious gases not noticeable by ordinary sense perception."[14] Women, that is women who are not "mutilated, muted, moronized . . . docile tokens mouthing male texts . . . Athena-like accom-plices," are of a piece with "the earth, the sea, the sky"—all "victimized as the Enemy of patriarchy."[15] Men, then, are de-mons; women, unless they are demonized, rendered moronic, and turned into "fembots," embody by definition another principle with its own inherent dynamic. This dynamic, if it is not blocked, requires that a woman become a Lesbian, a homosexual of a particular kind. Anyone, Daly argues, who is not Lesbian is "heterosexist," still "male defined."[16] This creates a dilemma,

[13] Mary Daly, *Beyond God the Father*, p. 172.

[14] Mary Daly, *Gyn/Ecology: The Metaethics of Radical Feminism*, p. 3.

[15] *Ibid.*, pp. 5, 8, 28, and 31. Cf. Susan Griffin, *Woman and Nature: The Roaring Inside Her*. In this evocative prose poem, Griffin traces patriarchal views on women and nature in Western culture. Her work serves as a history of scientific attitudes on questions of matter and spirit. The problem here as elsewhere is that radical feminists unfold what they see as the destructive historic effects *on* women of the view that women are closer to, or assimilated with, nature and that both must be conquered and dominated, and condemn those who held such views. Then they go on to excoriate the patriarchal culture they are angry at being excluded from—or that women were excluded from. As a final step, they embrace the terms of their historic exploitation by saying, in effect, "Yes, women are closer to nature or are one with nature. We must escape, transcend, or destroy culture for it is male," and so on. Griffin's book is a perfect example of powerful literature which would make for a sectarian or futile politics.

[16] Daly, *Gyn/Ecology*, p. 376.

even on Daly's terms: if male and female natures have an onto-logical status, how can the woman's Be-ing be stymied and blocked? Daly must explain, for example, why so many women do not share her views: simple, they have been taken over by the demons. But she allows for no similar alteration or mutation of male nature through contact with women. For Daly, women are clearly the weaker sex. History is one long tale of perfidy by men against women. Those women—the Hags, Spinsters, and Crones—who, argues Daly, attempted to revolt, were burned at the stake or destroyed in other ways. Women who weren't thus destroyed had sided with the enemy and come in for Daly's vitriolic scorn.

The status accorded male and female natures in Shulamith Firestone's radical feminist text, *The Dialectic of Sex*, diverges somewhat from that of Atkinson, Brownmiller, and Daly.[17] Firestone traces all of culture and history to a "rock bottom" that shares with methodological individualism the presumption that all social explanation can be couched in terms of "facts" about individuals. Firestone locates woman's historic oppression *in biology itself*, even before gender differences can arise. The sex distinction—the division of human beings into males and females—constitutes a *biological tyranny*, a "fundamental inequality." Firestone extends this "tyranny" to nonhuman animals; thus, within her perspective, one could speak of an "oppressed" female cocker spaniel, oppressed *because* she is female. Inequality, tyranny, and oppression are located within nature with social structures and arrangements reflecting this original distinction. These terms lose their meaning as part of the evaluative language of political discourse as they are placed in nature. The closest Firestone comes to defending her methodological individualism and reversion to prepolitical categories is with the following query: "Why pos-

---

[17] Shulamith Firestone, *The Dialectic of Sex*. Firestone traces her intellectual heritage to Simone de Beauvoir's *The Second Sex*. De Beauvoir, in turn, has praised Firestone's book: most unfortunately given its celebration of terrible forms of male-dominated scientism and technological authoritarianism. I take up what seem to me to be the most salient features of de Beauvoir's book, one that defies easy categorization, in Chapter 6 below. Much of de Beauvoir's discussion, for an American woman, seemed strained even when it first appeared in translation in 1953, particularly the sections on sexuality.

tulate a . . . concept of Otherness . . . when one has never seriously considered the much simpler and more likely possibility," namely, that the "fundamental dualism" from which all oppression springs lies in nature, in "the sexual division itself." With this declaration Firestone joins hands with anti-feminist biological reductionists in declaring that all human culture, society, and history "sprang directly" from the biological distinction between the sexes with its subsequent domination of one "sex-class" (males) over another (females).[18] I take up Firestone's way out of a biologically based "tyranny" and "oppression" below.

One further example shall suffice to clarify and complicate the problem of male and female nature in radical feminist discourse. Monique Wittig, in an essay entitled "One is not Born a Woman," criticizes the biological approach adopted by other radical feminists. Drawing upon Marxist discourse, Wittig insists that "women are a class, which is to say that the category 'woman,' as well as 'man,' is a political and economic category, not an eternal one." Those feminists who argue for a "natural" division between women and men, for an ontic account of the sexual distinction, "naturalize history . . . making change impossible."[19] Wittig's "materialist" alternative would allow women, first, to constitute themselves as a universal class and second, to move *beyond* the category of sex entirely by becoming Lesbian," the only concept I know of which is beyond "the categories of sex (woman and man)."[20] One finds in Wittig an urge to transcend a "sexed identity" altogether, rather than to celebrate being "born Woman." Wittig would escape being a "woman" by creating "Lesbian societies" in which women can designate themselves as new beings who do not have to interact with men in any way. In another variation on this theme, Marge Piercy, in her utopian feminist novel *Woman on the Edge of Time*, treats males with

---

[18] *Ibid.*, pp. 7-8. Anti-feminists have always wielded a biologistic fallacy with relish.

[19] Monique Wittig, "One is not Born a Woman," in *The Second Sex—Thirty Years Later: A Commemorative Conference on Feminist Theory*, pp. 70 and 72-73.

[20] *Ibid.*, p. 70.

hormones so they, too, can suckle infants.[21] There have been, and are, suggestions that women could reproduce parthenogenically if science were not in the hands of patriarchs who have hidden this knowledge from them, or that the male body should be tampered with—surgical introduction of wombs, for example, would enable or require men to go through what Firestone calls the "barbarism" of pregnancy.

The urge to escape sexual identification altogether, or to celebrate it as *fully* definitive of the self, share in common a blurring of any distinctions between public and private identities. Radical feminist discourse is infused with that "terribly unreal" notion of freedom criticized by Charles Taylor (see Chapter 4 above) that is at work in the notion that the "opacity, division, indirectness and cross-purposes of social life" can be "quite overcome."[22] The social world, from top to bottom, is one long, unmediated conduit permeated throughout by male oppression of the female, whether the male is defined as a natural aggressor, a demon, a member of the universal male sex-class, or a simple oppressor who has throughout history taken advantage of his superior physical strength. For radical feminists, human beings cannot be both "this" and "that" depending upon the social context, the purposes they have in mind, the ends they seek, the underlying motives or reasons for their actions in diverse spheres. We are instead "this" *or* "that": victims or victors, oppressed or oppressor, exploited or exploiter. Their simplistic understanding of human nature becomes even more evident as one moves to examine the core categories of radical feminism as social and political explanation. What one finds, astonishingly, is a reversion to patriarchal explanation reminiscent of Filmer!

It is important to recall that *patriarchy*, as a historic way of life, was a precapitalist social form. The mode of production was based on land-holding; social relations were characterized by primogeniture and entail and defined by status rather than by contract.

---

[21] Marge Piercy, *Woman on the Edge of Time.* Many women have had the distressing experience of finding men as well as women who endorse this horrific intrusion on the human body and life processes. The men who embrace the possibility of having their bodies "made over" evince deep self-loathing.

[22] Taylor, *Hegel*, p. 557.

All of life was suffused with a religious-royalist ideology which was patriarchal in nature. A kingly father reigned whom no man could question for he owed his terrible majesty and legitimacy to no man but to God. All lesser fathers within their little kingdoms had wives and children, or so patriarchal ideology would have it, as their dutiful and obedient subjects even as they, in turn, were the faithful and obedient servants of their fatherly-lord, the king. For radical feminism, patriarchy still exists as a universal, pancultural fact, a description of all human societies, and an explanation of why each society is what it is in all its aspects. Radical feminists have resurrected an unrelenting patriarchal ideology.

Millett, for example, who rejects an ontology of male and female natures, seeing men and women as the "sum total" of their respective gender identity development, nonetheless declares that all of contemporary America, "family, society, and the state" is patriarchal.[23] Patriarchy, for Millett, is a category with which to characterize and explain the social world. Radical feminists revert to that family analogy which involves seeing the state and all its arrangements as the "family writ large" and which was overthrown as the preeminent mode of political argumentation with the victory of liberal-contractarian discourse. Millett's views are shared by contemporary male *defenders* of patriarchy. Steven Goldberg, for example, adopts premises identical to Millett's and shares her description of the social world in his book, *The Inevitability of Patriarchy*. With Millett and other radical feminists, Goldberg claims to have found the elements to which "every society that has ever existed" conforms.[24] According to Goldberg, the universality of patriarchy is an acknowledged anthropological fact.

The theoretical problem with attempts to explain and describe every society with a single notion are many. Comparing the way of life of Mbuti Pygmies with that of a complex, technological modern society like our own, for example, and labeling both patriarchal is rather like trying to derive an elephant from an earthworm. At a certain point differences in complexity beget

---

[23] Kate Millett, *Sexual Politics*, p. 33.

[24] Steven Goldberg, *The Inevitability of Patriarchy*. See also Jean Bethke Elshtain, "The Anti-Feminist Backlash," *Commonweal*, pp. 16-19.

differences in kind. To use a single category to explain the social organization of all societies is to place oneself, in the case of feminist and anti-feminist argument alike, on a Procrustean bed and to distort the variability, diversity, and manifold richness of different ways of life, then and now. A monocausal explanatory approach also ignores the nuances of linguistic communities and the fact that the same word (in translation) may mean very different things to alternative ways of life. Rather than studying history, patriarchalists, then and now, caricature it. Martin King Whyte, who did a scholarly study on the status of women in preindustrial societies, concludes that there is no "pattern of universal male dominance but much variation from culture to culture in virtually all aspects of the position of women relative to men."[25]

Within a patriarchal *Weltanschauung*, feminist or anti-feminist, the public and private recede as basic notions and guiding orientations to the world. Other notions and images move to the foreground either as corollaries or spin-offs of the patriarchal presumption or as implicit or explicit contrast models. One contrast model frequently favored by radical feminists is matriarchy, which is seen as a female-dominated Golden Age before male perfidy led to its downfall. This is a feminist variant on the Garden of Eden. The aim of radical feminist politics is to return to, or recreate, the matriarchal heaven when women held absolute power but were absolutely pacific, at least towards one another. I shall take up this theme in my treatment of the utopian impulse in radical feminist thought in a moment, but first I shall make a final claim *against* the category of patriarchy as it is used in radical feminist social explanation. Then I shall ask if the term nevertheless serves an important function on the level of metaphor, or as an expression of some psychic or emotional truth.

The following were the conditions for patriarchy historically: (1) the father's power was absolute and, sanctioned by religious or official authority, "political" in its essence; (2) women and children were (said) to be dutiful and obedient subjects; (3) male

---

[25] For a critique of oversimplified, ahistoric approaches to women's history, see Martin King Whyte, *The Status of Women in Preindustrial Society*.

children alone could inherit property, be educated, and have a public role; (4) female children were told when they could be married, and to whom, even as they were kept uneducated, disinherited, and privatized; (5) this patriarchal structure was kept in place through a reinforcing ideology which permeated all levels of society, up to and including its absolutist monarchy.

Should one or more of these criteria of the historic patriarchal order pertain within contemporary American society, the case for patriarchy *as social explanation* would have a kernel of theoretical coherence. But not a single one of the above conditions pertains. The result of the most cursory comparison between Filmer's sixteenth-century world and our own makes it clear that whatever it is we now have, and however we may finally choose to characterize it, post-mid-twentieth century life in an advanced capitalist, pluralist society is so far removed from the contours of the paradigmatic case that to label both "patriarchal" is to muddle and distort reality. The conceptual fiat involved in labeling a society patriarchal doesn't make it so: the analyst is obligated to show why, how, and where this is true. The analyst who insists upon the appellation should tell us why such usage remains apt despite the revolutions brought into being in the wake of industrialization—democratization; the technological explosion; formal-legalistic equality for women; the ideology (and, to be sure, imperfect practice) of equal opportunity; the breakdown of barriers to female education, employment, and political participation (imperfectly realized, as yet); the triumph of a secular over a religious world-view—all these phenomena and others which eroded the props of historic patriarchy.

Suppose one shifts the term "patriarchy" to another level—that of metaphor, or as the expression of a truth with emotional resonance, a piece of psychic reality, although patriarchy as a social form no longer holds, at least not for advanced industrial societies. (This is *not* to argue that male dominance of various professions, activities, and roles has ended. Male dominance and an absolute patriarchy are not the same thing, though the one may be a concomitant of the other.) Iris Marion Young points to a problem with metaphors: that they may initially enable us to see the world in new and startling ways, but as "they become worn, too familiar to be visible, they assume a constraining power."[26] The excessively deferent wife, for example, who concurs with everything her husband says and does, supports him in every wifely way imaginable, professes herself to be happy, yet weeps for "no reason" may find the terms "patriarchy" or "male dominance" or "sexism" liberating in that they help her to rethink the terms of her personal and social experience. But to substitute these terms, or any other, for ongoing reflexivity, ongoing rethinking of one's experience and one's basic notions, after a time makes one's thought and analysis go flat, stale, dogmatic. This helps to explain "the broken record" syndrome one experiences as one works one's way through radical feminist texts. One begins to see that repetition of key words, whether as explanation or metaphor, can become a substitute for thought.

There is yet another level in the puzzle of patriarchal ideology, claims that the male is everywhere "supreme," in the hands of feminists. For the flip side of the image of absolute male dominance is one of absolute female subordination. Let me note the following as a possibility for why the term patriarchy has become such a ubiquitous catchall in radical feminist discourse. Recall for a moment the discussion of the dynamics of internalization and projection in the critique of John Stuart Mill. The salient feature of that discussion was an argument that external reality is not, crudely, what is "out there," but complicatedly both inner and outer: reality as "perceived." That perceived reality may begin as some inner image, fantasy, fear, or desire which is first projected outwards, then taken in as external reality. I suggested that part of what women have suffered from over the years is man's inability to tolerate his feminine aspect with the subsequent development of "hard" social forms, all the life-denying paraphernalia of the modern state replete with a vast engine of death (also known as the military "hardware"), to counter his own "softness."

Clearly, there is a similarly defensive aspect in feminist evo-

---

[26] Iris Marion Young, "Is There a Women's World?—Some Reflections on the Struggle for Our Bodies," in *The Second Sex—Thirty Years Later*, p. 44.

cations of patriarchy—absolute male supremacy everywhere, total female subjugation everywhere. What may be at work is the inability of some women to tolerate their "masculine" side: a serious problem as each one of us is inescapably both male and female. The repudiated masculine aspect is projected outward as a piece of negative identity. As such it becomes a screen behind which the fearsome images of *them* appears, and is then internalized as external reality. *They*, males everywhere and for all time, stand *against us* as remorseless foes or as Brownmiller's deceptive nonrapists who claim to be opposed to violence against women yet use rapists as their "shock troops" to keep women down. Perhaps there is also at work a defense against politics and a public world for so long associated with men. This defensive posture may lead to a celebration of female separatism that requires a retreat from the world as well as a wholesale condemnation of it. The reversion involved is into a world where all is warm, supportive, uncritical, a world, in Daly's words, "beyond compromise."[27]

A second key imperative of radical feminist explanation is the erosion of any distinction between the personal and the political. Note that the claim is not that the personal and political are interrelated in important and fascinating ways previously hidden to us by sexist ideology and practice; nor that the personal and the political may be analogous to one another along certain axes of power and privilege, but that the personal *is* political. What is asserted is an identity, a collapse of the one into the other. Nothing "personal" is exempt, then, from political definition, direction, and manipulation—neither sexual intimacy, nor love, nor parenting. There is a total collapse of public and private as central categories of explanation or description. The private sphere falls under a thoroughgoing politicized definition.

If there are no distinctions between public and private, personal and political, it follows that no differentiated activity or set of institutions that are genuinely political, that are, in fact, the bases of order and of purpose in a political community, exist. What does exist within the radical feminist script is pervasive force,

[27] Daly, *Gyn/Ecology*, p. 40.

coercion, and manipulation: power suffusing the entire social landscape, from its lowest to its loftiest points. Just as the personal
is political, politics is power. Because power is everywhere so
is politics. Power, Millett toughly declares, is "the essence of
politics";[28] it follows that politics is ubiquitous, that politics is
everything, because power defines all relationships.[29] Nancy Henley interprets the "personal is political" this way: "Basically it
refers to the position that there is nothing we do—no matter how
individual and personal it seems—that does not reflect our participation in a power system."[30] For Henley the options appear
to be either dominance or submission and this is consistent with
the power-definition she adopts. For Atkinson, "Politics and political theory revolve around [this] paradigm case of the Oppressor
and the Oppressed."[31] What is subjected to a thoroughgoing politicization in this perspective is the relationship between the two
"universal sex-classes" on all levels everywhere, including the
family. It is important to note that the politicization of the family
takes place *under* the presumption that the "patriarchal" family
serves essentially and preeminently as a power arena and bastion
of male supremacy.

What follows from the "personal is political" and the relentless
power definition of social reality? For Atkinson, in her world of
Oppressor and Oppressed, the only alternative is to reverse who
is oppressing or metaphysically cannibalizing whom. There is no
reconstructive or transformative vision; rather, we are presented

[28] Millett, *Sexual Politics*, p. 25.

[29] By confining politics to power, Millett links herself with status quo political
scientists who have been the target of radical or nonmainstream scholarship for
several decades. Anti-status quo thinkers have struggled to defend the view that
thinking about politics in substantive rather than instrumentalist terms requires
going beyond the confines of power to a consideration of justice, equality, the
"good society." Millett and other radical feminists who celebrate a power definition of politics represent a retrograde force, if they are situated within current
debates in the field of political science.

[30] Nancy Henley, *Body Politics: Power, Sex, and Nonverbal Communication*,
p. 197. I wish to commend Henley's book in other ways as it offers a fascinating
peek into what it is we are doing with our bodies when we stand, move, touch,
etc., in certain ritualized ways.

[31] Ti-Grace Atkinson, "Theories of Radical Feminism," p. 37.

with the ugly form of politics as *ressentiment*. In Brownmiller's hard world, all of the central features of the male power structure remain intact but women come to control these structures coequally. This will mean a cease-fire in the sex war. That war can never end, however, given its location in male being. Brownmiller casually indicates that armies will probably be around for a while and they, too, "must be fully integrated, as well as our national guard, our state troopers, our local sheriffs' offices, our district attorneys' offices, our state prosecuting attorneys' offices—in short the nation's entire lawful power structure (and I mean power in the physical sense) must be stripped of male dominance and control—if women are to cease being a colonized protectorate of men."[32] Women must prepare themselves for combat and guard duty, for militarized "citizenship." Brownmiller began plans for the Brave New World by learning "how to fight dirty" and, as a bonus, learning that "I loved it."[33] The striking thing about Brownmiller's response to the male will to power is its own machismo cast: raw power, brute force, martial discipline, uniforms, militaristic law and order with a feminist face.

Firestone's future—and with this I shall lead into the disturbing question of an antidemocratic impulse in radical feminist politics—offers us the cybernetrician as the modern saviour.[34] Her scenario for salvation runs roughly like this: (1) free women from

[32] Brownmiller, *Against Our Will*, p. 388. [33] *Ibid.*, p. 403.

[34] I shall point out one example of Firestone's irresponsibility as a scholar. She claims, in a note on page fifteen of *The Dialectic of Sex*: "For example, witches must be seen as women in independent political revolt: Within two centuries eight million women were burned at the stake by the Church—for religion was the politics of that period." Leaving aside the claim that witches were, simply, women "in independent revolt," and passing over the claim that these witches were "burned by the Church" (the Church was forbidden to shed blood so executions were all carried out by the secular arm), in order for eight million women to be burned at the stake over a span of 200 years (Firestone never says *which* two centuries) means that an average of 109 women per day, 365 days per year, for 200 years were put to the torch. Firestone's claim is not only implausible, it is impossible and flies in the face of evidence. I have found no responsible scholar of this period, male or female, who affirms her rhetorical assertion. I shall simply note one of the recent major studies: Richard Kieckhefer, *European Witch Trials: Their Foundation in Popular and Learned Culture, 1300-1500*.

biological "tyranny"; (2) this freeing will undermine all of society and culture which is erected upon biological "tyranny" and the family; (3) all systems of oppression, including the economy, state, religion, and law erected upon the family will erode and collapse. The woman who internalizes Firestone's ideology can work to achieve Firestone's future by *seizing control* of reproduction and *owning* her own body. A hard-edged, calculated intrusion of market language into all aspects of life—once the private is deprivatized—is characteristic of Firestone's evocation of the future.

Ultimately, Firestone continues, test-tube babies will replace biological reproduction as the chief means of reproduction, pregnancy having been declared "barbaric" with the "fat lady" being peered at by strangers, laughed at by insensitive children, and deserted by feckless husbands. Full victory is achieved when every aspect of human life rests in the beneficent hands of a "new elite of engineers, cybernetricians."[35] This cybernetic elite will wield its totalistic control for good and benevolent ends. It is only fair to note that Adrienne Rich, in her exploration of motherhood, repudiates calls for technological control of reproduction and state takeover of child care. The problem with Rich's account, one that is very moving in places, is her insistence that "under patriarchy" the family and mothering will remain terrible and debased. Since "under patriarchy" is where we all are, in her view, it is hard to see any way out save the one she favors: separate female communities.[36]

What happens to politics in Firestone's new world? Like the family, it has disappeared, though of course there was no real politics in her prefuturistic society either, just control, oppression, and tyranny, natural-*cum*-political. Within her cybernetized utopia, a series of isolated human calculators of marginal utility run rampant. Abstract Man, Woman, and Child engage in a hard-edged pursuit of the best deal. The child, for example, with no

[35] Firestone, *Dialectic of Sex*, p. 201.

[36] Adrienne Rich, *Of Woman Born: Motherhood as Experience and Institution.* Rich is on target in arguing that mass child-care "in patriarchy has had but two purposes: to introduce large numbers of women into the labor force, in a developing economy or during a war, and to indoctrinate future citizens," p. xiv.

need to be "hung up" by authoritarian parents, may bargain for the latest deal in contracted households. Firestone calls this total breakdown of community "freedom," yet insists that this total freedom is also total community. Her feminist future emerges as a hybrid admixture of the "hard" and the "soft." This becomes clear in her discussion of male and female modes, the "hard" and the "soft" on a grand scale. Firestone discusses these abstractions as if they had real agency in the world. At one point a "cultural revolution" occurs, a fusion of masculine and feminine modes resulting in an explosive "sum of their integration," characterized thus: "A matter-antimatter explosion, ending with a poof! culture itself."[37] This yearning for the apocalypse, for some totalistic solution of all human woes, for a thoroughgoing fusion of all principles, represents a utopian fantasy with regressive implications: at least that is the way it plays politically.

In order to evoke my sense of foreboding at the implications of tendencies internal to radical feminist discourse as political prescription, I must pick up another thread which weaves its way through radical feminism. The thread is an anti-intellectualism flowing from acceptance of the split in empiricist epistemology between thought and feeling, reason and passion, experience and knowledge. From its inception, radical feminism has eschewed what it called male-identified structures of thought. A politics that "begins with our feelings . . . that's how we know what's really going on,"[38] proclaimed one radical feminist manifesto. What ends do feminists who celebrate a politics of feeling have in mind insofar as political theory and practice is concerned? There is, first of all, a yearning for a *societas perfecta*, a sisterhood of the "feeling," purified from male rationality. The tendency to promote what Susan Sontag has called a "rancid and dangerous antithesis between mind . . . and emotion," a bifurcation which is not only banal but serves as "one of the roots of fascism," is my concern.[39]

---

[37] Firestone, *Dialectic of Sex*, p. 190.
[38] "Our Politics Begin with Our Feelings," in Roszak and Roszak, *Masculine/Feminine*, p. 285.
[39] Susan Sontag and Adrienne Rich, "Feminism and Fascism: An Exchange,"

male-identified woman = radical feminist term (?)

There is more: I mentioned the regressive utopian urge to return to a womb-like community where no voices speak in discord, where there is only harmony and agreement and love. Such communities provide a total definition of the person: everything one does or says is personal/political. One no longer speaks as an autonomous individual but as woman-identified woman, fused with others, seeking union finally with the Great Mother. Charlotte Beradt, in a chilling volume, *The Third Reich of Dreams*, reports on dreams she recorded in the early years of the Third Reich. The dreams demonstrate the conflicts that arose as individuals strove "to keep politics from robbing their existence of its meaning."[40] The politics that was robbing lives of meaning was a totalistic edifice which aimed to consume all of life, to allow for a single *public* identity. The most poignant aspect of the dreams was the anxious flight into the only sphere of privacy remaining, the dream, only to discover, in some instances, that one's dream-thoughts had taken on the cast of the public world. "I dreamt I was no longer able to speak except in chorus with my group," said one dreamer to Beradt.[41] The means of expression characteristic of the totalitarian milieu or the "total community" is the *Sprechchor*, the chorus, not individuals but vehicles. This is where dreams of fusion wind up; this is the way they play politically.

Cut off from a political imperative, such dreams evoke uncon-

---

New York Review of Books, p. 32. Sontag had been taken to task by Rich for her putative lack of feminist fervor.

The conceptual connections to an authoritarian impulse go beyond this, however. As J. P. Stern points out in his brilliant study, *Hitler, The Fuehrer and the People*, fascism begins and ends with an *overpersonalization of politics* ("the personal is political" with a vengeance), a process which leads to a stress on personal "authenticity" as "the chief value and sanction of politics" (p. 24). All "impersonal" dimensions of political thought and action, including public law, relatively stable and secure social institutions, and contestable terms of political discourse, are first scorned and then destroyed as the product of overintellectualized, inauthentic, unnatural beings, or, in radical feminist terms, males and male-identified females. (See also Elshtain, "Review of *Against Our Will*," n. 8, pp. 240-241.)

[40] Charlotte Beradt, *The Third Reich of Dreams*, p. 32. Cf. Norman Mailer's plaint, not unjustified, against Millett's distortion of the literary works of Lawrence, Miller, and Mailer himself. See Norman Mailer, *The Prisoner of Sex*.

[41] Beradt, *The Third Reich of Dreams*, p. 87.

scious memories of union with the mother, what Freud called the "oceanic feeling," and lie at the heart of romantic discourse. Adrienne Rich, for example, writes of "The drive to connect,/ The dream of a common language," in her poem, "Origins and History of Consciousness."[42] The impulse to fuse may work itself out in utopian novels like Charlotte Perkins Gilman's *Herland*, a humorous satire on masculine and feminine.[43] But the radical feminist texts I have criticized as being suffused with regressive urges are not proffered as romantic dreams but as genuine blueprints for a realizable future, including Marge Piercy's *Woman on the Edge of Time* which, though a utopian novel, is nonetheless to be taken seriously, as a vision of the future. What I am saying here is that the way it plays poetically may or may not, depending in part on the author's intent, in part on the reader's mind-set, in part on the social context, usher in politically dangerous demands. This is a problem radical feminists have yet to consider seriously, in part because their discourse gets in the way.

There are several radical feminist approaches to language: one is a tough, hard language filled with talk of power, exploitation, manipulation, and violence. The other is an overblown ontological language which represents the flip side of Hobbesian nominalism. The best example of this genre is Mary Daly's metaphysical or "metaethical" language of demonology. It may be well to recall that Hobbes was reacting against metaphysical language within which individuals were suffocated by, or suffused with, ontic categories. His own solution—to reduce humans to matter in motion—was extreme. Daly returns to a mode of discourse which is the verbal equivalent of military overkill. She sees herself as creating a new language, the old being totally male-dominated, thus breaking and alienating every female 'I' who must speak and write it.[44] The other possibility is to move to a realm beyond

---

[42] Adrienne Rich, *The Dream of a Common Language: Poems 1974-1977*, p. 7.

[43] Charlotte Perkins Gilman's *Herland* is an example of feminist utopianism emerging from the first feminist wave. In her introduction to this previously lost fiction, Ann J. Lane discusses nineteenth- and twentieth-century utopian novels as one perennial mode of feminist expression.

[44] Daly, *Gyn/Ecology*, p. 19.

language, to a language that does not differentiate or classify objects of reference but is the medium of fusion with some greater whole. Again, conceptual similarities to fascism, which also insisted that the old language and reason was thoroughly false, debased, and unacceptable, arise. Anti-democratic politics utterly rejects human discourse. Language must no longer serve, *as it must* for otherwise it would not be language, as a "divisive instrument,"[45] as an expression of diversity and variability. Perhaps the apogee of this mistrust of language is Daly's insistence that Lesbians must imitate/learn from the language of "dumb" animals, "whose nonverbal communication seems to be superior to androcratic speech."[46] Daly cites several conversations she has had with animals and translates a few of those conversations; needless to say, all the animals shared her perspective and none contested her position.

One final turn of this troubling issue and that is the language of radical feminist description—the way the social world is characterized and the way woman is portrayed as debased, victimized, deformed, and mutilated, as a cunt, a hag, and a piece of ass. Description always takes place from a point of view and hence is evaluative. We describe situations on the basis of those aspects of the situation we deem relevant or important. In this way, we always evaluate under a certain description.[47] Description is to a purpose and constitutes an evaluation that either opens events up for critical scrutiny from a moral point of view or forecloses our capacity to examine them in this way. A serious problem of choice emerges for the thinker who wishes to describe a situation in a way that simultaneously condemns it. If the descriptive language is too muted—saying, for example, that workers on an assembly line are not "fulfilled"—the moral and political point may be

---

[45] Lessing's moves to give up language and to celebrate telepathic or nonverbal communication as superior may be found in *The Four-Gated City* and, most prominently, in *Briefing for a Descent into Hell*. Having given up, first on language and then on those who use it, Lessing has now junked the entire planet and is sending messages from outer space. See Doris Lessing, *Shikasta: Canopus in Argos: Archives, Re: Colonised Planet 5.* Cf. Jean Bethke Elshtain, "Doris Lessing: Language and Politics," *Salmagundi*, pp. 95-114.

[46] Daly, *Gyn/Ecology*, p. 414.

[47] Julius Kovesi, *Moral Notions*, p. 63.

lost. Overstating the descriptive case, saying that such workers are "hideously enslaved, reduced to robots" may backfire as the overinflated description raises in the reader's mind the suspicion that the describer "protests too much," that things can't possibly be all that bad. Most troubling of all, some feminists who set out to describe in order to condemn may, in their very description, embrace the terms of their own degradation. This is a complicated point and I shall try to unfold it.

Powerlessness begets a distortion of self-understanding. The slave may come to see himself as the master sees him, he may, for example, embrace his own slavishness. Similarly, "the woman, by willfully defining herself as 'the exploited,' as 'victim'; by seeing herself as she was reflected in the male's perception of her," may seek thereby to attain some power over men, some measure of control.[48] This process varies from one social epoch to the next as the terms of male perceptions of women change. What is distressing is the repeated evocation in feminist discourse of images of female helplessness and victimization. The presumption is that the victim speaks in a pure voice: I suffer therefore I have moral purity.[49] But the belief in such purity is itself one of the effects of powerlessness.

What most disturbs me about certain radical feminist characterizations of women—and they are not alone, they are simply most prominent in this respect—is a tendency to function like pornography in repeatedly describing brutalizing sex-power horrors tied together with a thin narrative. Brownmiller's book is one striking example. I recall attending a conference on the new feminist scholarship and listening to a litany, lovingly detailed, of mutilating practices against women, some of which had long since been outlawed. I found myself growing nauseated that so many women seemed so eager to revel in details of their own brutalization. Although Midge Decter overshoots her target and lacks any understanding of the subtle ways in which sexism may flourish even in a system of formal-legalistic equality, there is a measure of truth in her pronouncement that "an expression of self-hatred"

---

[48] Helen Moglen, *Charlotte Brontë: The Self Conceived*, p. 30. Cf. Ann Douglas, *The Feminization of American Culture*, p. 10.

[49] Rosenthal, "Feminism Without Contradictions," p. 29.

can be found to inform many statements of women's liberation. She also notes that much of it has a "desperately nihilistic" quality.[50] The challenge to create a language of description that evaluates critically and morally without wallowing in the very terms of victimization remains. Indeed, it has a long history in scholarship *by* women, *of* women's history, and I shall make a brief detour into that area before moving on to liberal feminism.

There has long been an alternative to seeing the history of women as an unbroken tale of victimization. Mary Beard, in 1946, described *Woman as Force in History*,[51] distinguishing carefully between rationalizations of female subjection, particularly as these became imbedded in the common law, and actual social practice in which women played an important and meaningful role *in culture*, including what successive epochs understood as public life. Beard argues that it was with the advent of industrialization and the growth of the middle class that a virulent form of male domination arose in which women, or women of the privileged classes, became more clearly both the "possession" of a husband and a status symbol of his position in society.

Even a cursory glance at historic evidence demonstrates that there have always been women whose thought and action does not mesh with an image of downtrodden subordination. The medieval period, for example, is presumed by most feminists to be an age of *machismo* par excellence with knights, Crusades, feudalism, and an antifemale theology. They see an ideology that either damned women as Eve-like temptresses or placed them on pedestals surrounded by troubadours singing moonstruck verse about purity, grace, delicacy, and all the rest. Yet large numbers of women routinely participated in economic life, land ownership, estate management, and even political movements throughout medieval history.

Women, according to the medievalist Eileen Power, "per-

---

[50] Midge Decter, *The New Chastity and Other Arguments Against Women's Liberation*, p. 212.

[51] Mary. R. Beard, *Woman as Force in History*. Sheila Rowbotham, *Women, Resistance and Revolution*, details women's involvement in some twentieth-century revolutions from a Marxist feminist perspective.

formed almost every kind of agricultural labour'' and carried on a variety of trades in the towns.[52] Power notes that most historic evidence for the medieval period is slanted to the upper classes where the wife began to serve as a symbol of privatization and refinement, but that this image does not accurately reflect what women, even in that class, actually did. Women could inherit and hold land and offices. Given the frequent absence of men of the noble class on military adventures, women frequently represented their husbands and ran the fief or manor.[53] Power concludes that the ''dogma of the subjection of women'' which became embedded in the common law and, it must be added, in both feminist and anti-feminist discourse, has distorted the past even as it plagues the present and future. The medieval woman ''had a full share in the private rights and duties arising out of the possession of land and played a considerable part in industry. . . . The education of the average laywoman compared very favorably with that of her husband. . . . In every class of the community the life of the married woman gave her a great deal of scope, since . . . the home of this period was a very wide sphere.''[54] More recently, Ann Douglas has detailed the manner in which nineteenth-century American women, relegated to a particular sphere,

---

[52] Eileen Power, ''The Position of Women,'' in *The Legacy of the Middle Ages*, ed. C. G. Crump and E. F. Jacob, p. 411. Feminists in our time have tended to adopt as historic truth certain ideological portraits by men of the historic past; thus they see it, as at least some men, no doubt, would like to see it, as one long, unbroken record of male supremacy.

[53] Collections of medieval wills show that wives were often made executrixes of their husbands' wills. Cf. Power, ''The Position of Women,'' p. 419. See also David Herlihy, ''Land, Family and Women in Continental Europe, 701-1200,'' *Traditio*, pp. 89-119. Herlihy demonstrates that women played ''an extraordinary role in the management of family property in the early Middle Ages'' (p. 89). The matronymic or female title to property grew increasingly common from the eighth to the eleventh centuries—no small matter in a land-based society. Herlihy concludes that women ''appear with fair consistency as land owners and land managers and apparent heads of their families at all times and places in the early medieval period'' (p. 110). See also Eileen Power, *Medieval Women*; and Michael W. Kaufman, ''Spare Ribs: The Conception of Women in the Middle Ages and the Renaissance,'' *Soundings: An Interdisciplinary Journal*, pp. 139-163.

[54] Power, ''Position of Women,'' pp. 432-433.

embraced it, broadly defined, as their unique prerogative and attempted to turn a passive definition into an active vocation.[55]

Given a growing body of evidence, some of which has been extant for many years, demonstrating that women have played a variety of active roles throughout history—activities *in* culture—one must wonder about the motivation which underlies a depiction of women as incapable, helpless, demeaned, victimized. The issue is one of vital concern, for our beliefs about ourselves and our world are constitutive of social practices and individual actions. Told she is the Universal Victim; told that an implacable foe will frustrate her at every turn; told she is an "object"; told she will fail to take her place in the world as it is presently organized unless she becomes a grim militant or a "woman-identified woman"; told relations of mutuality between men and women are not only difficult but impossible; she can only wonder whose interests and needs, public and private, are being served through such distortions, since clearly those of women pummeled with such propaganda are not.

LIBERAL FEMINISM: WHY CAN'T A WOMAN BE MORE LIKE A MAN?

Unlike many of their radical counterparts, liberal feminists always have at least one foot securely on political turf—most often in a particular pluralist activity, like lobbying for a law, litigating in court, promoting ERA campaigns, campaigning for favored candidates, conferring on the next strategical and tactical moves. Liberal feminists, in action, behave like other interest groups bent on "maximizing [their] effectiveness." The ultimate aim of such groups is integration of group members into the ongoing political structure—the public sphere—with its attendant schedule of benefits and rewards. This, at best, is how things are supposed to work. Betty Friedan, for example, the founder of the current wing of liberal feminism, asked feminists recently to join her in a mutual

---

[55] Douglas, *Feminization of American Culture, passim.*

affirmation, something she calls the "New Yes." The door has opened, she claims, and women have but to walk through.

Liberal feminist thought shares the strengths and weaknesses of the liberalism I assayed in Chapter 3, including a particular split, to certain ends and purposes, between the public and the private. I will not repeat those arguments here, but simply note that liberal feminists follow their utilitarian predecessors—Bentham comes to mind—in holding that all principles of action finally devolve to a single point of personal interest, the concatenations of which, on a society-wide scale, are to redound to the benefit of everybody or the greatest good for the greatest number. I shall examine liberal or reformist feminism beginning with an analysis of the strengths and weaknesses of the nineteenth-century struggle for woman suffrage, a movement that was essentially middle-class, concentrating upon those themes clustered around the public-private split as it became infused with Machiavellian imperatives. My exploration of the presumptions and ideology propounded by women's suffrage advocates serves as the historic background for my subsequent consideration of contemporary liberal feminist thought.

The majority of nineteenth-century Suffragists engaged in a long and arduous struggle for formal-legalistic equality for women, many in the hope that other changes would follow quickly upon the heels of reform in those statutes discriminating against women's holding of property, bringing action in civil suits, and exercising the franchise. I shall argue that Suffragist failure to bring about structural change can be traced, first, to the manner in which they analyzed their dilemma and, second, to the proposed remedies which followed from their initial understanding.

On what terms did the Suffragists lodge their battle for formal-legalistic equality? In what categories did they analyze their mutual dilemma and propose remedies? With few exceptions, the Suffragists accepted, implicitly if not explicitly, the already dominant presumptions of a particular split between the public-political world of power and action, and a private-apolitical realm of sentiment and feeling; they simply placed a different interpretation on the relative value of these features of the dominant ideology.

By proceeding from, or accepting, the assumptions of their opponents, Suffragists unwittingly perpetuated many of the distortions and unexamined presumptions which rigged the system against them. The following, for example, is a typical anti-Suffragist argument:

Man assumed the direction of government and war, woman of the domestic and family affairs and the care and training of the child. . . . It has been so from the beginning, throughout the whole history of man, and it will continue to be so to the end, because it is in conformity to nature and its laws, and is sustained and confirmed by the experience and reason of six thousand years. . . . The domestic altar is a sacred flame where woman is the high and officiating priestess. . . . [T]o keep her in that condition of purity, it is necessary that she should be separated from the exercise of suffrage and from all those stern and contaminating and demoralizing duties that devolves upon the hardier sex—man.[56]

The statement sets into high relief the notions that man and woman are different in essence and hence must have separate spheres of activity. (Or, man and woman have separate spheres of activity *because* they are different in essence.) Politics is by definition the man's sphere; it follows a fortiori that woman has nothing to do with politics. To the man alone belong those "stern . . . contaminating . . . demoralizing" duties. Those women who moved outside the private realm were "semi-women, mental hermaphrodites." Women were separate but equal. Suffrage opponents elaborated on this theme:

. . . the Creator has assigned to woman very laborious and responsible duties, *by no means less important* than those imposed upon the male sex, though entirely different in their character. . . . While the man is contending with the sterner

---

[56] Elizabeth Cady Stanton, Susan B. Anthony, Matilda Joslyn Gage, eds., *History of Woman Suffrage*, 2:145.

duties of life, *the whole time* of the noble, affectionate and
true woman is required in the discharge of the delicate and
difficult duties assigned her in the family circle, in her
church relations and in the society where her lot is cast. . . .
I believe that they [women] are better than men, but I do not
believe that they are adapted to the political work of this
world. . . . I would not, and I say it deliberately, degrade
woman by giving her the right of suffrage. I mean the word
in its full signification, because I believe that woman as she
is today, the queen of home and of hearts, is above the political collision of this world, and should always be kept above
them.[57]

What was the response of the Suffragists to arguments that
woman was pure, private, and apolitical and man was immoral,
public, and political (because his sphere was)? Rather than rejecting the conceptual system from which these dichotomies were
a predictable outgrowth, the Suffragists turned anti-Suffrage arguments upside down to serve as the basis for a pro-Suffrage plea.
Yes, man was evil and bad and he had made something nasty out
of politics. True, woman was purer and more virtuous—look at
the way she had ennobled the private sphere. What must be done,
therefore, is to throw the mantle of private morality *over* the
public sphere by drawing women into it. Women would be politicized and politics would be transformed in one fell swoop.
Thus public language—not unique to the Suffragists—underwent
a sentimentalization.

Elizabeth Cady Stanton, the most important of the early Suffrage theorists, espoused the female-superiority view with vehe-
mence.

---

[57] Susan B. Anthony and Ida Husted Harper, eds., *History of Woman Suffrage*,
4:95, 106-107. The first two sentences are drawn from an 1887 anti-suffrage
speech by Sen. George Vest; the remainder is taken from a similar speech by Sen.
Joseph E. Brown. There were radical thinkers in the nineteenth-century movement,
including Elizabeth Cady Stanton herself in her attacks on religion. A second
thinker who cannot simply be described as liberal, Charlotte Perkins Gilman, was
important in the later stages of the movement, but the radical voices were finally
swamped. I deal here with the prevailing themes of Suffragist discourse.

The male element is a destructive force, stern, selfish, aggrandizing, loving war, violence, conquest, acquisition, breeding in the material and moral world alike discord, disorder, disease and death. See what a record of blood and cruelty the pages of history reveal! Through what slavery, and slaughter, and sacrifice, through what inquisitions and imprisonments, pains and persecutions, black codes and gloomy creeds, the soul of humanity has struggled for the centuries, while mercy has veiled her face and all hearts have been dead alike to love and hope! The male element has held high carnival thus far, it has fairly run riot from the beginning, overpowering the feminine element everewhere, crushing out the diviner qualities in human nature until we know but little of true manhood and womanhood, of the latter comparatively nothing, for it has scarce been recognized as a power until within the last century. . . . The need of this hour is not territory, gold mines, railroads, or specie payments, but a new evangel of womanhood, to exalt purity, virtue, morality, true religion, to lift man up into the higher realms of thought and action.[58]

The image enunciated by Stanton holds that the male element—destructive and selfish—is in control. The female element—loving and virtuous—is enslaved and intimidated. If social chaos is to be prevented, the balance must be tipped to the feminine element.

As the Suffrage fight progressed women increasingly proclaimed their purity in religious terms and flatly contended that Christ himself received his "sweet, tender, suffering humanity . . . wholly from woman." Women, consequently, "have a greater share of Him than men have."[59] If elected to public office, women would "far more effectively guard the morals of society, and the sanitary conditions of cities."[60] There were Suffragists who admitted that the vote for women would not cure all society's ills, but they believed it would mean that governments responsible to women would be more likely to conserve life and preserve morals.

[58] Stanton, Anthony and Gage, *Woman Suffrage*, 2:351-352.
[59] Stanton, Anthony and Gage, *Woman Suffrage*, 2:785.
[60] Stanton, Anthony and Gage, *Woman Suffrage*, 1:19-20.

The remedy for the evil of the liquor traffic, for example, lay in woman's suffrage. The social triumph of Christ's Golden Rule would be a corollary achievement. Sentimentalization bore with it a tendency toward a sometimes censorious moralism, the voice of strained piety.

Why did the Suffragists feel constrained to celebrate their nobility and the purity of women? Why did they make such outrageous claims for the power of the ballot and their abilities, armed with the ballot, to transform public life? They readily admitted to being "dreamers" (again the adoption of an epithet turned on its head to create a presumed virtue): "We are told that to assume that women will help purify political life and develop a more ideal government but proves us to be dreamers of dreams. Yes, we are in a goodly company of dreamers, of Confucious, of Buddha, of Jesus, of the English Commons fighting for the Magna Charta. . . .''[61] The answer to these troubling questions becomes somewhat clearer if one remembers that the dominant ideology set forth controlling presumptions for both politics and the private realm. For women to reject its terms would have meant a rejection of the Victorian version of marriage and family life which revolved around the image of a saintly, sexless, wife-mother. The sexual Manichaeism of the nineteenth century was so deeply entrenched that the Suffragists, with few exceptions, did not consider the manner in which this image served to reinforce male dominance.

Certain scholars see the increased emphasis by the Suffragists on their superior virtue as one indication of a shift in the movement from arguments for the vote based on "justice" to arguments based on "expediency." Aileen Kraditor contends that the early Suffragist arguments demanded political equality "on the same ground as that on which men had based their demand for political equality with their English rulers two generations before."[62] I agree with Kraditor that a shift in emphasis did occur. But I do not see this, as she apparently does, as a major qualitative change; rather, it seems to me an altered emphasis within a single tradition.

[61] Ida Husted Harper, ed., *History of Woman Suffrage*, 5:126.

[62] Aileen S. Kraditor, *The Ideas of the Woman Suffrage Movement 1890-1920*, pp. 38-39. See also Sheila M. Rothman, *Woman's Proper Place: A History of Changing Ideals and Practices 1870 to Present*.

Kraditor herself points out that most of the Suffragists belonged to the same native-born white, middle to upper-middle class, Anglo-Saxon Protestant group as the male-dominant group of American society. She sees the expediency argument as put forth to appeal to that group. Because the Suffragists shared the same class status as the dominant males, they also shared their class prejudices—without, however, sharing in the political power of the males of their class. The following statements are representative of the expediency approach to votes for women.

You did not trust the Southern freedman to the arbitrary will of courts and States! Why send your mothers, wives and daughters to the unwashed, unlettered, unthinking masses that carry popular elections?[63]

We ask for the ballot for the good of the race. . . . When you debar from your councils and legislative halls the purity, the spirituality and the love of woman, those councils are apt to become coarse and brutal. God gave us to you to help you in this little journey to a better land, and by our love and our intellect to help make our country pure and noble . . .[64]

Woman's vote is needed for the good of others. Our horizon is misty with apparent dangers. Woman may aid in dispelling them. . . . She desires the homes of the land to be pure and sober; with her help they may become so . . .[65]

The dangerous experiment has been made of enfranchising the vast proportion of crime, intemperance, immorality and dishonesty, and barring absolutely from the suffrage the great proportion of temperance, morality, religion and conscientiousness; that, in other words, the worst elements have been put into the ballot-box and the best elements kept out . . .[66]

We point to the official statistics for proof that there are more white women in the United States than colored men

---

[63] Stanton, Anthony and Gage, *Woman Suffrage*, 3:88.
[64] Anthony and Harper, *Woman Suffrage*, 4:39.
[65] *Ibid.*, 4:84. [66] *Ibid.*, 4:xxxvi.

and women combined; that there are more American-born
women than foreign-born men and women combined; that
women form only one-eleventh of the criminals in the jails
and penitentiaries; that they compose more than two-thirds of
the church membership, and that the percentage of illiteracy
is very much less among women than among men. Therefore
we urge that this large proportion of patriotism, temperance,
morality, religion and intelligence be allowed to impress itself upon the government through the medium of the ballot-
box.[67]

The shift in emphasis to expedient rationales for women's suffrage is further evidence of the effects on women of the distortions
imbedded within the dominant perspective. The way in which the
original justice argument was framed contained the seeds of the
expedience justification because it meant the Suffragists had implicitly accepted a set of beliefs about themselves and their society.
Their failure lay in an initial conceptualization which was tied to
the dominant ideology and helped to shape Suffragist practice.
With the achievement of suffrage, this ideology remained and
continued to gloss over the inequalities of the system with the
claim that these inequalities emerged "naturally" and therefore
lay outside the sphere of politics. The Suffragists accepted their
dematerialization, the terms of sexual Manichaeism. They wished
to draw "their" men into this rarified realm and to exclude the
more "bestial" underclasses (whose "overbreeding" constituted
a clear and present danger to Anglo-Saxon dominance). Dematerialization was a function of both their sex and their social class.

Political power—associated with war, force, and violence—
was anathema to the Suffragists. Such power was an aspect of
the public, male sphere they wished to join and by joining, transform. Rosemary Radford Ruether points out that by the mid-
nineteenth century and the beginning of Suffragist protest, the
splits between public and private spheres and moralities had already had a devastating, impoverishing effect on both realms.
Moral virtues had been so "sentimentalized and privatized they

---

[67] Harper, *Woman Suffrage*, 5:77.

ceased to have serious public power."[68] Morality was identified with the feminine sphere. In the rough and tumble world of politics, such morality was deemed "unrealistic." The political world demanded "hard, practical aggressivity, devoid of sentiment or moralizing." A male participates in this world during the day; in the evening he repairs "to the idealized world of the 'Home' where all moral and spiritual values are confined."[69] What the Suffragists did by accepting a definition of themselves that arose out of their powerlessness, that meant embracing their purity and suffering, was to reinforce a set of presumptions which were strongly arrayed against female political participation and socioeconomic equality.[70]

Suffragist insistence on their purity and their dependence upon moral suasion as the means to reform meant they could avoid taking a hard look at political power: What was it? How was it gained? To what ends was it or could it be used? In their scheme of things, if women gained political power, that power would be transformed automatically into a moral force. Women would therefore never have to face issues arising from those ambiguous situations in which political judgments must be made with no clear-cut division of the "good" and the "bad" on one side or the other. Women would use the votes to change society, but the vote would not change women.

That woman will, by voting, lose nothing of man's courteous, chivalric attention and respect is admirably proven by the manner in which both houses of congress, in the midst of the most anxious and perplexing presidential conflict in our

[68] Rosemary Radford Ruether, "The Cult of True Womanhood," *Commonweal*, p. 131.

[69] *Ibid.*

[70] Rosenthal, "Feminism Without Contradictions," p. 29. Rosenthal points out that a victim is "supposed to have moral authority or purity because the exploitative terms in which her suppression is couched have been imposed on her by others. . Her real voice has been silenced." The majority of Suffragists did not "break the silence" by speaking with their real voices. Instead, they made, in Hegelian terms, a virtue out of historic necessity by celebrating the qualities which arose from their oppression.

history, received their appeals from twenty-three States for a sixteenth amendment protecting the rights of women.[71]

I will say to woman's credit she has not sought office, she is not a natural office-seeker, but she desires to vote . . .[72]

Woman's work during the nation's various wars showed that "women were clearer and more exalted than the men, because their moral feelings and political instincts were not so much affected by selfishness, or business, or party consideration . . ."[73]

Because the Suffragists assumed that moral high-mindedness was almost exclusively a female trait, they could only treat obliquely, or not at all, the argument that moving into public life would force women into a change of habits, attitudes, and standards. Women would remain guileless. Once the private had become public, politics in the traditional sense would come to an end.

The form, language, and mode of Suffragist protest was set by the objective conditions of female oppression and by their response to those idealizations and distortions which rationalized continuance of the status quo. This led, for example, to the fallacy of attributing the political position of men almost exclusively to their position *under the law*. Political power was seen as something which automatically flowed from legal power. Legal change, therefore, was the path to political goals. The Suffragists (with a few notable exceptions) failed to recognize that men could use the law in this way because of a set of economic and social conditions that lay outside the law itself but which provided the context within which the law was applied.

The power of men to achieve their objectives was power with a legal component but the law itself was not the sole root of that power. The Suffragists concentrated upon the trappings rather than the substance of political power. The end result was the failure of the Suffragists to achieve an original political vision.

[71] Stanton, Anthony and Gage, *Woman Suffrage*, 3:67.

[72] Anthony and Harper, *Woman Suffrage*, 4:117.

[73] Stanton, Anthony and Gage, *Woman Suffrage*, 2:17.

They said they wanted equality within the extant structure. But that structure by definition was one of male dominance. They therefore were proposing change with a presupposition of stasis or stability. They apparently did not see that the ideal of "woman" which they celebrated included the idea of "man" which they denigrated, and that these concepts were necessarily connected. The controlling images of "woman" and "man," in turn, were linked to a larger matrix, a social structure within which these relations made sense. As Winch has pointed out, the idea we form of an object includes the idea of connections between it and other objects.[74]

The Suffragists' ultimate conclusions were that private morality could be applied to the public level; that public persons ought to be judged by the rigorous standards of the private sphere; that the public (im)moral qualities men exhibited were probably innate to the male character, but that men, too, could be transformed as could public life by the entry of women into it; that the qualities women exhibited were innate and were not merely an outgrowth of their enforced domesticity; that these same qualities were the qualities that would invest the political sphere with a sanctified aura. In the Suffragist future, if a man wished to be a "good" citizen he would have to take on the cloak of selflessness and private virtue. Most Suffragists wanted to take the identifying terms of the private sphere and ramify these terms through the public sphere. As Ann Douglas argues, a "male-dominated theological tradition" was "largely defeated" in popular culture by "an anti-intellectual sentimentalism purveyed by men and women." Unfortunately, the denouement of a patriarchal Calvinism did not entail "gaining a comprehensive feminism."[75]

Demoralization set in among Suffragists when votes for women did not achieve all the miracles they had claimed it would. Women could vote, but structures were largely unchanged; indeed, both the ideas and the economic and political realities underpinning them retained their viability. Women did not vote as a bloc nor organize into political movements to promote their "interests"

[74] Peter Winch, *The Idea of a Social Science and Its Relation to Philosophy*, p. 124.

[75] Douglas, *Feminization of American Culture*, p. 13.

by translating certain needs into interests. All of this is unsurprising given the assumption that women were to stay pure and to purify politics at the same time. When the vote for women did not see the victory of private morality in the public sphere, it led to a reversion to the full defining terms of the dominant ideology with the exception that women could vote without completely losing their "femininity" or claims to private virtue. Participation beyond the level of the vote did present such a danger, however. How much has changed for their contemporary liberal heirs?

Liberal feminists share with others of a pluralist persuasion a commitment to an incremental politics of "running repairs," reforms which do not involve a major alteration in the social system's basic schedule of benefits and rewards. They share with mainstream defenders of the status quo in political science a set of positivist presumptions which define, delimit, structure, and gear their analyses and their conclusions in certain directions and toward particular ends. Briefly: positivist commitments include a split between description and evaluation, between statements of "fact" and statements of "value." Values are privatized—couched on a par with individual preferences and feelings amenable neither to rational defense nor to adjudication.[76] It follows that what a person calls "good" will depend upon values or biases for which he can make no rational truth claims nor defense; thus a feminist is free to lodge charges of bias or sexism to her heart's content, as an expression of what she wants or finds good, but she can never make a serious moral claim and defend it.

These issues permeate liberal feminist discourse as they did earlier forms of liberal thought. One finds liberal analysts alternating between the "hard facts" of discrimination and institutionalized sexism and the "soft appeal" to feminine opinions and values. Elizabeth Janeway, for example, can only proffer, as support for her feminist position, an "appeal to opinions," to

---

[76] The behaviorist persuasion in political science holds that the facts of political life and the values one appends to those facts are different kinds of propositions that must be kept analytically separate. A bifurcation between "statements of fact" and "statements of value" lies at the heart of the enterprise. Within these epistemological presumptions, to describe and to evaluate, to characterize what is and to press for what ought to be, are two entirely distinct activities.

tenets we declare to be true because *"we feel they ought to be"* (emphasis mine).[77] She herself doesn't feel too badly about this state of affairs because even "the most dedicated social scientists" cannot wholly rid themselves of values. They, too, "find it difficult to get rid of the idea that some human situations are better than others."[78] One might have supposed that the whole point of a feminist dissent was precisely an appeal to an alternative state of affairs as defensibly better than others, including what presently exists.

I shall focus my exploration of liberal feminism by concentrating upon the images of persons, the purposes assigned to politics or public activity, and the scope and importance given the private sphere within liberal feminist discourse. Liberal feminists, unlike those radicals discussed above, give the problem of human nature, male and female, relatively short shrift. If pressed, the liberal feminist stance is a rather thoroughgoing environmentalism. All persons are held to be initially the same but are then shaped, molded, conditioned, and socialized within diverse environments and propelled towards contrasting roles, activities, values, and relationships. The centrally defining human characteristic in this schema is the presumption of an almost boundless adaptability—hence the emphasis on "socializing to nonsexist roles," "positive role models," and so on. At times liberal environmentalism is overly deterministic and children are treated as human Play-Doh to be shaped at will by social engineers in the person of parents, school teachers, and other "socializing agents."

The liberal feminist commitment to environmentalism is not consistent, however, for if it were, they would have to concede

---

[77] Elizabeth Janeway, *Man's World Woman's Place*, pp. 12-13. Janeway's revolution isn't quite so empty as that of another liberal feminist, Gayle Graham Yates, whose conclusion to *What Women Want: The Ideas of the Movement* is a bit of a fizzle: ". . . in the final analysis, what is true is what we believe individually, academically and socially" (p. 189). What, one might ask Yates, of the sexist who sincerely believes women are inferior, or the racist who believes he must oppress the blacks he finds less than human, or the fascist who believes he has a mission to rid the world of Jews, or even the neurotic who believes he will be struck dead if he does not incessantly perform a series of time-consuming rituals?

[78] Janeway, *Man's World*, p. 136.

that as women forsake that private sphere which formerly defined and shaped them and enter a very different public arena which now defines men—who are seen as tougher, more aggressive, assertive, active—women, too, would take on the "male" characteristics appropriate to that sphere. Few liberal feminists desire this outcome: thus one finds that to certain ends and purposes they locate the source of women's woes in her privatization and see her salvation in going public, but to other ends and purposes they celebrate women's "softer attributes" without specifying the origin, development, and institutional support for those attitudes, as that would mean that female privatization carried certain benefits and values, that it was, in some ways, "good." Liberal feminists fail to treat squarely and cogently the problem of "separate but equal" and different, or "not-separate but equal" and the same, which plagued the nineteenth-century Suffragist movement.

If radical feminists deal with the public-private, personal-political dilemma by eliminating all distinctions between diverse spheres, relationships, and activities, liberal feminists retain an implicit public-private division but hope to erase the harmful results the traditional split has had, they argue, for women. Few harbor the illusion which permeated the thinking of many nineteenth-century Suffragists—that if women ran politics, politics would automatically be transformed in the direction of goodness—nor do most believe that the erection of a single uniform standard by which to assess, evaluate, and explain both public and private activities and relationships is either possible or desirable. Just what, then, do liberal feminists want to change along public and private dimensions? What values do they hold dear and which would they realize more fully in either or both spheres of life? Answers to these questions turn on each thinker's assessment of the source and scope of the problem for women, and her defense of a set of values and desired outcomes for change.

A public world is not necessarily a political one; to confound the two, to collapse them into one another, is once again to fail to identify political sets of institutions, activities, and purposes. The classic version of the public-private split involved demarcating the household or the family, spiritual institutions, and commercial or economic institutions from the arena within which adult males, or *citizens*, in their political capacity, met together to strive to arrive at mutually beneficial arrangements. The individual played other *public* roles, as a merchant, perhaps, or a lawyer, a clerk, or a teacher, but in his *political* role he was the citizen and his politics was instrumental in its means and in its ends. To be a *citizen* meant to participate meaningfully in the body politic, to have a voice, to have a say.

Contemporary liberal feminists, however, rarely speak of *citizens* or *citizenship*. Kirsten Amundsen is one exception and she resurrects citizenship only to impoverish its meaning as a "one resource that . . . is equally distributed" just like any other.[79] This is not unlike the calculus she applies to family ties which become one among many desires whose satisfaction humans seek rationally to maximize.[80] Amundsen simultaneously reduces the political character of citizenship and drains the private world of whatever noninstrumentalist value, resonance, and meaning it retains. What remains is a single self-interested calculus roaming freely over the social landscape as both the polity and the family are denuded of the normative significance and legitimacy they continue to possess. This drive, a substitute for a geniune politics, becomes, in practice, the only "politics" around: a further fracturing of social ties under the imperatives of "equal opportunity," "meritocracy," "progress," and "liberation." I discuss this *politics of displacement* in greater detail later in this chapter.

The best entry into the world of liberal feminism is through an exploration of their terms of discourse: How do they describe and explain public and private phenomena? What motivations, potentialities, and desired outcomes are held out for women? One is struck immediately by the depoliticized language liberal feminists deploy in characterizing persons, male and female, in their public and private capacities. The most commonly used term is the notion of "role." No one would disagree that persons play a number of different parts at different times to different purposes in their social capacities, but liberal feminists' exclusionary focus on the notion of *role* carries with it important implications for their social analysis.

[79] Kirsten Amundsen, *The Silenced Majority*, p. 63.
[80] *Ibid., passim*. This presumption underlies the entire argument.

Persons are not essentially mothers, fathers, lovers, friends, scholars, laborers, eccentrics, dissidents, or political leaders in liberal discourse, but *role-players*. Society is a collection of aggregates, social atoms performing roles. A flattening-out of social life and the human subject results when one thinks exclusively in terms of role-players. Each role seems equal to another in a kind of leveling process, a homogenization of description and evaluation. Cynthia Fuchs Epstein, for example, dubs motherhood a "role" like any other, a socially constituted and sanctioned activity with a relatively fixed range of operation. The effect is to distort the full meaning of mothering. Mothering is *not* a "role" on par with being a file clerk, a scientist, or a member of the Air Force. Mothering is a complicated, rich, ambivalent, vexing, joyous activity which is biological, natural, social, symbolic, and emotional. It carries profoundly resonant emotional and sexual imperatives. A tendency to downplay the differences that pertain between, say, mothering and holding a job, not only drains our private relations of much of their significance, but also oversimplifies what can or should be done to alter things for women, who are frequently urged to change roles in order to solve their problems.

The liberal feminist devaluation of the private sphere and the woman's place within it is a curious thing. On the one hand, it involves a recognition of ongoing social realities, as families are less and less "havens in a heartless world" and all that implies. But to reduce motherhood to a "role" is to speed up and enhance the process of eroding the private sphere and its social relationships of their significance and value, with nothing, one must point out, to take its place. On the other hand, feminist discussions of the motherhood "role" are frequently coupled with anger at the social "value system" for not supporting or valuing the mothering "role," thus placing mothers under "cross-pressures" which make it more difficult for them to play both "professional roles" to "fully exploit [her] potential" as well as to derive value from their mothering "role."[81] The reason it is bad not to exploit fully one's potential, Epstein argues, is because the "exploitation of

[81] Cynthia Fuchs Epstein, *Woman's Place*. See the discussion in chap. 3, pp. 86-150.

an individual's potential is beneficial to society" by definition—
a liberal article of faith Epstein repeats but fails to defend.

Janeway, in turn, reinforces a depoliticization of the public
sphere even as she holds up that sphere as the only true and secure
arbiter of human values. Janeway's privatized women are caught
in a cultural lag. They find themselves in roles (wifehood, mothering) which puts them at odds with the American ethos, a condition distressing to Janeway.[82] The result for women is a severe
attack of anomie, a Durkheimian concept used by Janeway to
explicate that insecurity which results when one does not receive
rewards in conformity with "pre-existing standards of judgment."[83] Women languish because they are not in the running for
the prizes; the standards of the marketplace are deployed and the
private sphere is found wanting.

Why do men have it better? In order to appreciate Janeway's
simultaneous depoliticization of the public sphere and an insistence on that sphere as an alternative locus of value, it is necessary
to appreciate what she means by a "role." She adopts a functionalist definition—a role "is the aspect of what the actor does
in his relationship with others seen in the context of its functional
significance for the social system."[84] Men have it better, she
contends, because their public roles allow them to receive rewards
and "there are pre-existing standards of judgment by which a
verdict of 'well-done' can be pronounced."[85] With other liberal
analysts, Janeway takes the social system—with the exception of
its exclusion of women from the echelons of power and privilege—as a given; thus it comes as no surprise that rather than
questioning the "pre-existing standards" by which men are
judged, she celebrates that standard and prescribes it for what ails
women. Men, having become what they do, know who they are
in a rather reified route to self-identity. She notes approvingly:
"Men participated in the drama of life by . . . receiving earnings,
in money or status or respect. *Modern economic man knows where
he stands. Because of this . . . he values himself* by the return his
work brings in, and he expects to enjoy it himself" (emphasis

---

[82] Janeway, *Man's World*, p. 99.   [83] *Ibid.*, p. 74.
[84] *Ibid.*, p. 70.   [85] *Ibid.*, p. 74.

mine).[86] One further observation about Janeway's notion of a
"role." As her discussion proceeds something rather bizarre happens. Janeway makes roles, abstract categories, agents in the
world. She grants them the power to engage in complex social
operations. She argues, for example, that roles do not submit to
change readily; or that a role (not a person, remember, but the
role itself!) can be found in a *"struggle to endure and to reproduce
the same sort of relationship in which it was first conceived"*
(emphasis mine).[87]

Janeway joins Epstein in advising women to "go public," to
take on new roles, to become "role-breakers" and thus to become
integrated into the standards of the public world. "Role-breakers," in turn, are "role models" and as such help others to "break
roles." Throughout this interaction of disembodied roles, the social structure does not change, but "role-breakers" move out and
up within it, pursuing their own individual ends and purposes.
Janeway's feminist strategy is intensive individualism—she doesn't
even allow her role-breakers to join with others to form a pressure
group, the modus vivendi of pluralist politics. Although her individualist "solution" to the feminist dilemma does not threaten
any given political status quo, Janeway insists it "threatens the
order of the universe."[88] Unfortunately, Janeway never lets us in
on how individual role-breakers might mount a challenge to the
universe.

The language of roles, and those terms and notions clustered
and associated with it—functional differentiation, systems maintenance, social deviance, dysfunctional, and so on—is a depoliticized language. A political perspective must be couched in a
political language. Janeway, again, is an excellent example of
depoliticizing language. She explicitly repudiates a resonant term
of political discourse, "equality," as a way to characterize the
aims of the feminist movement. Equality, she chides, is "too
small a word" to capture what she has in mind.[89] The real problem,
of course, is that equality is potentially too highly charged a
political term for one who neither seeks nor desires genuine struc-

---

[86] *Ibid.*, p. 168.
[88] *Ibid.*, p. 124.
[87] *Ibid.*, p. 129.
[89] *Ibid.*, p. 217.

tural change. We have already seen what Janeway has in mind: intentional role-breaking to gain status and a sense of identity for exceptional women who, through their activities, mount an unspecified challenge to the universe.

There are liberal analysts who openly advocate an explicit political role for women beyond Janeway's. But just as the Suffragists were constrained in their articulation of a transformative feminist vision by their absorption of sentimentalist notions as to the correct means and ends of politics, contemporary liberal feminists have difficulties in part because of their embrace of the liberal presumption that all values, ends, and purposes are simple private values or compounds of such values.[90] Liberal feminists share with other liberal pluralists an insistence on the overall social benefits of self-interest.

The problem—or one of the problems—with a politics which begins and ends with mobilization of resources, achieving maximum impacts, calculating prudentially, articulating interest group claims, engaging in reward distribution functions, and so on, is not only its utter lack of imagination but its inability to engage the reflective allegiance and committed loyalty of citizens. Oversimply: no substantive sense of civic virtue, no vision of the political community which might serve as the groundwork of a life in common, is possible within a political life dominated by a self-interested, predatory individualism.

Liberal feminist analysis when it becomes explicitly "political," rather than merely public, presumes that the aims and the purposes of politics are given. The only problem for feminists is how to "get in on the action." The feminist solution is thought to rest in the formation of a well-defined interest group.[91] But whose interests will be served? Those of "all women" again?

[90] Wolff, *Poverty of Liberalism*, p. 197.

[91] Jo Freeman, *The Politics of Women's Liberation*, *passim*. Freeman accepts the constraints of positivist discourse which disallow for a critical in-depth exploration of human beings and their social world. See Jean Bethke Elshtain, "Methodological Sophistication and Conceptual Confusion: A Critique of Mainstream Political Science," in *The Prism of Sex: Essays in the Sociology of Knowledge*, ed. Julia A. Sherman and Evelyn Torton Beck, pp. 229-252.

What about the problems of race and class? Liberal feminists tend to ignore or slight these issues even as they acknowledge their existence with the depoliticizing rubric, "social stratification." It is clear, however, that the full range and dimensions of the problems of poverty and injustice are never joined, or Amundsen, one of the liberal analysts who takes up the problem, could not proffer her assurance that "*the feminist program . . . can be enacted without too much straining or radical transformation of the present economic structures*" (emphasis mine).[92] This is the case *only* if the feminist program consists of integrating relatively few, well-educated, privileged, and, most often, white women into the extant structure. "Equality" and "liberation" come too easily in the liberal feminist world. To give these words substance is to mount a challenge liberal politics cannot, in its present form, accommodate.

The liberal feminist tendency to reduce substantive debates to matters of "style" or "organizational" structure, thereby cooling these debates, is evident in Jo Freeman's treatment of those she variously labels "reformist" and "revolutionary" feminists. It turns out, in her view, that there really are no differences at all between these groups, no potentially incompatible or competing views of the political world. All differences are redescribed by Freeman under the rubric of "style."[93] Conflict is minimized and genuine debate goes by the board. Freeman argues that the diverse activities of these branches of feminism are not really relevant or important—they are simply incongruous. In her discussion of "disagreements over strategy and priorities" between feminist groups, Freeman recharacterizes the differences as either being "complementary" or—even better—"irrelevant."[94]

Individualism, self-interest, role-changing—these are the hallmarks of liberal feminism. But middle-class liberal feminists are divided on many issues, not least of which is the relative value and importance of the public and private spheres and what part women should play within each. They reject a separation which

[92] Amundsen, *Silenced Majority*, p. 164.
[93] Freeman, *Politics of Women's Liberation*, p. 9.
[94] *Ibid.*, p. 231.

cuts them out of the many prizes the public world has, or seems to have, to offer: power, status, the opportunity for public discourse, and important public responsibilities. Yet most liberal feminists are reluctant to thoroughly politicize or publicize the private sphere, a realm they associate, not without reason, with gentler virtues and with values not dominated by those of exchange relations and self-interest. Thus they would purify the private realm, make it better, by allowing women to play both public and private roles, as if this would not importantly alter the private values they cherish. The questions are: How can women partake equally of both spheres? To what ends and purposes would they do so? Proposals for role-sharing and role-reversal are attainable only by a few. To advocate and provide full-time public day care for children from the age of two (or younger) would allow some women to stride full-time into the public arena much sooner than if they had to wait until their children reached school age, but the takeover of child-rearing by public institutions would also denude the private sphere of its central raison d'être and chief source of human emotion and value. Similarly, to externalize all housekeeping activities, to make them public activities, would vitiate the private realm further. "All persons would, so far as possible, be transformed into totally public persons, and the sundering of the forms of social life begun by industrialization would be carried to completion by the absorption of the private as completely as possible into the public."[95] This is the completion of the liberal imperative. If attained, the result would be enormously unattractive: an extension of thin, instrumental relations to all spheres of life. Given such alternatives, it is not surprising that one finds implicit desires on the part of liberal feminists to hold on to many traditional characteristics of femininity, which means as well to cling to the social locus of that femininity. But it is impossible to indefinitely have things both ways: to condemn woman's second class status and the damaging effects of her privatization and, simultaneously, to extol or celebrate the qualities that have emerged within the sphere women are to be "freed" from. The result of all this is a confused admixture: a tough-minded market

[95] Wolff, "Nobody Here But Us Persons," pp. 140-141.

language of self-interest coupled with evocations to softer virtues, precisely the combination which plagued the Suffragists. Because the only politics liberal feminists know is the rather crass utilitarianism they implicitly or explicitly adopt, they have thus far failed to articulate a transformative feminist vision of public and private.

Perhaps the clearest example of liberal feminism's conceptual dilemma, and it is with this I shall conclude the section, is afforded by the work of Betty Friedan, frequently referred to as the "mother" of women's liberation. In her 1963 text, *The Feminine Mystique*, Friedan argued that women in the decades after World War II suffered from an identity crisis: they were assured that they should feel happy and "fulfilled" as full-time wives and mothers; they felt guilty if they pursued careers; they were unhappy; they had a problem which had "no name." Women were victimized, goes Friedan's thesis, by a self-perpetuating myth, a mystique that was so pervasive women's lives were shaped and controlled by it unawares. Those responsible for the destructive mystique included women's magazines, television, advertising, newspapers, child psychologists, sociological and psychoanalytic popularizers, and Margaret Mead. The most serious problem was that the mystique was so pervasive and so powerful that women's views of themselves and the world were distorted and inhibited subliminally. The mystique and the suburban life style tied to it led to a "stunting or evasion of growth."[96] Friedan went on to detail the results of this takeover of women by the mystique: women "of fine mind and fiery spirit" accepted uncritically the message of "sex-directed educators" and fled "college and career

Friedan (handwritten marginal note)

[96] Betty Friedan, *The Feminine Mystique*, p. 77. I shall omit a discussion of Friedan's distortions of psychoanalytic theory. The problem with her approach and that of many other feminists is their condemning a theory they haven't taken the trouble to understand from the inside out. They overassimilate the theory to established, medically-controlled psychiatric practice in the United States. (Freud, of course, opposed a takeover of psychoanalysis by the medical profession.) This overeasy condemnation disallows coming to grips with what the relation between psychoanalytic theory and American psychiatric practice might be. Does the practice really reflect the theory or grossly distort it? One other imperative is at work, particularly in liberal feminism, and that is a deeply rooted antitheoretical, overly pragmatic and utilitarian focus.

to marry and have babies."[97] Frustrated and unhappy in their marriages, they turned to alcoholism, divorce, and adultery. Children suffered being in the company of distraught mothers and so on, a litany of misery.

The great strength of Friedan's 1963 account is her attack on ideology—though she doesn't call it that—the ideology she characterizes as the "feminine mystique." She puts her finger on an enormously vexing theoretical and political question: How do people come to hold views of themselves as members of the moral universe and social world which incorporate a self-image of helplessness, excessive deference, inability to stand up to authority, incapacity to act in the world? Marxists call this the problem of "false-consciousness" with specific reference to the proletariat acting, thinking, and behaving in ways conducive to the continuation of their own oppression and exploitation. One weakness of her account, a weakness shared by many Marxist thinkers as well, is that she fails to articulate the criteria whereby one can sift out what, in a person's view of herself and the world, constitutes a *totally* false and distorted image; what represents important truths cast, perhaps, in a distorted form; and what authentically embodies and represents the truth about herself and her social location.

Friedan's elaboration of the feminine mystique led to facile notions about true and false images of the feminine and ushered into a rather breezy elitism whereby women who were already privileged by education and class could impose upon other women their own analysis of other women's discontents; could presume that all women felt as they did, or *would* so feel if they would drop their false-consciousness and shuck the constraints of the feminine mystique. This is a very complicated problem and Friedan must not be singled out as a particular offender. Few social and political thinkers have come to grips with this question in satisfactory ways, though I shall attempt to do so in Chapter 6 below.

A second difficulty with Friedan's analysis lies in her implicit, and at times explicit, contrast model to what women in the 1950s

[97] *Ibid.*, p. 173.

and early 1960s had to suffer as victims and perpetrators of the feminine mystique, a victimization and mystique tied on both political and conceptual levels to what it was men were doing, to how they saw and understood themselves in the world. (A point of caution: the men to whom Friedan refers and to whom I shall refer in criticizing her analysis are educated, mobile men of the upper-middle class. The working class and underclasses in American society are omitted from her purview or figure only derivatively.) Rather than extending her analysis of "mystiques" to include the male mystique of success, she embraces it as the alternative for women. She assaults the housebound condition of wives and celebrates the success-impelled condition of husbands, all those "... able, ambitious men" who go off to the big city and keep "on growing."[98] Her book is a paean of praise to what Americans themselves call the "rat race": she just wants women to join it.

No one, then or now, would disagree with Friedan's assertion that the identity of a totally housebound wife is frustrating and, in many ways, empty (although the identity as "mother" which Friedan overclosely assimilates to that of "housewife" cannot be thus characterized, or is so characterized only by perpetrating a serious distortion). But to argue that the man's identity, because it is carried on outside the home in the bowels of corporate America is automatically exciting, fulfilling, and worthwhile is to create another mystique, the "masculine mystique," and to give up one distortion only to embrace another. Friedan, in 1963, denigrated as "sex-directed" opponents of American corporate capitalism and the uncritical acceptance of what was called "progress." By accepting the values of male-dominated, individualistic society, Friedan was forced by the logic of her analysis to advocate what might be called a turnover in personnel—women bureaucrats for male bureaucrats, women corporate executives for male corporate executives, women generals for male generals. She has since backed off this view somewhat. I shall consider the revisions in her position in a moment.

A third problem with Friedan's liberal feminist classic is her

---

[98] *Ibid.*, p. 201.

excessive environmentalism. With other liberal thinkers—anyone who embraces, whether explicitly or not, the Lockean *tabula rasa*—Friedan presumes that we are *totally* shaped by culture; that human identity is always and fully explained with reference to certain external criteria and can be identified by such criteria. This ties Friedan to one group of nineteenth-century feminists and Suffragists and separates her from another which claimed that male and female, masculine and feminine, were, in part, diverse principles, modes, or ways of being.[99] Mary Wollstonecraft's *A Vindication of the Rights of Women*, for example, is an early defense of the environmentalist thesis. Agreeing that women in her own day were frivolous and useless creatures, Wollstonecraft located their misery in a system of education which made them pitiful and stupid. She wanted women to acquire the "manly virtues" of moral courage and disinterestedness; true virtue, Wollstonecraft said, was reserved to men.[100] Sex differences would diminish if education were identical for the two sexes.

Friedan's variant on environmentalism not only allows her to gloss over the questions of identity as in part a bodily or an embodied identity, but it also enables her to articulate an overly simplistic and overly optimistic theory of how change is to be brought about. She glorifies education as the key to breaking the chains of the suburban prison. Only education can save women from the feminine mystique and lead to a new integration of female roles with male roles. She cites with approval something called the Danish Folk-High School movement which brought housewives back into the "mainstream of thought with a concentrated six-week summer course, a sort of intellectual shock

[99] Among the feminists who embraced a vision of male-female divergence that went deeper than environmental "conditioning" was Margaret Fuller who, in a famous 1844 essay, "Woman in the Nineteenth Century," argued that women were different from men and needed freedom to assert their unique qualities. She expressed an intensely felt notion of woman's "especial genius." Her protests against the status quo were enlivened by an assertion that the "electrical, the magnetic element in Woman" was being denied expression. See Margaret Fuller, *The Writings of Margaret Fuller*, ed. Mason Wade, esp. p. 176.

[100] Mary Wollstonecraft, *A Vindication of the Rights of Women*, ed. Charles W. Hagelman, Jr., p. 33.

therapy.''[101] The shallow philosophy of mind imbedded in this prescription retains its capacity to stun the reader, for Friedan's implicit presumption is that human identity—despite that vast and enormous paraphernalia she singles out as implicated in the feminine mystique in the first place—is a surface phenomenon, readily remedied, readily discarded. The other presumption, of course, is her view that what is desirable for women and the social world is women's full integration into the extant structure: hence the stated aim of Friedan's National Organization for Women (NOW), founded in October 1966, is to gain "truly equal partnership with men."

One of the *necessary* conditions for such "equal partnership," according to NOW's Bill of Rights, is the establishment of *government-sponsored* child-care centers open twenty-four hours a day for all children and the right to abortion on demand: the first "right" often involved a utilitarian approach to children and parenting (setting women "free" without sufficient consideration for the well-being of children, coupled with the unexamined claim that children were automatically "better off" in public child-care centers than at home); the second, as stated, evinced an insensitivity to the working-class and religious woman whose self-identity and sense of self-worth is tightly linked to the activities of mothering. By seeing such proposals as unalloyed goods and remedies, reflecting or conducing towards every woman's "true needs" even though many women from the start said they wanted none of it, Friedan's liberal feminist movement provides evidence of the pervasive effects of one of the most powerful mystiques of all: that of class.

What has changed in Friedan's view? She called several years ago for feminists to move from the "Old 'No' to the New 'Yes.' " Yet her new "Yes" is suspiciously like the old "No" with one exception: she now insists feminists must focus on the family rather than flee from it. In an article, "Feminism Takes a New Turn," Friedan recalls the halcyon days of 1970 when thousands of women marched down Fifth Avenue in the "first nationwide

[101] Friedan, *Feminine Mystique*, pp. 370-371.

women's strike for equality" carrying various banners, including "24 Hour Child Care." Their agenda then, she muses, was "so simple and straightforward," or seemed so. To see the problem with that first agenda as its simplicity is to miss the boat: Friedan's rethinking fails to reflect on the presumptions imbedded in those early demands.

Friedan goes on to insist that now, ten years later, "our daughters take their own personhood and equality for granted."[102] I shall focus on this claim for a moment. Friedan constantly buttresses her points from personal experience, and I shall mine. I am the mother of four children including three teen-age daughters, daughters of a professional and feminist mother. None of them takes her identity, or what Friedan calls her "personhood," for granted. I find the claim that they do, or should, troubling and condescending to all young women. If feminism is about a woman's struggle with, and against, prefabricated identities, why should Friedan presume that the mother's achieved identity should, or can be, adopted uncritically by her daughters as part of a phenomenon one might call the new "*feminist* mystique"? She would *deprive* daughters of the struggle for personhood she earlier claimed as *essential* to human identity; moreover, she ignores the evidence that human identity is *always* with (and against), always towards (and away from). No daughter, if she is to become her own person, particularly in a transpositional era, can simply adopt her mother's identity, whether feminist or not.

For Friedan, the feminist struggle seems largely to have been won and female identity secured. One nowhere finds in her celebration of what feminism has done—the movement even gets credit for the improved health of middle-aged women—a discussion of two troubling sorts of evidence about the young women whose identities feminism has ostensibly secured. I refer to the current epidemics in teen-age suicides, especially those of young women, and in teen-age pregnancies and live births despite the accessibility of birth control and abortion. Clearly many young

---

[102] Betty Friedan, "Feminism Takes a New Turn," *New York Times Magazine,* p. 40.

women find the world horribly confusing, depressing, even intolerable; clearly many young women, particularly those of the working-class and underclasses, *know* that despite Friedan's new "Yes" the route to success American-style is denied them. Thus, they are reaffirming a very militant *female* identity: I am Woman. Friedan takes credit for the "good" things but fails to examine flaws in the image: that is one reason why her rethinking is so terribly insular, even precious.

One final comment to illustrate the failure of middle-class feminism to come to grips with larger issues including consideration of the structural dimensions of our current crisis that lie in specific practices of the culture of productivity and problems of political accountability, and in social stratification along lines of ethnicity, class, and race as well as sex. Friedan embraces a view of the family I shall call the "corporate family." Although she calls for "restructuring of the institutions of home and work," her restructuring amounts to an overall accommodation to the prerequisites of corporate capital which can surely take account of dual sex, upper-middle class professionalism. Although Friedan seeks greater social services for parents on all income levels,[103] that call is tied to her acceptance of the American mobility myth and based on the belief that if lower income people would just change themselves in ways more suitable to the demands of professionalism—what Lillian Rubin in her examination of life in the working-class family, *Worlds of Pain*, calls "people-changing programs"—if they would only adopt the mores, manners, and life styles of the upper-middle class, they too could "move into more privileged sectors of the society."[104] Rubin proves this a gross illusion. Friedan, despite her rethinking, perpetuates a class-blind view. All her concrete examples of couples "making it" in ways that allow both to be parents and both to succeed are drawn from individuals in the top ten to fifteen percent of the population. This problem, the problem of class, is one Marxist feminists explicitly address and it is to their mode of analysis that I now turn.

[103] *Ibid.*, p. 94.
[104] See the concluding chapter of Lillian Rubin, *Worlds of Pain: Life in the Working-Class Family.*

MARXIST FEMINISM:
WHY CAN'T A WOMAN BE MORE LIKE A PROLETARIAN?

There is no single Marxist feminist perspective but several, depending upon which dimension of Marx's thought is being turned to feminist purposes and why. All Marxist feminist analyses, however, share the view that sex *and* class are critical determinants of women's place. For some this leads to an abstract notion of sex-class, which, like the radical feminist version, tends to collapse the categories "sex" and "class" into one another. For most, however, sex and class are complex factors that interrelate in a number of ways, public and private, for women, depending on their class standing and their relation to the mode of production, as well as the fact of their sex. There are Marxist feminists who share the sanguine hope that the total absorption of women into productive labor will provide ultimately for their complete emancipation.[105] Others, however, disagree with this optimistic view. There are hard-line Marxist feminist voluntarists who would "go it alone" as a vanguard movement; others find such strategies destructive and call for women to unite with oppressed men to bring about human emancipation, even as women struggle with specific features of their own oppression.

The basic notions public and private do not move as guiding orientations through Marxist feminist literature—at least not as such. Rather, in most (but not all) cases public and private are recast into spheres of production and reproduction respectively. In this recasting the meaning of public and private is remarkably transformed. That will be one basis of my critique. Another will be the inadequacies of Marxist feminism as an explicit political perspective. Marxist feminists share, with Marx, a tendency to treat politics as derivative, epiphenomenal, or symptomatic of the social relations of capitalism to be dispensed with altogether in some future classless order. I shall link these considerations with Marxist feminist accounts of the life-worlds of males and females—the logic of their analysis prevents Marxist feminists from

[105] See V. I. Lenin, *The Emancipation of Women: From the Writings of V. I. Lenin.*

taking the easy way out and positing separate male and female natures as the underlying explanation for the existence of such diverse social spheres—and the project of human emancipation to which they give rise. This, in turn, leads to another cluster of concerns over what might be called the "Marxist feminist subject"—who is she, what does she want, and what sort of action shall she undertake? Is she a human being who can give a spoken account of herself? If so, what language does she speak, according to Marxist feminism? If her language is distorted, how do Marxist feminists propose an alternative, undistorted self-identity and self-comprehension cast in and through language? (For that is the only way it can be cast.)

In order to probe these issues it will be necessary to step back into the nineteenth century and to take up the single text in the classical Marxist lexicon devoted to the "problem of women." Marx himself wrote very little on women or the family and what he did write is ambiguous and fragmented.[106] Engels took up the challenge of women and, he claims, stated what Marx himself would have said had he gotten around to saying it. Because subsequent Marxist feminists explicitly or implicitly range themselves for or against Engels' method and conclusions, and because *The Origin of the Family, Private Property and the State* forms the major conceptual link between the Marx-Engels corpus and contemporary Marxist feminism, it is worth treating in detail.

Engels develops a theory of the relationship between the public and the private, recast into Marxist terms as the spheres of production and reproduction. In his "Preface to the First Edition, 1884," Engels sets forth the postulates that delimit his inquiry: "According to the materialistic conception, the determining factor in history is, in the last resort, the production and reproduction of immediate life. But this life itself is of a twofold character. On the one hand, the production of the means of subsistence, of food,

[106] See Marx's frequently ignored, "On the Divorce Bill," an 1842 essay published in *Rheinische Zeitung* in which Marx argues against liberalization of divorce laws on the grounds that marriage—a *true* marriage creating something new, a *family*—is indissoluble. Marx and Engels, *Collected Works*, 1:307-310. See my discussion in chapter 4 above.

clothing and shelter and the tools requisite therefore; on the other, the production of human beings themselves, the propagation of the species.''[107] He goes on to trace what he takes to be a universal law of cultural development, namely, that the less developed the society ''the more . . . does the social order appear to be dominated by ties of sex.''[108] As social complexity based upon a division of labor and increased productivity supercedes structures based on ties of sex, and as private property, exchange relations, class inequality and antagonisms emerge, the ''old society based on sex groups bursts asunder'' and ''in its place a new society appears, constituted in a state, the lower units of which are no longer sex groups . . . *a society in which the family system is entirely dominated by the property system*'' (emphasis mine).[109]

Engels' starting point of inquiry is the premise that the ''first class antagonism which appears in history coincides with the development of the antagonism between man and woman in monogamian marriage, and the first class oppression with that of the female sex by the male.''[110] The subjugation of woman to man did not exist in premonogamous, preprivate property familial modes; thus neither did antagonism between males and females. This antagonism enters with monogamous marriage. Engels reverts to a ''family analogy'' mode of discourse but with a twist. His analogy is not from family to polity but the inverse: from the public sphere, conceived as the sphere of production upon which political institutions are affixed like parasites having no autonomous existence of their own, to the sphere of reproduction, the realm of women. The analogy also carries within it the presumption that the private class of oppressed persons, women, are analogous to the class of exploited workers, the proletariat, in the sphere of production. There is an analogous subordination of working class *men* and of all *women*.

---

[107] Frederick Engels, *The Origin of the Family, Private Property and the State*, pp. 25-26. For a reading of Engels which sets up the anarchist feminism of Emma Goldman as a term of contrast and comparison see Kathy E. Ferguson, ''Liberalism and Oppression: Emma Goldman and the Anarchist Feminist Alternative,'' in *Liberalism and the Modern Polity*, ed. Michael C. Gargas McGrath, pp. 93-118.

[108] Engels, *The Origin of the Family*, p. 26.

[109] *Ibid.*   [110] *Ibid.*, p. 75.

Following the linear anthropological formulations of L. H. Morgan (one of that species sometimes called "armchair anthropologists"), Engels begins with a secular Garden of Eden, a stage of "original . . . promiscuous intercourse," followed, in turn, by consanguine, punaluan, pairing, and, finally, monogamian family systems. Familial evolution corresponds to evolution in modes of production in a lock step fashion following a set of universal historic laws; thus, with the stage of the monogamian family, or capitalist class society, the family itself displays "in miniature . . . the very antagonisms and contradictions in which society, split up into classes . . . moves."[111] Like such latter-day thinkers and ostensible antagonists as the functionalists of the Parsons school, Engels presumes a series of "ideal-typical" family systems that are rigidly interdependent with the macrostructure, or mode of production. As the one, the mode of production or macrostructure, transmutes the other, the mode of reproduction or microsphere, a dependent variable, inescapably falls into line as well. Thus the functionalist devoted to social equilibrium and the Marxist devoted to social revolution meet on common terrain, for each views all forms of human social relationships, including the family, from the perspective of the functional prerequisites of capitalism rather than from the point of view of social participants themselves or from a perspective which can incorporate their point of view. For Engels, as for Talcott Parsons, the family (private but pulled along by a public teleology) is the creature of the social system. There can be no holdouts to the totalistic subsumption of all of life under the ineluctable imperatives of the productive sphere, the macrostructure, the public world.

Parsons, like Engels, concentrates upon forces impinging upon the family which compel it to comply in its inner structure and outer function with a higher schema, one unavailable to social actors. Family structure and function are determined by the needs of the macroorder: functionalism, like Marxism, involves an explicit or implicit teleology writ large. The family performs requisite functions for the society. As these requisites change, the family reacts appropriately. For example, the ideal-typical family

---

[111] *Ibid.*, p. 76.

prior to industrialization emphasized particularism and ascription. But this placed undue restraint on the needs of capital for a mobile labor force; ergo, the family altered to meet these demands. Or because, in Parson's view, it is only through isolation from wide social networks of friends and kin that it is possible to create the type of personality which can thrive on mobility and tielessness, "socializing agents should not themselves be too completely immersed in family ties."[112] I am not here questioning the moments of truth imbedded within functionalist analyses. What is at stake is a set of unexamined presumptions which undergird an insistence that families are helpless to resist change, to provide alternative values to those which prevail, or to create subjects who are critical of their social world rather than merely reactive puppets who jump, willy-nilly, whenever the macrostructure or mode of production blows the whistle.

Engels and Parsons alike see opposition to structural changes as futile, doomed to failure, and, in Engels' case, worthy of contempt.[113] Neither questions *why* a *particular* institution exists. The answer is given in advance: to meet the needs of the macrostructure or of capitalism. No good inheres in the institution itself (say, the family) or in those social relations for which it is the locus. As with the utilitarians, good resides in states of affairs and is signalled by a calculus of inexorability, whether couched as industrialization, modernization, or capital accumulation. The result is an iron-cage approach to social analysis, as Engels' dis-

[112] Talcott Parsons, "The Family in Urban-Industrial America," in *Sociology of the Family*, ed. Michael Anderson, p. 59. See also Talcott Parsons, "Age and Sex in the Social Structure of the United States," in *Selected Studies in Marriage and the Family*, ed. Robert F. Winch and Robert McGinnis, pp. 330-345.

[113] For example, Engels assaults the aspirations for self-determination of people "without a history," that is, those without a history that meshes with Engels' teleology which requires, in order to have a history, that one's course of development leads to capitalism. He and Marx supported German hegemony over the Slavs and American expansionism at the expense of "lazy Mexicans" because, Engels argued, Slavs and Mexicans "lacked the historic requisites for independence." The "chief mission" he assigns to "all other races and peoples—large and small [that is, all who have not played an active role in history] is to perish in the revolutionary holocaust," chilling words from our tragic vantage point. Cited in Diane Paul, "In the Interests of Civilization: Marxist Views of Race and Culture in the 19th Century."

course on private property, sexual love, and monogamy demonstrates.

Although Engels traces the emergence of modern individual "sex love" to monogamy, he denies the existence of such love among the nineteenth-century bourgeoisie for whom marriage is "determined by the class position of the participants, and to that extent always remains marriage of convenience."[114] Male dominance characterizes bourgeois marriage and persists because of the existence of private property. Monogamy among the bourgeoisie is, by definition, the subjugation of females by males under the imperative of property; however, monogamy sans property is "love" or "sex love." This condition, he declares, exists only among the proletariat, for among the proletariat monogamy *cannot*, by *definition*, entail male dominance given the "complete absence of all property" among the working classes. The safeguarding of private property is the sole reason, for Engels, that bourgeois monogamy exists. One problem he never treats is the following: if property is the primary motivation for monogamy, why doesn't a propertyless proletariat revert back to the halcyon, preprivate property days of group marriage?

Proletarian monogamy is not perfect. Its complete realization will occur only with the disappearance of private property and the total transformation of "private housekeeping" and the "care and education of the children" into fully public activities. At that point reproduction will no longer be a mere analogue of production but will become a species production. Within a propertyless society, sex love—no longer tainted by property considerations—will rule supreme and perfect monogamous relations will prevail. Like all utopian visions, this one requires a suspension of disbelief. Engels, remember, insists that male domination requires as a prior condition, the holding, safeguarding, and inheritance of private property. The economic imperatives which flow from private property serve as a stimulus to male domination and this domination is protected in bourgeois law. Among the proletarians, however, male domination has "lost all foundation." Engels adds a brief caveat concerning "that brutality towards women which

[114] Engels, *The Origin of the Family*, p. 79.

became firmly rooted with the establishment of monogamy" and which persists among the working class but he fails to explain why a phenomenon which has lost its economic base should continue to exist at all.[115] It follows, in Engels' view, that proletarian marriage is monogamous only in an etymological or formal sense, "but by no means in the historical sense." His formula is: monogamy minus property equals love. Proletariat monogamy is love, not brutality or dominance, but because individuals can't live by love alone, Engels introduces as a "first premise for the emancipation of women" the absorption "of the entire female sex" into public industry.[116]

Engels ignores counterevidence that would put pressure upon his lock step ordering of human history. His account of historical change and the interpenetration of the family, private property, and the state is flat and mechanical, a ritual in self-confirmation. For example, he locates the source for women's oppression both in their exclusion from the mode of production and their exclusive inclusion in the sphere of reproduction. The solution to the women question will occur when the laws of history have worked themselves out, production for private profit ends, class antagonisms melt away, and reproductive functions are taken over, or subsumed by, the sphere of production or society in toto (not the state, which will have withered away, if not immediately then imminently). "Along with them [private property, class antagonisms, and so on] the state will inevitably fall." In what was formerly the private sphere (there can be no private sphere proper without a public sphere as a contrast model and these divisions, together with politics, will have disappeared) a romanticized version of monogamous sex-love will reign supreme in a pure state unattainable under the conditions of bourgeois oppression.

Although politics vanishes in Engels' text the political implications of his determinism are very much alive. Nowhere does one find a complex, self-reflective human subject in his account of the past, his descriptions of the present, or his paeons to the future.[117] Human beings are stimulus-response creatures. Even

---

[115] *Ibid.*, p. 80.   [116] *Ibid.*, p. 82.

[117] What one does find is *animal laborans*, man as essentially and preeminently a laboring animal. One interesting dimension involved in labor is the human

those who are in revolt must, in Rosenthal's words, "shut up and fight" as discourse itself belongs to the history of exploitative relations.[118] The problem of the Marxist subject, or a subjectless Marxism, is treated in greater length below. At this point I shall proffer one disturbing example from *The Origin of the Family, Private Property and the State* to illustrate Engels' amoral consequentialism. In his discussion of the Iroquois gens, Engels intones: "Let us not forget . . . that this organization was *doomed to extinction.* . . . Impressive as the people of this epoch may appear to us . . . they are still bound, as Marx says, to the umbilical cord of the primordial community. *The power of these primordial communities had to be broken, and it was broken*" (emphasis mine).[119] Engels' claim isn't that, given the combination of forces arrayed against them, the Iroquois' chances of survival were slim; neither does he condemn their ruthless slaughter. Rather he insists that this assault *had to occur.* The Iroquois had to be destroyed to make way for the next wave in civilization leading, ultimately, to the classless utopia.

Presumably one can no more lament that state of affairs than bemoan the fact that an apple detached from a tree by a sudden gust of wind falls to the ground under the laws of gravity. Through an act of historical alchemy and under a set of laws within an overarching teleology, the base dross of common metals ("The lowest interests—base greed, brutal sensuality, sordid avarice, selfish plunder of common possessions") is transformed into a shining thing of gold ("the new, civilized society").[120] Engels' insistence that sordid brutality serves as the prelude to free, just, and liberated societies strikes me as most undialectical. I shall return to the problem of historic agency, moral limits, and social change in Chapter 6 below. One final comment must suffice for

---

relationships to nature. Engels' approach negates a supple relationship of man to nature: he stresses only mastery. Indeed, he signals mastery as the catalyst which changed ape into man and separates us from "lesser" creatures. Thus man is the master of nature and human beings are distinguished from nature to the extent that they master it. Read Mary Midgley's brilliant *Beast and Man* for witty and cogent criticisms of such arrogance.

[118] Rosenthal, "Feminism Without Contradictions," p. 31.

[119] Engels, *The Origin of the Family*, p. 101.　　　　[120] *Ibid.*

now. It is drawn from John Dunn's discussion of the failure of Marxism as a full and coherent account of the human future. He writes that a "license to evade" is built from the start into any Marxist account "which contrives to unite a despondent historicism about the human past with a gratuitously optimistic historicism about the human future."[121]

There is another serious problem, Engels' prescription for the emancipation of women. He fails to treat cogently the possibility that the full integration of women into the productive sphere may "universalize the envy and egotism that is from a Marxian perspective the defining characteristic of bourgeois civil society."[122] What Richard Krouse calls Engels' "abstract collectivism" permits him to sweep aside this question, and the problem of *children*, by simply assuming that turning over children to be cared for by "society" will produce a humane state of affairs: ". . . in order to emancipate women from the ghetto of the home, Engels would relegate children to the ghettos of the state (or its postrevolutionary equivalent). But it is by no means clear, to put it mildly, that the values of individual autonomy and self-consciousness prized in the more reflective versions of the Marxian ideal would flourish in this context."[123] The inadequacies of Engels present a daunting challenge for Marxist feminists. How have they responded?

As I mentioned above, Marxist thinkers tend to recast the public and private spheres as the spheres of production and reproduction. This translation is not viewed as a serious problem in terms of loss of meaning, given the characterization of social life and history to which Marxists commit themselves, totally or in part.[124] By dropping the notion of the private, Marxist feminists (with a

---

[121] Dunn, *Western Political Theory*, p. 101.

[122] Krouse, "Patriarchal Liberalism and Beyond."

[123] *Ibid.*

[124] I am not analyzing works from feminist historical scholarship that use Marxism as a powerful conceptual wedge into the history of women; rather, I am concentrating upon those texts that offer a Marxist feminist political perspective. For a Marxist perspective on comparative politics see Heleieth Saffioti, *Women in Class Society*. For a critique of so-called "classless" societies, see Heide Scott, *Does Socialism Liberate Women?*, and Gregory J. Massell, *The Surrogate Proletariat: Moslem Women and Revolutionary Struggles in Soviet Central Asia 1919-1929* for a discussion of Soviet perceptions of female inferiority.

few exceptions) lose, simply wash away, a host of related concepts, particularly those clustered around familial imagery, emotions, and ties. Marxist feminists locked into a narrow econometric model see the family only as a basic economic unit defined by its role in "the provision of domestic labor and the reproduction cycle of labor-power through which it relates to the functional prerequisites of capitalism."[125] What of family loyalty? Intimacy? Responsibility? Cross-generational ties? Love? Hate?

The most compelling example I can think of against Marxist feminism's infusion of econometric terms into the sphere of family ties and relationships would be to ask any mother whether she would accept "producing the future commodity labor power" as an apt characterization of what she is doing. One's fears and love for children are drained of their meaning, their emotional significance, when they are recast as relations between "reproducers" and "future labor power." By their choice of an abstracted, reductionist language, Marxist feminists confound ordinary language and evade the serious questions that arise when one attempts to express and examine the depth and complexity of family relations. Within the boundaries of econometric discourse, issues that emerge when one takes the human subject and her relations as a starting point simply disappear.

There is a simultaneous loss of meaning and coherence in orthodox Marxist feminist treatments of the public sphere. Public life as a political life and the person in the public aspect of a citizen, do not figure in these analyses. The citizen is dropped and human beings are designated exclusively by their relations to the means of production. The notion of "citizen" is, necessarily, a somewhat abstract term. Yet a "citizen" is by definition a person playing a political part. Such terms of Marxist discourse as "commodity labor force," "petit bourgeoisie," "lumpen pro-

---

[125] Jane Humphries, "The Working Class Family: A Marxist Perspective," in *The Family in Political Thought*, ed. Jean Bethke Elshtain. Humphries, an economic historian working from a Marxist feminist perspective, offers a discussion of the working-class family based on historic case studies and evidence which is at odds with the econometric model she criticizes. The econometric approach is chiefly concerned with whether surplus value is created within the household economy or mode of production.

letariat,'' or, again, ''reproducers of future commodity labor power'' are not simply abstract but, and here I am searching for the most appropriate characterization, ''aggregate.'' The person is not even thought of as an individual role-player—another abstract notion—but as a reactive member of a *collective* category. Whether Marxist feminists who repudiate the econometric model have an alternative that enables them to see and to conceptualize a subject will be explored in a moment. Also lost are notions of authority and law, and, most unhappily, considerations of political power, how it is attained, to what ends it may be deployed, through what means it can be controlled. Although Marxist feminists who use the abstracted language I am criticizing fail to take up the question, it is clear that the translation from public and private as basic notions to an abstract, econometric language in which these terms and all notions related to them are dropped, not only impoverishes their work as social analysts, it conduces to the overoptimism of their prescriptions for change. It is always easier to issue clarion calls for social revolution when there is no one to shout back—the speaking human subject, one's potential ally or protagonist, having been silenced before one starts to yell.

As one moves away from the rigidity of orthodox Marxist feminism, questions begin to surface that are treated obliquely or not at all within that model. One of these is the question of human nature I have already discussed at length in my section on Marx in Chapter 4. But Marx did not concern himself with the problem of the ways in which the diverse social locations of men and women lead to differences in consciousness or self-identity even among male and female members of the same class. Although Marxist feminists, particularly those indebted to the early, philosophical writings of Marx, grapple with the problems of men's and women's worlds, their respective self-identities, and possibilities or strategies for change, they haven't moved that far from Marx's basic presumptions that human nature is largely, if not exclusively, determined by the social relations of production. Given the distortions brought on by having to live and find one's being within a world of oppressive and exploitative relations (all of human history, remember, is the history of class oppression and conflict), human nature can be said to be alienated. Alienation "refers to the relationship of the individual to elements of his social and natural environment and to his state of mind, or relationship with himself."[126] Alienation is, to follow Steven Luke's summary argument, a social phenomenon; an individual state of mind; a hypothesized relationship between the two; and, finally and most importantly for our purposes, a presupposed or implicit picture or image of what the relationship between social phenomena and states of mind could or should be. Man (understood generically) is alienated from himself and will be restored to himself once he is no longer alienated. Alienation degrades and dehumanizes individuals and denies them their natural potentialities, or the actualization of those potentialities. If part of one's agenda, as a Marxist feminist, is to end the alienation of the female subject, one has already adopted an implied contrast model of what women will be once they are free to be "truly human."

An example of a humanist Marxist feminist account which takes the alienated and distorted human subject in the capitalist, commodity system for its subject is Sheila Rowbotham's *Woman's Consciousness, Man's World.* It is Rowbotham's view that this distortion can only be understood by focusing on the "outer world of production and the inner world of the family and sexuality." Note that the public world becomes "outer" and is reduced to relations of production and that the private world becomes an inner zone of privacy and intimacy out of place in the outer world. Marxist theory in our own time, she continues, is sadly lagging behind political practice, including the "new forms of organization"—her examples are women, gay, and student liberationist movements—whose politics express the "interaction between commodity production and other aspects of life under capitalism." Capitalism, and here comes Rowbotham's implicit model of alienation, "does not only exploit the wage-earner at work, it takes from men and women the capacity to *develop their potential fully in every area of life*" (emphasis mine).[127] What has capitalism taken away? What does a Marxist feminist solution promise to

---

[126] Steven Lukes, "Alienation and Anomie," in *Social Structure and Political Theory,* ed. Glen Gordon and William E. Connolly, p. 195. See also Ollman's *Alienation: Marx's Concept of Man in Capitalist Society.*

[127] Sheila Rowbotham, *Woman's Consciousness, Man's World,* p. xv.

restore? Can this restoration be specified more succinctly than with the notion of full development of one's potential in all areas, a vague promise at best?

Rowbotham begins by considering human beings, particularly women, on the basis of those features or aspects which characterize them in the specific social conditions of capitalist society. In vivid, ordinary language she describes what it means to be a "Living Doll," a description of becoming female that includes an illuminating example of what Marxists call reification, a process of objectification, in a woman's relationship to her eye makeup. "A Dog's Life" details the dehumanizing aspects of wage-labor under capitalism for men and "Sitting Next to Nellie" describes the even worse situation for women who lack the right, as Rowbotham puts it, to "equal exploitation." "A Woman's Work is Never Done" evokes tellingly the "inner world" of domestic work and the sense of endless repetition coupled with the little respect it commands.

But Rowbotham isn't satisfied with what feminists, at this time, actually know of how and why things are the way they are. "We need to know much more of the specific manner in which particular little girls perceive themselves in particular families in particular forms of society," she writes.[128] Women must become more visible to themselves, they must "break the hold of the dominant group over theory," indeed over language itself.[129] She would understand the ways in which society penetrates individual consciousness. She would challenge the sexual division of labor, the prevailing "order of fantasy," by understanding "the relationship of the various elements within the structure of male-dominated capitalism."[130] She repeats her claims and her agenda by insisting, first, that "our most private, personal experiences are affected by external social relations" and that, given this interpenetration, feminists must look at "the specific manner in which the dominant relations and values of capitalist society penetrate all the "supposedly 'personal' areas of human life," questions which remain "largely unexplored."[131]

[128] *Ibid.*, pp. 31-32.
[130] *Ibid.*, p. 122.

[129] *Ibid.*, p. 33.
[131] *Ibid.*, p. 55.

Two inescapable questions emerge: the first is how thoroughly the private sphere is dominated or infused with the values of the public world. If the relationship between the two is not simply asymmetrical but totally determinative, it would lead, surely, to a kind of despair, for Rowbotham characterizes the world of "commodity production" as totally debased and sees that as the central defining feature of the public world. The second is to ask how Rowbotham proposes to fulfill her agenda, her promissory note, to develop alternatives on the level of theory and language itself to power-riddled and distorting discourse, fantasy, and self-identity. "If we are ever to end the spiraling whirlwind of simply economic inroads into the structure of capitalist society which are recouped by the political power of the ruling class, we need to develop *notions of what an alternative society will be like*" (emphasis mine).[132] Part of this task for Rowbotham or anyone who would transform the present to some alternative order is to distinguish between those aspects of social life and relations that express something so fundamental about human beings they either cannot be changed or should not at our peril, and those which represent the detritus of coercive relations which can be swept under the historic rug.

I shall tie together my response to the two salient questions I have put to Rowbotham, for she forges links throughout her text between her characterization of the present condition of public and private relations and her promise of some alternative way of life. That link, specifically, is through language, particularly the sort of language that women must "break" and the sort they must come to embrace. I shall argue, finally, that her commitment to a thoroughgoing epistemological or conceptual relativism vitiates the coherence of her argument both as explanation and as future vision.

At times Rowbotham describes private relations as being "affected" by external social relations; as being in a "completely subordinate and dependent relation" to the dominant mode of production; as being penetrated ("all supposedly personal areas of human life") by the dominant relations of the society; as

[132] *Ibid.*, p. 101.

"defined" by external forces. But each of these is a different way, with diverse implications for understanding the present and reaching for the future, to treat the same reality or series of relationships. Being "affected" by an external force or being "completely subordinated" to that force are very different sorts of relationships. The first holds out the possibility that, for example, the family or our private worlds can serve not just as havens in a heartless world, occupying a totally defensive posture, but as partially autonomous arenas within which authentic human alternatives to market relations and values continue to hold, however shakily and imperfectly. Rowbotham moves back and forth between these alternatives depending upon whether she is seeking, forcefully, to condemn what is or moving, fitfully, to envisage what might become. But this won't do because the way in which we describe what *is* necessarily and ineluctably gears expectations and possibilities for how we think about what might be.

At times, Rowbotham depicts movingly the importance of the family, particularly for working-class people, as a "sanctuary for all the haunted, jaded, exhausted sentiments out of place in commodity production. . . . The family is the only place where human beings find whatever continuing love, security and comfort they know."[133] In the family, in Marxist language, women create "use value," not market or exchange value. But Rowbotham alternatively celebrates and condemns this fact: celebrates it because the inner world of "reproduction" and domesticity isn't thoroughly absorbed into market imperatives where things have only a price but no inherent dignity; condemns it because, even though women create "surplus value" (a claim incompatible with her notion the family isn't thoroughly consumed by the market), they are still devalued—not having a market price they are allowed no dignity. Perhaps, given the complexity of this question, there is no alternative but to condemn and celebrate. If this is the case, it should be articulated clearly rather than emerging, as it does for Rowbotham, somewhat ad hoc.

Rowbotham's sensitivity to the private sphere in the emotional lives of human beings is not finally incorporated into a compelling

---

[133] *Ibid.*, p. 59.

explanatory theory perhaps because she is determined to make her case entirely in untheoretical language. There is enormous strength in using ordinary language and resisting the move, certainly in some ways a power move, to couch one's arguments in an abstract language unavailable to most social participants. But Rowbotham goes too far in seeing the language of theory simply as an instrument of domination which must be repudiated even as she exhorts the oppressed to take over language and make it their own in order to express their reality.[134] The "language of theory—removed language—only expresses a reality experienced by the oppressors."[135] Surely this cannot be wholly correct unless she wishes to draw Marx himself into her indictment: no ordinary proletarian ever depicted his dilemma in the highly complex theoretical language of *Capital*. Language, or theoretical language, is seen by Rowbotham solely as a weapon in the hands of dominant groups. But at times she claims, or seems to, that the language of everyday reality is also reflective of the "words of the powerful" in so thoroughgoing a manner that the powerful "define and control reality for themselves."[136]

It is true that those in power have a greater opportunity to get across their assessments of social reality but it does not follow that all language, including the language of theory must spring from, or serve only, the dominators. If Rowbotham's claims were true it would follow that once the oppressed have gained power they, too, would deploy language as a tool of domination; they, too, would impose a view of reality on others, unless she is willing to advocate what she elsewhere calls the "sentimentalism" which assumes that the oppressed are purer and more noble because they have suffered.

When Rowbotham enjoins women to "change the meanings of words,"[137] or calls for revolutionary movements to "break the hold of the dominant group over theory," she proffers an important insight. But words are not changed *de novo* by single persons or groups. Meanings evolve slowly over time as changing social practices, relations, and institutions are characterized in various

---

[134] *Ibid.*, p. 32.
[135] *Ibid.*, pp. 32-33.
[136] *Ibid.*
[137] *Ibid.*, p. 33.

ways leading ultimately to an altered reality, part of which is a transformed characterization of that reality. In this process women are placed in an odd, inconsistent position by Rowbotham. She begins by excluding them "from all existing language" and depicting them as profoundly alienated *"from any culture"* (emphasis mine)[138] despite the fact that they are language-using, culture-bearing, self-interpreting beings. It would seem that women had nothing to do with the emergence of language and culture and the passing on of historic traditions. To press this point requires seeing women as existing outside of culture in a state that is at best quasi-natural. Rowbotham nowhere makes this claim for she sees, clearly, the sort of celebration of a separatist female culture and society, an enclave in male-dominated world, it would lead to and the futility that move would embody.[139] But her argument does lead inescapably to another claim: given the contradiction between private and public, production and reproduction, men's and women's experiences are, quite literally, opaque to one another. The alternative she proposes since she views women as the producers of "surplus value"—therefore a proletariat unto themselves, an oppressed and revolutionary class—is the transformation of the sphere of reproduction into the battleground of change. She posits a struggle which is both individual and collective on the terrain of production and reproduction alike. Yet she never addresses the manner in which a struggle in all arenas of human existence might wind up over-politicizing every aspect of that existence and in so doing wipe out rather than preserve the human values she cherishes.

Rowbotham's dilemmas emerge, in part, because her questions are so difficult. But that is only part of the story. Another aspect lies in the fact that her opening conceptual moves cancel out many of her explicit ends. She begins her analysis from a stance of eclectic tolerance from which she proffers praise for a list of feminist texts which are by no means in agreement with one another on any central issue, including some whose views she explicitly counters elsewhere in her discussion.[140] Most tellingly, however, her epistemic relativism (which is never, simply, a rel-

---

[138] *Ibid.*, p. 34.   [139] *Ibid.*, p. xiii.   [140] See *ibid.*, n. 12 on p. 9.

ativism on the level of theories of knowledge but which exudes a moral relativism as well) emerges in her treatment of Freud's "rather odd ideas." Because this discussion reflects a larger problem with Rowbotham's approach I shall spend a moment detailing it.

Rowbotham's condemnation of Freud's theoretical views, other than her insistence on their oddity, is erected on the foundation of a thoroughgoing relativism in the sphere of ideas. She nowhere discusses Freud's ideas from his own texts but cites as evidence of his oddity a bowdlerized excerpt from a letter Freud wrote his fiancée in 1883, a letter originally quoted out of context by Friedan in the *Feminine Mystique*. That initial distortion is simply repeated by Rowbotham.[141] But the more important dimension of her discussion lies in the fact that she positions herself utterly against claims she says are Freud's, though they are Marx's as well and those of nearly all political and social theorists, namely, that certain conceptual categories or forms of mind may have universal and transhistorical status. Indeed, she praises the cultural relativism of Karen Horney (a psychoanalytic thinker who rejects Freud's account of female development) by arguing, correctly, that this relativism led Horney, and those who adopt her stance, to critique Freud.[142] With this, Rowbotham has placed herself in a bind the nature of which she fails to appreciate. Anyone who attacks a thinker because he or she has made claims for the cross-cultural or transhistorical application of certain categories of explanation, and does so from a stance of total cultural and epistemic relativism, places herself on the shifting sands where she has placed others.

[141] The particular passage Friedan and Rowbotham find offensive is one in which Freud, in a moment of romantic effulgence, implores his bride-to-be to "withdraw from the strife into the calm, uncompetitive activity of my home." As if this weren't enough to condemn him as "odd"—a condemnation itself odd given Rowbotham's insistence in viewing individuals and their thought in a historic context and Freud here certainly reflects that context—Freud also is guilty of criticizing John Stuart Mill, a posture Rowbotham finds "reactionary within its own time." But she doesn't trouble herself over the substance and nature of Freud's criticisms of Mill. She does not seem to know that Freud had translated Mill's *On the Subjection of Women* into German. See Freud's comments on Mill in Chapter 3, note 94 on page 141 above.

[142] Rowbotham, *Woman's Consciousness*, p. 10.

This is a precarious position from which to launch one's own claims and arguments—unless one is prepared to explore explicitly why one's own arguments are *not* undermined by the relativistic claims one deploys against others with whom one disagrees.

For example: Rowbotham contends that Freud had a tendency to "make generalizations . . . without recognizing that he spoke from a particular sexual and cultural point of view,"[143] a claim that is incorrect on its own terms but, more important, is incompatible with other aspects of Rowbotham's text, including her claim that rich specifications of particular existence can usher in universal postulations of a life without oppression and exploitation. By eliding the difficulties which inhere in her own position she avoids wrestling with how it is possible to develop a set of concepts with which to characterize a particular reality—in her case that of all women in all societies dominated by commodity capitalism—that has cross-cultural application. By decreeing relativism a good thing she does not find it necessary to defend her own perspective as more rational, internally coherent, and valid on the basis of certain standards of rationality against those points of view she counters and with which she disagrees.

Despite these problems, there are enormous strengths in Rowbotham's analysis. She recognizes that human beings struggle to retain their humanity under conditions of oppression and that they preserve, however shakily, a capacity for reflective and critical self-awareness. Her individuals are not so thoroughly overdetermined that they emerge as mere reactors or passive role-players. She proffers a human subject conceived concretely and having agency, not abstractly and incapable of action. Human subjects experience pain at estrangement from their fellows and this pain and unhappiness speaks powerfully, if indirectly, of human needs either not met or distorted within ongoing social reality. But she does not tackle the tough ones: How much of human needs and potentialities are natural or given and how much are socially constituted? How much of human unhappiness and anxiety is simply part of what it means to be human and how much can be attributed to faulty and exploitative social forms? These important

[143] *Ibid.*

questions force a rich description of the terms of public and private reality and identity and are necessary to *any* treatment of the subject from a cogent feminist perspective.

I shall now examine a very different sort of Marxist thinker, Juliet Mitchell, who writes and argues in the abstract language of theory Rowbotham sees as inherently alienating. (Though, given her tendencies towards relativism, Rowbotham might exempt Mitchell, as a feminist, from her condemnation.) In her 1971 feminist classic, *Woman's Estate*, Mitchell proposes to ask the feminist questions and come up with some Marxist answers, answers shorn of the sentimentalism rife within other feminist perspectives which celebrate the terms of female oppression by romanticizing the characteristics taken on by the oppressed. With this opening gambit, Mitchell throws down the gauntlet to the radical feminists and cultural separatists.

Yet despite her explicit disavowal of the key categories and conclusions of radical feminism, she shares with these analysts a presumption that a sharp disjuncture exists between nature and culture or the "natural-biological" and the "cultural-historical." This has implications for her arguments on how, and under what terms, women gain entrance into culture, that human order she equates with patriarchy; namely, via the inexorable workings of a set of abstracted, ahistorical, universal laws. Mitchell's laws have causal efficacy. They are universal in their form and application and can be deployed to explain any and all particular, diverse events and phenomena in divergent cultures. Theory, "scientific Marxism" or "scientific Freudianism," in turn, explains the laws. If Rowbotham falls prey to overrelativism, Mitchell embraces a set of presumptions which are iron-clad in their operation. She creates a formalistic universality which transcends or bypasses the rich diversity of extant cultural and social forms— past and present.[144] Even as a relativist gives the diversity of ways of life the status of an incorrigible reality, Mitchell downgrades

---

[144] The quest for lawlike explanations in the social sciences presumes that a symmetry of logic of explanation pertains, or ought to, between natural and human sciences and, moreover, that within lawlike explanations a symmetry of explanation and prediction exists. Thus every "true explanation" must have predictive power.

diversity to the level of mere appearances beneath which lies a
set of *"necessary* laws of human society,"[145] necessary in the
sense that all disparate phenomena have an invariable relation to
one another and thus to a set of laws independent of historic
specificities and determinations. I shall argue that Mitchell's laws
are couched in such abstracted terms that the initial conditions
that do not explain laws but must be present within her explanation
in order for the laws to operate, can *always* be found to pertain.
The relationship between theory and evidence is extremely loose
in Mitchell's analysis. She completes her embrace of positivistic
social science by insisting that her explanations commit her to no
normative stance; indeed, she explicitly separates value judgments
from scientific laws and facts.[146]

Although Mitchell's scientific theory is far more complex and
demanding than the crude empiricism she critiques, it shares with
its less complex cousin the omission of individual and social
meaning as a central concern. In this she implicitly follows rather
than rebuts Engels and the functionalists. Mitchell's explanations,
including her treatment of sex and class, omit a self-reflective
human subject. An explanation that includes self-interpretation
and self-identity cannot emerge from claims to iron-clad, lawlike
predictability. To explain and to understand human social systems
as diverse, replete with multiple meanings and particular determinations which cannot be understood in the absence of a rich
characterization of persons and their social reality, requires an
interpretive and critical social theory. Mitchell, however, presumes that she can advance lawlike claims *in advance of any
study of human beings, within particular cultures, who are en-*

cf Geertz ?

[145] Juliet Mitchell, *Psychoanalysis and Feminism*, p. xvi. Further examples of
the structuralist approach may be found in a journal published in Australia, *Working
Papers in Sex, Science and Culture*. See especially Elizabeth Gross, "Lacan, The
Symbolic, The Imaginary and The Real," pp. 12-32; and Mia Campioni, "Psychoanalysis and Marxist Feminism," pp. 33-60.

[146] Mitchell's approach allows her to criticize such simplistic empiricism as that
of Naomi Weisstein who, in a much reprinted piece, "Kinder, Küche, Kirche as
Scientific Law: Psychology Constructs the Female," *Motive*, pp. 78-85, condemns
Freud for not doing what he never pretended to do, provide replicable controlled
experiments on human beings that would mesh with the narrow standards of a
crude verificationistic model of science.

gaged in determinate relations and speak both "the same" and a "different" language given the diversity of social and individual meanings.

I shall assess Mitchell's contributions to feminist debates on the public and the private by pointing out how her conceptualization of woman's estate and, later, *Psychoanalysis and Feminism* suffers from an excessive abstractedness. Like those structuralist thinkers to whom she is indebted, notably Louis Althusser, Jacques Lacan, and Claude Lévi-Strauss, for Mitchell structures, laws, and ideological formations rather than human subjects are the agents of history. Mere persons become vehicles for the ongoing operation and transmission of structures and laws—if, indeed, people can be said to exist at all. Because one of my concerns in assaying competing perspectives on the public and the private is to determine whether a theorist incorporates within her analysis, or expunges from her vision, a rich view of the human subject, Mitchell's turn to structuralist discourse is troubling. Monique Wittig is correct in saying that Marxism, historically, by refusing to grant a subject to oppressed classes, is implicated in preventing "all categories of oppressed peoples from constituting themselves historically as subjects."[147]

Mitchell's persons, whether as members of a class or a sexual category, emerge as objectified entities subject to universal laws. In *Woman's Estate*, Mitchell's concern is to explain woman's condition as that of being under the sway of a "complex totality" of objective conditions, a unity of different elements she calls "Structures." She writes: "Because the unity of woman's condition at any time is in this way the product of several structures, moving at different paces, it is always 'overdetermined.'"[148] These welded together structures, which march through her pages capitalized as proper nouns, are Production, Reproduction, Sexuality, and Socialization. Women play roles within each structure and this defines women's condition. An ideology or "ideological formation" presents a role as given; thus women are denied any authentic understanding of their situation. Their self-understand-

---

[147] Wittig, "One is not Born a Woman," p. 73. Wittig's critique is explored as I articulate my theoretical alternative in chapter 7 below.

[148] Juliet Mitchell, *Woman's Estate*, p. 101.

ing is defective as they remain unaware of the deep structures or laws at work which can only be captured within the terms of a scientific theory available to an elite few. It ultimately matters little whether women have a correct or distorted understanding of social formations because Structures, not women themselves, are credited with historic agency, despite calls by Mitchell to struggle. Sectors have their "own autonomous reality," although each is "ultimately . . . determined by the economic factor."[149] Structures "move" at different paces and "reinforce" one another. One day their contradictions will "so reinforce one another as to coalesce into the conditions for a revolutionary change" and the Structures will "rupture."[150]

Although Mitchell explicitly and insistently incorporates the private realm—Sexuality, Reproduction, and the Socialization of Children—into her scheme of things, to treat Sexuality, for example, a powerful and profoundly resonant human activity, as an abstract Structure in "rapid evolution" and the weakest link in the chain,[151] is to distort social relations by treating abstractions like real things. It is also to lose our centuries-old complex language of private reality. Given Mitchell's conviction that all Structures must be attacked simultaneously (insofar as they are monolithic) she espouses, by way of change, further diversification of the functions of the family fused in the Structures of Sexuality, Reproduction, and Socialization. Thus, despite her expressed and brave defense of the needs of children for nurturant socialization, Mitchell's structuralism, like its cousin, functionalism, can only prescribe or foresee as a cure for social ills a healthy dose of the current disease, with a predictable further breakdown of possibilities for human beings to have rich, continuing, social relations in either their private or public worlds.[152]

Mitchell's programmatic agenda for the feminist struggle juxtaposes a "scientific socialist" analysis with liberal feminist demands—apparently in the belief that such demands, including the right to equal employment and child care, will deepen contradic-

[149] *Ibid.* [150] *Ibid.*
[151] *Ibid.*, p. 147.
[152] Mitchell is familiar enough with psychoanalytic theory in this early work to be sensitive to the child's need for constant, nurturant care in its developing years.

tions within the current order and hasten the day of an apocalyptic rupture. But it is difficult, within the terms of her analysis, to determine why a woman who is a wife and mother should be motivated to seek further differentiation of the functions fused within her family life, the locus of her most meaningful, if frustrating, social relations and activities, particularly when all she has to look forward to as an alternative is absorption into the Structure of Production castigated by Mitchell (correctly!) as one in which uninspiring, demeaning, and—in the case of the woman worker—ill-paid and unprotected wage-labor prevails. Most women's real alternatives are limited. The emotional costs of stripping down her private world and draining its current profusion of demands, activities, and meanings are potentially great.

If a woman is told she should make these moves nonetheless because she will be deepening the contradictions of capitalist society in order that one day its fused Structures will rupture and a new order will emerge, she will quite correctly wonder what sort of religious certainty sans spiritual comfort she is being asked to embrace in the absence of a clear and compelling vision of the future alternative. Here Mitchell's refusal to turn to political theory, from which she might have drawn enrichment, support, and meaning, is apparent in the impoverishment of her analysis. She has no notion of a political community, no concept of a citizen, no apparent understanding of the meaning to human beings of their loyalty and allegiance to families, communities, and country. There are, finally, neither persons nor politics within Mitchell's abstract Marxist structuralism. There is only a rigid interdependence of structures and functions with men and women as role-players who do not possess self-reflexive awareness concerning their roles and the beliefs that sustain them. Like Parsons, Mitchell agrees that the fully socialized person doesn't so much play a role as *become* the role he plays.[153] We are, for Mitchell, the functions we perform; indeed, we are their features. For example, ". . . the family does more than occupy the woman: it produces her."[154]

[153] See Parsons, "Age and Sex in The Social Structure of the United States," *passim*.

[154] Mitchell, *Woman's Estate*, p. 151. Parsons' use of Freud to functionalist

Mitchell's abstraction from an embodied human subject is especially ironic given the fact that she is preeminently the thinker linked to an incorporation of psychoanalytic theory—as a theory of, or for, the private sphere—into feminist and Marxist thought. But Mitchell's positivism leads her to adopt psychoanalysis as a set of scientific laws operating in the sphere of reproduction, a kind of analogue to those laws of production provided by her Marxism. The human beings who emerge with such profuse complexity and multileveled senses of meaning within Freud's case studies are stripped by Mitchell to abstract bare bones, to objects which acquire laws as unaware, passive reactors. Despite Freud's repeated warnings that unconscious mental process should not be reified and made thinglike or lawlike, Mitchell writes of "The Unconscious" as the "object" of psychoanalytic science. Like her Structures, The Unconscious, rather than a fully fleshed-out person, has agency in the world. When Freud deployed the language of laws he meant that probabilities, regularities, and tendencies could be found in human mental life. He denied that psychoanalysis could be a predictive science.[155] Freud's complex

---

ends—the little girl grows up to be an expressive nurturant like Mommy and the boy to be an instrumental adaptive like Daddy—ultimately diverges little from Mitchell's use of Freud to structuralist ends. For example, "The girl will grow up like her mother, but the boy will grow up to be another father" (*Psychoanalysis and Feminism*, p. 170). As Richard Bocock put it (in a critique of Parsons which is equally apt for Mitchell): "All signs of conflict are eliminated in the oversmooth workings of Parsonian social, cultural, personality and organic systems. They all seem to integrate with one another. . . . Life has been removed from Parsonian systems theory" (*Freud and Modern Society*, p. 54). Mitchell eliminates conflict by integrating and fusing structures into an overdetermined totality even as she postulates deep conflict, even contradiction, between structures. The moment of conflict, however, is unbelievable to the reader who realizes that overdetermination builds a kind of meta-homeostasis into the system. For Mitchell, an opponent of capitalist society who has a revolution in mind, and Parsons, a celebrant of capitalist society who desires the maintenance of equilibrium, to share a basic set of presumptions and concepts does not necessarily mean that they must share the same interpretation of any given set of phenomena, although a strong tendency for such interpretations to converge does exist.

[155] Mitchell's structuralist imperatives as scientific theory allow her to claim that psychoanalysis has its own "laws" and that these "laws" can somehow be extracted "from their specific problematic" (*Psychoanalysis and Feminism*, p.

human subject gives way before an objectified Unconscious and an ahistorical woman inculcated into the human order under the inexorable laws of patriarchy. Although Mitchell's woman is present at the initiation ceremonies she is an unself-aware initiate, being a child. Her unreflectiveness continues into adult life. The Law of the Father she carries about is held in The Unconscious, and this Unconscious operates with no regard for the human subject it inhabits; it is more a machine in the ghost than a ghost in the machine.

Culture is treated as an unspecified whole, a massive, diffuse conglomerate. Beneath all the "apparent" variations in economy, ecology, history, religion, politics, art, and language, an adamantine deep structure, universal and formal, operates. What do all human cultures share in common? The "law of the father" or patriarchy. But if, for example, the "law of the father" can be deployed to explain the life of the Zuni, the life of the suburban American housewife, and the life of the queen of England, what, ultimately, has been explained? These women—and all others—fall under Mitchell's universal edict of patriarchy and its laws. What is her evidence? Simply this: that, as members of the human order, women *by definition must* be operating under the laws of patriarchy. Patriarchy is *culture* itself. Mitchell states: "This symbolic law of order defines society and determines the fate of every small human animal born into it."[156] Freud's stress on psychic

___

xx). What this means in practice is that the subject matter to be explained and the logic of explanation can be severed without losing anything important in the process. To extract laws of psychoanalysis from its "specific problematic" is to throw out the very phenomena Freud would explain—the complex human subject, the human mind, and personality. Freud's subject was never "The Unconscious" but the mind within which unconscious mental processes were one aspect of a set of dynamic forces that work in descriptive, topographic, economic and structural dimensions and relations. In Freud's mature thought, in his move to the structural theory with its postulate of id, ego, and superego as agencies of mind, the power of the ego, of substantive reason, and self-reflection, is stressed. Yet this capacity appears nowhere in Mitchell's impressive but, finally, linear and abstract rendering of Freud. She insists that the social-historical matrix in which the theory emerged itself fails to explain or critique the theory fully—fine—but then she has gone on to eliminate from Freudian theory its very subject matter and we are confronted with the curious case of the missing mind.

[156] *Ibid.*, p. 391.

bisexuality and the child's identification with both parents fades into the background. The Oedipus complex becomes the child's acquisition of "the patriarchal social order."[157] For Freud there was no such thing as "*the* Oedipus complex." There were as many Oedipus complexes as there were human beings—the ambivalent conflicts of infantile sexuality could be resolved in an infinite variety of ways.[158] Once again a feminist analysis posits an irresistibility of the phallus dreamt of by males in fantasies of omnipotence. When Mitchell equates patriarchy with "human history" she joins ranks with those radical feminists she criticized for their ahistorical understanding of patriarchy. The human subject, amidst all this scientific, tough-minded lawfulness must attempt somehow to assault the edifice of universal laws—patriarchal, capitalist—which operate everywhere and to at least one shared end: the oppression of women.

Mitchell's way out of her structural iron cage is a move to Lévi-Strauss's claim that women have been universal objects of exchange.[159] This becomes, strangely, a ray of hope. It turns out, stranger yet, that the law of patriarchy, including the taboo on incest, operates to maintain a situation in which women are universal exchange objects. (Surely, though, the incest taboo had its raison d'être in human beings coming to grips with their frequently imperious sexual and aggressive urges.) Women are exchange objects *in all* cultures and patriarchy "describes the universal culture," Mitchell proclaims.[160] Evidence as to diverse ways of life is bypassed or brought into line with a purely abstract claim, an "unwarranted teleology, reminiscent of eighteenth-century social-contract theorizing," belied by actual anthropological and historical evidence.[161] Eleanor Burke Leacock points out that all acts of reciprocity between men and women are *reinterpreted* by Lévi-Strauss (and hence Mitchell) under the rubric of asymmet-

[157] *Ibid.*

[158] See, for example, Sigmund Freud, "The Dissolution of the Oedipus Complex," *Standard Edition*, vol. 19, p. 179. Freud writes: "I have no doubt that the chronological and causal relations here discussed . . . are of a typical kind; but I do not wish to assert that this type is the only possible one."

[159] Mitchell, *Psychoanalysis and Feminism*, p. 393.

[160] *Ibid.*, p. 409.

[161] Eleanor Burke Leacock, "The Changing Family and Lévi-Strauss, or Whatever Happened to Fathers," *Social Research*, p. 250.

rical "exchange"—despite the fact that Lévi-Strauss's own work contains evidence of symmetrical, reciprocal relations in which women are not exchange commodities. The result of this "universal law," like all the others, is a distortion of real societies, real distinctions, genuine diversity, and the ambivalent complexities of the public and the private dynamics of real men and women.

By adopting ahistorical, universal categories subject to no counterfactuals, nor contested evidence, Mitchell's only way out of the patriarchal laws and monolithic unities of Structures is the deus ex machina of universal women's exchange. This leads Mitchell to her most implausible conceptual move and indefensible claim: that the incest taboo, though essential to precapitalist societies, is "irrelevant" under capitalist economies which do not turn on woman exchange. The contemporary "ban on incest," Mitchell argues, is stressed so "loudly" (actually, one rarely hears it stressed at all—it is simply assumed if social life and our most basic and intimate relations are not to become brutal and exploitative at their core) because we no longer, on a market calculus, require it. That a thinker who claims to be presenting a reading of Freud against prior feminist distortions should treat the most powerful, fearful, repressed constellations in human psychic life as parasitic upon, or an outgrowth of, a set of calculated, external considerations of exchange designed to assure male dominance (thereby requiring that the incest taboo itself be a *consciously selected manipulative strategy* set forth to buttress these relations) is astonishing.

Change, clearly, if Mitchell is to be consistent, requires doing away with the Oedipus complex, the incest taboo, and hence women's feminization. If the incest taboo is but an artifact of the exchange of women capitalism has made redundant, it appears that our best bet lies in recognizing this fact and undoing the tangled web of patriarchal lawfulness lodged in the taboo itself. But given Mitchell's tie-up of the incest taboo with human culture, it is difficult to imagine what will supercede it. A primal horde? A self-limiting polymorphously perverse paradise? Or will we rationally choose to pretend "as if" such a taboo still existed in order to prevent the exploitation of children by adults on whom they are dependent? Mitchell backs off a massive assault against the by-now superfluous incest taboo. Instead she speaks vaguely of a "cultural revolution" which will usher new structures and free potentialities into being. "It is a question of overthrowing patriarchy," she concludes, a desideratum with about as much chance of success, given the inexorability of her own analysis, as overthrowing the law of gravity.[162]

I would suggest that there is in fact rather more hope for change than feminist writers who would challenge the order of the universe or overthrow the universal patriarchal order allow for. My hope begins with a very different understanding of the human subject and social realities, one indebted to an interpretive approach to Marx and Freud.[163] A person, after all, is not merely or exclusively (if at all) an objectified role-player or abstracted object of inexorable laws, but a thinking, acting being engaged in particular relations with others within a specific historic time and place. To assimilate the public and the private into universal laws and abstracted structures requires Abstract Man, Abstract Woman, and Abstract Child in turn. Within this rarified, undifferentiated realm one searches in vain for a recognizable person and a redeemable politics.[164]

---

[162] Mitchell, *Psychoanalysis and Feminism*, p. 416. Ironically, Mitchell winds up with the same kind of determinism and totalism she so astutely critiqued as features of radical feminist analysis. In *Woman's Estate*, she observed that the radical feminist version of patriarchy was "all-pervasive: it penetrates class divisions, different societies, historical epochs. Its chief institution is the family: having the shakiest of biological foundations. . . . Different societies have never offered real alternatives. . . .'Patriarchy' then is the sexual politics whereby men establish their power and maintain control. All societies and all social groups within these are 'sexist' . . . in the far more fundamental sense that their entire organization, at every level, is predicated on the domination of one sex by the other. *Specific variations are less significant than the general truth*" (emphasis mine; *Woman's Estate*, p. 65).

[163] Two articles drawing upon aspects of Marx's thought in an attempt to take up the questions Mitchell evades or denies as crucial, Dorothy E. Smith, "A Sociology for Women," in *The Prism of Sex*, ed. Julia A. Sherman and Evelyn Torton Beck, pp. 135-188; and Virginia Held, "Marx, Sex, and the Transformation of Society," in *Women and Philosophy*, ed. C. Gould and M. Wartofsky, pp. 168-183, figure in my discussion in the last chapter.

[164] Joan Landes first labeled Mitchell's female an abstract woman in her Ph.D. dissertation, "The Theory Behind Women's Liberation."

PSYCHOANALYTIC FEMINISM:
GENDER, IDENTITY, AND POLITICS

The final major category of contemporary feminist thought, psychoanalytic feminism, has emerged as a force to be reckoned with in this country only over the past five years. One might have thought feminist thinkers, in their attempts to conceptualize inner/ outer, me/not-me, and issues of male and female identity, would have turned at the outset to psychoanalytic theory. Unfortunately, thinking psychoanalytically was an activity interdicted by feminists given what was considered Freud's misogyny and the antiwoman conspiracies of American psychiatry, traceable, it was claimed, to Freud himself. Radical, liberal, Marxist—nearly everyone repudiated psychoanalysis, most often from a stance that indicated no understanding of the theory being rejected.[165] Ironically, in this repudiation of Freud, feminists were reflecting, not countering, the prevailing tendencies in American social and political science that dictated a rather crude empiricism and an antitheoretical approach to social issues. Feminist thinkers who are responsible for the "psychoanalytic turn" not only had to come to grips with an extraordinary complex body of thought but also had to fight the ignorance and hostility of their colleagues in doing so.

What are the fruits of the turn to psychoanalysis? The record at this point is incomplete as the field is in ferment. My comments will be couched from my stance as a political thinker attuned to and sympathetic toward the psychoanalytic approach. Psychoanalysis is being deployed as a way to understand the individual, particularly the female individual, in society and to appreciate

[165] See, for example, Friedan, *Feminine Mystique*, p. 77; Firestone, *Dialectic of Sex*, chap. 3; Rowbotham, *Woman's Consciousness, Man's World*, p. 10. One additional example must suffice: Barbara Deckard, after what one hopes was a meticulous reading of one excerpt from a single Freudian essay, dismisses psychoanalysis with startling shallowness. She is tempted to "dismiss Freud and his theories as a sick joke" (*The Women's Movement*, p. 17). One other fascinating development in contemporary feminist thought should be mentioned and that is the voluminous literature flowing out of the French feminist turn to psychoanalysis. Because this is literally a field unto itself, I have decided to stay on ground more familiar, at this time, to Americans in my own discussion.

more richly than possible under perspectives that concentrate on "externality," the inner connections between individuals and their social worlds within particular or "universal" historical situations. The two psychoanalytically oriented thinkers I will focus upon briefly—Dorothy Dinnerstein and Nancy Chodorow—take as their subject for critical dissection the nature of contemporary "gender arrangements" with specific reference to female dominance of the "mothering" process. Rejecting a biological deterministic model as an explanation for what is seen as a universal pattern in which females are primarily responsible for child care, Dinnerstein and Chodorow speculate as to why our private and public situations have remained, in some ways, so constant; what can or should be done to transform the situation, for it is one they and all feminists find unacceptable in whole or in part; and what the effects of such transformation would be. If their arguments are to be *politically* compelling, there must be a relatively tight and concretely specified connection between the *particular nature of private social arrangements and public outcomes both by way of explanation as to what is wrong and by way of prescription for what must be changed.*

Dinnerstein, a psychologist, foresees the very end of civilization itself if something isn't done, and soon, to "break the female monopoly over early child care."[166] Dinnerstein correctly observes that ". . . the private and public sides of our sexual arrangement are not separable, and neither one is secondary to the other. Both have their psychological roots in a single childhood condition."[167] But does this claim, couched as an imperative and an article of faith, follow coherently? She states that both our private and public arrangements "will melt away when that condition is abolished."[168] In order to explore her contention, it is necessary to assay the malaise that Dinnerstein locates exclusively in gender

---

[166] Dorothy Dinnerstein, *The Mermaid and the Minotaur*, p. 33.

[167] *Ibid.*, p. 159. But ". . . a single childhood condition" is a terribly abstract notion and the question must be posed, though Dinnerstein doesn't pose it, whether in fact mothering in each instance is a single condition whatever the socio-economic contrasts between, say, a single welfare mother of four and a married upper-middle class mother of two.

[168] *Ibid.*

distinctions in the first place. Here Dinnerstein presumes a private-public arrangement in which private psychological imperatives, instilled from the first, given female mothering, flow upward and outward and lead, in adult life, to women depending "lopsidedly on love for emotional fulfillment because they are barred from absorbing activity in the public domain," even as "men can depend lopsidedly on participation in the public domain because they are stymied by love."[169] This outcome is inexorable, "woven into the pattern of complementarity between male and female personality that emerges from female-dominated early childhood."[170] Rooted into these patterns, then, is male privilege and female oppression ("universal exploitation of women"). Why? Because—and here I condense the pattern of Dinnerstein's argument that is unsystematic, evocative, and intuitive as well as theoretically grounded—female power is so potent, so dangerous, given women's exclusive mothering role and the overwhelmingness of it for male and female infants alike (but with differential results for each) that it will always be hard, if not impossible, "for mother-raised humans to see female authority as wholly legitimate."[171]

I am not going to attempt to counter Dinnerstein's argument on the level of psychological truth, in part because I find much of it compelling, in part because to do so would require a search of clinical evidence to articulate a counterthesis. But what I am going to question is the alternative she proposes and the outcome she foresees. There is in Dinnerstein, and necessarily in all feminist thinkers indebted to psychoanalytic theory, an ambivalence about what women are to give up in order to gain much of what men have had. With Dinnerstein this ambivalence, because it isn't clearly articulated and confronted, results in a deep fissure in her thinking that weakens it as a viable feminist politics, or even as the basis for one.

Let me be specific. Dinnerstein's characterization of the public world is thoroughly abstract and denunciatory. She never distinguishes between the kinds of activities that fall within the public domain; nor does she indicate which of these activities may be

[169] *Ibid.*, p. 70.   [170] *Ibid.*, p. 210.   [171] *Ibid.*, p. 179.

properly seen as "political" and which are something else. In other words, she has no political account of the public world. For a political theorist this is a serious shortcoming at the outset. But there is another problem. Dinnerstein describes the public world as, alternatively, history-making and "nature-assaulting"; indeed, for her, history-making is coterminous with those assaults against nature she deplores. Women, excluded from history-making, have also refrained from nature-killing. Dinnerstein writes:

> What has kept women outside the nature-assaulting parts of history—what has made them (with striking exceptions, to be sure) less avid than men as hunters and killers, as penetrators of Mother Nature's secrets, plunderers of her treasure, outwitters of her constraints—may well be not only the practical procreative burden that they have carried, but this special compunction too. [The compunction to which she refers is the special relationship women have had towards "mother."] Certainly *it seems reasonable to suppose that if men had felt all along more closely identified with the first parent—as they will be if time permits us to make the necessary change in our child-care arrangements—we would not now be so close to the irrevocable murder of nature* (emphasis mine).[172]

There are several imperatives at work in this passage. Dinnerstein first provides a devastating and angry description of the public world of history-making that women have been excluded from; and second, insists that if women had not been excluded, that public world would not be, nor would it have become, the deadly business it was and is. The reason she can make this claim lies in the underlying presumption that had women been incorporated into history-making, and should they be, this would require as a necessary and (almost) sufficient prerequisite a break in "the female monopoly over early child care."

If women and men were to "mother" equally and to participate in the public world in full parity, public and private would be

---

[172] *Ibid.*, p. 103.

transformed in one fell swoop. Children would no longer be distorted; nature would no longer be assaulted. Dinnerstein sees this not only as a desirable outcome but a perfectly workable one as it requires but two kinds of conditions—the first *psychological* (just described) and the second *technological*. The technological condition is characterized as "the practical possibility of making parenthood genuinely optional, the concrete feasibility of adult work life flexible enough so that men and women can take equal part in both domestic and public life"—something, she insists, that is "already available," just as the restructuring of child-rearing, if we really want it, is equally available.[173] On the road to sexual equality something very interesting has happened: a series of important considerations involving the structure of the American political economy are drawn in ad hoc—the "possibilities" quoted from Dinnerstein above appear in a brief note on the bottom of a page—and labeled "technological," not political or economic factors. In this we find Dinnerstein reflecting a dimension of the public world she deplores—the tendency to reduce important human and social issues to problems of technology and to presume we can find a quick technological fix to nearly everything. But surely the public conditions she requires for her solution are not technological ones but profoundly, inescapably, political. Dinnerstein, however, has no way to handle these issues because she has no political analysis at all.

There is one final, serious problem with Dinnerstein's way of seeing and that is her extraordinary overoptimism when she comes to prescription and prophecy, given the despair of her description of the present. She moves into the future in a way that is far too facile, even as it is at times touching and playful. Of course, none of us is in a position to foretell the psychological and social outcomes were our gender arrangements to be restructured overnight with males and females involved equally in parenting. In one way this question is a provocative and important one; in another it is utopian, for the *political* preconditions, including the consciousness and self-identity of women themselves, stand in the way of such a dramatic, or traumatic, overhaul. But that is

[173] *Ibid.*, p. 256n.

not the most important critique. I refer the reader back to Dinnerstein's claim that it is women, over the years, who have not been the hunters, killers, plunderers of Mother Nature. They have not been because of their procreative activities and the special relationship, *given precisely the gender arrangements Dinnerstein wishes to overturn*, to "Mother" and thus to All Women. Recall, if you will, that what Dinnerstein foresees, after having prescribed a gender revolution, is a situation of perfect parity in which all the current deadliness, plunder, exploitation, nature-assaulting she rightly deplores have melted away. She foresees this result because men, no longer overwhelmed by potent female power in the child-rearing process, will no longer be under a felt exigency to control the "female" in their public role as history-makers.

But what will have happened to the women? They, it seems, will stay as "sweet as they are" even as they gain public roles, authority, power. They, apparently, will *not* become infused with any of the previously denied to them male qualities (denied *because* of their intense relationship to Mother, according to Dinnerstein) including the need to control the Mother. Something has dropped out of Dinnerstein's equation on the road to the future. The nastiness has evaporated. I am not suggesting that Dinnerstein's argument is altogether unconvincing. I am insisting that it is ingenuous from the point of view of politics and unconvincing from the point of view of psychology, particularly if that psychology is psychoanalytic which has never flinched from exploring the darker sides of human nature and asking: Why? Dinnerstein has come up with too simple an answer and thus too easy and apolitical a resolution. This derives, in part, from the *necessary* intensity of psychoanalysis's concentration upon the individual subject, not upon social wholes. If the psychoanalytically indebted thinker is going to make claims concerning the public world, as Dinnerstein does, she must reach for a richer characterization of that world than Dinnerstein has.

A second important feminist thinker indebted to psychoanalysis is Nancy Chodorow, a sociologist, whose concern, like Dinnerstein's, is the nearly exclusive responsibility of women for child care. In *The Reproduction of Mothering*, Chodorow approaches what she calls the "sociology of gender" by examining the relationship between male dominance and the sexual division of labor. Indebted to the post-Freudian schools of ego psychology and object relations, Chodorow presents a closely reasoned case for the emergence of a gender identity which leads to the reproduction of particular social roles, notably mothering ("Women come to mother because they have been mothered by women").[174] She concludes that "the social organization of parenting produces sexual inequality, not simply role differentiation." With Dinnerstein, Chodorow insists that our public and private identities and activities are set, congealed, in the early stages of childhood development given women's responsibility for child care, a responsibility linked irrevocably to "male dominance." Chodorow states: "Psychologists have demonstrated unequivocally that the very fact of being mothered by a woman generates in men conflicts over masculinity, a psychology of male dominance, and a need to be superior to women."[175] Citing cross-cultural studies by anthropologists, Chodorow buttresses her psychoanalytically based claims with evidence that the "more father-absence (or absence of adult men) in the family, the more severe are conflicts about masculinity and fear of women."[176]

Chodorow's analysis immediately suggests a counterfactual argument, namely, that in societies in which men were not mothered by women, at least not exclusively, a psychology of male dominance would not take root and neither would the need to be superior to women be a felt imperative of male life. Given that no such world has ever existed, Chodorow must turn to social situations in which the hard and fast gender identities and activities she analyzes are somewhat ameliorated. She finds, for example, that if the mother carries on her activities in a supportive network of "women kind and friends," and if she "has meaningful work and self-esteem" she will "produce daughters with capacities for nurturance and a strong sense of self."[177] What is less clear, because Chodorow doesn't spell it out, is what happens to male children under these circumstances—circumstances which by no means represent her ideal. But the ameliorative dimensions Cho-

---

[174] Nancy Chodorow, *The Reproduction of Mothering: Psychoanalysis and the Sociology of Gender*, p. 211.
[175] *Ibid.*, p. 214.   [176] *Ibid.*, p. 213.   [177] *Ibid.*

dorow finds fitfully extant in some societies do not and cannot exist under the terms of "capitalist industrial development." That is, in societies such as our own the development of capitalism has diminished the conditions under which women can "do meaningful productive work, have ongoing adult companionship while they are parenting, and have satisfying emotional relationships with other adults."[178] This means, in turn, they are more likely to overinvest in children.

The stresses and shortcomings of our present arrangements, for both sexes and for children, have been bountifully documented. Chodorow presents one of the strongest cases for where, and how, these strains get reproduced. But how convincing is it, finally, to lay the developments she links to "capitalist industrial development" on that doorstep rather than to see these alterations as endemic to modernity itself. The examples of societies in which women have the things Chodorow mentions—meaningful productive work (what is meaningful work is not specified), kin, and close social network ties—either belong to some preindustrial age, or to simpler tribal societies that we compare with our own, or with *any* industrial society at our peril. Students of contemporary Russian society, for example, frequently point to the extraordinary overprotection and what Chodorow, rather unfortunately, calls "investment" or "overinvestment" in children that takes place in the Soviet Union.

If one begins to view many of the problems Chodorow over-assimilates to the capitalist mode as part and parcel of a set of social changes ushered in with modernity, a range of political and theoretical issues she does not take up in her discussion suggest themselves. These include the vexing questions I posed at the very beginning of this book. Given that we cannot turn back to a less dynamic age when mobility was foreclosed and tighter networks of kin and neighbors were a given aspect of social reality, we must ask which of the social arrangements and institutions we have inherited represent impositions upon us of "artifacts" we can and should change in order to become individuals

[178] *Ibid.*, p. 212.

or societies of some other kind, and which embody instead necessary or vital human ends that we drop or manipulate at our peril? Chodorow—and this is a strength she shares with other psychoanalytically oriented feminists—recognizes the extraordinary importance of early childhood and of providing nurturant, secure, stable units within which children can develop and move through the conflicted stages of development. We usually call such units families. But her alternative to what we now have emerges none too clearly: not only does she fail to specify the politics of the current situation, she also refuses to spell out the political implications of alternative modes she hints we ought to set about emulating.

One example of the thin account of politics in a work that provides a rich account of the emergence of gender identity must suffice. At the conclusion of her text, Chodorow sets about linking women's mothering and women's liberation. She poses as alternatives to contemporary American society ''more collective child-rearing situations.'' Specifically, she mentions studies done in Israel, China, and Cuba, which ''suggest that children develop more sense of solidarity and commitment to the group, less individualism and competitiveness, are less liable to form intense, exclusive adult relationships, than children reared in Western nuclear families.''[179] Here Chodorow implicitly links gender identity in American society to what might be called social identity—though it is not a specifically *political* identity—and she means to portray it as debased given that its fruits are ''individualism . . . competitiveness.'' The terms used to describe what emerges from the gender arrangements she criticizes are crucial. Another observer might, utilizing many of the same studies Chodorow cites, speak of ''being an individual'' or of having a sense of ''moral autonomy'' as the result of our child-rearing arrangements when they are working well. We would respond very differently in that case because none of us applauds individualism, which has a bad name, and rightfully so given the predatory forms it frequently takes, but all of us save those most blind to concerns of

[179] *Ibid.*, p. 217.

human freedom and responsibility want children to grow up to be, in the best sense, *individuals*, persons with a sense of moral responsibility, who can be held accountable for their deeds. What of Chodorow's alternatives—do they produce *individuals* without *individualism*? Surely Cuba and China offer small comfort to the political theorist concerned with freedom and responsibility. The sight of three- and four-year-olds chanting in unison and waving Mao's little red book, or of their Cuban counterparts raising their arms and shouting allegiance to Fidel is a disturbing one, if we remain concerned with individuals and moral development—with a process of development that allows for, if it does not guarantee, the possibilities for the emergence of a *critical* political conscience and consciousness, for individuals who will, if need be, march against the state, not simply fall into line for it. Here the fears of the radical feminists like Rich about state control of child care are well-placed. Although Chodorow doesn't cite the studies she insists lead to the results she applauds in Israel, China, Cuba (a strange omission, by the way, in such a well-documented volume) there is at least one study that raises questions about the kibbutzim and allows us to spell out the potential political implications of moves towards "more collective child-rearing arrangements." I refer to Bruno Bettelheim's *The Children of the Dream.*

Bettelheim emerged with some startling information and troubling speculations following his study of child-rearing in the kibbutzim. On the positive side, he discovered that children grow up with a strong sense of security within the perimeters of an entire social matrix that is somewhat like an extended family. The kibbutz as a whole "stands for providing, controlling, educating": the kibbutz is a kind of collective mother.[180] No child ever has to go hungry or without basic care. There is, Bettelheim found, a floor beneath which none is allowed to fall. There are not, as there are tragically and inexcusably in our society, "severely neglected children."[181]

But there are costs in this collectivism. All children tend to be

---

[180] Bruno Bettelheim, *The Children of the Dream*, p. 70.
[181] *Ibid.*, p. 297.

treated alike regardless of individual differences in response to developmental pressures. Bettelheim found slavish following of schedules in some kibbutzim to the detriment of the children. The strong, cohesive community—which provides that network of supportive kin Chodorow desires—also makes for a situation in which dissent is either discouraged or repressed, or the eccentric or dissident is ostracized. The voice of conscience that emerges is a kind of collective superego: morality is tied to the need to cooperate and be at one with the peer group. Given the intensity and bustle of daily life, children "must develop a high threshold against sensations, must screen out the finer nuances"; thus, capacities for a rich intimacy, capacities for being intimate *with oneself*, for privacy, remain underdeveloped or fail to emerge.[182] The homogeneity of the social system disallows children of the kibbutz to identify, through empathic imagination, with those different from themselves. Bettelheim learned that kibbutz young people found it impossible to move outside themselves, to take alternative perspectives even in the imagination.

When Bettelheim asked them to imagine life as someone else or life somewhere else, he found that the question "what would my life be like if . . .," one essential to all creative thought, seemed to kibbutz young people either inexplicable or too dangerous to even consider.[183] If any one of them expressed or uttered a divergent opinion, a defense was thrown up immediately: "It's only a joke," "I'm not being serious," they would say. In other words, there is little chance for a multiplicity of perspectives to emerge for there is no locus for it; indeed, the very qualities of mind necessary to entertain diversity fail to develop. It is not surprising that individualism, construed by Bettelheim as meaning developing one's own point of view and defending it, is discouraged. The young person who revolts is ostracized by the group. The meaning and purpose of life is given, not questioned. The result: security and a sense of *duty* and *obedience* so great that the kibbutzim inordinately supply Israel with members of its officer corps (at the time of Bettelheim's study four percent of the Israeli population lived in kibbutzim but kibbutzniks provided

---

[182] *Ibid.*, p. 123. [183] *Ibid.*, p. 172.

forty percent of the officer corps), and with its dead in Israel's wars (in the 1967 war Israel suffered 800 deaths of which 200 or twenty-five percent were kibbutzniks). It seemed to work best, for purposes of fighting morale and soldierly solidarity, to allow those from a particular kibbutz to soldier together in the same units. They fight bravely and die unhesitatingly. But, Bettelheim discovered, creative thinkers, innovators, critics do not emerge from the kibbutz and its "more collective child-rearing."

My point is this: if we want to go Chodorow's route, we had best be clear about what we are doing and what sort of people we are likely to get. Bettelheim, troublingly, concluded that the original aims of the kibbutzniks were not met and never can be. He writes: "Essentially they wanted both for their children: utter egalitarianism and highest individuation." It comes hard to realize, he concludes, that these "are contradictory values."[184] Even if one concludes that Bettelheim has overdrawn his argument, it is nonetheless the case that Chodorow has underdrawn hers. She stacks the deck against the qualities that emerge from the child-rearing modes she finds damaging ("individualism . . . competitiveness") and fails to tackle the tough questions about the mode she favors. If she had linked up gender identity and political identity more specifically, asked not only how and why little girls become mothers and little boys men who put down those who mother, but how and why both little girls and little boys see themselves as Americans or Russians or English or Irish, the political issues implicit in her study would have emerged with greater clarity. There is another point at which Chodorow fails to follow through on the implications of her conclusions: she insists, repeatedly, that it is in father-absent families that young boys suffer the most severe conflicts about their masculinity and are more likely to fear and despise women. But she fails to draw the obvious point for contemporary America in which a variety of child-rearing and familial arrangements are being experimented with, and that is that single-sex families based on a feminist politics of gender (that is, all female communes or households) may be engaged in a self-defeating activity.

[184] *Ibid.*, p. 319.

What is interesting in the psychoanalytic feminist works that have thus far emerged is the fact that the conceptual categories internal to psychoanalysis have not yet been put to full use to feminist ends—rich, dynamic concepts like projection, displacement, regression, and transference. The "feminist ends" I have in mind include the articulation of a philosophy of mind that repudiates the old dualism with which we are still saddled in favor of an account that unites mind and body, reason and passion, into a compelling account of human subjectivity and identity, and the creation of a feminist theory of action that, complicatedly, invokes both inner and outer realities. A third feminist end to which psychoanalysis could make a major contribution is the amplification of a theory of language as meaning and truth, as the articulation of a coherent logos of female experience. If psychoanalytic feminism begins to move in these directions, it will make contact with speech, identity, and action along the whole range of public and private possibilities. At this point, however, psychoanalytic feminists, in their attempts to derive everything from private imperatives buttressed by social compulsion, are creating, paradoxically and unwittingly, a patina of defenses against politics, or against thinking "the political." Political history gets overassimilated to domestic dynamics and family history. Their turn towards preindustrial societies, past and present, to buttress their conclusions facilitates this tendency, as one of the things to be said of such societies, with their less complex and differentiated social worlds, is that direct explicit connections between domestic and "public" (whether properly political or not) are more readily apparent. Despite these shortcomings as a political account, feminist psychoanalytic theory is one of the most promising developments in current feminist thought.

As with the Western tradition of political thought, contemporary feminism is alive with competing ways of seeing and contrasting images of public and private realities. In my final chapter I shall remain faithful to the complexity imbedded in alternatives drawn from feminism and the Western political tradition as I move toward a critical theory of women and politics.

Chapter 6

Toward a Critical Theory of Women and Politics: Reconstructing the Public and Private

Striking for the gentle, striking for the kind
Striking for the guardians and protectors of the mind
An' the unpawned painter behind beyond his rightful time
An' we gazed upon the chimes of freedom flashing.*
—*Bob Dylan*

We all carry within us our places of exile, our crimes
and our ravages. But our task is not to unleash them on
the world: it is to fight them in ourselves and others.
—*Albert Camus*

I have set for myself a daunting task. In bringing feminist imperatives to a critical exploration of the tradition of Western political thought and going on to locate the insights and concerns
of political theory in the heart of the feminist enterprise, I implicitly and, at times, explicitly indicated that I had an alternative
to offer which would forge links between the Western tradition
and feminist thinking in a way that served to illumine the past,
instruct the present, and presage a reconstructive future. I am now
faced with making good on these promises. In our parlous age
it is not enough to critique what is, vital as that task may be. The
political thinker, as witness, must imagine a livable future, must
proffer coherent proposals for reordering our public and private
worlds if he or she is to make a claim on the attention of others.
One telling critique of Marxist politics, for example, has been its
"persistent readiness to allow intensity of moral distaste for a
present state of affairs to excuse a weakening of the determination

to understand (or even to reflect seriously upon) the causal prop-
erties of the future social order with which it is hoped to supplant
the present."[1] That criticism is justifiably levelled at much contemporary feminist politics: too often the present is assailed but
proposals for the future are neither specified with coherence nor
consistent with one another or the ends being sought. Wildly
visionary futures are portrayed but no cogent way to move from
the horror of the present to the heaven of the future is provided.[2]

I have no heaven to offer perhaps because I have not discovered
in ordinary reality the irredeemable hell many feminists have seen
in present social arrangements and experiences. Yes, there is much
that is unconscionable and cries out for relief. There is much that
is ugly, sordid, and violent; tragic, pathetic, and heartbreaking.
There are events that arouse horror, outrage, and disbelief. There
are realities that encourage cynicism, disconcern, and despair. At
times one is overwhelmed by madness and corruption in high
places and like a wrathful, avenging god one would topple the
secular temple, call down lightning upon the unjust, humiliate the
arrogant who gamble with the lives of the innocent, and rid the
world of opportunistic ruthlessness, whether it calls itself democratic, socialist, revolutionary, or holy. Nothing, at such times,
seems sweeter than vengeance. Nothing, at such times, seems
more fitting than cold wrath. Nothing, at such times, seems more
enchanting a prospect than an ''apocalypse now.'' It is at precisely
such times that the political imagination must come to life and
the moral sentiments awaken from slumber not simply as personal
exigencies, to save oneself from cynical escapism and corrupting
delusions of death and glory, but as a *public imperative and
responsibility*.

Our century is piled high with bodies: victims of the deadly
politics of the right (fascism), the left (Stalinism and other so-
called Marxist regimes that create burying grounds and call them
people's republics), and the less immediately fatal but ultimately
coarsening and life-denying politics of liberal complacency and

[1] Dunn, *Western Political Theory*, p. 97.

[2] Think of Daly's Hagocracy, Brownmiller's militarized Sparta with its standoff
in the sex-war, Firestone's cybernetic Brave New World, even the much sober
Dinnerstein's alteration of parenting and gender arrangements.

benign neglect. The task of the political imagination must be to serve as witness for the victims, all those the final solutions, ends-of-history, and politics-as-usual either eliminate, manipulate, degrade, or deny, without at the same time falling into a political identity, language, and mode of practice that sentimentalizes their victimization and repeats the terms of their degradation. From the Biblical warning that those who live by the sword shall perish by it to the rock group Who's expression of postrevolutionary working-class cynicism, "Meet the new boss/just like the old boss," warnings have been issued to social-changers and their would-be beneficiaries to eschew a politics of violence and coercion, to be suspicious of false promises, and to be unremittingly skeptical of boldly stated but thinly defended claims. Feminists and their political constituents, being human, are no more exempt than anyone else from the lures of vanguardism or the false comfort of delusory faith.

My moral guides for future reflection include those great witnesses from our recent past, Camus, Bonhoeffer, and Weil. It is from them, and from my diverse experiences as a student, writer, teacher, scholar, feminist, traveler, activist, wife, mother of four children, child of my parents, sister to my brothers and sisters, that I learned to repudiate theory-building as the construction of an overarching *Weltanschauung* which, as Freud observed, "leaves no question unanswered and no stone unturned." Those with a need for absolute certainty must force intractable human material into the mold of their hubris in order that life mesh with abstraction. The search for what is called the "totality" is uncomfortably close to this century's term for unmitigated political terror, totalitarianism. Life is too various, diversity too dear, to give it over to a single definition or purpose. There are no ultimate solutions though there are those arrogant or dangerous enough to attempt them. In calling for a reconstruction of public and private, I do so within the frame of a theory and a politics of limits, not because I can envisage only limited possibilities from politics but precisely the opposite: because I know that politics too easily becomes an engine of limitless, destructive possibilities as the face of Leviathan dons an executioner's mask. For feminism to save its soul it can have nothing to do with the creation of a new order that *requires* sacrificial victims for its achievement.

We must actively urge individuals to act in common to agreed upon and worthy ends. We must unalterably and with a clear voice oppose ends that are unworthy, that in the name of *future* justice or freedom destroy human beings in the present. Without illusions, we are neither world-weary nor abject. As for charges of pessimism, I offer Camus's response as my own: "The idea that a pessimistic philosophy is necessarily one of discouragement is a puerile idea."[3] Part of the struggle involves reflecting on whether our current misery and unhappiness derive entirely from faulty and exploitative social forms that can, and therefore must, be changed or whether a large part of that unhappiness derives from the simple fact of being human, therefore limited, knowing that one is going to die. In these matters and others, as Wittgenstein put it, "Light dawns gradually over the whole." Every reflective person who has struggled to see more clearly knows the truth of this saying. Light dawns, but only if one persists.

The discussion which follows is divided into two sections in which I attempt to discover and illumine for others a number of vexing, interconnected puzzles and problems from a stance informed by feminism and political thought. In the first section I take up the question of feminist theory and the project of creating a reflective feminist discourse. The activity of theory is, literally, about seeing.[4] *Theorein*, the Greek word from which our own derives, meant to watch or to look at. "Seeing" is a complex activity, transformed, like mind, over time. Although it is impossible to reproduce precisely one's own process of seeing for others, I shall try by looking first at the activity of the theory itself. In the second part of this chapter, I move imaginatively from particular to universal, from concrete to abstract, from public to private as I envisage a reconstructive ideal of public and private.

The terrain traversed in this chapter is not *about* political theory but is itself an example of what it means to *do* political theory

---

[3] From Camus's *Notebooks*, cited in Jacobsen, *Pride and Solace*, p. 145.
[4] Gunnell, *Political Theory: Tradition and Interpretation*, pp. 136-139.

in our time. Too often scholars in the field of political theory devote themselves entirely to the task of probing the texts of "the fathers." Too often this yields works of filiopiety rather than original rethinking and confronting the political problems we face at present. I am not urging that we kill the fathers but that we recognize that we cannot remain forever in the house of the fathers. Lincoln said it best: "The dogmas of the quiet past are inadequate to the story present. . . . As our case is new, so we must think anew, act anew. *We must disenthrall our selves*" (emphasis mine).[5] Although the past was by no means quiet for our ancestors in political theory, that past, as dogma, is a refuge for us now compared to the storm of the present; hence my call to disenthrallment.

POLITICAL DISCOURSE AND ITS DISCONTENTS

This is what we need: we need an account of women's liberation which can incorporate the self-understanding of the female subject as an essential feature of its overall logic of explanation. We need to be able, cogently, to articulate the bases and steps in the creation of female identity, public and private. We need a way to explore female speech and language along public and private vectors. We need to create a mode of political thinking that helps women redescribe social reality from a vantage point that allows for, and sustains, critical reflection. We need to conceptualize plausible alternatives. We need to avoid powerful tugs toward repetition of the compulsions of the past, including the sentimentalization and oppressions of women under some new guise. This is a large order indeed.

There is no single, overarching logic of explanation which can do everything for us. Those who make monistic claims fail to distinguish between explaining and interpreting human life in all its diversity and denying or quashing the diversity as they "explain" human life. There are times when we need to examine the

---

[5] Cited in *The Collected Works of Abraham Lincoln*, ed. Roy Basler, 1:488; 5:537.

individual female subject in her particular social location and probe her inner and outer realities; there are other times when the individual female subject will be submerged within some aggregate category like sex, race, or class, because our theoretical aim is the explanation of systemic or structural features of an overall social order. Psychoanalytic theory can no more account for the political economy of women under capitalism than Marxist economic theory can offer a coherent understanding of women's psychology and sense of self-identity.

The search for the female subject is simultaneously a quest for a form of inquiry that serves the ends of explanation, understanding, and critique along public and private vectors. This means that the theorist must reject out of hand any mode of explanation which requires or sanctions the imposition upon the female subject of the theorist's own views as to who she is, what she wants, and what she should have in advance of any attempt to probe that subject's self-understanding. To take a human being as the object of political inquiry without patronizing, manipulating, or distorting her world must be every critical feminist thinker's concern. Too often those whose chief delights include abstract formulation, as Freud ironically reminded us, wind up treating real "objects," including human beings, as abstractions and treating abstractions as if they, not human beings, had real existence, agency, and importance in the world.[6] One cannot survey the human race from a great and learned distance, proclaiming loudly that one has found the truth for the good of all the nameless, faceless abstractions one has nevery really bothered to take seriously, and go on to provide the account of women's liberation I have called for.

One must first *locate* the female subject in creating a feminist political theory *for* and *about* her.[7] One must refuse to accept the political silencing of women under terms that either take their social position, traditionally a particular, local and concrete one, for granted or label it and move on to other, more "important"

---

[6] Freud, "The Unconscious," p. 204.

[7] Compare the provocative essay by Smith, "A Sociology for Women," pp. 135-188. I have relied on Smith's reconstruction of the sociological subject as a "problematic" for my own discussion.

matters. One must find out how the female subject in our time sees herself, or would, were she given the opportunity to provide a spoken account of her existence. The feminist political thinker aims to transform her discipline as well as her social world in important ways. This necessitates locating the woman as subject of political and social inquiry, moving away from the abstracted, disembodied "product" of social forces featured in much contemporary social science.[8] This female subject, as the object of inquiry, must be approached as an active agent of a life-world of intense personalization and immediacy.

As the female subject explores her life-world, dimensions of her daily existence which fell previously under the interdiction of silence will be opened to scrutiny. This dynamic of consciousness poses a serious problem for the political analyst: How active and intrusive a part should she play in the process of the self-discovery of others? Dorothy Smith, a feminist sociologist, locates herself at the activist end of a range of alternatives when she writes: "We might attempt to develop *for* women analyses, descriptions, and understandings of their situation, of their everyday world, and of its determinations in the larger socioeconomic organization to which it is articulated."[9] This is a task the subject cannot undertake alone as the very terms of her privatization and particularity prevent her from making the conceptual linkups Smith would develop *for* her.

Smith's approach avoids the arrogant presumption that the analyst, in advance of either seeing or listening to her subjects, can proffer an accurate description of their world. Instead, she promulgates what I shall call a part-whole-part hermeneutic in which inquiry begins with the self-descriptions of subjects in context, a discourse made possible only after silences are broken. This is followed by the analyst's rendering of those self-descriptions in a manner that makes them more widely and generally accessible by assimilating them into a theoretical framework that gives them explanatory power at a more abstract level of understanding. I

---

[8] See Dennis Wrong's still important critique of the disembodied subject in his seminal essay, "The Over-Socialized Conception of Man in Modern Sociology," *American Sociological Review*, pp. 183-193.

[9] Smith, "A Sociology for Women," p. 173.

suggest a third step though Smith does not. The conceptual formulations based upon the subjects' self-interpretations should then be shared with the subjects to elicit whether, on their view, the analysis seems intelligible and responsible, or whether it is distorting in some serious or, most unhappily, demeaning way. This raises many problems, including the force of *resistance* by subjects based on distortions of their own self-understanding, or, simply, on the need to "defend" themselves. These are not easily dealt with but they must be faced, not denied.[10]

There is one final vexation Smith hints at but shies away from confronting and that is: Why should a personalized, localized, particular female subject be brought into the more abstract, rationalized, universal mode? To be sure, the realm of particularity, which I will recast here as the private, exists in a determinate relation with a wider social organization whether private subjects recognize this or not. But the private world also exudes its own values and imperatives in part because it *is* the theater of particularity and everyday concrete meaning. If that mode were suppressed altogether in favor of the exigencies and demands of abstract personhood and the pull towards rationalization, technological definition, and universalism, who would tend to the little world, keeping alive its life-redeeming joys and tragedies? In other words, does Smith, or does any feminist political thinker, really want to so relocate female subjects and reconstruct the matrix of their traditional identities by substituting the terms of universal, bureaucratic socio-economic imperatives that, as women achieve a public identity, they lose this other world and the values imbedded with it entirely?

If we can bear to turn our thoughts to this problem we shall perhaps come close to seeing, perhaps experiencing within ourselves a queasiness or twinge of regret in sympathy with the fears and ambivalences of many women about the feminist movement and a proposed way of being that, it is claimed, shall serve as their liberation, shall "free" them from their domestic prisons. It may help us to understand what the militant activist's single-

---

[10] Rubin's *Worlds of Pain* is a moving example of the dynamic I have here described.

mindedness disallows: that there are no gains without losses; that assaults on a given order sweep along in their trail much that makes life livable, diverse, and charming as well as that which makes it exploitative and unjust. And the truth of the matter is that no one can predict the fruits of major social change, though all social changers want their potential constituencies to focus only on the most optimistic possible outcomes.

An illuminating contrast-model to a mode of inquiry that incorporates female self-understanding as central, having both as method and aim helping women become conscious of themselves through a process they actively undertake, is the form of social analysis undertaken by a renowned world-changer, Simone de Beauvoir, in her feminist classic, *The Second Sex*. At first glance it might seem that de Beauvoir and I are engaged in similar activities: both of us have the modern woman-in-society as our concern; both of us want that woman to alter her inherited and, in some ways, restricting or damaging views of herself; both of us want change in a direction that would transform her world for the better. But de Beauvoir's analysis emerges from a stance of great distance cast in a mode of disquieting abstractedness. The difference between political inquiry *for* women and de Beauvoir's theory *about* women is apparent when de Beauvoir chooses as her central terms of social description and analysis Sartrian categories which have no meaning in ordinary discourse, terms that are unavailable to social participants themselves. To be sure, the woman who makes her way through de Beauvoir's lengthy tome may pick up the language of "Immanence" and "Transcendence." But if she then wishes to state her case to others, to persuade them of her point of view rather than pummel them with her superior knowledge, she *must* be able to make that case in terms of personal, political, and social discourse that are commonly shared.

Rather than beginning with the female subject's self-understanding, de Beauvoir labels her subject by fixing her in that cement she calls Immanence, a variant on Sartre's Being-in-itself (not, by the way, the Being-to-be). With Sartre, she identifies woman with nature, the practico-inert, the sphere of Immanence. This world of everyday life is first treated as an abstraction and then condemned as a morass, a bog, noncivilization. De Beauvoir contrasts Immanence with all that is light, worthy, civilized (and the work of men!), the realm of Transcendence (Sartre's Being-for-itself, definitely the Being-to-be). De Beauvoir's subjects are pictured in a matrix of the local and particular. But rather than framing her analysis from the point of view of the subject's self-understanding, de Beauvoir compares them unfavorably to men who undertake "free projects" in the realm of Transcendence. Although de Beauvoir declares women free and autonomous a priori (a metaphysical construction having no bearing on their social identities, a noumenal category, sundered from phenomenal reality), she consigns them to a region declared to be one of determination, totally lacking in autonomy.[11]

De Beauvoir launches volleys against her subjects in the name of liberating them. Women are consistently and invidiously compared with men. For example, de Beauvoir approvingly cites the claims of one male writer who hit upon the notion that the body of man had its own integrity and "makes sense" apart from woman; however, the woman's body, what Sartre called woman's "unfortunate anatomy," is a body that " 'seems wanting in significance by itself.' "[12] This narcissistic male view, reminiscent of the Greek misogynists who saw women as misbegotten men and not fully human, is repeated by de Beauvoir as a serious piece of wisdom rather than probed as the male's "advertisement for myself."

As the price of admission to the realm of Transcendence de Beauvoir's female subjects must shuck off their female identities. Civilization de Beauvoir declares to be male and men its essential parts; women, the flip side of the coin, lie outside civilization and are inessential. The formulation is an existentialist recasting of the Aristotelian typologies of "necessary conditions for" and "integral parts of." The reader who objects that my critique of de Beauvoir is misplaced because she is simply describing "what is" has failed to appreciate the insistence, argued and exemplified throughout this book, that description is never from a neutral point

---

[11] de Beauvoir, *The Second Sex*, p. 642.
[12] *Ibid.*, p. xvi.

of view. Instead, description may be framed from a moral or critical point of view that allows us to question and to probe "what is," or description may be framed from an abstract, all-knowing point of view that explicitly aims to liberate humanity but in the process demeans, labels, or undermines human dignity, self-identity, and the social bases of our humanity.

De Beauvoir's choice of descriptive terms carries moral and political implications for the female subject she characterizes as stuck in Immanence within a body "wanting in significance by itself." De Beauvoir adopts a set of terms that silences the vast majority of women in advance or gives them an implicitly coercive alternative. They can either speak the language of Immanence, in which case they remain outside civilization babbling, as it were, from the bog, or they can begin to speak in the voice of civilization which is a *male* voice, framed by, for, and about males. Given these alternatives, de Beauvoir enjoins women to throw off the veils of Immanence, enter the world of Transcendence, and become as Sartrian men who declare that the world is theirs to do with as they will.[13] Rather than a slow process of self-discovery and reflection on the terms of their life-worlds, de Beauvoir holds out the lure of the world-historic figure as a way to force women to recognize the pettiness of their own existence. She proclaims:

> The men we call great are those who—in one way or another—have taken the weight of the world upon their shoulders; they have done better or worse, they have succeeded in re-creating it or they have gone down; but first they have assumed that enormous burden. . . . *To regard the universe as one's own . . . one must belong to the cast of the privileged; it is for those alone who are in command to justify the universe by changing it . . .* (emphasis mine).[14]

---

[13] For a critique of Sartrian man as the recasting and militant adoption of a vision of abstract individualism, and of human liberation as freedom for the grandiose Self, see Jean Bethke Elshtain, "Liberal Heresies: Existentialism and Repressive Feminism," in *Liberalism and the Modern Polity*, ed. Michael C. Gargas McGrath, pp. 37–41. Mary Midgely writes: "The really monstrous thing about Existentialism . . . is its proceeding as if the world contained only dead matter (things) on the one hand and fully rational, educated, adult human beings on the other—as if there were no other life-forms," *Beast and Man*, p. 18.

[14] de Beauvoir, *The Second Sex*, p. 671.

Her adoption of the male mode as normatively superior is complete when de Beauvoir urges women to take up the instrumental use of sex now practiced by "busy men." A busy woman, she writes, one who "expends her energy, who has responsibilities, who knows how harsh is the struggle against the world's opposition, needs—like the male—not only to satisfy her physical desires but also to enjoy the relaxation and diversion provided by agreeable sexual adventures."[15] Women are urged to maintain their dignity throughout, however.

This celebration of male heroes, sexual instrumentalism, and modes of male-defined identity is framed within a work that concludes with a call for the "complete economic and social equality of women"; the precondition of that equality is the "inner metamorphosis" of women. The problem is that de Beauvoir knows in advance the trajectory of that metamorphosis. Like the terms under which Plato admitted female Guardians, de Beauvoir's require female self-denial.

De Beauvoir's capitulation to silencing terms and female self-denial is painfully evident in her discussion of "The Data of Biology" which opens *The Second Sex*. She holds female embodiment at arm's length as if it were repugnant to her and distant from her. Woman is portrayed as "the victim of the species." Man is portrayed as imbued with a sense of virile domination that extends to reproductive life (for example, the life of the male is "transcended" in the sperm, and so on). The female subject, simply by being born female, suffers an alienation grounded, not as Marx would have it, in oppressive and exploitative social structures and arrangements, but in her biological capacity to bear a child. Pregnancy is described in foreboding terms as the alienation of woman from herself (the woman is not "transcended" through her procreative capacity as the male is through his sperm).

The fetus is characterized as a "tenant," a parasite upon the mother's existence. Menstruation is horrific and disgusting. Nursing merely exhausts the mother—de Beauvoir nowhere acknowledges that it, or any other female reproductive or nurturant activity, can have meaning or profound emotional importance *to* and *for* the subject herself. One particular statement reveals the depth

---

[15] *Ibid.*, p. 646.

of de Beauvoir's loathing, projected onto all of female humanity. She calls a woman's breasts "mammary glands" that "play no role in woman's individual economy: *they can be excised at any time of life*" (emphasis mine).[16] A male physician who expressed such cavalier disregard for the sensibilities of a woman about to undergo the ordeal of mastectomy would, correctly, be denounced for his sexism. No analyst who approaches her subject from the stance of abstractedness, peevishness, and disdain evinced by de Beauvoir could begin to truly see and to hear her subjects as they broke silence on matters of particular concern to them—for women this invariably includes, as thousands of women in consciousness-raising learned, reflecting upon one's body and one's feelings of socially induced shame or repugnance about that body, and how to attain a sense of biological integrity through self-affirmation, not denial.

Rejecting de Beauvoir's approach for one that incorporates the self-understandings of female subjects as central does not, in itself, tell us what political discourse is for. How can political discourse embody as an essential feature, a means and an end, a process of arriving at transformative knowledge of self and other—truth not as a thing-in-itself abstractly couched but as the active creation of meaning between two or more people?[17] If the search for truth or meaning is not to replicate those approaches, whether feminist or not, in which passive subjects simply receive "truth" as uncovered by some expert or visionary, it must be construed as a dynamic, social search for transformative and reconstructive knowledge.

This suggests another rich way feminists, particularly those concerned with feminism as a process or a means as well as an end, may draw upon psychoanalytic discourse, grounded as it is in a theory which embodies a moral and theoretical imperative of truth-telling and truth-seeking. For example: Wolfgang Loch, a psychoanalyst and philosopher, describes truth as the active *construction* of something that makes sense and permits the subject to rely on it, to live a life wide-awake, not sleep-walking. To

---

[16] *Ibid.*, p. 24.

[17] Wolfgang Loch, "Some Comments on the Subject of Psychoanalysis and Truth," in *Truth, Consciousness and Reality*, ed. Joseph R. Smith, M.D., p. 221.

reach this truth, with its profound implications for political discourse and political action, a particular sort of dialogue that is itself a feature of the truth that finally emerges must be undertaken. The means of truth-seeking cannot be bifurcated from the ends of truth-construction. For Loch, this dialogue's vital end is to reach a truth from, by, and for the subject-herself, but within a social frame of uncoerced communication which becomes, as in the Hebrew tradition, a rock to stand on.[18] This dynamic process includes but is not merely interpretation, the drawing out of a hidden meaning; instead, it implicates both subject and analyst (or political thinker by analogy) in the construction or reconstruction of truths whose trajectory aims toward the future.

This means that political discourse aimed at the construction of new meanings, at enabling subjects to become more intelligible to themselves, must take place within an arena in which human speech or discursive reflection is undominated, uncoerced, unmanipulated, in an approximation of Jürgen Habermas's "ideal speech situation."[19] The salience of this ideal for a critical account of women's liberation is that it offers a motive *for* that liberation framed from the point of view of the individual subject as one actively seeking meaning and purpose. This search will be distorted if it occurs under manipulative, coercive, or silencing conditions. The implication for political discourse is simply this: the political thinker who wants to find out "the truth" must approximate as closely as possible in her work the uncoercive terms of the psychoanalytic dialogue as a locus of "ideal speech." The relevant features of the "ideal speech situation" for political discourse include the repudiation of shaming, guilt-inducing moralisms, and the absence of abstracted assessments. To those who insist that my terms would make political discourse nearly impossible, I would argue that the notion is offered up as a worthy picture of reality and as a standard against which we can assess our own efforts. Although we can never realize perfectly the "ideal speech situation," our construction of transformative meaning through political discourse requires such an ideal as a mode of inquiry and an end in itself.

[18] *Ibid.*, p. 237. Cf. Sigmund Freud, "Constructions in Analysis," *Standard Edition*, 23:255-270.

[19] Jürgen Habermas, *Legitimation Crisis*.

The feminist analyst who takes the self-understanding of the female subject as a central feature of political inquiry and goes on to affirm an ideal of noncoercive human discourse as a touchstone from which to assay silencing considerations, is, for example, ideally equipped to explore critically the anti-abortion Right-to-Life movement in the United States. This movement has encouraged thousands of never-before-political women to take an active role in organizing, marching, leafletting, petitioning, politicking, maintaining vigils, sitting-in, lobbying Congress, even heckling and harrassing (though much less of that than feminist targets of Right-to-Lifers claim from their own spirit of *parti pris*). Right-to-Life women have been assailed by many feminists, or those sympathetic to the pro-abortion or "pro-choice" position from a stance of superiority and portrayed stereotypically as reactionaries and right-wingers; ignorant dupes of the Catholic Church; fanatics; misguided and male-identified opponents of progress, enlightenment, and all that is rational and good. One recent article by a feminist on the "pro-life" movement termed them "neofascists."

I am not suggesting that there is no truth in the charges lodged by feminists and their supporters. But I am saying, and this is the crux of the matter: without allowing Right-to-Life women to speak the truth as they understand it; without engaging them from a stance that respects their human possibility for the creation of meaning through uncoerced dialogue, which requires of the investigator a stance of empathy, openness, and a willingness to entertain and explore alternatives she may not share, we will continue to treat them in distorted, presumptuous, and prejudicial ways (there is a vein of anti-Catholic prejudice to be found in pro-choice characterizations of Right-to-Lifers as robotized minions of the Church).

A sympathetic willingness to see and to hear the Right-to-Life woman and understand her position as she herself perceives it as the beginning point, remember, not the end point of critical exploration, prompts a second suggestion for theoretical investigation. It would be enlightening to explore feminist orthodoxies on the abortion question by determining whether feminists share the arguments for abortion made in the case of *Roe versus Wade* which guaranteed abortion rights.[20] This exploratory inquiry would probe feminist self-understanding on the abortion question; whether, for example, this self-understanding includes a vision of the human being as a possessor of self, cut off from ties that bind her to a community or tradition, or a commitment to a militant notion of privacy that undercuts any serious political claims launched from a moral point of view by deploying a notion of tolerance construed as the insistence that the private opinions of others can exert no claims over us. My point is that the pro-abortion and Right-to-Life positions may both be unreflectively held and thus require probing and exploratory reexamination. My further point is that the current *political* situation that pits these two groups of women against one another as implacable and hostile foes embodies the mirror image of the ideal speech situation: it is a highly charged milieu riddled with coercive, manipulative, and silencing considerations on both sides in which each accuses the other of placing herself against liberation, justice, equality, choice, freedom on the one hand, and morality, human community, family ties and values, and the reaffirmation of the sanctity and importance of human life or potential life as unassailable on the other.

Finally, one must find a way to move coherently from self-understanding and the social construction of reality and meaning, to critique. Brian Fay offers a set of criteria for a critical account of women's liberation. I have drawn on that account for my own purposes.[21] Fay's arguments are dense and I shall offer a condensation of their central features. First, he argues that ideas help to make us and our social worlds what we and they are. Second, he claims that any action by a human agent is motivated and can be interpreted. Third, and related to the first two, that it is through action—Fay stresses *political* action, presuming, as he does, that politics has some primary claim on us among diverse human activities—that human beings reveal themselves to one another; therefore, such action is essential to becoming and being seen as a person. Fourth, that our actions, ideas, and the activities which

[20] *Roe v. Wade*, 410 U.S. 113 (1973).
[21] Fay, *Social Theory and Political Practice, passim.*

flow from them may, in trivial or important ways, be muddled, distorted, or confused. Fifth, and Fay's bedrock, that there are real human needs, as well as wants, purposes, intentions, and desires; that these needs have motivating force; that they can be distorted and damaged; that they are essential even if distorted; finally, that they serve as the presuppositional basis for *any* form of social existence and, it follows, for transformative social possibilities as well.

To make good on his tall order, Fay begins by insisting, as I did in my critique of de Beauvoir, that the knowledge claims of the critical thinker must in principle be translatable into ordinary language and that it must be possible for those claims to be grounded in the human subject's self-understanding even if one's critical aims are, finally, to persuade these subjects to conceive of themselves and their situations in different ways.[22] Fay resolutely rules out vanguardism as a stance which can have a place in a critical venture from a moral point of view. His critical posture includes neither coercion nor manipulation of the lives of those he is struggling to alter. Fay's social theorist is a kind of educator, who draws upon an image of the "ideal speech situation" as a contrast to coercive and manipulative models and goes on to connect understanding and critique to human potentialities and democratic aims.

The dimension of Fay's account I shall look at more closely here is his notion of "ideology critique," the process of unmasking the distorted modes of self-understanding and probing the twisted forms of self-identity of his subjects. Ideology critique is a central pillar in Fay's proposed agenda for a critical theory of women's liberation, for any such theory must articulate the ways in which a sexist social order has damaged and deformed individual women, and go on to clarify the ways in which they, and it, can be changed and liberatory possibilities opened up.[23]

The most provocative dimension of Fay's ideology critique is his insistence that ideology is never merely or simply a distortion or falsehood, but that expressions of ideology, like neurotic symp-

[22] *Ibid.*, esp. chap. 5, pp. 92-110 inclusive.
[23] *Ibid.*, p. 100. See Jean Bethke Elshtain, " 'Thank Heaven for Little Girls': The Dialectics of Development," *Politics* 10:139-148, for an example of such critique.

toms to the psychoanalyst, are clues to and features of a complex structure comprised of manifest and latent, apparent and more deeply rooted exigencies. No analyst who disregarded a symptom as the expression of a totally false belief (for example, the conviction on the part of a patient that his left ear had fallen off though it was demonstrably attached to his head), to be ignored as he treated the disorder, would get very far. The symptom, like all our beliefs however muddled, inconsistent, incoherent, magical, or merely misinformed, is our entree to underlying motivations, authentic needs, and less distorted views of self and others. The political theorist must listen carefully and observe sympathetically for everything that individuals do, say, or believe is important and has meaning. This uncovering of true or less distorted meaning, ideology critique, is a process of reclamation.

An example may clarify this important point. Many women, particularly feminists, find a phenomenon which calls itself "total womanhood" shocking, stupid, even repugnant and an expression of female "false-consciousness." The movement's founder, Marabel Morgan, wrote a book in 1973 called *The Total Woman* that became one of the ten bestsellers of the decade (by the end of 1979 103,000 hardcover and 2,700,000 paperback copies were in print). The "total woman" movement appears to enlist thousands of restless, unhappy, bored, confused, dissatisfied, and resentful women who are then encouraged to "talk out" their miseries after which they are offered a prescription for ending their woes. From a critical, feminist perspective the cure looks suspiciously like a heavy dose of what helped to make the woman miserable in the first place. Women are enjoined to become "happy housewives" as well as seductive sexpots, to approach every vexation with an understanding smile, a soothing voice, and a boundless capacity for selflessness. (Clearly, my descriptive terms indicate a stance toward this phenomenon that is already critical.) Ignored, so far as I can tell, by social thinkers and condemned by feminists, we can only hazard plausible guesses as to *why* so many women have signed up to become "total women," what meaning this movement offers that was previously denied them, and how it has helped them to attain a self-identity they can use as the basis for living their lives.

A critical inquiry into the "total woman" would draw out from its participants their own motivations as these propelled them into the movement. To presume that the "total woman" ideology is *thoroughly* debased would be not only a bad beginning point that would preclude a sympathetic stance for listening to participants, but also a way to do social theory that is presumptuous. If, with Fay, we see ideology as a clue to underlying meaning and truths, investigation of "total womanhood" could help us assay the hopes, fears, desires, aims, anxieties, boredom, purposelessness, confusion, or despair that have spurred so many to seek to become "total women." These beliefs and attitudes, uncovered through dialogue and probing, would be taken seriously. Finally, it might be possible to persuade a "total woman" of the contradictory or inconsistent nature of the beliefs she espouses, in part because life in modern society is such that no woman could ever live up to the "total woman" ideal or find a secure locus for herself and social identity within it. This, as I say, is a possibility, but it demands as a preliminary step encouraging the subject to reach down into her own self-understanding and to draw out aspects of her own social situation. In this way we may come to see the structural pressures on her family and herself and how these became implicated in her felt misery and her desire to change herself.

If she decided, after revealing herself in speech, and having another revealed to her who held a different view of women in modern society, that what "fulfilment" is supposed to mean for the "total woman" and the organization of contemporary social life were fundamentally at odds, the onus of her restlessness would undergo a shift to consideration of those social forces that lay at the basis of her own confusion.[24] If she did not move from self-understanding to critique, it would not be the theorist's prerogative to compel or manipulate her in any way. Although on the basis of tests of coherence, internal consistency, and plausibility, the political thinker may have the better case, if that case isn't accepted by the subject whose life-world and self-identity it aims to interpret, explain, and move towards transformation, to coerce agreement would subtly but irreparably undermine the connection between means and ends the critical thinker must preserve. One

---

[24] Fay, *Social Theory and Political Practice*, p. 101.

recalls Eugene O'Neill's "The Iceman Cometh" and Hickey's dogged and fanatical insistence that his illusion-ridden comrades learn to face the painful truth about themselves and their situation. The result is disaster. Some illusions may be necessary, for some people, at some times, just to keep on living.[25]

RECONSTRUCTING THE PUBLIC AND PRIVATE

I ask readers to picture in their minds' eyes, a time long ago and far away, the scene described by Richard E. Leakey and Roger Lewin in *Origins*. Perhaps this passage may serve as a benchmark amidst the confusions and tumult of the present.

. . . from the Shanidar Cave in the Zagros Mountain highlands of Iraq, . . . on a June day *some sixty thousand years ago a man was buried* in unusual circumstances.

The humidity of the cave was far from favorable for preserving the bones of the dead man; but pollen grains survive very well under these circumstances, and researchers at the Musee de l'Homme in Paris who examined the soil around the Shanidar Man discovered that *buried along with him were several different species of flowers*. From the orderly distribution of the grains around the fossil remains, there is no question that the flowers were arranged deliberately and did not simply topple into the grave as the body was being covered. It would appear that the man's family, friends, and perhaps members of his tribe had gone into the fields and

---

[25] Sigmund Freud, "Introductory Lectures on Psychoanalysis," *Standard Edition*, vols. 15 and 16. The discussion in question occurs in Freud's account of the moral dilemmas of psychoanalytic therapy and the intimate intervention in people's psychic lives that is never, simply, an involvement in their psychic lives alone but involves a whole social network. The case was that of a young woman who "fell ill" from time to time to escape a husband unsympathetic to her needs and her wifely and motherly burdens and responsibilities. Given the patient's objective lack of options, and the fact that there was no way she could break her economic and emotional dependency on her husband, Freud found it better to allow the woman her "escape into illness" than to confront her with the self-serving nature of her periodic incapacity.

brought back bunches of yarrow, cornflowers, St. Barnaby's thistle, groundsel, grape hyacinths, woody horsetail, and a kind of mallow (emphasis mine).[26]

This deliberate burial, with its nonutilitarian sensibility and delicate specificity, is described by Leakey and Lewin as an act by human survivors that "betrays a keen self-awareness and a concern for the human spirit." Later, the coauthors remark that the sociality of human beings runs like a vital thread through our most distant origins. The human being, they declare, is "an animal with its own unique reasons for living in communities."[27] What all this means is not simply that we are social beings but that we are, profoundly, beings with certain needs or yearnings of spirit as well as body. We possess an inborn imperative, power as *potentia*, to find and to create meaning.

I begin my final reflections with several presumptions that may be taken as axiomatic though they are neither arbitrary nor the end product of a formal exercise in abstract logic. First, human beings have a need to live with and among others in relations of concrete particularity, in space, extending over and through time. If we are deprived of such relations we are damaged and distorted in body and spirit. My second presumption is that human beings, and here the evidence stretches from prehistory through the present, experience an imperative—Freud termed it an epistemic instinct—to discover, to understand, and to create meaning. That drive, too, can be damaged and deflected and to the extent that it is we become less fully human. Clearly those ancestors of ours, as they gathered their offerings of thistle and hyacinth, horsetail and groundsel, had no utilitarian calculus in mind; they didn't plan to eat the flowers and grains nor feed them to animals. No, they scattered these remembrances in orderly fashion over the grave of a loved one: a family member, a tribesman, one of their own. This action can only be explained with references to my presumptions or similar reasons which might plausibly form the basis of human morality and social existence.

[26] Richard E. Leakey and Roger Lewin, *Origins: What New Discoveries Reveal About the Emergence of our Species and its Possible Future*, p. 125.
[27] *Ibid.*, p. 157.

In thinking of the present and recasting the future there are those, and one finds feminists in their ranks, who see past epochs as so much human waste, perhaps a remorseless tale of patriarchal horror or pervasive class conflict. They would create a future in which there will be no more of whatever it is that makes human history, for them, a litany of debasement, and the present an unconditional war against enemies. I am not one of these. The struggle over tradition—what is it, how ought we to regard it— is central to reconstructive notions of public and private. Those I disassociate myself from believe history has no claim upon us at all. There are others to whom tradition embodies sanctity, has unchallenged claims on us, and serves as a sanctuary from the present. My ideal neither repudiates the present in toto nor seeks, nostalgically, to return to the past but faces the more difficult task of evaluating its claims upon us. Does the fact that a particular social form, the family for example, is traceable to prehistory, all of recorded history, and is present in all known societies, constitute an important claim on us because it can be presumed to express something so fundamental about human beings that to reject it is either folly or madness? This question cannot be answered abstractly. Rather one must take up evidence from the past, like the burial in the Shanidar Cave, as clues to a vast and awesome mystery that embodies, at one end of a range of alternatives, authentic human imperatives, those basic notions with which this inquiry began.

Stuart Hampshire has sketched a nonutilitarian starting point for reflection on human beings and their universe—I have already cited one clue, 60,000 years old, that human motivations cannot be subsumed within utilitarian categories or calculations—and that is that *every way of life* will be built up on notions of morality that contain "prohibitions, barriers to action, in certain quite distinct and clearly marked areas of action; these are the taking of human life, sexual functions, family duties and obligations, and the administration of justice according to the laws and customs of a given society. . . . A morality is, at the very least, the regulation of the taking of life and the regulation of sexual relations."[28] Each way of life will embody within its social forms a

---

[28] Hampshire, *Morality and Pessimism*, p. 12.

cluster of basic notions as the moral grounding required, in the first instance, for the creation and sustenance of *any way of life*. Without such a set of moral rules and prohibitions, basic notions and symbolic forms, no *human* society could exist.

The free-floating pictures of human life that emerge from such feminist texts as Firestone's or Daly's present an abstract plan of a society to come that is not threaded through and through with the warp and woof of a set of basic moral notions and prohibitions that tie us to past and present. Thus their pictures of present and future become rhetorical in relation to social and human reality; everything is cast too much in the abstract, is alternately visionary and banal with respect to the concreteness of what is, of what human beings not only are but must in some ways remain. The exercise of the political imagination must take root in those moral concepts and categories in which people think and which serve as the touchstones of respective ways of life. This means one must repudiate rhetorical claims that the past can be quite overcome and declarations that it must be, in order to preserve the complexity involved in moral reevaluation, in distinguishing between the notions, rules, and prohibitions essential to *any* way of life and those that embody a *particular ideal of a way of life*. For example, one must distinguish relations between women and men in public and private spheres that one finds, in some ways, destructive and incompatible with an ideal of a way of life, and the inescapability of *necessary* relations between men and women if social life in any form is to survive.

To make these distinctions one must first accept the reality of limiting conditions; one must recognize that we are not thoroughly untrammeled in our imaginings, though we may self-indulgently entertain the view that we are. In this way one not only opens up the possibility for, but accepts the irrevocability of conflict, given our diverse assessments of the moral imperatives embodied in ideas of ways of life. Too often, feminist utopians and revolutionists throw out not the baby *with* the bathwater, but the baby *rather than* the bathwater. That is, they junk all notions of what is essential, of limiting conditions, in the creation of the future by concentrating exclusively on what must, they believe, change in order for women to be "free." They will brook no disagreement for to disagree is to exhibit the poison of "male identification." Yet conflicts involving moral claims are part of what it means to be human. To end all such debates, as some feminists would by articulating a single, overarching lodestone of Truth, is to undermine that restless urge towards the creation of meaning as an ongoing adventure of the human spirit.

Thus when we think about public and private and its reconstruction, if we are to avoid the presumptuous and the abstracted, we are thinking about a multiplicity of moral claims and about competing human values concerning what an ideal way of life ought to be. Such conflict is unavoidable. A harmony of purposes, ends, virtues, and identities is achievable *only* if we so thoroughly erode the bases of human existence that we willingly engage in radical and destructive social surgery. In our own century, the Nazi and Stalinist experiments have been the most destructive instances of this sort.[29] If everything, every basis of human existence, every rule and prohibition, not excluding the incest taboo, is "up for grabs," those who unscrupulously grab will inherit the earth and we will no longer have the earth as our inheritance.

The upshot of such reflection is a recognition that each succeeding generation must respect some moral necessities, must have some "taken for granteds," rules without which even the minimal aspects of a human existence that propelled our prehistoric ancestors to place flowers on the graves of their beloved, will be jeopardized. Tradition does have claims on us; history does limit us. But moral debate, hence political conflict, can and should arise concerning competing *ideals* of human existence: these may be debated, rethought, overridden so long as the debate makes reference to, and builds upon, a necessary moral foundation. The horror of fascism was its total overturning of all fundamental prohibitions. The great emblem of that terror, the symbol of all such exercises in horror and hubris, is the death camp.

It is on the basis of my recognition of the existence of limiting conditions and the inescapability of moral rules in fundamental areas of human existence, together with my presumptions con-

---

[29] See Hampshire, "Public and Private Morality"; and "Conversation with Bernard Williams," in *Modern British Philosophy*, ed. Bryan Magee, pp. 150-165.

cerning human sociality and the imperative to create meaning that I turn, first, to a reconstructive ideal of the private world. I shall treat the private not in instrumentalist terms, as the necessary condition for some other ideal or end embodying no good or end in itself, nor as a taken-for-granted, nor as something to be overcome in order to attain unity in the ideal state of total social justice, but as a locus of human activity, moral reflection, social and historical relations, the creation of meaning, and the construction of identity having its own integrity.

To talk of an ideal of the private world within the context of contemporary American society is to talk about the family. The family is the linchpin in all visions of future alternatives, often as something to be reformed or overthrown. It is *the* institution singled out must frequently by feminists as one of the keys to female oppression.[30] The image which has emerged from feminism's treatment of the family, although shifts are now being signalled, reflects a distortion symptomatic of the diseases of the present it seeks to cure. One of the key symptoms of our present disease— our "legitimation crisis"—is a widespread draining of our social institutions, public and private, of their meaning and significance. In stripping away the old ideological guises that celebrated motherhood yet denigrated women, extolled an ideal of private life yet disallowed parents the means with which to live in decency and with dignity, feminists and other social critics have played a vital role.

But unmasking ideological distortions is not synonymous with constructing an alternative that does not incorporate its own silencing and repressive effects. What reconstructive ideal of the private can serve as an alternative to the romantic ideologies of the past that required and rationalized a picture of women as inferior or as beings engaged in second-rate, albeit necessary activities, and to feminist ideologies in the present that promote the erosion and meaning of private family life in the absence of

---

[30] I recognize that there is no such thing as "the family" but that there are multiple variations on this theme. Nevertheless, in discussing the imperatives that must be infused within *any* familial form in order for it to serve the humanizing functions I explicate it is more economical simply to speak of "the family."

any viable alternative? To envisage such an ideal one must examine the question on several levels. First, because there are those who adamantly insist the family is not a necessary feature of human life, one must demonstrate coherently that some form of familial existence is a presuppositional feature of social existence. Second, one must go on to articulate a *particular ideal* of family life that does not repeat the earlier terms of female oppression and exploitation. I shall treat the most fundamental level first for it is the foundation of any reflective, reasoned inquiry into the question.

I ask readers to return once again to a previous epoch, in this case the eighteenth and early nineteenth centuries. The savants and philosophers of that time, heirs of the Enlightenment, were not timid men. They posed, quite unabashedly, the most fundamental of questions: What is the nature of man? The question admits, as we have seen, of no easy answers for the human being is, from birth, a being profoundly influenced by culture. How is one to disentangle man's natural nature from his social nature? Few opportunities for direct observation, for what scientists call "controlled experiments" ever present themselves. (Though, in a sense, families and alternatives to families including institutionalization provide constantly powerful evidence with observable results.) Contests raged between those who held to the notion that man in the state of nature was a Rousseauian "noble savage," pure in heart, affectionate, as yet untainted by a corrupt society and those who argued that apart from human social relations there would be no "human" nature at all. The case of "le jeune sauvage de l'Aveyron," the wild boy of Aveyron, promised to help settle, once and for all, the nature of man.

The wild boy of Aveyron was captured in 1800 in a district of southwestern France. After a series of escapes and recaptures during which a naturalist made a detailed description of him which has survived, the wild boy was placed in the Institute for Deaf Mutes in Paris under the tutelage of Abbé Sicard, an authority on the retraining of the deaf and a member of the Society for Observers of Man which had taken a special interest in the case. The society believed that the wild boy would help to resolve their philosophic speculations concerning human nature, the relationship between nature and nurture, whether there were innate ideas, and so on.

The abbé himself shortly gave up on the wild boy as hopeless. This being who had aroused such initial curiosity and enthusiasm rapidly invited disinterest and disgust. For, rather than the incarnation of Rousseau's noble savage, what those who observed the wild boy discovered was a "disgustingly dirty child affected with spasmodic movements and often convulsions who swayed back and forth ceaselessly like certain animals in the menagerie, who bit and scratched those who opposed him, who showed no sort of affection for those who attended him; and who was in short, indifferent to everything and attentive to nothing."[31]

At this juncture a remarkable young man, a twenty-six-year-old doctor, Jean-Marc-Gaspard Itard, enters the picture. In 1800 he undertook responsibility for the wild boy's education and developed a rigorous program for the approximately twelve-year-old youth who had been deprived of human company, as closely as could be determined, from the age of three on. Those, like the Abbé Sicard, who had given up on the wild boy, insisted that he had been left in the wild because he was an idiot. Itard took precisely the opposite tack: he saw in the wild child one who was an idiot *because* he had been left in the wild. Itard's arduous, painful, finally despairing efforts to educate and humanize the wild boy of Aveyron are among the most poignant records left us from that epoch.

Itard discovered that outside human social relations and cut off from the organizing structure of language, even the most basic human senses of sight, touch, and hearing remain unfocused and unintegrated, centered upon the stomach only. He had to attend to each of Victor's (as the wild boy came to be called) sensory modalities separately—first to arouse or tap them and then to organize them. But with the onset of puberty all these efforts came to an abrupt halt. Unfocused, unbound sexuality proved to be too much; earlier efforts were swamped and the boy regressed

---

[31] Jean-Marc-Gaspard Itard, *The Wild Boy of Aveyron*, p. 4. Cf. Harlan Lane, *The Wild Boy of Aveyron, passim*.

back into a "wild," unsocial, unreachable condition. Itard finally gave up. Victor was turned over to an institution where he lived out the remainder of his less-than-human existence. This extraordinary tale powerfully suggests that outside the bounds of human nurture human beings would not be like the beasts—who are adroit and adept within their habitats—but less-than-human human beings. Our debt to nurture extends even to our most elementary sensory discriminations.

Cut-off from human society and language we could neither identify objects, nor establish categories, nor engage in social relations. But surely, the reader will cavil, no contemporary social critic ever advised that we return to a presocial existence, ever advocated a new state of nature. Perhaps not, at least not in such terms. But the past fifteen years have seen a number of visions of family-less, asocial existence celebrated. These have taken several forms, including one in which, not having biological, nuclear families, all individuals, including children, would be "free" to look for the best contractual deal in living arrangements. Firestone, for example, egregiously negates any legitimate moral claims of children on others, or moral obligations of adults to children, not only by her strategy for technocratic child-rearing by experts, but by celebrating the "good old days" in which a concept of the child did not exist—and, one might add, in which children were systematically exploited, crushed by back-breaking labor, physically and psychologically abused as a matter of course rather than a matter of concern, and stunted in their human capacities from birth. She romanticizes ghetto life because in it black children live unrepressed lives unlike their up-tight, less fortunate white counterparts. Surely, this is a contemporary version of the state of nature, looking backwards to a mythic golden age in which children were "free from" adults and finding in the present, in a patronizing celebration based on racist stereotypes, a state of nature enclave in the midst of the oppression of blacks in the ghettoes of America's cities in which a large minority of our fellow citizens are condemned to unemployment, welfare dependency, marginal existence, and inferior education.[32]

[32] Firestone, *Dialectic of Sex*, p. 101.

A second variation of the end-of-family ideology grew out of the counterculture commune movement in the 1960s, one to which many social rebels turned as an alternative to the nuclear family. The motivations for these moves lay primarily in restructuring male-female relations and presuming, from a stance lacking in moral concern and reflexivity, that these changes would a fortiori be "good for the children" as the child would be the "child of all" and not the "possession of two." The force of this ideology is apparent in a study on the children of the counterculture in which the authors provide "an overall portrait of children almost uniformly neglected, deprived, and tormented; many are uneducated, disorganized, and disturbed; a pervasive boredom and lack of joy and serious problems of mal- or undernourishment were prevalent. After such a sad portrait, it comes as a shock to find the authors concluding that communes are a success in child-rearing because they have done away with materialism and competitiveness."[33] This is reminiscent, though it is a far less coherent claim, of Chodorow's insistence that communal alternatives are *presumptively* preferable to private familial child-rearing because they result in less "individualism."

Another claim and aim of social critics in family elimination or radical transformation is an instrumentalist one: in order for other political ends to be achieved. The idea here is that devotion to the family and to private ties and purposes not only takes the edge off radical commitments to change (coopting is the favored term with which to describe and simultaneously disparage) but also means one is pressed into service by a society that has the family as one of its structural supports. By implication, and here a counterfactual argument is implied, *in the absence of any viable private life public life would be transformed for the better*. I shall take up this claim, as I link public and private, at the conclusion of the chapter.

I begin with a reaffirmation: familial ties and modes of child-rearing are essential to establish the minimal foundation of human, social existence. What we call human capacities could not exist

[33] Alice S. Rossi, "A Biosocial Perspective on Parenting," *Daedalus*, p. 16. Rossi is discussing a book by Joan Rothschild and S. B. Wolf, *The Children of the Counterculture*.

outside a familial mode; for human beings to flourish a particular ideal of the family is necessary. I shall take up that challenge in a moment. But first, the family's status as a moral imperative derives from its universal, pan-cultural existence in all known past and present societies. We are not dealing with a tangential, episodic cultural form but a transhistorical one. To state a presumptive case for familial ties, to argue that they are required to make us minimally human, is *not* to detail the specific forms within which the creation and nourishment of humanity may take place. Aristotle and all the other political theorists down through the centuries who asserted the primacy of politics, and viewed man (the male, at any rate, if not generic humanity) as preeminently a political animal even as they downgraded or simply took for granted the private sphere, were guilty of a serious distortion. It is the family which "pervades all our perceptions of social reality." It is the family that constitutes our "common humanity," for our use of language, the basis of that humanness, has its origin in family forms. This makes the family "the universal basis of human culture. . . . As language constitutes the essence of man as a species, and not reason, so the family and not the social order, is the setting that humanizes him."[34]

Those who claim that humanization and the creation of identity

[34] Stuart Hampshire, "Joyce and Vico: The Middle Way," *New York Review of Books*, p. 8. Some might develop a counterargument based on tradition by claiming that infanticide is as old as human history. Does this not mean, by my logic, that there is a presumptive force in its favor? It is true that infanticide is evident as a practice. But it is a practice that always required atonement or justification. There were specifications as to types of infants to be abandoned and conditions under which abandonment could occur. This is not a practice on which a moral code that made life itself or the ideal of a way of life possible but one that societies, even as they engaged in it, had a bad conscience about, hence the need for justification and denial. The abandonment of that practice is universally taken as one sign of moral advance; moreover, it has been shown that if the situational catalysts, particularly direct economic exigency, are eased or removed the more "natural" human instinct is not to abandon infants but to care for them. See Maria W. Piers, *Infanticide, Past and Present*. See also George B. Forgie, *Patricide in the House Divided: A Psychological Interpretation of Lincoln and His Age* for a brilliant treatment of the nexus between family metaphor and symbol and American politics and culture in the mid-nineteenth century. Cf. Jean Bethke Elshtain, "Family Reconstruction," *Commonweal*, pp. 430-431.

could be done as well in some alternative to familial ties ignore the counterevidence provided by abandoned, neglected, or abused children, many of whom exist in shells that are families in the formal sense alone; children reared totally in institutions; children separated from their families during critical periods because of war or social calamity; children neglected under the guise of not "hanging them up" in counterculture communes; together with a vast body of evidence from history, anthropology, social theory and psychoanalytic case studies. To be sure, the feminist political thinker must sift what gets "packed into" the family as understood by non- or anti-feminist thinkers. But to ignore the evidence because she would alter a familial form in the direction of more egalitarian relations between the sexes is likely to result in a dauntingly optimistic image of the future which feeds on a distortion of the present and a silencing of discourse on vital moral imperatives. This is reminiscent of the suppression of debate on a whole range of issues by nineteenth-century Suffragists under the felt demand that they be both social rebels and "ladies." Feminism, until recently, has tended to view as anti-feminist or, minimally, as suspect, open, reflective discussion of heterosexual ties and eroticism, the needs and identities of children considered as ends-in-themselves and not merely as means, and accounts of the normative meaning and richness of being a parent.

Children will incur an assault to their humanness, an affront they will know in the tissue of their bio-psychic beings, if they suffer from the diseases of neglect and nonattachment. A being without a presumptive need for attachments of a special kind— concrete, particular, and continuing—*would not suffer distortion and damage if such relations were absent*. Just as Marx's theory of alienation presupposes an ideal of human existence that holds, or would hold, in the absence of damaging exploitative and oppressive social structures, so the knowledge we now have of what happens to children *in the absence of strong, early attachments to specific adult others*, allows us to assert that we are dealing with a categorical imperative of human existence.

If children are to be morally and socially responsible and potentially self-reflective adults, they must be reared in a highly charged emotional setting in which they are loved in a manner that establishes basic trust. This requires the continuing presence of specific beloved others. It is only through powerful, eroticized relations with specific others, parents or their permanent not temporary surrogates, that children will be nurtured and protected in a way that allows their creation of self and other to be structured and mediated by parental care and concern. It is only through the child's internalization of specific others that he or she can later identify with nonfamilial human beings. These powerful early ties serve as the template of conscience that makes possible adult empathy, the qualities of pity and compassion of which Rousseau spoke. These ties cannot emerge, *pace* Plato and Firestone, in abstract, diffuse, nonfamilialized settings. In the absence of special, specific ties, familial feelings cannot be suffused into or displaced throughout a wider social network. The child will have lost the capacity for human identification. Not every neglected and abused child becomes a Charles Manson, but every Charles Manson was an abused and neglected child. "The jailhouse was my father," Charles Manson cried. For us to ignore these as the rantings of a madman is for us to repress moral reflection on the most basic things of all. One needs a family history to have a social history. As Stanley Hauerwas puts it:

. . . the family is morally crucial for our existence as the only means we have to bind time. Without the family, and the inter-generational ties involved, we have no way to know what it means to be historic beings. As a result we become determined by rather than determining our histories. Set out in the world with no family, without a story of and for the self, we will simply be captured by the reigning ideologies of the day.[35]

The child's helplessness, Freud once remarked, is the first stirring of moral motives. Deprivation of deep and profound emotional ties in infancy causes irreparable damage to our later capacities for creating and sustaining human bonds and social

---

[35] Stanley Hauerwas, "The Moral Meaning of the Family," *Commonweal*, p. 435.

concern. If these are not developed very early in life they cannot be reclaimed. The poor wild boy of Aveyron is an extreme case, but every twelve-year-old adolescent who murders without remorse is a stark reminder of this truth: the diseases of nonattachment lead to the inability of the child to modify his or her aggressive impulses and to find "alternative modes of expression that are sanctioned by love."[36] Selma Fraiberg writes: "The distinguishing characteristic of the diseases of non-attachment is the incapacity of the person to form human bonds . . . the other striking characteristic of such people is their impoverished emotional range. There is no joy, no grief, no guilt, no remorse. In the absence of human ties, a conscience cannot be formed; even the qualities of self-observation and self-criticism fail to develop."[37]

Totally institutionalized forms of child care, or modes that call themselves familial but replicate family ties through hollow, sentimentalized repetition of terms for family relations—"brother," "sister," "family"—rather than a serious attempt to recreate and resituate genuine intergenerational, not simply peer or generation-specific bonds, have damaging effects upon children that result from the diseases of nonattachment. Child-rearing in which children are raised primarily by and within institutionalized structures, perhaps with the family serving an adjunct function, avoids some of the diseases of nonattachment but is more likely to create obedient, oversocialized rule-followers who unquestioningly do their "duty" and do not challenge authority as adults. To push children prematurely into a group context results in more, not less, pressure for adaptation to conformist pressures given the routinization of tasks, regimentation of schedules, and group-dominant values which underlie these settings in the first place. Children who grow up in institutionalized structures frequently have a diminished capacity for empathic identification with others,

---

[36] Selma Fraiberg, *Every Child's Birthright: In Defense of Mothering*, p. 46. Sadly, this book has come under attack from some feminists as simply a reproduction of a "mothering ideology." It is, instead, a powerful theoretical and clinical argument *for* the needs and rights of children that does *not* require or demand female subordination.

[37] *Ibid.*, p. 47.

for they have "internalized" an abstract, diffuse authority not amenable to the reality-testing, the tumultuous "with" and "against," "love" and "hate," of parental and sibling attachments.

It is to be thoroughly muddled, confounded in fact, to assume that it is easy to separate out what one sees as the "good" that may inhere in family life from what one decrees "bad," either by eliminating biological familial ties altogether or "recreating" them in quite different social arrangements. To call some abstract structure, or a loose collection of like-minded, unrelated peers "families" is to treat our most basic human relationships frivolously, as mere historic accidents, or as the excreta of oppressive relations having no deep inner logic, meaning, or purpose of their own. "The minimum guarantee for the evolution of the human bond is prolonged intimacy with a nurturing person" or persons.[38] Fraiberg concludes on a solemn note: "But to a very large extent the diseases of non-attachment can be eradicated at the source by ensuring stable human partnerships for every baby. If we take the evidence seriously we must look upon a baby deprived of human partners as a baby in deadly peril. This is a baby who is being robbed of his humanity."[39] The feminist political thinker must similarly ask at what price she would gain the world for herself or other women, utterly rejecting those victories that come at the cost of the bodies and spirits of human infants. Unless this reflexivity is ongoing and central, feminism is in peril of losing its soul.

The feminist concerned with a reconstructive ideal of the private sphere must begin by affirming the essential needs of children for basic, long-term ties with specific others. Only then should she move to a second level of exploration and challenge by pursuing the creation of her ideal on this moral foundation. The second level begins with the articulation of a rich, concrete description of contemporary social reality. The American feminist who looks at the "real world" finds that families are centrally responsible for rearing children in our society. I am familiar with statistics sometimes cited to "prove" that only seven percent or only four-

[38] *Ibid.*, p. 56.   [39] *Ibid.*, p. 62.

teen percent of American women live in the "ideal-typical nuclear family of husband-earner and wife non-earner with two dependent children." Such figures are misleading if they are taken as evidence that the family is on the way out. They are misleading because they imply that families with a female wage-earner are somehow not families at all. They are misleading because they suggest that those single parent families required by the repressiveness of the welfare system don't count as families. Finally, they are misleading because they take *all* women as the base from which to calculate and this includes millions of unmarried young women who continue to live in their parents' homes; moreover, to cite contestable statistics is not the same as posing serious alternatives. This "evidence" in family breakdown is frequently cited with glee as "proof" of family decomposition, as if this boded only good for the future. Even if the statistics were unquestionable, one could interpret them as evidence of the extent to which contemporary, capitalist society has so undermined our capacities or our ability to act upon our deepest human imperatives, that it has made the sustenance of rich, long-lasting, cross-generational ties difficult or impossible for many to attain.[40]

The reflective feminist, then, begins her considerations with the important, not trivial, fact that Americans remain committed to family life and that it would require major social coercion and manipulation to destroy that commitment. Those thus committed include children as well as adults. Accounts of the search of displaced, abandoned, or neglected children for "mothers" and "fathers" is one of the most heartbreaking and telling one can imagine of the familial-imperative and the deep, emotional operations of familial imagery. Studies done by such observers as Robert Coles and Myra Bluebond-Langner demonstrate the pervasive force of "family," either as daily reality or as fond dream, and give powerful evidence of familial commitments.[41] The con-

---

[40] See Kenneth Keniston and the Carnegie Council on Children, *All Our Children: The American Family Under Pressure*, for a dire report on the inegalitarian pressures that bear down disproportionately on some of this nation's families.

[41] I refer here to Robert Coles's monumental five-volume contribution published under the title *Children of Crisis*. Volume 5, the final one in the series, was published in 1977. Myra Bluebond-Langner's *The Private World of Dying Chil-*

crete reality of the lives of American children, their self- and social understanding, includes a devotion to an ideal of the family that sometimes implicates them in criticisms of their own. But the salient point is their affirmation of the ideal to be preferred: it is not a family-less or nonfamilial ideal, but a familial one. The reflective feminist must be as concerned with the concrete existences and self-understandings of children as she is with female subjects. Her mode of theorizing and posing alternatives must locate this concern as central.

To attain and affirm an ideal of family life as the locus of humanization is, contrary to certain unreflective radical orthodoxies, to put pressure upon social structures and arrangements, not to affirm them. For to the extent that the public world, with all its political, economic, bureaucratic force, invades and erodes the private sphere, it, not the private world, should be the target of the social rebel and feminist critic. To promote a politics of displacement that further erodes the terms of the private sphere and all that stands between us and a coarse power or market-ridden definition of all of life, is to repress discourse on public, political issues even as one simultaneously takes the symptoms of its destructive effects as the "good news" that radical change is just around the corner.

It is the isolation and debasement of women under terms of male-dominated ideology and social structures that must be fought, not the activity, the humanizing imperative, of mothering, or of being a parent, itself. Too frequently mothering has been overassimilated to what feminists call "the shitwork." Mothers were demeaned under the guise of "liberating" them. In many early feminist accounts mothering was portrayed as a condition of terminal psychological and social decay, total self-abnegation, physical deterioration, and absence of self-respect. Women, al-

---

dren sensitively probes the life-worlds of children with terminal disease and the way in which they and their families experience this tragedy. Also important is Herbert G. Gutman's *The Black Family in Slavery and Freedom 1750-1925* which documents the drive of the enslaved to create familial ties and bonds under profoundly de-civilizing circumstances. The aim of slaveowners, of course, was to erode and break those ties and the moral sustenance and courage they helped to provide.

ready victims of an image that denigrated their social identity under the terms of the male American success ethos, now found themselves assaulted by the very group that would liberate them. "I'm only a mother," is a comment I have heard from many women not engaged in professional activity, and it reflects this socially decreed diminution of self-respect.

Back in the late 1960s a friend and I, struggling with our identities as mothers and graduate students, an anthropologist-and political theorist-in-becoming, decided to attend a feminist group being formed which billed itself as dedicated to transformative purposes in thought and action. At the first session each of us was asked, in turn, to give her reasons for being there, to briefly tell the story of how she came to this place at this time. When my friend's turn came, and she began to speak of her conflict over public and private values, commitments, and purposes, of her guilt and her confusion over whether that quest was a reflection of male-dominated social values, or a genuine response to an ambiguous situation, she was cut off abruptly and publicly shamed with this silencing declaration from the group's "facilitator": "We will have no diaper talk here. We're here to talk about women's liberation." My friend and I left, for we could not treat our children as abstractions, as nuisances to be overcome, or as evidence of our sad capitulation to the terms of patriarchy. Fortunately, we later found and became part of a consciousness-raising group that did not require, as the price of entry, the disarticulation of our moral sensibilities and the denial of our diverse and sometimes conflicting public and private purposes. We were able to engage in "truth-telling" of a special and powerful kind. It is interesting that many feminists now deny that the prevalent force of feminism was ever—save for a few "fringe lunatics"—antifamilial and see such claims as anti-feminist. This convenient forgetting of the immediate past, sadly, makes such feminists no different from those who want to put Vietnam and other conflicts "behind us." That is another term for repression. That is another way to silence debate.

To affirm a vision of the private-familial sphere as having its own dignity and purpose is to insist that particular experiences and spheres of social relations exude their own values and purposes, and have ends not attainable by, or within, other spheres. To assert the continued necessity of such relations and a particular notion of their reconstructed vitality is to recognize that we are all impoverished if all of life falls under a single set of terms. It is to adopt a perverse version of the Platonic epistemology that calls for other ways of seeing to be suppressed, literally exiled, or taken as inferior when compared with a supreme, powerful way of seeing beyond and above everyday human existence.

I am here calling for *the redemption of everyday life*, a recognition of its joys and vexations, its values and purposes, and its place in becoming human. I am embracing what George Steiner calls the " 'personal lexicon' in everyone of us" which "inevitably qualifies the definitions, connotations, semantic moves current in public discourse. . . . The language of a community, however uniform its social contour, is an inexhaustibly multiple aggregate of speech-atoms, of finally irreducible personal meanings. The element of privacy in language makes possible a crucial, though little understood, linguistic function. . . . Obviously, we speak to communicate. But also to conceal, to leave unspoken."[42] A world without the possibility for concealment, a world, as the Nazi imperative had it "without shadows," with no hiding places, nor refuge, nor solace, nor alternative to the force of the public sphere, is a world that invites barbarism or sterility or both. Hélène Cixous argues that women's "political urgency" must be "caring about what seems to be of no importance, to be the insignificant, to be the well-known, the familiar . . ."[43] Compared to the heady power of de Beauvoir's World Historic figures this seems paltry stuff. But "seems" is not "is" and the fact it seems so indicates our continued enchantment by certain public imperatives, male-created, sustained, and celebrated that we ostensibly would repudiate or alter radically.

If it is the case that women have a distinct moral language, as Carol Gilligan has argued, one which emphasizes concern for others, responsibility, care, and obligation, hence a moral language profoundly at odds with formal, abstract models of morality

[42] Steiner, *After Babel*, p. 46.
[43] Hélène Cixous, "Poetry is/and (the) Political," in *The Second Sex—Thirty Years Later*, p. 37.

defined in terms of absolute principles, then we must take care to preserve the sphere that makes such a morality of responsibility possible and extend its imperatives to men as well.[44] If Gilligan finds women's inner lives more complex, and learns that women have a greater ability to identify with others, to sustain a variety of personal relationships and to attain genuine reciprocity in those relationships, and locates these qualities and capacities in women's involvement with families and the protection of human life, we must think about what would be lost if the private sphere erodes further or if we seek to alter our intimate relations entirely.

One moral and political imperative that would unite rather than divide women, that would tap what is already there but go on to redeem and transform it, would be a feminist commitment to a mode of public discourse imbedded within the values and ways of seeing that comprise what Sara Ruddick has called "maternal thinking."[45] Such thinking need not and must not descend into the sentimentalization that vitiated much Suffragist discourse. For women to affirm the protection of fragile and vulnerable human existence as the basis of a mode of political discourse, and to create the terms for its flourishing as a worthy political activity, for women to stand firm against cries of "emotional" or "sentimental" even as they refuse to lapse into a sentimental rendering of the values and language which flow from "mothering," would signal a force of great reconstructive potential. It would require of feminists moves toward those women they now tend to classify, along with men, as "Other." Feminists should be among the first to recognize that individuals who are put on the defensive, made to feel inadequate, as women-as-mothers now feel, will respond in defensive, even reactionary ways unless or until others begin to approach them as ends-in-themselves rather than simply pawns in the game or enemies in the war.

There is, of course, an irritant in the image as I have thus far presented it, and that is that in order to provide trust and security for their children parents, in turn, must experience trust and security themselves in their relations with one another and with the

[44] Carol Gilligan, "In a Different Voice: Women's Conceptions of the Self and Morality," *Harvard Education Review*, pp. 481-517, *passim*.

[45] Cited in Christine de Stefano, "Legitimation Crisis Reconsidered: Women, Personal Identity, and the State," pp. 54-57.

"outside world." Parents who are frustrated and demeaned, rendered dependent and helpless in work-life and citizenship, will have difficulty instilling such bedrock beliefs and ways of being inside their families. Conflicts that originate "outside" get displaced "inside," perhaps into the very heart of the family's emotional existence. We know, for example, that the incident of wife- and child-battering rises in times of unemployment and economic recession. That is all too often our current reality. What this means is that political thinkers, including feminists, devoted to the family reconstructive mode cannot carry out their supremely important tasks unless or until there are structural changes in American life. That is where the heart of "politics and the family" should lie—not in overpoliticizing our most intimate relations and turning the family into the war of all against all to be negotiated by contract, but in fighting the pressures at work from the outside which erode, impoverish, or preclude the flourishing of our most basic human ties. Richard Sennett argues that the "erosion of a strong public life . . . deforms the intimate relations which seize people's wholehearted interest."[46] It is to public life and possibilities for its reconstruction that I now turn.

I shall spend somewhat less time discussing a reconstructive notion of the public because it stands in less need of a defense and reaffirmation within feminist political discourse than our besieged sphere of the private. In moves to treat the existence of a particular disjuncture between public and private that has in the past and remains in the present unacceptable to a feminist vision, some feminists have explored alternative societies to ascertain how they interrelate or oppose public and private. Anthropologists have taken the lead in this effort and I shall briefly take up the argument from anthropology, as articulated by Michelle Zimbalist Rosaldo. Then I turn to the tradition of political theory, examining what I find it necessary to repudiate and important to reclaim. I conclude with an exercise of the political imagination that "dwells in possibility," the possibility of what I shall call the "ethical polity."

---

[46] Richard Sennett, *The Fall of Public Man*, pp. 6-7. Sennett sees public and private as "concurrent human modes of expression, located in different social settings . . . correctives to each other" (p. 91).

Rosaldo uses the term "domestic" to refer to the institutions and modes of activity organized around mothers and children. "Public refers to activities, institutions, and forms of associations that link, rank, organize, or subsume particular mother-child groups" within a larger, frequently overarching framework.[47] Rosaldo insists that examination of these twin loci provides the "necessary framework" for evaluating male-female roles in society, an insistence I share from my own perspective as a political thinker. Rosaldo's anthropological model leads her to conclude that women's status "will be the lowest in those societies where there is a firm differentiation between domestic and public spheres of activity and where women are isolated from one another and placed under a single man's authority in the home," a conclusion I would not quarrel with. But then she adds that "perhaps the most egalitarian societies are those in which public and domestic spheres are only weakly differentiated, where neither sex claims much authority and the focus of social life itself is the home."[48] Later, she concludes that an egalitarian ethos turns on men taking on domestic roles, as she has defined them. Finally, she compares American society unfavorably with a tribe which still practices head-hunting with this statement: "Unlike the Ilongot, however, American society is in fact organized in a way that creates and exploits a radical distance between private and public, domestic and social, female and male."[49]

My quarrel is not with the accuracy of Rosaldo's anthropological description and her characterization of her tribal contrast model; rather, I question the use of such a model in the first place. Even if one ignores the fascinating fact that Ilongot men, or some of them, are head-hunters and women are not, surely an activity that expresses certain destructive human possibilities in a manner that may plausibly have as part of its underlying motivation an assertion of "maleness" and "male-differentness" given the

[47] Michelle Zimbalist Rosaldo, "Women, Culture and Society: A Theoretical Overview," in *Woman, Culture and Society*, ed. Michelle Zimbalist Rosaldo and Louise Lamphere, pp. 23-24. See Rosaldo's rethinking of this position in "The Use and Abuse of Anthropology: Reflections on Feminism and Cross-cultural Understanding," *Signs*, pp. 389-417.

[48] Rosaldo, "Women, Culture and Society," p. 36.   [49] *Ibid.*, p. 42.

greater assimilation of domesticity and the public in Ilongot society that Rosaldo praises, a tribe cannot provide us with a viable model. As human social forms and the human mind grow more complex, nuanced, and structured within civilization, filled with multiple identifications and envisagements (mind), and multiple possibilities and roles (social forms), and this brings in its wake altered public and private modes of expression and action, one cannot revert to a simpler way of life as a serious alternative.[50] In holding the Ilongot up as a preferred contrast model to our own arrangements between the sexes, Rosaldo is forced by the logic of her argument to downplay the *qualitative*, not merely quantitative differences between our way of life and theirs.

Søren Kierkegaard once remarked that politics in the modern age was imperilled and doomed because the modern subject had become too complex to be merely represented. The shifts involved in moving from tribal forms to our sprawling, vast, literally mind-boggling technological, industrial, political-economic-social order are *qualitative*, not simple quantitative alternations. We have, to take up Rosaldo's formulation via Kierkegaard, become too complex to establish a *simple* set of egalitarian terms of division of labor and exchange. Our divisions of private-public contain within them a whole range of meanings unavailable to the Ilongot, plus, to be sure, a set of pan-cultural, bedrock imperatives involving the nurturing and caring for infant children by specific others in space and over time.

Packed into our concept of the private or domestic is a complex set of recognitions of the perils and pitfalls of child-rearing experts who cajole, warn, instruct, and applaud us. The Ilongot woman doesn't need her well-thumbed copy of Dr. Spock. The contemporary American parent requires it, or similar assistance and assurance. Ilongot society didn't spawn a league devoted to encouraging and supporting women in breast-feeding their infants. It doesn't require the whole edifice of modern medicine, or a struggle against that edifice with its depersonalization and its robbing women of the process of giving birth. It didn't need years

[50] See Eli Sagan's powerful account of moral transformation in *Cannibalism: Human Aggression and Cultural Form, passim.*

of protest and agitation to enable women to be surrounded by kin, at least the husband, as a supportive environment for birth. It didn't require a protest spearheaded by women rebels, including but not exclusively feminist, to allow women to keep their babies with them following birth, rather than packing them off to a central nursery. It didn't require court cases and social struggle for fathers to assert their rights to domestic involvement. The "equality" the Ilongot experience bears such a thin relation to whatever concepts finally characterize relations between men and women in our society that I doubt Wittgenstein would see it as bearing a "family resemblance" to our own.

If we cannot be "retribalized," can we be repoliticized? The question requires consideration of the terms of repoliticization. Recalling quickly the alternatives in Western political thought: Plato's archetypes represent not a re- but a depoliticization, creation of an earthly world in which no voice is raised in dissent and the Guardians may lie because they know better. I know many will find this unacceptable because Plato is a profound thinker, a great writer, and a man of vision, but, whatever Plato's justifications, the fact is that the Guardians lie in order to deceive the public, or to prevent it from being unnecessarily aroused or tormented by doubt. Whatever Plato's motives, there is little doubt that the frequently less than profound practitioners of modern politics would have but one aim in mind: keeping and maintaining themselves in power and treating adult citizens as infants to be cajoled or lied to "for their own good." That is what is called "the bottom line." Bypassing Aristotle and Christian political thinkers for a moment, there can be no wavering on the fact that the terms of the Machiavellian "deal," with its coarsening effects for both public and private life, must be repudiated. Once again, the bottom line, despite all attempts to show that Machiavelli either meant less than he said or said less than he meant, is tortuous and finally deceiving. Alasdair MacIntyre demolishes the sentimentalization of Machiavelli:

A great deal of effort has been expended to show that, contrary to the Elizabethan dramatists, and in spite of his notorious admiration for Cesare Borgia, Machiavelli was not a bad man. This is partly because his was clearly an attractive personality, and it is widely although incorrectly felt that somehow one cannot be both bad and attractive. But more importantly it is because Machiavelli's private and personal preferences were certainly for democracy (in his sense of the word—that is, *extended*, limited rule, with small masters sharing power with larger merchants, excluding of course servants and propertyless men) [and I would add though MacIntyre does not, women] . . . But none of this must be allowed to confuse the issue. For Machiavelli the ends of this social and political life are given. They are the attainment and holding down of power, the maintenance of political order and general prosperity, and these latter, in part at least, because unless you maintain them, you will not continue to hold power. Moral rules are technical rules about the means to these ends.[51]

Anyone who accepts or opts for a "Machiavellian deal," including those feminists who incorporate as central a "Machiavellian moment"—Atkinson with her ontic enemies and sex-war or Brownmiller with her militarized Sparta and learning to love to "fight dirty"—have already given themselves over to nihilism. The perversity of Machiavellianism is not simply or only its vision of public life but the fact that promulgation of that vision helps to bring about Machiavellian methods at their most destructive. Taking one's opponents as enemies, for example, as a recent American president did, viewing every political debate or conflict as a personal assault equivalent to an assault on the state, led to the Nixon administration's inglorious use of "reasons of state" and "executive privilege" for cynical and thoroughly despicable purposes; moreover, our embrace of an implicit Machiavellianism in our public and private evaluations meant that Nixon's assault upon the foundations of American constitutional integrity, his criminal offenses of covering-up, lying, and obstruction of justice, were finally pardoned or glossed over by many citizens because "the man has suffered enough" and, despite overwhelming evidence to the contrary, because he had "meant well," or had the bad luck to "get caught."

[51] MacIntyre, *Short History of Ethics*, p. 127.

A muddling of public and private purposes, terms, and moralities was also in evidence when revelation of the late President Kennedy's alleged involvement with a number of women not his wife was treated by some as "proof" that "he was as bad as Nixon." Kennedy's alleged peccadilloes were given a status identical in their import and seriousness for the future of American democratic social forms as Nixon's creation of enemies lists, plumbers, a secret police force, plundering of public funds, subversion of the Constitution, and so on. This confusion also explains the late J. Edgar Hoover's simultaneous obsession with possible "communist" infiltration of the Reverend Martin Luther King's Southern Christian Leadership Conference and with the details of Dr. King's sex life as being equally the justification for defaming him and declaring him unworthy of the public trust. It should be noted that a cramped and cribbed, narrow-minded set of Christian moralisms frequently affixes itself to the terms of the Machiavellian deal: a marriage not made in heaven. Under the guise of bringing morality to politics this deal only brings moralisms to the private lives of political figures and ignores a public morality altogether. As Sennett puts it, ". . . confusion has arisen between public and intimate life; people are working out in terms of personal feelings public matters which can be properly dealt with only through codes of impersonal meaning."[52]

Liberal political theory demands a more complex, ambiguous response. It turns on the public-private distinction and the *particular* terms of that distinction, forged in liberal thought and practice, are unacceptable as the bases of a reconstructive idea. They require too much precious exclusion of the private sphere; they turn on too little recognition of the invasion of politics itself by great forces of unaccountable public power, largely economic, that make a mockery of the politics liberalism professes to embrace. Liberalism's public-private split, as Marx devastatingly pointed out, denies real social distinctions and artificially bifurcates politics and economics whose pas de deux (some would say *danse macabre*) has been the predominant feature of Western society since the triumph of Calvinism.

[52] Sennett, *Fall of Public Man*, p. 5.

But a reconstructive ideal indebted to liberalism also demands what Ronald Dworkin calls "taking rights seriously."[53] Too often radical social critics and activists, with what seems an unerring eye for opening moves that immediately cancel out their proclaimed ends, call "rights" the phony rationalization of bourgeois ideology, or the last refuge of pernicious individualism. Yet we cannot do without a robust and vibrant understanding of rights unless we are prepared to accept the dangerous presumption that individuals are nothing more than the products of social forces, having no dignity, meaning, or inherent presumptive force of their own against abuses of public power. Feminist political discourse needs a defense of rights within the framework of a reconstructive public sphere. Women have struggled for too long to be included within the range over which rights operate, and the understanding of persons' rights implies, to junk "rights" as mere ideology without substantive value and meaning. Finally, liberalism, imperfectly, nurtures the conviction that life consists of a plurality of worthy activities and ends and that these—art, for example— must not be brought under the domination of political power.

Rousseau's ambivalent legacy offers us a public life as the vibrant focus of citizenship, the locus of the highest human ideals, and a troubled and troubling picture of that pervasive, inescapable *force majeure*, human sexuality and the emotions attendant upon it. Hegel provides a dialectic of self-consciousness as the dynamic concatenation of mediated private and public meanings. We need not accept his precise characterization of the household, civil society and the state which finally gives much too much to the state, fails to come to grips with the corrosive effects of civil society, and treats the family both as the stepping stone to universal ethics and the realm in which women are consigned to a shadow world, to call upon his account of mind and embodied selfhood. From Marx we can draw little for an explicit political vision but we can learn much about linkages between diverse social spheres and the pervasive force of ideological distortions which justify exploitative and inegalitarian social relations.

[53] See Ronald Dworkin, *Taking Rights Seriously*. The essays are Dworkin's articulation of a substantive theory of law that serves as an alternative to legal positivism and natural law theory alike.

Marx's category "class" can be adopted variously depending upon one's reconstructive aims. As a powerful tool of social analysis, a category necessary in any critical assessment of social reality, class is inescapable. But as the basis for a theory of political renewal in contemporary America, class has limited critical purchase. Americans do not see themselves primarily as members of a class even as they are aware of what the Marxist would call "class-divisions" in the larger social order and in their personal lives. The Marxist feminist, if she is genuinely interested in reaching a potential constituency in and through politics rather than creating an ideal order "in speech" alone, must take the self-definition of that constituency into account. If she does she will find that the pervasive, rock-bottom sense Americans have of being "individuals" is not to be eradicated by fiat or through a few intensive years of Marxist political education. I concur with Monique Wittig's critique of the Marxist sacrifice of the historical subject and share her insistence that individuals must constitute themselves as subjects, as active agents of their own destiny. They must not be reduced, as Camus once cried, to historical terms.[54] Efforts can and should be made to take the edge off the predatory aspects of individualism, but to sacrifice the concept of the *individual* is to guarantee in advance the failure of one's reconstructive ideal and to invite unchecked political terror. Class does not and cannot characterize individuals in their political aspects as *citizens* because, through the lens of class, they are seen as non-individuated members of an abstract, collective category. To call for class to exclusively define the individual's terms of entry into public life is to limit and confine one's concerns to those considered members of one's own class and to neglect visions of the "common good." If, however, class analysis leads to the demand for a revitalized and more egalitarian polity in which citizens can debate the public business on the basis of greater equality of respect and treatment than pervasive class inequity allows, it serves the reconstructive purposes I have in mind.

American social identity is not only profoundly individual, it

---

[54] The whole of Albert Camus's *The Rebel* is devoted to exploration of this theme.

is also intensely linked to the belief that being an American means or ought to mean "something." It means one has claims against a society that refuses to treat one with respect. It means this country has historically stood for certain worthy ideals. In 1962 when the Students for a Democratic Society issued their challenge to the public world, they did so as Americans urging their fellow citizens to fully implement our own ideals by revitalizing a participatory ethos and making possible genuine responsibility, of citizens, over the decisions that affect their lives. They recalled Jefferson, Lincoln, and John Dewey. They did not, in 1962, fall into the orgy of self-contempt, social loathing, and mindless arrogance characteristic of later enemies of "Amerika," the "pig society." Martin Luther King and the great social movement he represented most forcefully fought for a specific, concrete American dream and asserted their rights, as Americans, to human dignity and to equality of respect and treatment. Strangely, few feminists have couched their political vision in terms of what it means to be an "American" or a "citizen" save in a thin, instrumentalist sense ("How to get yours"). Where is a feminist analogue of Dr. King's "I Have a Dream"? In whose behalf is the feminist dream being dreamt?

Interestingly, it is more frequently among the feminist rank and file, those "ordinary women" who support the ERA and embrace some aspects of traditional femininity, that one finds both the affirmation of a feminist identity as a specifically American identity and the demand that America make good on its commitments to human rights and equal justice. The struggle is to do what our revolutionary forebears did during the early days of the American Revolution; what slaves and abolitionists did during the dark, tragic, yet profoundly ennobling struggles of the Civil War; what working men and women did as they fought for decent wages and a "fair deal"; what the ancestors of slaves and many American young people, including feminists, did in the 1960s to insist with Camus that they would love their country and also love justice. In all these cases it is the individual who is the basic unit of action even as the ideal of politics is a participatory one. The Christian social gospel, a potent force in American consciousness and history, adds force to this ideal for it sees individuals, not as lost in some aggregate abstraction, but as unique, irreplaceable beings with inalienable human dignity as well as immortal souls. A robust rather than insipid, reactionary, or moralistic Christian social language as part of a revitalized political discourse would satisfy my insistence that the terms of this discourse be neither abstract nor ahistorical but concrete, available to social participants, involving a potentially transformative dimension and critical edge.

I earlier embraced those aspects of Aristotelian thought that turned on the imperative that acting in common together with others to agreed upon ends is a worthy form of human life. I shall simply reiterate that Aristotelian moment here. Unfortunately, the most pervasive manner in which Aristotelianism enters discussions of citizenship and a "public space" involves a sentimental rendering of the Greek tradition. More importantly, it requires putting at the heart of one's political vision a great void, the absence of something (a Greek "public space") as one's contrast to "all lesser" forms of citizenship, including democratic citizenship. There never was a "public space" as celebrated in romantic notions of the Greek way in any case: that space was pervaded by the terms of Greek social existence, including the privatization and misogynist treatment of women, the presence of despised but "necessary" slaves and underclasses, and the condemnation of non-Greeks as "*barbaroi*," less than human beings to be dominated, plundered, or destroyed. It is important to remember, as one shines a light through the romantic mists obscuring Aristotle's Greece, that most of the debates in the "public space" had little to do with great or noble ends, and much to do with jockeying for position and pelf, raising monies "by any means necessary," and going to war under the conviction that to be a hero, one of those warriors Arendt celebrates as he displays himself before his fellows, one must die young and leave a beautiful memory.

To pursue the trail of this nostalgia leads to the conclusion that "There is no longer a public space," or that our "public space" is infected and thereby undermined by social concerns. To lament the absence of a "public space"—even the notion of a "space" conveys an aura of pristine exclusion, apart from, floating above the concerns of everyday life—becomes a self-fulfilling prophecy as well as self-indulgent nostalgia. It means one is blinded to authentic instances of citizenship within one's own society. It means one nurtures the concept of the "citizen" in a hothouse of purity so as to keep it untainted by the struggles of the present.[55] Citizenship, like a robust social gospel, must dirty its hands in the tasks of the present. It must, with Lincoln, "disenthrall itself"; it must cast off the image of noble figures disinterestedly debating final ends. Perhaps the most cogent way to put my objection to attempts to hold on to and reclaim the concept of politics as a "public space" and "citizens" as those who inhabit it, is to state that it is as inappropriate to the realities of the present as that tribal analogy I critiqued earlier. Public imperatives, competing public claims, public morality, public duties, responsibilities, goods, yes: a "public space," no. The public world I am claiming for my reconstructive vision is very much *in* and *of* the world, not cut asunder from it in a presumption of its own uniqueness, not parasitic on spheres it despises as those of necessity even as it drains them of dignity and meaning.

In our own time we have seen America's handicapped citizens, a minority dispossessed and deprived of most basic dimensions of human existence—dignity, the right to work, the right to use of public transportation and buildings, the right to education, the right to intimacy—organize themselves into a viable political force and break through invisible walls of public unconcern and private disgust, barriers of silence and shame, stigmata of helplessness and dependence that we forced upon them. Are these not citizens? When they march in public or stage a sit-in—some in wheelchairs, others on crutches, some blind, others minus limbs—have they not created a politics that aims simultaneously to attain their group ends and to reach out so that others may identify with them as individuals and citizens? Their movement transcends a politics of self-interest for it represents in practice a powerful participatory ideal and embodies a less exclusionary definition of the moral and political community. The handicapped movement is an exercise

---

[55] For Arendt, one example of the improper "politicizing" of a social issue was the struggle surrounding school desegregation. Hannah Arendt, "Reflections on Little Rock," *Dissent*, pp. 45-55. See also the critiques of Arendt's position by David Spitz and Melvin Tumin in the same issue.

in democratic political education. What of Ralph Nader and the consumer movement he initially catalyzed and has spearheaded? This movement from its inception has been a grass-roots one, organized around issues of both local and national concern, and is not reducible to a politics of self-interest or self-aggrandisement. Are these not citizens? Have they not created a politics, a "space" populated by real, engaged people rather than exhibitionistic warriors?

Once we political thinkers escape the iron cage of the agora, we can say, paraphrasing a religious ideal, "Where any number of citizens is gathered in the name of acting together in common towards ends they debate and articulate in public, there is citizenship." The quadriplegic who wants simple entrance and egress from the public buildings accessible to us all, just like the black youths who sat in at the lunch counter twenty years ago, or the women struggling for equal respect, are heroes and heroines of another mold, not militarized citizens, not world-historic leaders who take the world as "their own," but individuals who fit another mold different from the Greek one.

Women have a stake in all of this because the Greek way and its nostalgic re-creation exclude and debase them and because its maintenance means most of women's traditional concerns, passions, and responsibilities will fall outside the grid of a "public space." The activation of a female participatory capability must begin with her immediate concerns, go on to give a robust account of them, and then bring these concerns to a transformed vision of the political community. The vision of citizen of which I speak is inclusive, not exclusive; it reaches out to include the young, the old, the infirm, to enlist all on terms of an equality guaranteed by their humanness that does not, at the same time, deny the inegalitarianism of the society in which that equality of participation is affirmed. Such an ideal, and again women's stake is great, must embrace a strong, dignified vision of nonviolence that holds that even as one may find it necessary to break particular laws, one must simultaneously affirm the moral law openly, in the light of day, not under cover of darkness and without public debate and scrutiny. In the words of Dr. King:

A nonviolent army has a magnificent universal quality. To join an army that trains its adherents in the methods of violence, you must be of a certain age. But in Birmingham, some of the most valued foot soldiers were youngsters ranging from elementary pupils to teen-age high school and college students. For acceptance in the armies that maim and kill, one must be physically sound, possessed of straight limbs and accurate vision. But in Birmingham, the lame and the halt and the crippled could and did join up. Al Hibbler, the sightless singer, would never have been accepted in the United States Army or the army of any other nation, but he held a commanding position in our ranks.[56]

The armies of nonviolence, participatory citizens informed by reconstructive ideals that grant inalienable dignity to human beings and to their everyday lives as well as to their political commitments and ends, are ideally suited for women to join their ranks. Camus cried that perhaps we cannot prevent a world in which children are tortured by we can lessen the number of tortured children: If you do not do this who will do this?[57] Given the concrete realities of their social life-worlds, women are uniquely placed to affirm this imperative and make it binding on others. Finally, a reconstructive ideal must fight the enchanting lures of resentment and the poisonous destruction of rage. Martin Luther King expressed, unyieldingly, moral outrage but he never raged at others for he hoped to draw them into his moral and political vision. A feminist politics that does not allow for the possibility of transformation of men as well as women is deeply nihilistic; it does not truly believe in transformative possibilities nor the ideal of genuine mutuality.[58]

A politics of compassion may not be the stuff that leads us to excoriate enemies or march in assurance of our own rectitude to

---

[56] Martin Luther King, Jr., *Why We Can't Wait*, p. 38.

[57] Albert Camus, "The Unbeliever and Christians," in *Resistance, Rebellion and Death*, p. 73.

[58] Through a diverse route this is the conclusion arrived at by Virginia Held in her essay "Marx, Sex and the Transformation of Society."

do battle with foes, but it does allow for the possibility of good faith and it does recognize that no good can come from the widespread dehumanization and destruction of others. Hate is easy; arousing the regressive urges and instincts of one's fellow men requires little more than a capacity for spite. What is difficult, what is the most daunting task of the political imagination in our time, is to fight the allure of hate, particularly when it comes to us in the name of the revolution.

One of the best examples from our recent past of a situation in which a politics of compassion sought to draw out from others a spirit of renewed commitment to a set of moral and political ideals was Sen. Robert F. Kennedy's extemporaneous remarks in Indianapolis, Indiana, in the heart of that city's black community, on learning of the death of Martin Luther King. Kennedy first acknowledged the bitterness, hatred, and desire for revenge his audience would feel and the polarization between white and black that we, as a country, could be moving towards. He indicated to his listeners that he could "feel in my own heart the same kind of feeling [of hatred and distrust] at the injustice of such an act," after the assassination of his older brother. After first acknowledging, and neither denying nor belittling these powerful urges and reactive forces, he carried his listeners to an ideal "beyond these rather difficult times," to an insistence that what was needed was not hatred or violence "but love and wisdom, and compassion toward one another, and a feeling of justice toward those who still suffer within our country, whether they be white or they be black."[59]

So as not to make things easier or simpler than they were, he reminded his fellow citizens that difficult times lay ahead; that they had not seen the end of violence and disorder. Finally, coming full circle and reaffirming the ideal of the man who had died, Kennedy stated: "Let us dedicate ourselves to what the Greeks wrote so many years ago: to tame the savageness of man and to make gentle the life of this world. Let us dedicate ourselves to

[59] Robert F. Kennedy, "Statement by Senator Robert F. Kennedy on the Death of the Reverend Martin Luther King, Rally in Indianapolis, Indiana, April 4, 1968," in *An Honorable Profession: A Tribute to Robert F. Kennedy*, ed. Pierre Salinger, Edwin Guthman, Frank Mankiewicz, and John Seigenthaler, p. 7.

that, and say a prayer for our country and for our people."[60] Those who can see in these words only cynical political advantage or a mushy refusal to face the dire facts have fallen into the despair and cynicism that a politics of compassion must most robustly and firmly oppose, for we can have no illusions about its seductiveness.

None of us lives in what I shall here call the "ethical polity." But we can conceive of that possibility. And if our thinking refuses to capitulate to coercive terms, to be condescended to or hectored, if we refuse to be drawn into utopian pipe-dreams or bullied prematurely into action, our reflections may yet become part of a reconstructive vision of a future social world in which civility and complexity prevail. Such a world would require private spheres bearing their own intrinsic dignity and purpose tied to moral and aesthetic imperatives, all the textures, nuances, tones and touches of a life lived intimately among others. A richly complex private sphere requires, in order that it survive, freedom from some all-encompassing public imperative, but in order for it to flourish the public world itself must nurture and sustain a set of ethical imperatives, including a commitment to preserve, protect, and defend human beings in their capacities as private persons, and to allow men and women alike to partake in the good of the public sphere on an equal basis of participatory dignity and equality. Rather than an ideal of citizenship and civic virtue that features a citizenry grimly going about their collective duty, or an elite band of citizens in their "public space" cut off from a world that includes most of the rest of us, within the ethical polity the active citizen would be one who had affirmed as part of what it meant to be fully human a devotion to public, moral responsibilities and ends.

My ideal is the preservation of a tension between diverse spheres and competing ideals and purposes. There is always a danger that a too strong and overweening polity would swamp the individual, as well as a peril that life as lived in a polity such as our own, faced with delegitimation, will decivilize us. That is, the crises of our time may erode within us the possibility of civic

[60] *Ibid.*, p. 8.

virtue as we increasingly come to substitute private pleasures and asocial inwardness for any sort of public involvement and obligation to others. Within an ethical polity the individual would, or could, have many irons in the fire. The prevailing image of the person would be that of a human being with a capacity for self-reflection as to the ends and means of public and private action. Such persons could tolerate the ineradicable tension between public and private imperatives, thought and action, aesthetic standards and ethical principles. He or she could distinguish between those conditions, events, or states of affairs which are part of a shared human condition—grief, loss through death, natural disasters, and decay of the flesh—and those man-made injustices which can be remedied, or which one can work to remedy. Above all the human being within the ethical polity never presumes that ambivalence and conflict will one day end, for he or she has come to understand that such ambivalence and conflict is the wellspring of a life lived reflectively and that we are all enriched by the messy reality which is our lot. A clear notion of what ideals and obligations are required to animate an authentic public life, an ethical polity, must be adumbrated: authority, freedom, public law, civic virtue, the ideal of the citizen—all those beliefs, habits, and qualities which are integral to a political order.

We will have kept the moral wager and affirmed our humanity only if, with Camus, we refuse to capitulate to the plague. We must embrace a politics of limits. There are things we must not do for in so doing we will not only further cheapen already fragile human ties in the present but undermine the very humanitarian ends we claim to seek. Each of us has the responsibility of making judgments between competing visions of the political imagination, rejecting those which tap primitive rage from those which have as their template our earliest memories of needs met and succor provided within a social context that was our secure universe. Only in this way can envisagements of hope and compassion—private and public—ideals the more clamorous pictures of the rageful would expunge from our world—be kept alive. It is, of course, possible that our language of political inquiry, including its emerging feminist variant, is not adequate to the task of uniting the material and the spiritual, the public and the private, by achieving a dialectics of choice, variability, and possibility grounded in a conviction which disallows absolute certitude and the destruction it brings in its wake.

The task of the political imagination is possible if civility is not utterly destroyed, if room remains for playful experimentation from deep seriousness of purpose free from totalistic intrusion and ideological control. For even when notions of sexual equality and social justice are not realized and seem far-off ideals, freedom preserves the human discourse necessary to work toward the realization of both. One day as our children or their children or their children's children stroll in gardens, debate in public places, or poke through the ashes of a wrecked civilization, they may not rise to call us blessed. But neither will they curse our memory because we permitted, through our silence, things to pass away as in a dream.

Bibliography

Allen, Christine Garside. "Plato on Women." *Feminist Studies* 2 (1975):131-138.

Amundsen, Kirsten. *The Silenced Majority.* Englewood Cliffs, N. J.: Prentice-Hall, 1971.

Anthony, Susan B. and Harper, Ida Husted, eds. *History of Women Suffrage*, vol. 4. Indianapolis: Hollenbeck Press, 1902.

Aquinas, St. Thomas. *The Political Ideas of St. Thomas Aquinas.* Edited by Dino Bigongiari. New York: Hafner Publishing, 1953.

Arendt, Hannah. *The Human Condition.* Chicago: University of Chicago Press, 1958.

————. "Reflections on Little Rock." *Dissent* 1 (Winter 1959):45-55.

Aristotle. *Metaphysics.* Translated by Richard Hope. Ann Arbor: University of Michigan Press, 1968.

————. *The Politics.* Edited and translated by Ernest Barker. New York: Oxford University Press, 1962.

————. *The Student's Oxford Aristotle.* Vol. 5: *Ethics [Ethica Nicomachea].* Translated by W. D. Ross. London: Oxford University Press, 1946.

Atkinson, Ti-Grace. "Theories of Radical Feminism." In *Notes from the Second Year: Women's Liberation*, edited by Shulamith Firestone. N.p., 1970.

Augustine. *City of God.* Edited by Etienne Gilson. Garden City, N. Y.: Doubleday, 1958.

————. *City of God.* Edited by David Knowles. Baltimore: Penguin Books, 1972.

————. *The Political Writings of St. Augustine.* Edited by Henry Paolucci. Chicago: Henry Regnery, 1967.

Barber, Benjamin R. "Rousseau and the Paradoxes of Imagination." *Daedalus* 107 (Summer 1978):79-95.

Basler, Roy, ed. *The Collected Works of Abraham Lincoln.* 9 vols. New Brunswick, N. J.: Rutgers University Press, 1975.

Beard, Mary R. *Woman as Force in History.* New York: Collier Books, 1972.

Beauvoir, Simone de. *The Second Sex.* Translated by H. M. Parshley. New York: Bantam Books, 1968.

Bentham, Jeremy. *The Principles of Morals and Legislation.* New York: Hafner Publishing, 1965.

Beradt, Charlotte. *The Third Reich of Dreams.* Chicago: Quadrangle, 1966.

Berlin, Isaiah. "The Question of Machiavelli." *New York Review of Books,* 4 November 1971, pp. 20-32.

Bettelheim, Bruno. *The Children of the Dream.* London: Collier-MacMillan, 1969.

Blanchard, William H. *Rousseau and the Spirit of Revolt.* Ann Arbor: University of Michigan Press, 1967.

Bloom, Allan. "The Education of Democratic Man: Emile." *Daedalus* 107 (Summer 1978):135-154.

Bluebond-Langner, Myra. *The Private Worlds of Dying Children.* Princeton: Princeton University Press, 1978.

Bocock, Richard. *Freud and Modern Society.* London: Thomas Nelson and Sons, 1977.

Bodin, Jean. *Six Books of the Commonwealth.* Translated by M. A. Tooley. Oxford: Basil Blackwell, 1956.

Bonhoeffer, Dietrich. *Letters and Papers from Prison.* Edited by Eberhard Bethge. Rev. ed. New York: Macmillan, 1967.

Brown, Norman O. *Love's Body.* New York: Vintage Books, 1966.

Brownmiller, Susan. *Against Our Will: Men, Women and Rape.* New York: Simon and Schuster, 1975.

Butler, Melissa A. "Early Liberal Roots of Feminism: John Locke and the Attack on Patriarchy." *American Political Science Review* 72 (March 1978):135-150.

Calvin, John. *On God and Political Duty.* Indianapolis: Bobbs-Merrill, 1956.

Campioni, Mia. "Psychoanalysis and Marxist Feminism." *Working Papers in Sex, Science and Culture* 1 (November 1976):33-60.

Camus, Albert. *The Rebel*. New York: Vintage Books, 1956.
———. *Resistance, Rebellion, and Death*. New York: Alfred A. Knopf, 1961.
Cassirer, Ernst. *The Question of Jean-Jacques Rousseau*. Bloomington: Indiana University Press, 1967.
Castoriadis, Cornelius. "From Marx to Aristotle, From Aristotle to Us." *Social Research* 45 (Winter 1978):667-673.
Chapman, Richard Allen. "Leviathan Writ Small: Thomas Hobbes on the Family." *American Political Science Review* 69 (March 1975):76-90.
Charvet, John. "Individual Identity and Social Consciousness in Rousseau's Philosophy." In *Hobbes and Rousseau*, edited by Maurice Cranston and Richard S. Peters. Garden City, N. Y.: Doubleday Anchor Books, 1972.
Chodorow, Nancy. *The Reproduction of Mothering: Psychoanalysis and the Sociology of Gender*. Berkeley: University of California Press, 1978.
Cîxous, Hélène. "Poetry is/and (the) Political." In *The Second Sex—Thirty Years Later: A Commemorative Conference on Feminist Theory*. Mimeographed. New York: Institute for the Humanities, 1979.
Coles, Robert. *Children of Crisis*. 5 vols. Boston: Little, Brown, 1967-1977.
Cooke, Joanne; Bunch-Weeks, Charlotte; and Morgan, Robin, eds. *The New Woman*. Greenwich, Conn.: Fawcett, 1969.
Copelston, Frederick J., S.J. *A History of Philosophy*, vol. 2, *Medieval Philosophy*. Garden City, N. Y.: Doubleday, 1962.
Daly, Mary. *Beyond God the Father*. Boston: Beacon Press, 1973.
———. *Gyn/Ecology. The Metaethics of Radical Feminism*. Boston: Beacon Press, 1979.
Dante. *Monarchy and Three Political Letters*. Translated by Donald Nicholl and Colin Hardie. New York: Noonday Press, 1954.
Deckard, Barbara. *The Women's Movement*. New York: Harper and Row, 1975.
Decter, Midge. *The New Chastity and Other Arguments Against Women's Liberation*. New York: Berkeley Medallion Books, 1972.

Demos, John. *A Little Commonwealth: Family Life in Plymouth Colony*. New York: Oxford University Press, 1970.

De Stefano, Christine. "Legitimation Crisis Reconsidered: Women, Personal Identity, and the State." Graduate seminar paper, University of Massachusetts, Amherst, 1979.

Descartes, René. *Meditations on First Philosophy*. Translated by Lawrence J. Lafleur. New York: Bobbs-Merrill, 1960.

Dillenberger, John, ed. *Martin Luther: Selections from His Writings*. Garden City, N. Y.: Doubleday Anchor Books, 1961.

Dinnerstein, Dorothy. *The Mermaid and the Minotaur*. New York: Harper Colophon, 1976.

Douglas, Ann. *The Feminization of American Culture*. New York: Avon, 1977.

Dover, K. J. *Greek Homosexuality*. London: Duckworth, 1978.

Duncan, Graeme. *Marx and Mill: Two Views of Social Conflict and Social Harmony*. Cambridge: Cambridge University Press, 1973.

Dunn, John. *Western Political Theory in the Face of the Future*. Cambridge: Cambridge University Press, 1979.

Dworkin, Ronald. *Taking Rights Seriously*. Cambridge, Mass.: Harvard University Press, 1977.

Elshtain, Jean Bethke. "Against Androgyny." *Telos* 47 (Spring 1981):5-21.

———. "The Anti-Feminist Backlash." *Commonweal*, 8 March 1974, pp. 16-19.

———. "Doris Lessing: Language and Politics." *Salmagundi*, no. 47-48 (Winter-Spring 1980):95-114.

———. "Family Reconstruction." *Commonweal*, 1 August 1980, pp. 430-431.

———. "Liberal Heresies: Existentialism and Repressive Feminism." In *Liberalism and the Modern Polity*, edited by Michael C. Gargas McGrath. New York: Marcel Dekker, 1978.

———. "Methodological Sophistication and Conceptual Confusion: A Critique of Mainstream Political Science." In *The Prism of Sex: Essays in the Sociology of Knowledge*, edited by Julia A. Sherman and Evelyn Torton Beck. Madison: University of Wisconsin Press, 1979.

———. "Moral Woman/Immoral Man: The Public/Private Distinction and Its Political Ramifications.'' *Politics and Society* 4 (1974):453-473.

———. ''Review of *Against Our Will*.'' *Telos*, no. 30 (Winter 1976-1977):327-342.

———. ''The Social Relations of the Classroom.'' *Telos*, no. 27 (Spring 1976):91-110. *probably in Studies in Socialist Pedagogy* ✓

———. '' 'Thank Heaven for Little Girls': The Dialectics of Development.'' *Politics* 10 (November 1975):139-148.

Engels, Frederick. *The Origin of the Family, Private Property and the State*. New York: Pathfinder Press, 1972.

Epstein, Cynthia Fuchs. *Woman's Place*. Berkeley: University of California Press, 1971.

Fay, Brian. *Social Theory and Political Practice*. London: George *p. 3/3* Allen and Unwin, 1975.

Ferguson, Kathy E. ''Liberalism and Oppression: Emma Goldman and the Anarchist Feminist Alternative.'' In *Liberalism and the Modern Polity*, edited by Michael C. Gargas McGrath. New York: Marcel Dekker, 1978.

Feuer, Lewis S. *Marx and Engels: Basic Writings on Politics and Philosophy*. Garden City, N. Y.: Doubleday Anchor Books, 1959.

Figes, Eva. *Patriarchal Attitudes*. Greenwich, Conn.: Fawcett, 1970.

Figgis, John Neville. *The Political Aspects of St. Augustine's City of God*. Gloucester, Mass.: Peter Smith, 1963.

Filmer, Sir Robert. *Patriarcha and Other Political Works*. Edited by Peter Laslett. Oxford, Basil Blackwell, 1949.

Firestone, Shulamith. *The Dialectic of Sex*. New York: Bantam Books, 1972.

Forgie, George B. *Patricide in the House Divided: A Psychological Interpretation of Lincoln and His Age*. New York: W. W. Norton, 1979.

Fraiberg, Selma. *Every Child's Birthright: In Defense of Mothering*. New York: Basic Books, 1977.

Freeman, Jo. *The Politics of Women's Liberation*. New York: David McKay, 1975.

Freud, Ernst L., ed. *The Letters of Sigmund Freud*. New York: Basic Books, 1975.

Freud, Sigmund. *The Complete Psychological Works of Sigmund Freud*. 24 vols. London: Hogarth, 1975. Hereafter called *Standard Edition*.

―――. "A Child Is Being Beaten." In *Standard Edition*, vol. 17, pp. 179-204.

―――. *Civilization and Its Discontents*. In *Standard Edition*, vol. 21.

―――. "Constructions in Analysis." In *Standard Edition*, vol. 23, pp. 355-370.

―――. "The Dissolution of the Oedipus Complex." In *Standard Edition*, vol. 19, pp. 173-179.

―――. *The Ego and the Id*. In *Standard Edition*, vol. 19.

―――. "Introductory Lectures on Psychoanalysis." In *Standard Edition*, vols. 15 and 16.

―――. *New Introductory Lectures on Psycho-analysis*. In *Standard Edition*, vol. 22.

―――. "On the Sexual Enlightenment of Children." In *Standard Edition*, vol. 9, pp. 129-139.

―――. *The Psychopathology of Everyday Life*. In *Standard Edition*, vol. 6.

―――. *Three Essays on the Theory of Sexuality*. In *Standard Edition*, vol. 7.

―――. "The Unconscious." In *Standard Edition*, vol. 14, pp. 166-204.

Friedan, Betty. *The Feminine Mystique*. New York: W. W. Norton, 1963.

―――. "Feminism Takes a New Turn." *New York Times Magazine*, 18 December 1979, p. 40.

Fuller, Margaret. *The Writings of Margaret Fuller*. Edited by Mason Wade. New York: Viking Press, 1941.

Gass, William. *On Being Blue: A Phenomenological Inquiry*. Boston: David R. Godine, 1976.

Gilligan, Carol. "In a Different Voice: Women's Conceptions of the Self and Morality." *Harvard Education Review* 47 (1977):481-517.

Gilman, Charlotte Perkins. *Herland*. Introduction by Ann J. Lane. New York: Pantheon, 1979.

Goldberg, Steven. *The Inevitability of Patriarchy*. New York: William Morrow, 1974.

Goodall, Jane Van-Lawick. *In the Shadow of Man*. Boston: Houghton Mifflin, 1971.

Gornick, Vivian and Moran, Barbara K., eds. *Woman in Sexist Society: Studies in Power and Powerlessness*. New York: Signet, 1971.

Greer, Germaine. *The Female Eunuch*. New York: McGraw-Hill, 1970.

Gregor, James. *The Fascist Persuasion in Radical Politics.* Princeton: Princeton University Press, 1974.

Griffin, Susan. *Woman and Nature: The Roaring Inside Her*. New York: Harper and Row, 1978.

Grimsley, Ronald. *Jean-Jacques Rousseau*. Cardiff: University of Wales Press, 1961.

Gross, Elizabeth. "Lacan, The Symbolic, The Imaginary and The Real." *Working Papers in Sex, Science and Culture* 1 (November 1976):12-32.

Gunnell, John G. *Political Theory: Tradition and Interpretation*. Cambridge, Mass.: Winthrop Publishers, 1979.

Gutman, Herbert G. *The Black Family in Slavery and Freedom 1750-1925*. New York: Vintage Books, 1976.

Habermas, Jürgen. *Legitimation Crisis*. Boston: Beacon Press, 1973.

Hampshire, Stuart. "Joyce and Vico: The Middle Way." *New York Review of Books*, 18 October 1973, p. 8.

———. *Morality and Pessimism*. Cambridge: Cambridge University Press, 1972.

———. "Public and Private Morality." In *Public and Private Morality*, edited by Stuart Hampshire. Cambridge: Cambridge University Press, 1968.

———. *Thought and Action*. New York: Viking Books, 1960.

Harper, Ida Husted. *History of Woman Suffrage*, vol. 5. New York: J. J. Little and Ives, 1922.

Hart, Herbert Leonidas. *Women's Suffrage and National Danger: A Plea for the Ascendancy of Man*. London: Alexander and Shepheard, 1889.

Hartmann, Klaus. "Hegel: A Non-Metaphysical View." In *Hegel*, edited by Alasdair MacIntyre. Garden City, N. Y.: Doubleday Anchor Books, 1972.

Hauerwas, Stanley. "The Moral Meaning of the Family." *Commonweal*, 1 August 1980, pp. 432-436.

Hegel, G.W.F. *Aesthetics: lectures on fine art*. Translated by T. M. Knox. Oxford: Clarendon Press, 1975.

———. *The Phenomenology of Mind*. Translated by J. B. Baille. New York: Harper and Row, 1967.

———. *Philosophy of Right*. Translated by T. M. Knox. London: Oxford University Press, 1973.

Held, Virginia. "Marx, Sex, and the Transformation of Society." In *Women and Philosophy: Toward a Theory of Liberation*, edited by Carol Gould and Marx Wartofsky. New York: G. P. Putnam, 1976.

Henley, Nancy. *Body Politics: Power, Sex, and Nonverbal Communication*. Englewood Cliffs, N. J.: Prentice-Hall, 1977.

Herlihy, David. "Land, Family and Women in Continental Europe, 701-1200." *Traditio* 18 (1962):89-119.

Hinton, R.W.K. "Husbands, Fathers and Conquerers: I." *Political Studies* 15 (1967):291-300.

———. "Husbands, Fathers and Conquerers: II." *Political Studies* 16 (1968):56-67.

Hirschmann, Albert O. *The Passions and the Interests*. Princeton: Princeton University Press, 1978.

Hobbes, Thomas. *Leviathan*. Edited by Michael Oakeshott. New York: Collier Books, 1966.

Hodge, John L.; Struckmann, Donald K.; and Trost, Lynn Dorland. *Cultural Bases of Racism and Group Oppression*. Berkeley: Two Riders Press, 1979.

Humphries, Jane. "The Working Class Family: A Marxist Perspective." In *The Family in Political Thought*, edited by Jean Bethke Elshtain. Amherst: University of Massachusetts Press, 1981.

Itard, Jean-Marc-Gaspard. *The Wild Boy of Aveyron*. Englewood Cliffs, N. J.: Prentice-Hall, 1962.

Jacobsen, Norman. *Pride and Solace: The Functions and Limits of Political Theory*. Berkeley: University of California Press, 1978.

Janeway, Elizabeth. *Man's World, Woman's Place*. New York: Delta Books, 1971.

Jerusalem Bible. Edited by Alexander Jones. Garden City, N. Y.: Doubleday, 1969.

Kaufman, Michael W. "Spare Ribs: The Conception of Women in the Middle Ages and the Renaissance." *Soundings: An Interdisciplinary Journal* 16 (Summer 1973):139-163.

Keniston, Kenneth and The Carnegie Council of Children. *All Our Children: The American Family Under Pressure*. New York: Harcourt Brace Jovanovich, 1977.

Kennedy, Robert F. "Statement by Senator Robert F. Kennedy on the Death of the Reverend Martin Luther King, Rally in Indianapolis, Indiana, April 4, 1968." In *An Honorable Profession: A Tribute to Robert F. Kennedy*, edited by Pierre Salinger, Edwin Guthman, Frank Mankiewicz, and John Seigenthaler. Garden City, N. Y.: Doubleday, 1968.

Keohane, Nannerl O. "The Masterpiece of Polity in Our Century: Rousseau on the Morality of the Enlightenment." *Political Theory* 6 (November 1968):421-456.

Kessen, William. "Rousseau's Children." *Daedalus* 107 (Summer 1978):155-166.

Kieckhefer, Richard. *European Witch Trials: Their Foundation in Popular and Learned Culture, 1300-1500*. Berkeley: University of California Press, 1976.

King, Martin Luther, Jr. *Why We Can't Wait*. New York: New American Library, 1964.

Kovesi, Julius. *Moral Notions*. London: Routledge and Kegan Paul, 1967.

Kraditor, Aileen S. *The Ideas of the Woman Suffrage Movement 1890-1920*. Garden City, N. Y.: Doubleday Anchor Books, 1971.

Krouse, Richard W. "Patriarchal Liberalism and Beyond: From John Stuart Mill to Harriet Taylor." In *The Family in Political Thought*, edited by Jean Bethke Elshtain. Amherst: University of Massachusetts Press, 1981.

Lakatos, Imre and Musgrave, Alan, eds. *Criticism and the Growth of Knowledge*. Cambridge: Cambridge University Press, 1970.

Landes, Joan. "The Theory Behind Women's Liberation: Problems and Prospects." Ph.D. dissertation, New York University, 1975.

Lane, Harlan. *The Wild Boy of Aveyron*. Cambridge, Mass.: Harvard University Press, 1976.

Lawrence, D. H. *Stories, Essays and Poems*. Edited by Desmond Hawkins. London: Dent Everyman's Library, 1973.

Leacock, Eleanor Burke. "The Changing Family and Lévi-Strauss, or Whatever Happened to Fathers." *Social Research* 44 (Summer 1977):235-259.

Leakey, Richard E. and Lewin, Roger. *Origins: What New Discoveries Reveal About the Emergence of our Species and its Possible Future*. New York: E. P. Dutton, 1977.

Lenin, V. I. *The Emancipation of Women: From the Writings of V. I. Lenin*. New York: International Publishers, 1966.

Lessing, Doris. *Briefing for a Descent into Hell*. New York: Bantam Books, 1972.

————. *The Four-Gated City*. New York: Bantam Books, 1970.

————. *Shikasta: Canopus in Argos: Archives, Re: Colonised Planet 5*. New York: Alfred A. Knopf, 1979.

Loch, Wolfgang. "Some Comments on the Subject of Psychoanalysis and Truth." In *Truth, Consciousness and Reality*, edited by Joseph R. Smith, M.D. New Haven: Yale University Press, 1974.

Locke, John. *Two Treatises of Government*. Edited by Peter Laslett. New York: New American Library, 1965.

Lukes, Steven. "Alienation and Anomie." In *Social Structure and Political Theory*, edited by Glen Gordon and William E. Connolly. Lexington, Mass.: D. C. Heath, 1974.

————. *Individualism*. New York: Harper and Row, 1973.

Luther, Martin. *Three Treatises*. Philadelphia: Fortress Press, 1960.

Machiavelli, Niccolò. *The Prince and The Discourses*. New York: Modern Library, 1950.

MacIntyre, Alasdair. *A Short History of Ethics*. New York: Macmillan, 1971.

Magee, Bryan, ed. "Conversation with Bernard Williams." In *Modern British Philosophy*. New York: St. Martin's Press, 1971.

Mailer, Norman. *The Prisoner of Sex*. New York: New American Library, 1971.

Malcolm, Norman. *Ludwig Wittgenstein, A Memoir*. London: Oxford University Press, 1972.

———. *Problems of Mind*. London: Allen and Unwin, 1972.

Marcuse, Herbert. *Studies in Critical Philosophy*. Boston: Beacon Press, 1973.

Marx, Karl. *Capital*. Edited by Frederick Engels. 3 vols. New York: International Publishers, 1975.

——— and Engels, Frederick. *Collected Works*. 10 vols. New York: International Publishers, 1975.

Massell, Gregory J. *The Surrogate Proletariat: Moslem Women and Revolutionary Struggles in Soviet Central Asia 1919-1929*. Princeton: Princeton University Press, 1974.

Masters, Roger D. "Jean-Jacques Is Alive and Well: Rousseau and Contemporary Sociobiology." *Daedalus* 107 (Summer 1978):93-106.

———. *The Political Philosophy of Rousseau*. Princeton: Princeton University Press, 1968.

McMurty, John. *The Structure of Marx's World-View*. Princeton: Princeton University Press, 1978.

Midgley, Mary. *Beast and Man: The Roots of Human Nature*. Ithaca: Cornell University Press, 1978.

Mill, John Stuart. *Auguste Comte and Positivism*. Ann Arbor: University of Michigan Press, 1973.

———. *Autobiography*. Indianapolis: Bobbs-Merrill, 1957.

———. *On Liberty*. Chicago: Henry Regnery, 1956.

———. *On the Subjection of Women*. Greenwich, Conn.: Fawcett, 1970.

Millett, Kate. *Sexual Politics*. Garden City, N. Y.: Doubleday, 1970.

Mitchell, Juliet. *Psychoanalysis and Feminism*. New York: Pantheon, 1971.

Mitchell, Juliet. *Woman's Estate.* New York: Vintage Books, 1973.

Moglen, Helen. *Charlotte Brontë: The Self Conceived.* New York: W. W. Norton, 1976.

Nietzsche, Friedrich. *The Birth of Tragedy and The Case of Wagner.* Translated by Walter Kaufman. New York: Vintage Books, 1967.

——. *The Genealogy of Morals and Ecce Homo.* Translated by Walter Kaufman. New York: Vintage Books, 1969.

O'Faolain, Julia and Martines, Lauro, eds. *Not in God's Image.* New York: Harper Torchbooks, 1973.

Okin, Susan Moller. *Women in Western Political Thought.* Princeton: Princeton University Press, 1979.

Ollman, Bertell. *Alienation: Marx's Conception of Man in Capitalist Society.* Cambridge: Cambridge University Press, 1973.

O'Shaugnessy, Brian. "The Id and the Thinking Process." In *Freud: A Collection of Critical Essays,* edited by Richard Wollheim. Garden City, N. Y.: Doubleday Anchor Books, 1974.

Parsons, Talcott. "Age and Sex in the Social Structure of the United States." In *Selected Studies in Marriage and the Family,* edited by Robert F. Winch and Robert McGinnis. New York: Henry Holt, 1953.

——. "The Family in Urban-Industrial America." In *Sociology of the Family,* edited by Michael Anderson. Baltimore: Penguin Books, 1971.

Pateman, Carol. "Sublimation and Reification: Locke, Wolin, and the Liberal Democratic Conception of the Political." *Politics and Society* 5 (1965):441-467.

Paul, Diane. "In the Interests of Civilization: Marxist Views of Race and Culture in the 19th Century." Paper presented at the 9th Annual Meeting of the Northeast Political Science Association, November, 1977.

Piercy, Marge. *Woman on the Edge of Time.* New York: Fawcett, 1978.

Piers, Maria W. *Infanticide, Past and Present.* New York: W. W. Norton, 1978.

Plato. *The Laws.* Translated by Trevor J. Saunders. Baltimore: Penguin Books, 1970.

————. *Meno.* Translated by W.K.C. Guthrie. Baltimore: Penguin Books, 1956.

————. *The Republic of Plato.* Translated by Allan Bloom. New York: Basic Books, 1968.

————. *Statesman.* Edited by Martin Ostwald. Translated by J. B. Skemp. Indianapolis: Bobbs-Merrill, 1957.

————. *The Symposium.* Translated by Walter Hamilton. Baltimore: Penguin Books, 1973.

→ Pocock, J.G.A. "Languages and Their Implications: The Transformation of the Study of Political Thought." In *Politics, Language and Time,* edited by Melvin Richter. New York: Atheneum, 1974.

————. *The Machiavellian Moment.* Princeton: Princeton University Press, 1975.

Power, Eileen. *Medieval Women.* Cambridge: Cambridge University Press, 1975.

————. "The Position of Women." In *The Legacy of the Middle Ages,* edited by C. G. Crump and E. F. Jacob. Oxford: Clarendon Press, 1948.

Rapaport, Elizabeth. "On the Future of Love: Rousseau and the Radical Feminists." In *Women and Philosophy: Toward a Theory of Liberation,* edited by Carol Gould and Marx Wartofsky. New York: G. P. Putnam, 1976.

Rich, Adrienne. *The Dream of a Common Language: Poems 1974-1977.* New York: W. W. Norton, 1978.

————. *Of Woman Born: Motherhood as Experience and Institution.* New York: W. W. Norton, 1976.

Rosaldo, Michelle Zimbalist. "Woman, Culture and Society: A Theoretical Overview." In *Woman, Culture and Society,* edited by Michelle Zimbalist Rosaldo and Louise Lamphere. Stanford: Stanford University Press, 1974.

————. "The Use and Abuse of Anthropology: Reflections on Feminism and Cross-cultural Understanding." *Signs* 5 (Spring 1980):389-417.

Rosenthal, Abigail. "Feminism Without Contradictions." *Monist* 51 (January 1973):28-42.

Rossi, Alice S. "A Biosocial Perspective on Parenting." *Daedalus* 106 (Spring 1977):1-32.

Roszak, Betty and Roszak, Theodore, eds. *Masculine/Feminine.* New York: Harper Colophon, 1969.

Rothman, Sheila M. *Woman's Proper Place: A History of Changing Ideals and Practices, 1870 to Present.* New York: Basic Books, 1978.

Rousseau, Jean-Jacques. *The Confessions.* Translated by J. N. Cohen. Baltimore: Penguin Books, 1954.

————. *Emile.* Translated by B. Boxley. London: J. B. Dent and Sons, 1956.

————. *Emile or On Education.* Edited and translated by Allan Bloom. New York: Basic Books, 1979.

————. *The First and Second Discourses.* Edited by Roger D. Masters. New York: St. Martin's Press, 1964.

————. *Government of Poland.* Translated by Willmoore Kendall. Indianapolis: Bobbs-Merrill, 1972.

————. *On the Social Contract, with Geneva Manuscript and Political Economy.* Edited by Roger D. Masters, New York: St. Martin's Press, 1978.

————. *Politics and the Arts: Letter to M. D'Alembert on the Theatre.* Translated by Allan Bloom. Ithaca: Cornell University Press, 1960.

———— and Herder, Johann Gottfried. *On the Origin of Language.* Translated by J. Moran and A. Gode. New York: Frederick Unger, 1966.

Rowbotham, Sheila. *Woman's Consciousness, Man's World.* Baltimore: Penguin Books, 1973.

————. *Women, Resistance and Revolution.* New York: Vintage Books, 1972.

✓ Rubin, Lillian. *Worlds of Pain: Life in the Working-Class Family.* New York: Basic Books, 1976.

Ruether, Rosemary Radford. "The Cult of True Womanhood." *Commonweal*, 9 November 1973, pp. 127-132.

Rupp, E. G. and Drewery, Benjamin, eds. *Martin Luther.* London: Edward Arnold, 1976.

Saffioti, Heleieth. *Women in Class Society.* New York: Monthly Review Press, 1978.

Sagan, Eli. *Cannabalism: Human Aggression and Cultural Form.* New York: Harper Torchbooks, 1974.

———. *The Lust to Annihilate: A Psychoanalytic Study of Violence in Ancient Greek Culture.* New York: Psychohistory Press, 1979.

Salkever, Stephen G. "Rousseau and the Concept of Happiness." *Polity* 11 (Fall 1978):27-45.

Schochet, Gordon. *Patriarchalism and Political Thought.* New York: Basic Books, 1975.

Scott, Heide. *Does Socialism Liberate Women?* Boston: Beacon Press, 1974.

Seigel, Jerrold. *Marx's Fate: The Shape of a Life.* Princeton: Princeton University Press, 1978.

Sennett, Richard. *The Fall of Public Man.* New York: Vintage Books, 1978.

Shanley, Mary Lyndon. "Marriage Contract and Social Contract in Seventeenth Century English Political Thought." *Western Political Quarterly* 32 (March 1979):79-91.

Shklar, Judith N. *Men and Citizens.* Cambridge: Cambridge University Press, 1969.

Simon, Bennett. "Models of Mind and Mental Illness in Ancient Greece: I. The Platonic Model." *Journal of the History of the Behavioral Sciences* 8 (October 1972):398-404.

Singer, Peter. *Animal Liberation.* New York: Avon, 1975.

Slater, Philip E. *The Glory of Hera.* Boston: Beacon Press, 1968.

Smart, J.J.C. and Williams, Bernard. *Utilitarianism For and Against.* Cambridge: Cambridge University Press, 1973.

Smith, Dorothy E. "A Sociology for Women." In *The Prism of Sex: Essays in the Sociology of Knowledge,* edited by Julia A. Sherman and Evelyn Torton Beck. Madison: University of Wisconsin Press, 1979.

Solomon, R. C. "Hegel's Concept of Geist." In *Hegel: A Collection of Critical Essays,* edited by Alasdair MacIntyre. Garden City, N. Y.: Doubleday Anchor Books, 1972.

Sontag, Susan and Rich, Adrienne. "Feminism and Fascism: An Exchange." *New York Review of Books,* 20 March 1975, pp. 31-32.

Spinoza, Benedict de. *A Theologico-Political Treatise and Polit-*

ical Treatise. Translated by R. H. Melwes. New York: Dover Publications, 1955.

Stanton, Elizabeth Cady; Anthony, Susan B.; and Gage, Matilda Joslyn, eds. *History of Woman Suffrage*. 3 vols. Rochester: Charles Mann, 1881-1891.

Steiner, George. *After Babel*. London: Oxford University Press, 1977.

Stern, J. P. *Hitler, The Fuehrer and the People*. Berkeley: University of California Press, 1975.

Tanner, Tony. "Julie and 'La Maison Paternelle': Another Look as Rousseau's *La Nouvelle Heloise*." *Daedalus* 105 (Winter 1976):23-45.

Taylor, Charles. *Hegel*. Cambridge: Cambridge University Press, 1975.

Tiger, Lionel and Fox, Robin. *The Imperial Animal*. New York: Holt, Rinehart and Winston, 1970.

Tocqueville, Alexis de. *Democracy in America*. Edited by Phillips Bradley. 2 vols. New York: Vintage Books, 1945.

Unger, Roberto Mangabeira. *Knowledge and Politics*. New York: Free Press, 1975.

Walzer, Michael. *Regicide and Revolution: Speeches at the Trial of Louis XVI*. Cambridge: Cambridge University Press, 1974.

————. *The Revolution of the Saints*. New York: Atheneum, 1973.

Warrior, Betsy. "Man as an Obsolete Life Form." *No More Fun and Games: A Journal of Female Liberation* 2 (February 1969):77-78.

Weil, Simone. *The Need for Roots*. New York: Harper Colophon, 1952.

Weisstein, Naomi. "Kinder, Küche, Kirche as Scientific Law: Psychology Constructs of the Female." *Motive* 29 (March-April 1969):78-85.

Whyte, Martin King. *The Status of Women in Preindustrial Society*. Princeton: Princeton University Press, 1978.

Williams, Bernard. "Are persons bodies?" In *Problems of the Self*. Cambridge: Cambridge University Press, 1976.

————. "Bodily continuity and personal identity." In *Problems of the Self*. Cambridge: Cambridge University Press, 1976.

———. "The Idea of Equality." In *Moral Concepts*, edited by Joel Feinberg. London: Oxford University Press, 1970.

Wilson, Edward O. *Sociobiology: The New Synthesis.* Cambridge, Mass.: Harvard University Press, 1975.

Winch, Peter. *The Idea of a Social Science and Its Relation to Philosophy.* London: Routledge and Kegan Paul, 1958.

———. "Man and Society in Hobbes and Rousseau." In *Hobbes and Rousseau*, edited by Maurice Cranston and Richard S. Peters. Garden City, N. Y.: Doubleday Anchor Books, 1972.

———. "Understanding a Primitive Society." In *Rationality*, edited by Bryan Wilson. New York: Harper Torchbooks, 1970.

Wittgenstein, Ludwig. *On Certainty.* Edited by G.E.M. Anscombe and G. H. von Wright. New York: Harper Torchbooks, 1979.

———. *Philosophical Investigations.* Translated by G.E.M. Anscombe. New York: Macmillan, 1978.

Wittig, Monique. "One Is Not Born a Woman." In *The Second Sex—Thirty Years Later: A Commemorative Conference on Feminist Theory.* Mimeographed. New York: Institute for the Humanities, 1979.

Wojtyla, Karol [Pope John Paul II]. *The Acting Person.* Translated by Andrej Potocki. Dordrecht: D. Reidel, 1979.

Wokler, Robert. "Perfectible Apes in Decadent Cultures: Rousseau's Anthropology Revisited." *Daedalus* 107 (Summer 1968):107-134.

Wolff, Robert Paul. *The Poverty of Liberalism.* Boston: Beacon Press, 1969.

———. "There's Nobody Here But Us Persons." In *Women and Philosophy*, edited by Carol Gould and Marx Wartofsky. New York: G. P. Putnam, 1976.

Wolin, Sheldon. "Political Theory as a Vocation." In *Machiavelli and the Nature of Political Thought*, edited by Martin Fleischer. New York: Atheneum, 1972.

———. *Politics and Vision.* Boston: Little, Brown, 1970.

———. "The Rise of Private Man." *New York Review of Books*, 14 April 1977, p. 19.

Wollheim, Richard. "Identification and the Imagination." In *Freud: A Collection of Critical Essays*, edited by Richard Wollheim. Garden City, N. Y.: Doubleday Anchor Books, 1974.

———. "Psychoanalysis and Women." *New Left Review*, no. 93 (September-October 1975):61-70.

Wollstonecraft, Mary. *A Vindication of the Rights of Women*. Edited by Charles W. Hagelman, Jr. New York: W. W. Norton, 1967.

Wrong, Dennis. "The Over-Socialized Conception of Man in Modern Sociology." *American Sociological Review* 26 (1961):183-193.

Yates, Gayle Graham. *What Women Want: The Ideas of the Movement*. Cambridge, Mass.: Harvard University Press, 1975.

Young, Iris Marion. "Is There a Woman's World?—Some Reflections on the Struggle for Our Bodies." In *The Second Sex—Thirty Years Later: A Commemorative Conference on Feminist Theory*. Mimeographed. New York: Institute for the Humanities, 1979.

Index

Library of Congress Cataloging in Publication Data

Elshtain, Jean Bethke, 1941-
  Public Man, Private Woman

  Bibliography: p.
  Includes index.
  1. Women in politics.   2. Political science—
History.   3. Knowledge, Theory of.   I. Title.
HQ1236.E47   305.4′2   81-47122
ISBN 0-691-07632-4   AACR2
ISBN 0-691-02206-3 (pbk.)

Jean Bethke Elshtain is Associate Professor of Political Science at the University of Massachusetts.